TAKING THINGS HARD

TAKING THINGS HARD

THE TRIALS OF

F. SCOTT FITZGERALD

ROBERT R. GARNETT

LOUISIANA STATE UNIVERSITY PRESS

BATON ROUGE

Published with the assistance of the V. Ray Cardozier Fund

Published by Louisiana State University Press
lsupress.org

Manufactured in the United States of America
First printing

DESIGNER: Michelle A. Neustrom
TYPEFACE: Source Serif Variable
PRINTER AND BINDER: Sheridan Books, Inc.

COVER IMAGE: Fitzgerald resting halfway up North Carolina's Chimney Rock, 1935.
Courtesy Department of Special Collections, Princeton University Library, Princeton, NJ.

LIBRARY OF CONGRESS CATALOGING-IN-PUBLICATION DATA

Names: Garnett, Robert Reginald., author.
Title: Taking things hard : the trials of F. Scott Fitzgerald / Robert R. Garnett.
Description: Baton Rouge : Louisiana State University Press, [2023] |
    Includes index.
Identifiers: LCCN 2022049633 (print) | LCCN 2022049634 (ebook) | ISBN
    978-0-8071-7934-5 (cloth) | ISBN 978-0-8071-8022-8 (pdf) | ISBN 978-0-8071-
    8021-1 (epub)
Subjects: LCSH: Fitzgerald, F. Scott (Francis Scott), 1896–1940. | Authors,
    American—20th century—Biography. | LCGFT: Biographies.
Classification: LCC PS3511.I9 Z6256 2023 (print) | LCC PS3511.I9 (ebook) |
    DDC 813/.52—dc23/eng/20221222
LC record available at https://lccn.loc.gov/2022049633
LC ebook record available at https://lccn.loc.gov/2022049634

CONTENTS

Preface vii

Prologue 1

1 A Dream of the South (1918–1920) 21

2 Honeymoon Years (1920–1924) 47

3 *The Great Gatsby* (1925) 77

4 The Riviera, the Actress, and Football (1926–1927) 108

5 Restlessness and High Seas (1928–1929) 155

6 A Novel Stalls, Zelda Crashes (1930) 175

7 The Vine-Curtained Veranda Meets the Jazz Age (1931–1934) 199

8 Crack-Up Drama (1935–1936) 225

9 Fitzgerald's Last Chapter: Hollywood (1937–1940) 260

   Epilogue 295

   Notes 303

   Index 329

Images follow page 138.

PREFACE

I am tired to the point of nausea of books on F. Scott Fitzgerald," Fitzgerald's Princeton mentor, friend, and "intellectual conscience" Edmund Wilson remarked in 1971. Anyone venturing to add another Fitzgerald book to the crowded shelf must be attentive to that cranky but perhaps reasonable complaint.

It had been Wilson who a half-century earlier gave currency to the comment, "to meet F. Scott Fitzgerald is to think of a stupid old woman with whom someone has left a diamond." This witticism came in 1924, the year Fitzgerald wrote *The Great Gatsby*. With the understanding that "stupid" for Wilson was vernacular for "non-intellectual," the diamond and stupid old woman analogy has a certain aptness. Fitzgerald was not an intellectual. He "has been given imagination," Wilson wrote, ". . . a desire for beauty . . . a gift for expression without many ideas to express." For Wilson, "ideas" were all-important. For Fitzgerald, the emotions of love and loss were far more compelling than any idea.

While the "diamond" gleams brightly in *The Great Gatsby,* it somehow lost its sparkle in the fifteen years that followed. *Tender Is the Night, Gatsby's* successor, has advocates; others believe the novel left unfinished at his death (later published in fragmentary state) would have been his finest. These remain minority views. Voting with their feet, as it were, readers since Fitzgerald's death have overwhelmingly preferred *Gatsby*. In these chapters I have tried to account for its surpassing achievement, and why—for all his genius, promise, ambition, and early accomplishment—his career afterwards petered out.

The sources for his biography are abundant—letters; notebooks; a ledger of his writing, income, and activities; contemporaries' reminiscences; scrapbooks; his personal essays; the copious records of his publisher and agent, and more. I rely as well on another biographical source, often slighted—his short stories. Fitzgerald himself and many since have divided his fiction into mutually exclusive categories, his four novels being literature, his stories commercial and pot-boiling (Fitzgerald once called them "trash"). The novels naturally receive the bulk of critical attention, but as a running record of Fitzgerald's moods, feelings, regrets, and enthusiasms across the years they are limited, with the stories exceeding them in frequency, immediacy, and bulk. Though many of Fitzgerald's stories are undistinguished, more than a handful are excellent. None is without some trace of his imaginative DNA. "I have asked a lot of my emotions," he would write—"one hundred and twenty stories. The price was high . . . because there was one little drop of something not blood, not a tear, not my seed, but me more intimately than these, in every story." Eventually he wrote about 180 stories.

Another source, often overlooked or ignored, is the journal of his secretary, confidante, and companion during the summer of 1935—the summer of his "crack-up." I devote more pages to this candid journal than many Fitzgerald scholars might think advisable, but while sometimes unpleasant, it deserves to be brought into daylight. More than twice as long as *Gatsby,* it documents months of unusual interest and gives by far the most detailed accounting of Fitzgerald's life for any stretch of time. If guilty of overemphasis, I hope that focusing on the journal in one chapter will help compensate for its burial in most other accounts.

As customary when writing about Fitzgerald, I transcribe his own writing *verbatim* and *literatim,* without editing his eccentric spelling.

I'm indebted to many early biographers and scholars. Nancy Milford, Arthur Mizener, Henry Dan Piper, and Andrew Turnbull all had the foresight to talk to or correspond with still-living contemporaries of Fitzgerald in the decades after his death. Anyone investigating Fitzgerald's life will also be grateful to those of his contemporaries who recorded their impressions of him. This study often cites the journals or memoirs of Laura Guthrie,

H. L. Mencken, Lawton Campbell, Alexander McKaig, Andrew Turnbull, Frances Kroll Ring, and Sheilah Graham. All who write about Fitzgerald today are indebted to these pioneering biographers, record-keepers, memoirists, and diarists.

Another debt is to those who, beginning soon after Fitzgerald's death, brought into print, or back into print, almost everything he wrote. These began with Maxwell Perkins and extend through Edmund Wilson, the indefatigable Matthew Bruccoli, and more recently James L. W. West III, general editor of the *Cambridge Edition of the Works of F. Scott Fitzgerald* and individual editor of sixteen of its eighteen volumes. Many of Fitzgerald's letters, as well, have been published, in a half-dozen sometimes overlapping collections.

My thanks also, and not simply *pro forma,* to the two readers at LSU Press, Professors James West and Kirk Curnutt, far more knowledgeable Fitzgerald scholars than I. Both commented extensively and in detail on the manuscript and offered cogent advice and criticisms, suggesting alterations or improvements as well as pointing out infelicities and errors. In almost all cases I've heeded their advice and concerns as well as I could. James W. Long, the press's acquisitions editor, has been uniformly receptive, reassuring, prompt, and helpful. Copy editor Stan Ivester's thorough vetting of the typescript reined in my erratic punctuation, inconsistent formatting, and occasional carelessness.

The two leading collections of Fitzgerald's archives and publications are those of Princeton's Firestone Library and the University of South Carolina's Ernest F. Hollings Special Collections Library. Both have been helpful—at Princeton, Emma Sarconi especially; at South Carolina, Elizabeth Sudduth. At the Morris Library of Southern Illinois University, Matthew J. Gorzalski went out of his way to accommodate requests. My home library at Gettysburg College patiently suffered my stripping the shelves of their Fitzgerald collection for such extended periods that by now they expect never to see the missing volumes again. I've also benefited from the Robert Harper Fitzgerald Collection in Gettysburg Library's Special Collections, where Carolyn Sautter, Devin McKinney, Ron Couchman, and Amy Lucadamo have been uniformly friendly and helpful.

Several colleagues at Gettysburg College encouraged this book. I've many times profited from the comments and reactions of my students in classes I've taught on Fitzgerald.

My wife, Joanne, has patiently endured my preoccupation with Fitzgerald while the grass grew and the paint peeled. Finally, a nod to my children—Meg, Olivia, Tom, Kate, Emily, Diana—for whom I'm very grateful.

TAKING THINGS HARD

PROLOGUE

Two or three great and moving experiences in our lives.

—"ONE HUNDRED FALSE STARTS"

In October 1934, *Redbook,* a thick, high-circulation, glossy magazine, printed a complete fifty-thousand-word novella by Ursula Parrott, a well-known, well-paid writer—a "high-powered fiction mill" in the words of one contemporary.[1] The same issue carried serial installments of two other novels, an installment of a book about former president Herbert Hoover, two articles, and nine stories. All this, and more, for twenty-five cents.

Redbook's editor was Edwin Balmer, a writer himself. The year before, he had coauthored *When Worlds Collide,* a science fiction novel said to have inspired the *Flash Gordon* comic strip. A sequel quickly followed, *After Worlds Collide.*

But while *Redbook*'s editor wrote rocket-ship sci-fi and Ursula Parrott had won notoriety with her debut novel, *Ex-Wife,* about a freewheeling 1920s divorcée, the lead story in *Redbook*'s October 1934 issue, beginning opposite a full-page advertisement for Bon Ami sink cleanser, was neither futuristic nor racy.

"In the Darkest Hour," relates the early adventures of a dispossessed French count fighting to reclaim his birthright.[2] It begins in 872 A.D., with twenty-year-old Count Philippe returning alone from Spain on horseback to his native France, from which he had been carried off as a young boy with his captive mother.

Stopping somewhere in the Loire Valley for a wayside dinner of flapjacks, Philippe overhears two yokels chatting in a hillbilly *lingua franca* anticipating *Li'l Abner*'s Dogpatch:

> "I heard tell of a thing up to Tours last market-day," one said. "It was when them there yeller devils messed up St. Hilaire."
> "I heard some talk of it," said the other man morosely.

Philippe accosts them in equally curious colloquial: "'Howdy,' he said. 'God save you!'"

When he inquires "where I'm at," one of the two locals, mixing backwoods and Wild West, replies: "You're in a place used to be called Villefranche, but they aint no village any more. . . . We aint had a market here nigh on to ten years."

This is gloomy news. "Many people live hereabouts?" Philippe inquires, to which the yokel replies: "Used to be a right smart lot of them. But since them yellow devils come through, and them red-headed heathen from the north, it sort of thinned us out a little."

> "But what about the King—this Charles they call 'Baldy'?"
> They both laughed.
> "Lot of good he does us! Haven't heard tell of him since my father's time—except he wants to be the Emperor of Rome."

Apparently better up on European politics than Count Philippe, the two locals conduct him to a local worthy, Le Poire, who at their approach grabs a club.

Blending piety and the hard-boiled argot of *The Maltese Falcon*'s Sam Spade, Philippe greets him: "God be with you! Don't get up on your ear." Noticing Le Poire's daughter, Philippe "reached out carelessly for the young girl who stood regarding him with awe, pulled her toward him and looked into her face," remarking, "You're a pretty little parcel."

Le Poire again glances at his club, and Philippe "released the girl with a short laugh."

> "Your meat's going to burn," he warned Le Poire.
> Le Poire's eyes smouldered like the brazier itself.

With this lusty interlude and trite simile, the story returns to business. Rounding up some local peasants, Philippe—a Hemingway hero of few words—announces his agenda: "'Well, men,'" Philippe said, "'here's the line-up: This happens to be my land. I am Philippe, Count of Villefranche, son and heir of Count Charles. I've come here to take over.'"

Resenting this flagrant power grab, Le Poire collects a rabble force to dispose of the new gun muscling his way into town.

Philippe is awakened in the night and warned:

> "Don't speak! They know where you're camped, and they're a-going to kill you. They been talkin' about it ever since you left—there's ten of them now, all full of wine."
> Philippe was on his feet in an instant.
> "Where are the dirty dogs?" he demanded furiously. "I'll—"

Outnumbered, he beats off the dirty dogs but then prudently retreats, threatening loudly, "I'll be back, you rats, I'll be back." And so on . . .

D eservedly unknown, "In the Darkest Hour" was written by F. Scott Fitzgerald ten years after he wrote *The Great Gatsby*. Only his name could have induced *Redbook* to print the story. Balmer the editor was skeptical, and "the owners of his magazine were not yet convinced that he was not partially crazy in buying these stories"—plural, because Fitzgerald intended to continue Philippe's adventures as a serial.[3]

The owners' instincts were sound. The Philippe stories—wooden, simplistic, puerile, awash in cliché and banality, with ninth-century colloquial rendered in a hodgepodge of cowboy-movie, hillbilly, and detective novel—are the worst things F. Scott Fitzgerald ever wrote for publication. "In the Darkest Hour" applies not only to ninth-century Europe, but equally to Fitzgerald.

Balmer despaired. Worse than the stories themselves was Fitzgerald's failure to deliver sequels on time, disrupting any sustained reader engagement. The second Philippe story did not appear until the following June, nine months after the first; the third in August. A fourth was promised and scheduled for the following month, and Fitzgerald's name appeared on the bright red cover of *Redbook*'s September 1935 issue—with no Fitzgerald story inside.

"The Red book is plenty mad at him for not letting them have that last story in time for the Sept. issue," Fitzgerald's secretary noted in her journal, "and the awful thing happened that his name was on the cover, along with Sinclair Lewis's."[4] Balmer never forgave Fitzgerald for this embarrassing slip, and *Redbook* printed the fourth story only after Fitzgerald's death five years later, a sad *in memoriam.*

The four Philippe stories are now hard to come by: since their publication in *Redbook,* only one has been reprinted. In eighteen volumes, *the Cambridge Edition of the Works of F. Scott Fitzgerald* includes almost everything Fitzgerald wrote for publication—but not Philippe. "Scottie Fitzgerald, the author's daughter, judged these stories to be so far below the level of writing that her father was capable of that they should not be reprinted," *Cambridge* editor James L. W. West explains. Scottie herself called them, more bluntly, her father's "most abysmal failure."[5]

How in ten years had the author of *The Great Gatsby* sunk so far? Plausible answers crowd the page. Marrying the equally festive and irresponsible Zelda Sayre, Fitzgerald with her exuberant assistance had eagerly devoted himself to spendthrift self-indulgence and pleasure-seeking. Unable to control their spending and continually pressed for money, he was compelled to waste time and energy writing lightweight magazine stories for ready cash.

An ardent devotee of Youth, ending precisely at thirty, he reached that calamitous age himself the year after *Gatsby.* A century earlier, William Wordsworth, mourning (at twenty-eight) the "aching joys" and "dizzy raptures" of *his* lost youth, claimed that "other gifts / Have followed; for such loss, I would believe, / Abundant recompense." Not so for Fitzgerald.

His livelihood, largely dependent on stories, began to dry up as his flair for young-love romance waned and as reading tastes and magazine economics shifted in the 1930s. Zelda's mental breakdown and decline, beginning in 1930, dragged him too down. Indifferent reviews and weak sales of *Gatsby*'s long-delayed successor, *Tender Is the Night,* were both demoralizing and financially ruinous. And even before Zelda's collapse, Fitzgerald was sliding into a crippling dipsomania.

There is truth in all these explanations—but neither singly nor together do they fully explain the anchor drop from *The Great Gatsby* to Count Philippe.

During his lifetime *Gatsby* was neither the best-known nor most popular of his novels. That was his first, *This Side of Paradise.* His longest was the second, *The Beautiful and Damned;* his most ambitious the last, *Tender Is the Night.*

But if not for *Gatsby,* the others would be out of print. There would be no *Cambridge Edition,* six thousand pages in its eighteen volumes—four of them variations on *The Great Gatsby,* a scholarly twist on "Thirteen Ways of Looking at a Blackbird." There would be no long shelf of biographies, correspondence, and critical studies, including a half-dozen books about Fitzgerald and Zelda together, and another half-dozen about his mostly one-sided friendship with Ernest Hemingway.

Despite all the ink-covered pages, however, the enduring appeal of his paramount achievement remains largely a mystery. Why is *Gatsby* America's favorite novel? For a book so widely read, so frequently studied and taught, so much enjoyed, admired, and beloved, it strangely eludes critical capture. Most explanations are unconvincing; some would be good reason to avoid it.

Gatsby first became popular after the Second World War, a revival beginning with ordinary readers. When the professional reading class—professors, literary critics, book reviewers, English teachers—took notice, they puzzled to find weighty meaning in a melodrama of mushroom millionaires, gaudy parties, New York love nests, bootleggers, and the fatally romantic obsession of a dreamy underworld parvenu.

Gatsby, they happily discovered, was about "the American Dream," a phrase coined and defined in infelicitous prose by historian James Truslow Adams in 1931:

> . . . the *American dream,* that dream of a land in which life should be better and richer and fuller for every man, with opportunity for each ac-

cording to his ability or achievement . . . not a dream of motor cars and
high wages merely, but a dream of a social order in which each man and
each woman shall be able to attain to the fullest stature of which they
are innately capable, and be recognized by others for what they are, regardless of the fortuitous circumstances of birth or position.[6]

With his relentless ambition and "extraordinary gift for hope," Jay Gatsby
exemplified both the aspiration and corruption of the Dream. Just as America often confused material prosperity—"motor cars and high wages"—with
a "better and richer and fuller life," so young James Gatz's quest for a better life materializes in vulgar trappings like his large glistening automobile
purchased with ill-got profits from bootlegging.

The professors had found what they needed, classroom fodder. A useful
and edifying theme, the American Dream has been poured or knocked into
the heads of generations of students. Writing *Gatsby,* Fitzgerald had never
heard of it.[7]

By contrast, his contemporary Thomas Wolfe *was* a novelist of the
American Dream. Running through his long posthumously published novel
You Can't Go Home Again are passages of Dream uplift: "So, then, to every
man his chance—to every man, regardless of his birth, his shining, golden
opportunity—to every man the right to live, to work, to be himself, and to
become whatever thing his manhood and his vision can combine to make
him—this, seeker, is the promise of America."

Fitzgerald was unimpressed. "The stuff about the GREAT VITAL HEART
OF AMERICA," he wrote of Wolfe's novel, "is just simply corny."[8]

Though Fitzgerald found the Dream corny, at least Wolfe's version of it,
"American Dream" has virtually become *Gatsby*'s subtitle. A 1999 "critical guide" trumpets "exciting alternative readings" and "dramatic new de-
velopments" in *Gatsby* criticism, but the hoary Dream prevails, especially in
classrooms. The index of a 2014 study, *So We Read On: How* The Great Gatsby
Came to Be and Why It Endures, cites the "American Dream" nine times.[9]

For less academic readers, however, romance among millionaires
trumps sonorous themes. "At its heart," ventures a journalist after reading

it at least twenty-five times, "*Gatsby* was a story of love and loss among the one-percenters."[10]

Fitzgerald himself explained the novel as neither romance nor American Dream, but much closer to the former. Early in its writing he described it as "a new thinking out of the idea of illusion . . . much more mature and much more romantic than This Side of Paradise." His previous novel, *The Beautiful and Damned,* had been "a false lead," he acknowledged. "The business of creating illusion is much more to my taste and my talent." Finishing a draft of *Gatsby,* he reiterated: "The whole burden of this novel" is "the loss of those illusions that give such color to the world so that you don't care whether things are true or false as long as they partake of the magical glory."[11] Critics and teachers generally ignore such explanations. For pragmatic and perhaps temperamental reasons most prefer canned, easily discussed classroom ideas to anything so airy as illusions of magical glory.

"Her voice is full of money," Gatsby observes of Daisy, and many have seized on this trope as the novel's keynote. A preeminent Fitzgerald scholar, Matthew Bruccoli, asserts, "An essential aspect of the American-ness and the historicity of *The Great Gatsby* is that it is about money." He detects other themes too, however. "Time is a major theme in the novel," along with "the related themes of mutability and loss." And: "Ultimately the novel is about American history, compounding the time theme and the aspiration theme."[12] Meanwhile, another scholar applauds *Gatsby*'s "profound commentaries on the national themes of race, class, and gender." Foremost among "the subjects . . . that I'll be exploring," she promises, is "Social class. . . . *The Great Gatsby* is America's greatest novel about class."[13] This jumble of themes—money, time, mutability, loss, aspiration, American history, race, social class, gender—illuminates the novel darkly.

We like to think of our favorite historical figures as rather like ourselves: concerned with the same issues, holding similar views. A fine intellectual biography of Fitzgerald by David Brown, a professor of history, "emphasizes Fitzgerald's historical imagination and sees him as a progressive era intellectual rather than simply a chronicler of the Jazz Age."[14] In other words Fitzgerald was at heart a history professor, with the standard ideas of his time. But how many novel readers open *Gatsby* eager for the reflections of a "progressive era intellectual"?

To the contrary, the zest and charm of Fitzgerald's writing often springs from his unacademic boyishness and fancy. His loyal friend and editor Maxwell Perkins observed that "Scott was always a child—terribly impressed by the most foolish things," and "a great deal of the good writing he has done has come from that very fact of a sort of adolescent romanticism." Fitzgerald was a creature of lively enthusiasms and hobbies. A one-time neighbor recalled, "He would take up wrestling and then drop it; shooting, fencing, etc. Interested in military problems." He collected miniature soldiers and deployed them for battle on the dining-room table. His conversation was harum-scarum. "Talking with him was like dropping pennies on a boardwalk & having them keep falling thru the cracks," another writer recalled. "Nothing seemed to stick."[15]

Perkins noted the same trait: "In talk he's all over the place. You can never finish up anything you start to talk about," and after Fitzgerald's death he recalled, "Scott never stayed on one subject more than a few seconds—always leaping to another. Never stayed still." Fitzgerald's compulsive showing off, noted by many, betrayed an ineradicable sophomorism: he himself once admitted that "outside interests generally mean for me women, liquor or some form of exhibitionism." A Princeton friend observed, "In many ways, Scott remained a perennial undergraduate."[16]

Reminiscing about his last year, his Hollywood mistress Sheilah Graham recalled, "With his battered collegiate hat and raincoat, his pullover sweaters and jaunty bow ties, he reminded me more and more of all I had read about American college boys of the twenties." To the end, he doted on Princeton football. Fritz Crisler, Princeton's coach in the 1930s, thought "there was something beyond comprehension in the intensity of his feelings. What he felt was really an unusual, a *consuming* devotion for the Princeton football team." At the moment of his death Fitzgerald was thinking about Princeton football.[17]

It does not diminish him to point out that he was neither philosopher, thinker, theologian, oracle, nor sage; still less to acknowledge that he was not even a garden-variety intellectual. He gives us something richer than classroom discourse.

William Butler Yeats noted the scholarly impulse to overanalyze and codify literature:

Bald heads forgetful of their sins,
Old, learned, respectable bald heads
Edit and annotate the lines
That young men, tossing on their beds,
Rhymed out in love's despair. . . .

Ransacking Fitzgerald's novels and stories for themes, ideas, and opinions misses the ardent, vulnerable sensibility behind them.

To imagine Fitzgerald as the despairing poet-lover of Yeats's poem would oversimplify but not wholly misrepresent him. He was a writer of a few emotional tempests and the gift to embody them in story. That his fiction began not in ideas but in emotion we have on his own authority. In an often ignored magazine article, "One Hundred False Starts," he explained clearly the seed of his stories. "Whether it's something that happened twenty years ago or only yesterday I must start out with an emotion," he wrote, "one that's close to me and that I can understand."[18]

An apparently good idea for a story often went nowhere, he continued, because he could not enter into the characters' feelings: "I can open a volume from a criminal law library and find a thousand plots. I can go into highway and byway, parlor and kitchen, and listen to personal revelations that at the hands of other writers might endure forever. But all that is nothing—not even enough for a false start." Fascinating plots, unusual experiences, or memorable characters did not by themselves inspire a story: "If a friend says he's got a story for me and launches into a tale of being robbed by Brazilian pirates in a swaying straw hut on the edge of a smoking volcano in the Andes with his fiancée bound and gagged on the roof, I can well believe there were various human emotions involved." But such emotions do not generate a story, because "I can't feel them."

If he could not sympathize with characters' feelings, had not known them himself, there was no story. As with most, his strong emotions were few: "Mostly we authors must repeat ourselves—that's the truth. We have two or three great and moving experiences in our lives, experiences so great and moving that it doesn't seem at the time that anyone else has been

so caught up and pounded and dazzled and astonished and beaten and broken and rescued and illuminated and rewarded and humbled in just that
way ever before." No single passage better illuminates Fitzgerald's fiction.
And for him—again, perhaps as for most—those great and moving experiences came in his youth.

P rofessor Bruccoli, who asserts that *The Great Gatsby* is about money, time,
mutability, loss, aspiration, and American history, also remarks—in
view of these abstractions, confusingly—that "Everything Fitzgerald wrote
was personal because, as he stated, he took things hard."[19]

Fitzgerald knew his fiction had little to say about larger issues. Novelists like himself "have love as a main concern," he wrote, "since our interest
lies outside the economic struggle or the life of violence, as conditioned to
some extent by our lives from 16–21."[20] In those five years of his own life,
two girls were seismic experiences, and for years to come his fiction registered the aftershocks.

Writing of Thomas Wolfe, Hemingway, and himself in 1934, he suggested that what they had in common was "the attempt that crops up from
time to time to recapture the exact feel of a moment in time and space . . .
an attempt at a mature memory of a deep experience."[21] In 1935 he wrote to
his agent Harold Ober, "All my stories are concieved like novels, require a
special emotion, a special experience."[22]

A Fitzgerald confidante "wondered why his thoughts went incessantly
back to youth and that love. . . . why did he continually mourn the way he
loved Zelda in the long, long ago."[23] "Taking things hard . . ." he noted of
himself, "That's [the] stamp that goes into my books so that people can read
it blind like brail."[24] Hemingway agreed. "We are all bitched from the start,"
he told Fitzgerald, "and you especially have to be hurt like hell before you
can write seriously."[25] He "dragged the great Gatsby out of the pit of my
stomach in a time of misery," Fitzgerald recalled.[26]

Two years before his death, he advised a young woman seeking his opinion on a story she had written: "You've got to sell your heart, your strongest
reactions, not the little minor things that only touch you lightly, the little
experiences that you might tell at dinner. This is especially true when you
begin to write, when . . . you have *only* your emotions to sell. . . . The amateur

can only realize his ability to transfer his emotions to another person by some such desperate and radical expedient as tearing your first tragic love story out of your heart and putting it on pages for people to see."[27] "Taking things hard," "hurt like hell," mourning a love of "the long, long ago," "tearing your first tragic love story out of your heart"—such strong emotions generated Fitzgerald's finest fiction.

In his first novel, *This Side of Paradise,* "I wrote about a love affair that was still bleeding as fresh as the skin wound on a haemophile," he testified.[28] That wound was his heartbreak over Zelda Sayre, who in the spring of 1919 had jilted him. But the novel also bled from an earlier wound.

G inevra King was the daughter of a patrician Chicago family, her father a wealthy banker and stockbroker. The Kings summered on a fifty-acre Lake Forest estate with stables for Mr. King's polo ponies and, just down the road, the exclusive country club Onwentsia. "Once I thought that Lake Forest was the most glamorous place in the world," Fitzgerald recalled years later. "Maybe it was."[29]

The rest of the year the Kings lived in a new, massive four-story Astor Street mansion, completed soon after Fitzgerald and Ginevra met. "One of the most popular girls in Chicago society," she was often mentioned in the society columns of the *Chicago Tribune.*[30]

A surviving photograph shows her father, Charles Garfield King, confident and robust, standing in jodhpurs and riding boots and holding a polo mallet, the very image of *The Great Gatsby*'s Tom Buchanan—like King a Yale alumnus, wealthy Chicagoan with a summer home in Lake Forest, and polo player with his own stable of ponies. King's Lake Forest estate—Kingdom Come Farm—with a large colonial-style mansion, expansive greensward, gardens and pond and fountain and stables, inspired the Buchanans' East Egg estate, "a cheerful red and white Georgian colonial mansion," Nick Carraway remarks, with a lawn that "ran toward the front door for a quarter of a mile, jumping over sun-dials and brick walks and burning gardens," and with Tom Buchanan's polo ponies nearby.

Fitzgerald met Ginevra at the end of the Christmas holidays of his second year at Princeton, at a dinner dance at the home of his Saint Paul friend Marie Hersey, Ginevra's schoolmate at their Connecticut boarding school,

Westover. He was eighteen, she sixteen. Their meeting seemed to him fated, for his ledger records "The name 'Ginevra King'" more than three years earlier, though she and Marie had not then been schoolmates.[31]

He went to Marie's party with suitcase packed and in his pocket a ticket for an eastbound night train. But young love kindled, and craving more time with the fascinating Ginevra, he let the train steam off without him. Next day, "Minneapolis & movies with Ginevra," he recorded on a scratch-paper record of his holiday social engagements, followed by a bobsledding party, supper, and "Dance at McDavitts."[32]

Reluctantly tearing himself away from the dance, he caught the train to Chicago, Ginevra seeing him off at the station. Accompanied, they were too shy to kiss.[33] A few weeks later she wrote to him, "Scott, I'm surprised! I hear you had plans for kissing me goodbye publicly. . . . (*Ans. This—Why didn't you?* (KISS ME)." To her diary she confided, "Scott perfectly darling. Am dipped about." Nonetheless, she rallied after his departure to resume the evening's gaiety: "Went for ride in R's car with Bug and J.J. Fun."[34]

Their romance lasted two years, mostly by correspondence. The boy-crazy Ginevra never limited her attentions to Fitzgerald. "There are some peachy boys here now," she wrote from Chicago two months after they met, and years later recalled, "At this time I was definitely out for quantity not quality in beaux, and although Scott was top man, I still wasn't serious enough not to want plenty of other attention!"[35]

He was not on top for long, and well before the decisive break she lost all interest. After their initial meeting they saw each other only a handful of times, seldom if ever alone. They exchanged dozens of letters, however, and later, before destroying the originals, he had hers transcribed. In that form they survive on 227 typewritten pages that he retained until his death. She destroyed or discarded his.

During the first winter and spring of their romance, in 1915, they wrote frequent long letters. His rambled on for up to 24 handwritten pages and more, sometimes packaged in multiple envelopes. She was soon signing hers with "Love," but he was an exhausting correspondent and she was hard-pressed to match his epistolary chatter.

The month after their Saint Paul introduction, he and a friend with his own Westover romance traveled together from Princeton to Connecticut to visit their respective girls. He invited Ginevra to the Princeton spring prom, but when her mother balked at coming from Chicago to chaperone, Ginevra had to decline. In June, though, when Mrs. King came east to escort her home for the summer, he and she, with her mother, spent an evening together in New York, with dinner at the Ritz-Carlton Roof Garden, a play at the Princess Theatre, and a late-night visit to the just-opened Midnight Frolic, a lavish supper club with elaborate scenery and dozens of chorus girls on the roof of the New Amsterdam Theater. (Mrs. King must have paid for everything.) Fitzgerald would remember the evening fondly.

On his way to Saint Paul later that month, he stopped in Lake Forest for a day and visited Ginevra briefly in a pouring rain. "Oh Scott, I've met such an attractive Yale fellow in town," she gaily informed him soon after. In August, spending several weeks at the Montana ranch of a Princeton friend's family, he noted in his ledger, "No news from Ginevra." Mail delivery at the ranch was evidently spotty, for she had in fact written two letters, teasing in one: "How are the village queens?" By autumn the romance and correspondence had notably slackened. In February she had sent him eleven letters; in October, two. In December she reported herself "*absolutely* heart whole. . . . I don't care so very much for anybody."

That same month, in ill health and academic free fall, Fitzgerald left Princeton and returned home to sit out the spring 1916 semester. In May, caught up in a teapot-tempest at Westover, Ginevra was removed by her father and sent home. With Fitzgerald in Saint Paul and Ginevra in Connecticut and Chicago, they continued to correspond, but she had cooled. The previous June she had been eager to attend the Princeton prom; now, in a letter gushing about a "wonderful" three-day visit to Yale, she declined with only perfunctory regret his invitation to "the Princeton thing" in June.

They apparently next saw each other in August 1916, when he again visited Lake Forest. He would tell a friend that "The best thing I did [that summer] was go to Lake Forest," but his ledger's unusually lengthy account, with remarks like "The bad day at the McCormicks" and "Dissapointment," suggests the visit was a failure.[36] It was on this occasion that he recorded the often re-quoted remark, "Poor boys shouldn't think of marrying rich girls," without noting context or speaker.[37]

Writing a week later, Ginevra, contrary to her usual chatty, hyperbolic style, had little to say about his visit. "It's been just a week exactly since I last saw you, just think of that!" her letter begins, and then notes: "I was so sorry that you didn't come around on Monday to give the glad hand, and say goodbye, but I suppose I'll have to bear up on it—." Since she remarks in the same letter that "I quite fell for Dawson—he was simply divine, also Maurice McLoughlin," and mentions a tennis dance, golfing, and swimming, she evidently bore up pretty well. That September, 1916, Ginevra had plans to visit Saint Paul, she claimed, but "then Mother came up and busted all my hopes." In November, however, she and her Lake Forest friend Peg, both attending finishing school in New York, visited Princeton for the Yale game.

Years later she admitted that, after Fitzgerald and a Princeton friend had escorted Ginevra and Peg back to New York's old Penn Station and said goodbye, the girls rendezvoused with two Yale boys lurking in wait nearby. In January 1917, two years after their first meeting, he noted in his ledger, "Final break with Ginevra," but she had cut loose earlier.

In July he asked her to destroy his letters. "They were harmless—have you a guilty conscience?" she replied scornfully. "I never did think they meant anything." They had meant something to him, though. He took it hard.

To explain Fitzgerald's failure with Ginevra, scholars have often seized on the quoted remark, "Poor boys shouldn't think of marrying rich girls." He was not actually poor, but among the Kings and their wealthy Lake Forest friends he was decidedly a nonentity. Ginevra might be swayed by his good looks, wit, vivacity, flow of chatter, and puppyish attentiveness; her parents possibly less so. Ginevra herself may have grown more sensitive to the class difference. She would eventually marry, successively, two wealthy Chicagoans from Lake Forest society.

But money and class oversimplify the matter. Though neither wealthy nor Episcopalian, Fitzgerald as a Princetonian had respectable credentials; there would have been no barrier to Mr. King bringing a son-in-law into King, Farnum & Co.; while losing *The Great Gatsby,* the world would have gained a stockbroker. Ginevra was young and played the field, but very likely Mr. King was already taking measure of the young men flitting about her.

He was a strong masculine, business-like presence. Fitzgerald's strengths ran along different lines. He was high-spirited, clever, romantic, literary, and amusing, and his long and numerous letters to Ginevra no doubt overflowed with such traits. The first scholar to examine her letters, James L. W. West, surmises that Fitzgerald's advantage over her other suitors was his epistolary talent. Because the Kings' circle was immensely wealthier, "His visits to Lake Forest must have been difficult for him," but "In the field of letter-writing . . . he was unrivaled. Here he shone, and he knew it."[38]

To be sure, Ginevra admired his letters—"Your last letter was divine!!"— but over the course of their correspondence she may have tired of his prolixity—variously playful, pestering, provocative, jealous, and egotistical— and come to perceive that his lively facility as a letter writer hinted at deficiencies elsewhere. A young woman unconsciously seeking stability, judgment, and responsibility in a prospective husband might have intuited Fitzgerald's unsuitability. One doesn't sign on for life with a shoebox full of witty letters.

She remained a stirring memory and regret. He never forgot the long-ago night with her in New York, "when She made luminous the Ritz Roof on a brief passage through," and her shadow appears in *Tender Is the Night*'s Nicole, who "could have had all the young men she wanted," Nicole's father remarks. "We were in Lake Forest—that's a summer place near Chicago where we have a place—and she was out all day playing golf or tennis with the boys."

Looking forward to seeing Ginevra again years later, Fitzgerald observed that "These great beauties are often something else at thirty-eight, but Ginevra had a great deal besides beauty." He was not disappointed. "I . . . met the love of my youth, Ginevra King (Mitchell), after an interval of twenty-one years," he told his daughter Scottie. "She is still a charming woman and I'm sorry I didn't see more of her."[39]

He never did.

F itzgerald's two most fertile emotions were closely intertwined: falling in love with the girl, and losing her: Ginevra first, then Zelda.

The lost girl lingers ambiguously in memory. Writing to his first love many years after she had jilted him, Charles Dickens fondly recalled the time "when you made me wretchedly happy." Or as Tennyson put it, "'Tis better to have loved and lost / Than never to have loved at all"—better at least for the incipient poet or novelist. Fitzgerald himself would recall his "dramatic and feverishly enjoyed miseries" when courting Zelda.[40] To re-suffer in memory a painful loss is also to relive the hopefulness of young love, even to reawaken the keen sensitivities of youth itself.

Like falling in love, romantic loss was an emotion Fitzgerald under-stood well and suffered intensely. From the beginning, his heroes pine for the lost girl or woman. In *This Side of Paradise,* he tore his first tragic love story out of his heart (in his words) and put it on the page—not the happy ending with marriage to Zelda, but the jilting that preceded it. Jay Gatsby is fatally possessed by memories of the lost girl from Louisville. The hero of Fitzgerald's half-written final novel is haunted by memories of a dead wife, and seeks not her successor but her reappearance.

His most deeply felt stories explore the ache of loss: stories like "Winter Dreams," "'The Sensible Thing,'" "Jacob's Ladder," "The Last of the Belles." In perhaps the most poignant, "Babylon Revisited," the hero mourns his dead wife and loses his daughter. Fitzgerald's final full-length story, "Last Kiss," ends with a woman in her grave and the protagonist mournful, regretful, haunted.

In a letter to his daughter just weeks before his death, Fitzgerald claimed for himself "the wise and tragic sense of life . . . that life is essentially a cheat and its conditions are those of defeat, and that the redeeming things are not 'happiness and pleasure' but the deeper things that come out of struggle."[41] This was the disillusion of a disappointed and (as it happened) dying man who had discovered too late the superficiality of "happiness and pleasure"; but even during his early and hopeful days he knew that love and loss were as closely linked as birth and death.

The early story "Winter Dreams" was inspired by his "memory of a fas-cination in a visit paid to a very rich aunt in Lake Forest," he explained a dozen years later. "Also my first girl 18–20 [Fitzgerald's age] whom I've used over and over and never forgotten."[42] Not the rich aunt so much as the Kings' opulent "Kingdom Come" actually fascinated him, and the first and unforgotten girl was Ginevra.

Like Ginevra, Judy Jones of "Winter Dreams" inhabits a world of country-club pleasures amidst "the dwellings of the rich." As a girl Judy has her own governess, as a young woman her own powerboat. Photographs show the young Ginevra with striking dark eyes, and "Winter Dreams" frequently mentions Judy's "dark" and "passionate" eyes. Indifferent to the men who spin through the revolving door of her favor, she jilts them all, as Ginevra with Fitzgerald.

But the differences between Ginevra and the story's Judy illustrate the risk of identifying Fitzgerald's characters with a single model, as critics and biographers sometimes recklessly do. Fitzgerald knew Ginevra as a six-teen- and seventeen-year-old girl living in a circumscribed world of board-ing schools, headmistresses, teachers, parents, and chaperones; as a pre-debutante, just beginning to venture into the world of boys.

The story's Judy Jones is about twenty and unchaperoned. She appears suddenly out of the night, alone, her "racing motor-boat" the very image of her freedom and dash as it spins around Black Bear Lake and with "re-verberate sound" throws up "two white streamers of cleft water." Judy is already a veteran siren, fickle and jaded, her eyes "plaintive with melan-choly." Enjoying conquest, she is cynical and unscrupulous in love, "the most direct and unprincipled personality with which he [Dexter, the hero] had ever come in contact."

This was scarcely the flirtatious but romantic sixteen-year-old Ginevra King. "Winter Dreams" is actually not about Ginevra at all, or even about Judy Jones, but about Dexter, through whose impressionable eyes we see Judy's—"the almost passionate quality of her eyes," "her passionate eyes," "the sad luxury of her eyes." It is Dexter who senses Judy's "passionate vital-ity" and "passionate energy"; who feels in himself "ecstatic happiness" and "the helpless ecstasy of losing himself in her." The story's many "ecstasy's" and "ecstatic's"—eight altogether—remind us repeatedly of Dexter's ready self-transport into stratospheric regions of excited feeling.

Intimations of ecstasy have struck him even earlier, in such routine occurrences as autumn: "October filled him with hope which November raised to a sort of ecstatic triumph"—this when he is "not more than four-teen," and before he has even seen Judy. He is already rapt in ecstasy, "a mood of intense appreciation, a sense that, for once, he was magnificently attune to life and that everything about him was radiating a brightness and a glamour he might never know again," when Judy's speedboat comes roaring out of the darkness, and his free-floating ecstasy crystallizes in "the girl."

Seeing Judy through Dexter's eyes, we are likely to credit his impressions of her loveliness and desirability, but there are hints that her fascination is a creation of his own fancy. While the name "Dexter Green" anticipates the hopeful green light of *Gatsby,* "Judy Jones" is pedestrian. And at the end Judy herself drops out. In a thousand-word postscript projecting seven years beyond the story's main action, she is absent. Long out of touch, Dexter randomly hears of her from a business acquaintance who happens to know her as Judy Simms, wife of Lud. The one-time enchantress, Dexter discovers, has dwindled into a misused housewife who "stays at home with her kids" while Lud "drinks and runs around" and "treats her like the devil."

Worse, Judy's loveliness has vanished. When Dexter's acquaintance blandly recalls that "She was a pretty girl when she first came to Detroit," Dexter is astonished: "A pretty girl! The phrase stuck Dexter as ludicrous." But all the acquaintance can muster in Judy's praise is that she is "all right" and "has nice eyes." She of the dark passionate eyes and passionate vitality has become washed out and plain, and Dexter's world pales correspondingly.

With his earlier ecstasies inspiring flights of lyricism, "Winter Dreams" anticipates *Gatsby:* "A lump rose in Dexter's throat, and he waited breathless for the experiment, facing the unpredictable compound that would form mysteriously from the elements of their lips. Then he saw—she communicated her excitement to him, lavishly, deeply, with kisses that were not a promise but a fulfillment. They aroused in him not hunger demanding renewal but surfeit that would demand more surfeit . . . kisses that were like charity, creating want by holding back nothing at all."

But like *Gatsby,* "Winter Dreams" ends with awareness of life's diminishment. "The dream was gone," Dexter grieves, and recalling the "ecstatic" past, ". . . tried to bring up a picture of the waters lapping on Sherry Island and the moonlit veranda, and gingham on the golf-links and the dry sun and the gold color of her neck's soft down. And her mouth damp to his kisses and her eyes plaintive with melancholy and her freshness like new fine linen in the morning. Why, these things were no longer in the world! They had existed and they existed no longer." No idea ever prompted such keen emotion.

Reading Fitzgerald as commentator on the American Dream, progressive-era intellectual, op-ed savant, historian of the Jazz Age, or expounder of textbook themes misses the emotional engine of his fiction. Dexter Green's youthful sensibility was Fitzgerald's—imaginative, poetic, highly colored, sensuous, erotic, rapturous. Success and wealth could not console him for its loss.

Fitzgerald began writing as a boy—stories, plays, poems—and at Princeton churned out lyrics for musical comedies, more stories, more poems, short plays. Most of this early writing is predictably juvenile or sophomoric, but he had wit, humor, fancy, verbal felicity, and ambition. He wanted to be a writer and possessed the talent and energy to make a good run at it.

What he lacked was something worth writing about. He had ordinary boyhood interests and enthusiasms—football, school, the Civil War; as time went on, girls too, but only with Ginevra King's advent did they fascinate. In *This Side of Paradise* a succession of girls populate Amory Blaine's youth, and while his chatty Princeton friends all sound much alike, the girls are sharply differentiated.[43]

Even so, Amory enjoys a yet more fascinating interest—himself. Returning from the East at one point, he "sat in the train, and thought about himself for thirty-six hours." As Fitzgerald admitted, the novel's "romantic egotist" was essentially himself: "'Amory Blaine' was the name of the character in my first novel to which I attached my adventures and opinions, in effect my autobiography."[44] If his reputation depended on *This Side of Paradise,* however, and any number of similar sequels, Fitzgerald would be long forgotten.

His moment came on a July evening in 1918 when he happened onto one of those great experiences—*the* great experience—that would possess him and inspire his writing for years. The country club in Montgomery, Alabama, was a large, two-story Craftsman-style bungalow, overhung by wide eaves, wrapped on three sides by a veranda, and propped up on large stone blocks, "a rambling brown-shingled building, discreetly screened from the public eye by an impenetrable hedge of mock oranges."[45]

There from Minnesota appeared army second lieutenant F. Scott Fitzgerald, while from 6 Pleasant Avenue, Montgomery, came Zelda, daughter of Anthony Sayre, justice of the Supreme Court of Alabama. At some point that evening they met on the dance floor. The material of literature, Fitzgerald would later observe, "however closely observed, is as elusive as the moment in which it has its existence unless it is purified by an incorruptible style and by the catharsis of a passionate emotion."[46] The incorruptible style would take time, but in Zelda Sayre, the passionate emotion had arrived.

1

A DREAM OF THE SOUTH

(1918–1920)

A Northern man's dream of the South.

—"THE LAST OF THE BELLES"

Fitzgerald spent his early years in Minnesota and upstate New York. As a youth and young man he gravitated to the Northeast, especially New York. Later, he lived in Delaware for two years and Baltimore for five, but even then "I think of myself always as a Northerner," he remarked.[1] His most fateful experience, however, began in the South.

Zelda Sayre was not simply from the South, but *of* the South, and he would forever associate her with her homeland. Ardently courting her, he was enchanted with the South; later, frustrated and angry with her, he extended his animus to the entire South. In North Carolina in the mid-1930s he "had a habit [when drinking] of calling all Southerners 'farmers.'" A few years later he would contemptuously refer to "feebs of the Confederacy."[2]

But in 1918 and 1919, Zelda's South was a fresh, paradisiacal landscape. Her southern-ness was fascinating—sensuous, lazy, exotic, picturesque, alluring. Opening a door to warmer regions of imagination and feeling, she seduced his imagination from the North.

He had grown up in cities of severe winters. His first eighteen months had been spent in Saint Paul, where during his first November the temperature dropped to 10 below zero. Two months later, in January, it fell to 26 below zero, and for five consecutive days never broke zero. In February it fell to 22 below; in March, 9 below.[3]

In April of his second year, the Fitzgeralds moved to Buffalo, less frigid than Saint Paul but snowier. During their first December in Buffalo, thirty inches of snow fell, and during the following winter, ninety-nine inches.[4] In January of their third eastern winter, the Fitzgeralds moved to Syracuse, snowier yet.

When he turned seven the family returned to Buffalo, and that winter, 1903–4, nine feet of snow fell. In three of the five winters the Fitzgeralds lived in Buffalo, temperatures sank to 8 below zero. In summer 1908 they returned to Saint Paul, where in January the following year the temperature fell to 27 below zero.

Later, Fitzgerald would create evocative scenes of returning home by train from school at Christmas, of snow falling, of horse-drawn sleigh rides— but during Minnesota's long winters he actually preferred the indoors. He did not ski, snowshoe, or ice fish; he was a poor skater and did not play hockey. On a visit to Montgomery one March he wrote to a Minnesota friend, "St Paul with three weeks more of winter must be hell. Down here it's heaven." A decade later he would tell a Saint Paul friend that the city "still is home, of course, in spite of the fact that I never want to spend another winter there," and a little later admitted that "I never did quite adjust myself to those damn Minnesota winters."[5]

At fifteen he went East to prep school, and for the next six years spent school terms in the chilly damps of New Jersey, where "February dripped snow and rain." Dropping out of Princeton and judged "qualified physically, morally, and in horsemanship," he was commissioned a second lieutenant in the army and in November 1917 reported to Fort Leavenworth for officer training. In December the temperature at Leavenworth fell to 9 below zero; in January, 16 below; in February, 14 below. In his ledger he remarked on "The intense cold," and wrote his mother, "This is the coldest state in the Union"—from a Minnesotan, high tribute.[6]

From Kansas, the army sent Fitzgerald progressively further south. In March 1918 he reported to Camp Taylor outside Louisville, in April to Camp Gordon outside Atlanta, where he "taught Wisconsin country boys the basic principles of 'squads right' through two chilly months," and in June to Camp Sheridan outside Montgomery.[7]

In *The Great Gatsby,* Jay Gatsby's army posting to Louisville proves fateful, for there he meets Daisy. Fitzgerald met his destiny in Montgomery, "where the emotions of my youth culminated in one emotion," he later reflected—the most ecstatic, exhausting, momentous emotion of his life.[8]

I n 1918 Montgomery was a quiet provincial city of forty thousand. In Fitzgerald's short stories it becomes Tarleton, "a little city of forty thousand that has dozed sleepily for forty thousand years in southern Georgia."

Years later, encouraging Scottie to visit the now-invalid Zelda in Montgomery, he would apologize: "Your mother most particularly asked to see you again. . . . I know it will be dull going into that hot little town early in September. . . ."[9] Fitzgerald's tastes and ambitions were urban; any place smaller than New York was "a little town." Except for one stunning experience in 1918, Montgomery too would have been, for him, little more than a dull, hot little town.

Though new to the South, he was predisposed to it. His father, Edward, born in 1853, had grown up in Maryland, south of the Mason-Dixon Line, and passed on his Confederate sympathies to his romantically susceptible son. In an early draft of *This Side of Paradise,* the narrator reports that "From father I acquired an extended and showy, if very superficial knowledge of the civil war (with an intense southern bias . . .)." Edward Fitzgerald liked to recount boyhood memories of the war. "He sat on the front fence all one morning, when he was a little boy, watching the butternut battalions of Early stream by on their surprise attempt at Washington, the last great threat of the Confederacy." Recalling such tales after his father's death, Fitzgerald claimed, implausibly, that his father "as a boy during the Civil War was an integral part of the Confederate spy system between Washington and Richmond," and recalled Edward's repertory of boyhood stories, "the story of the spy, the one about the man hung by his thumbs, the one about Early's march."[10]

In a magazine article of 1924, Fitzgerald asked rhetorically, "Whom could my generation look up to . . . when we were young?" Among those mentioned are a football player, two Catholic priests, Charles Dickens, a poet, and five soldiers, two of them Confederate generals—Stonewall Jackson and J. E. B. Stuart. No Union figure, military or civilian, made the list.[11] Fictionally, he later added another Confederate: "gallant Pelham." "You know who the Gallant Pelham was?" a character in "Her Last Case" asks. "He commanded Stuart's horse artillery at twenty-three. He was my hero when I was a boy."

Periodically, beginning in his youth, Fitzgerald wrote about the Civil War. In "A Debt of Honor," written at thirteen, a young Confederate soldier sentenced to death for sleeping on sentry duty receives a last-minute reprieve from General Lee. "General," the soldier responds, "The Confederate States of America shall never have cause to regret that I was not shot." Several weeks later at Chancellorsville he redeems himself by dying in a charge against a Union outpost. A few years later Fitzgerald wrote and acted in a Civil War play, "Coward," also turning on the theme of redemption. A posed photograph of the cast members in "Coward" shows him in the spruce dress uniform of a well-turned-out Confederate officer, with cavalry hat and saber.[12]

In the 1930s, he returned to his father's anecdote of the Confederate soldier hung by his thumbs and wrote an oft-revised story eventually reaching print as "The End of Hate" in 1940. "Did you see a very poor story of mine that was in Collier's a few weeks ago?" he asked his cousin Cecilia Taylor; ". . . it was founded on a family story—how William George Robertson [Edward Fitzgerald's cousin] was hung up by the thumbs at Glen Mary or was it Locust Grove? [farms near Rockville]. Aunt Elise would know."[13]

Aunt Elise was his father's sister. When she died he wrote a sympathy note to her daughter: "With Father, Uncle John [Edward's younger brother] and Aunt Elise, a generation goes. I wonder how deep the Civil War was in them—that odd childhood on the border between the states with Grandmother and old Mrs. Scott and the shadow of Mrs. Suratt. What a sense of honor and duty. . . . How lost they seemed in the changing world. . . ."[14]

Though spurred by family traditions and loyalties, Fitzgerald's southern sympathies were temperamentally congenial. In *This Side of Paradise,* Amory Blaine and his mentor Monsignor Darcy share a bias for the "romantic lost cause" of the South:

> "I was for Bonnie Prince Charlie," announced Amory.
> "Of course you were—and for Hannibal—"
> "Yes, and for the Southern Confederacy."

I n "The Last of the Belles," a 1929 story revisiting Fitzgerald's army duty in Montgomery a decade earlier, the narrator reports that, during his early weeks in camp outside Tarleton, Georgia, he seldom ventured into town, hearing about the local girls only second-hand. This seems an unlikely description of Fitzgerald, who at twenty-one would not have hesitated to investigate Montgomery's social possibilities for a young bachelor. Zelda's 1932 novel *Save Me the Waltz* remarks on "a busload of officers . . . free from camp for the evening to seek what explanation of the world this little Alabama town had to offer."

Like the narrator of "The Last of the Belles," he was initially underimpressed. Several days after arriving, he wrote to a cousin: "I believe that for the first time in my life I'm rather lonesome down here . . . lonesome for the old atmosphere—a feverish crowd at Princeton sitting up until three discussing pragmatism or the immortality of the soul—for the glitter of New York with a tea dance at the Plaza or lunch at Sherries—for the quiet respectable boredom of St. Paul."[15] His southern sympathies would have to contend with oppressive summer heat and a quiet slow-moving town lacking clever Princetonians, luxury hotels, and sparkling nightlife. He was lonesome only briefly, however. Making his way from camp into town, he discovered that, if nothing else, Montgomery offered attractive girls. One in particular would transform his life.

Zelda Sayre has long fascinated readers of Fitzgerald. His early, lighthearted story "Head and Shoulders" follows a scholarly prodigy who marries an exuberant chorus girl and drifts away from a brilliant academic career to become a circus performer. "I just brought in the chorus girl by way of a radical contrast," Fitzgerald would recall. "Before I'd finished she almost stole the story."[16] So too Zelda. "She was a great original in her way," he later observed, "with perhaps a more intense flame at its highest than I ever had."[17] We know of her only because she married Fitzgerald; but it may also be that we know Fitzgerald only because he met Zelda.

She was like no one he had known. Ginevra King, of Chicago and Lake Forest wealth, moved in society-page circles and attended expensive private schools in the East. A full-page photo of her appeared on the cover of *Town and Country*. She was a girl of intelligence and spirit—managing to get herself expelled from Westover, for example. But ultimately she did not stray far from her upbringing and class.

Zelda's circumstances were much less grand. Daughter of an Alabama Supreme Court justice, she came from Kentucky and Montgomery gentry, but by Chicago standards the Sayres were small-town and small-money. Her father's income was modest, and they lived accordingly. Like the Sayres, the heroine of Fitzgerald's story "The Ice Palace" lives on an unpaved "dusty road-street" in a small southern city, not on "opiate Millicent Place, where there were half a dozen prosperous substantial mansions."[18] Zelda's father, the distinguished judge, rode a streetcar to work; she and her siblings attended public schools.

Four years younger than Fitzgerald, she had just graduated from Montgomery's Sidney Lanier High School when he reported to Camp Sheridan. Amplified by legend, reminiscences of Zelda note her fearlessness, recklessness, and disdain for propriety. The youngest of five (a sixth had died in infancy) and cosseted by her mother, like Fitzgerald by his, she was incorrigibly self-willed. Earlier that spring her senior class had mounted a "Pageant-Masque of War and Peace" to raise funds for Alabama troops in France, and a clipping pasted in her scrapbook reports that "Zelda Sayre as War was excellent." Her assignment to that role was probably typecasting.

A history of Montgomery's Bell Building, the city's tallest during Zelda's youth, mentions her: "From the opening of the Bell Building [in 1910] until the mid 1930s, the entire 12th floor was occupied by the Beauvoir Club, the city's premier downtown club for men. The club also had a roof garden on top of the building where the ladies were invited for dances and parties. The folklore is that at several of these affairs, young Zelda Sayre danced on the parapet, showing early her penchant for living on the edge."[19] Though likely apocryphal, the story suggests her reputation.

Her good looks and zest made her popular with the golden youth of Montgomery and nearby colleges. Her high school graduating class voted her Most Attractive and Prettiest, distinctions noted in Fitzgerald's ledger. She regularly attended dances, football games, and commencements at Auburn, Alabama, and Georgia Tech. Pasted into her scrapbook are society-page clippings about herself, photos of officers, invitations, and telegrams—her name variously misspelled by confused telegraphers as Telda, Zellia, and Elda—with such messages as:

AM ALL IN THE AIR WITH EXPECTANCY BUT NOTHING HAPPENS WILL
YOU BE HERE THURSDAY PLEASE SAY YES—HAINES

ON MY WAY ARRIVE IN THE CAPITOL CITY NOON WEDNESDAY YOU WILL
HAVE LUNCH WITH ME CERTAINLY WILL PHONE YOU UPON ARRIVAL L
J WEAVER

CAN YOU COME UP FOR PRE-LENTEN DANCES ON FEBY 10TH AND 11TH
WE ARE GOING TO PULL SOME BIG PARTIES I WANT YOU TO COME
MIGHTY BAD AND AM LOOKING FOR YOU AM WRITING YOU TONIGHT
TELLING DETAILS FARNELL BLAIR[20]

The influx of officers at Camp Sheridan was a gift to Montgomery's young women. "The war brought men to the town like swarms of benevolent locusts eating away the blight of unmarried women that had overrun the South since its economic decline," Zelda would describe wartime Montgomery in *Save Me the Waltz*. She herself was not backward in welcoming the soldiers.

"Zelda said of herself that she cared for two things: boys and swimming," biographer Nancy Milford reports, and quotes an old boyfriend of her Montgomery days: "Zelda just wasn't afraid of anything, of boys, of being talked about; she was absolutely fearless. There was this board rigged up at the swimming pool and, well, almost nobody ever dived from the top. But Zelda did, and I was hard put to match her. I really didn't want to. She swam and dived as well as any of the boys and better than most of us. She had no more worries than a puppy would have, or a kitten. . . ."[21] She was equally reckless, it is said, in risking her reputation, but Judge Sayre's prestige and rectitude sheltered her.

In "The Last of the Belles," the narrator reflects on what he calls "the Southern type in all its purity": the story's heroine "had the adroitness sugar-coated with sweet, voluble simplicity, the suggested background of devoted fathers, brothers, and admirers stretching back into the South's heroic age, the unfailing coolness acquired in the endless struggle with the heat." Zelda may not have conformed closely to this type, but for all her reckless independence, her devil-may-care élan rested on the secure foundation of her family's status and respectability.

The officers from Camp Sheridan mingled with the local girls at Saturday night dances at Montgomery's country club, an establishment much unlike the opulent, sleekly groomed Onwentsia of Ginevra King's family. In Montgomery, "The clubhouse sprouted inquisitively under the oaks like a squat clump of bulbs piercing the leaves in spring," Zelda described it in *Save Me the Waltz:* "The ground around the place was as worn and used as the plot before a children's playhouse. The sagging wire about the tennis court, the peeling drab-green paint of the summerhouse on the first tee, the trickling hydrant, the veranda thick in dust all flavored of the pleasant atmosphere of a natural growth."

The clubhouse burned down in 1925, and "the fire destroying this shrine of wartime nostalgias may have been a case of combustion from emotional saturation," Zelda remarked. "No officer could have visited it three times without falling in love, engaging himself to marry and to populate the countryside with little country clubs exactly like it." Fitzgerald arrived at Camp Sheridan on June 15, 1918, and probably at a Saturday night dance soon after—his ledger first notes "Zelda" in July—he met the celebrated local belle.[22]

In two of his Tarleton stories we glimpse these dances, and a third story, "The Dance," a murder mystery, is also set in a small southern country club. In "The Jelly-Bean," a Tarleton story, Jim Powell, attending a country-club dance for the first time,

> . . . saw the girls emerge one by one from the dressing-room, stretching and pluming themselves like bright birds, smiling over their powdered shoulders at the chaperones, casting a quick glance around to take in the room and, simultaneously, the room's reaction to their entrance— and then, again like birds, alighting and nestling in the sober arms of their waiting escorts. . . . all the girls he had seen loitering down Jackson Street by noon, now, curled and brilliantined and delicately tinted for the overhead lights, were miraculously strange Dresden figures of pink and blue and red and gold, fresh from the shop and not yet fully dried.

A keen observer of young women, Fitzgerald would have been fascinated. Zelda loved to dance, and one easily imagines a queue of young officers eager to cut in. For Fitzgerald, her notoriety and popularity enhanced her allure.

On her eighteenth birthday, July 24, he took her to dinner. Years later she recalled the occasion with characteristic sensuality: "Wouldn't you like to smell the pine woods of Alabama again? Remember there were 3 pines on one side and 4 on the other the night you gave me my birthday party and you were a young lieutenant and I was a fragrant phantom, wasn't I? And it was a radiant night, a night of soft conspiracy and the trees agreed that it was going to be for the best. Remember the faded gray romance. . . . Darling. That's the first time I ever said that in my life."[23] Despite this romantic evening there was no Romeo-and-Juliet precipitancy, and even as he wooed Zelda he was also rushing one or two others. In July his ledger mentions "May Stiener" [Steiner], before "Zelda," and a little later, "May and I on the porch." In August, May appears yet again: "Zelda and May." Meanwhile, the ledger also mentions a Helen Dent in July; again in October in connection with a "Frenchman"; and again the following month: "Zelda's friend Dent & the stolen kiss on the stairs."[24]

By this time, however, as suggested by Helen's reduction to "Zelda's friend," his attentions were focused on Zelda. His infatuation was dated with business-like precision, his ledger noting in September, "Fell in love on the 7th." Why that particular day is a mystery, but from that fateful moment Fitzgerald earnestly courted Zelda, and only Zelda. If pedantically exact in logging the beginning, he was persistent, fervent, and even frantic in pursuit. His southern sympathies were supercharged by ardor for the southern girl.

A few years later, writing of a twelve-hundred-mile road trip he and Zelda made to Montgomery as newlyweds, he would recall "the unexpected sadness of the journey's end, of the south itself, of the past we two had had together in this town."[25]

Later yet, in "Basil and Cleopatra," he recalled the experience of associating a beloved girl with her surroundings: "Wherever she was, became a beautiful and enchanted place to Basil, but he did not think of it that way. He thought the fascination was inherent in the locality, and long afterward a commonplace street or the mere name of a city, would exude a peculiar glow, a sustained sound, that struck his soul alert with delight." The story's Cleopatra was "a Southern girl."

Discharged at Camp Sheridan in February 1919, Fitzgerald proceeded straight to New York, job seeking. Though they were informally engaged, Zelda did not pine, attending three dances at Auburn the weekend after he departed and in April the "Folly Ball" in Montgomery, which "opened with a charming playlet" in which "'Folly' was delightfully portrayed by Miss Zelda Sayre, one of Montgomery's most beautiful girls." In May she attended a week of commencement dances at Auburn and in June the Junior Prom at Georgia Tech, where "she caused quite a stir in the hearts of four Atlanta beaux."[26]

New York for Fitzgerald was less gala. Three times—in April, May, and June—he made the long train ride to Montgomery to court and encourage Zelda. Returning from one visit, he later claimed, he couldn't afford a sleeping car and to conceal his poverty from her "had to climb into a Pullman, and then sneak through into the day coach." During the June visit she broke their engagement. Eighteen and enjoying life, she had tired of waiting. "I've done my best and I've failed," he told a Saint Paul friend. ". . . Unless someday she will marry me I will never marry."[27]

In July, staking everything on his twice-rejected novel, he quit his New York advertising job and returned to Saint Paul to rewrite it again. Sequestering himself on the top floor of his parents' house, he plunged into a final attempt to salvage the novel and with it Zelda. "There's still a faint chance" of regaining her, he wrote to a friend. ". . . All through two hot months I wrote and revised and compiled and boiled down," he would recall, and in September 1919 Scribner's accepted *This Side of Paradise*.[28]

The more important objective, however, remained in doubt. In October he wrote to invite himself to Montgomery to renew his suit. Zelda responded with encouragement: "I'm mighty glad you're coming—I've been wanting to see you"—though noting also that his proposed visit conveniently fell between two college football weekends requiring her presence, and adding that "I'm just recovering from a wholesome amour with Auburn's 'starting quarter-back.'" "Zelda had known the greatest gaiety of her youth" at Auburn, Fitzgerald later remarked. ". . . In many hurried letters had she aroused my uneasiness with the news that she was just starting up to Auburn to attend a dance, watch a football game, or merely spend an idle day!"[29]

Undeterred by her amour with the quarterback, he pursued his plan to visit, confiding to a friend, "Im leaving here [Saint Paul] Saturday & going first to Montgomery then to New York. However not even the family know I'm going to Montgomery so keep it dark."[30]

Suitcase in hand, he stepped off the train at Montgomery's Union Station. Of the momentous week that followed his ledger notes only "Went to see Zelda." But now, with his novel forthcoming and "selling short stories right and left," he seemed to have a promising future, and she was persuaded to renew their engagement.[31]

Within three weeks he drafted a fictional tribute to her, a story titled "The Ice Palace," which his new agent, Harold Ober, sold to the *Saturday Evening Post.* No other story expresses his enchantment with Zelda so warmly.

The inspiration and writing of "The Ice Palace" are better documented than those of any other Fitzgerald story. When a trade magazine for writers, *The Editor,* asked him to contribute to a feature ponderously titled "Autobiographical Letters on the Conception, Genesis and Development of Short Stories," he complied, and his article discussing "The Ice Palace" appeared in July 1920.[32]

Fitzgerald was sometimes accused of "fatal facility" and would in more than one magazine article fill the pages with glib opinions and pronouncements. But still a neophyte and addressing *The Editor's* readership of earnest writers, he undertook his assignment seriously, and his description of the origins of "The Ice Palace" is specific and credible. Its earliest inspiration, he noted, lay in a friend's casual remark:

> The idea of "The Ice Palace" grew out of a conversation with a girl out in Saint Paul, Minnesota, my home. We were riding home from a moving picture show late one November night.
>
> "Here comes winter," she said, as a scattering of confetti-like snow blew along the street.
>
> I thought immediately of the winters I had known there, their bleakness and dreariness and seemingly infinite length, and then we began talking about life in Sweden.

"I wonder," I said casually, "if the Swedes aren't melancholy on account of the cold—if this climate doesn't make people rather hard and
chill—" and then I stopped, for I had scented a story.

For two weeks he revolved this notion without writing anything, but "I already had one atmosphere detail—the first wisps of snow weaving like
advance-guard ghosts up the street." Revealing Fitzgerald's genius for evok-
ing emotion by sensory detail, an eighty-five-hundred-word story subse-
quently grew from an image of blowing snowflakes seen in headlights.

For a story, though, he also needed a plot and point of view. These presently came to hand. "At the end of two weeks I was in Montgomery, Alabama, and while out walking with a girl I wandered into a graveyard." The
girl was of course Zelda. "She told me I could never understand how she
felt about the Confederate graves, and I told her I understood so well that
I could put it on paper. Next day on my way back to St. Paul it came to me
that it was all one story—the contrast between Alabama and Minnesota."[33]
In fact Zelda had put her feelings about the Confederate graves on paper
and sent them to him several months earlier. "I've spent to-day in the graveyard," she began. ". . . Isn't it funny how, out of a row of Confederate soldiers, two or three will make you think of dead loves—when they're exactly
like the others, even to the yellowish moss? Old death is so beautiful—so
very beautiful. . . ."[34] As he wrote "The Ice Palace" this passage was unavailable for plagiarizing, as he had already lifted it for *This Side of Paradise*
(changing "Confederate" to "Union"), but the story closely echoes Zelda's
graveyard sentiments, now in the more appropriate southern setting. His
absorption with her—her alluring femininity, southern-ness, and whimsi-
cal charms—pervades "The Ice Palace."

Back in Saint Paul he began assembling the story's leading elements: a
contrast between North and South, to be dramatized in a southern heroine
visiting the North, and her terror of the cold, to be connected with an ice
palace. Traveling north, he noted another small but chilling image, "snow
in the vestibule of a railway train."

Looking back years later, he recollected his trip to Montgomery not only
for his recovery of Zelda, but as the occasion confirming his vocation. "That
June [1919]," he observed, "I was an amateur—in October [actually Novem-

ber], when I strolled with a girl among the stones of a southern grave yard, I was a professional and my enchantment with certain things that she felt and said was already paced by an anxiety to set them down in a story—it was called 'The Ice Palace.'"[35]

The story involved modest research. "I had had the idea of using an ice palace in a story since several months before when my mother told me about one they had in St. Paul in the eighties," he writes. At home he canvassed family for their memories, and "at the public library I found a rough sketch of it that had appeared in a newspaper of the period." In the 1880s Saint Paul's winter carnivals had featured spectacular ice palaces; the last and largest, in 1888, featured high crenellated walls, elaborate arched gateways, a massive keep, and a central tower rising to 130 feet. Its footprint nearly an acre, it was constructed of fifty-five thousand blocks of ice, each the size of a steamer trunk and weighing 420 pounds.

These ambitious structures had been discontinued before Fitzgerald's time, but even if anachronistic, the ice palace of the story, larger than 1888's, was an apt symbol, a temple dedicated to Cold. At 170 feet, it overshadowed by 10 feet the parapets of the Bell Building, Montgomery's tallest, on which Zelda is said to have danced.

The rest of Fitzgerald's article in *The Editor* walks through the actual writing of "The Ice Palace." After finishing the first two (of six) sections, he jumped ahead to write the last two: "So there I had my beginning and end which are the easiest and most enjoyable for me to write, and the climax, which is the most exciting and stimulating to work out. It took me three days to do parts three and four, the least satisfactory parts of the story, and while doing them I was bored and uncertain, constantly re-writing, adding and cutting and revising—and in the end didn't care particularly for them." Of the four sections he enjoyed writing, one took place in the ice palace but the other three in the South, where the story begins "with an atmospheric sketch of the girl's life in Alabama" (forgetting that the story begins and ends "in southernmost Georgia").

Like Zelda, the story's heroine is comfortably placed among the gentry of a small southern city. Happy there and fond of the local boys, the ambitious Sally Carrol Happer nonetheless rebels against the prospect of stagnating in the poky little city. "There's two sides to me, you see," she tells her

friends. "There's the sleepy old side you love; an' there's a sort of energy—
the feelin' that makes me do wild things." For this fusion of wild energy
and languor, Zelda was the undoubted inspiration. Unlike 1918 Montgomery, Tarleton lacks army officers, but Sally Carrol has nonetheless managed
to meet a northerner ready to carry her away to the larger world she seeks,
and she is eager to go.

The action of "The Ice Palace" divides equally between South and North,
with three sections set in each. Sally Carrol and her northern beau Harry
make reciprocal visits to each other's home, he to Tarleton, she to Minnesota. The structure is circular, beginning with Sally Carrol lounging in Tarleton on a lazy September day, skipping ahead to November, then January,
and ending with her back in Tarleton on a lazy April day, lounging exactly
where we had seen her on the first page. Few if any of Fitzgerald's other stories are so carefully symmetrical and rounded. But the apparently closed
circle is ironic. Tarleton remains the same lazy town, but Sally Carrol has
become a different, wiser girl.

The Ice Palace" opens with kinetic imagery of warmth: "The sunlight
dripped over the house like golden paint over an art jar, and the freck-
ling shadows here and there only intensified the rigor of the bath of light"—
and more follows. By contrast, as Sally Carrol travels north to visit Harry,
"All night in the Pullman it was very cold. . . . The snow had filtered into
the vestibules and covered the floor with a slippery coating. . . . Sometimes
a solitary farmhouse would fly by, ugly and bleak and lone on the white
waste. . . ." "The 'Ice Palace' was written in the middle of a Minnesota winter," he would recall, "when I felt that I could have been blood-brother to
a warm-blooded ethiope."[36] (When he sent the story out on December 10,
Minnesota's winter was actually just beginning.)

Closely related to the South's warmth was its easy rhythm, its unhurried
lassitude. "Sally Carrol gazed down sleepily. She started to yawn, but finding this quite impossible unless she raised her chin from the window-sill,
changed her mind. . . ." Beyond, in Tarleton at large, ". . . the population
idled casually across the streets and a drove of low-moaning oxen were be-

ing urged along in front of a placid street-car; even the shops seemed only yawning their doors and blinking their windows in the sunshine before retiring into a state of utter and finite coma." With Fitzgerald's background of midwestern industriousness, Princetonian ambition, and New York hustle and push, and with his own nervous energy and drive, one might have guessed that he would have had little patience with such idling, yawning placidity. As background and setting for Zelda and as picturesque foil to wintry Saint Paul, it charmed him.

Sally Carrol's northern beau Harry, "tall, broad, and brisk," admires the robust hockey players of his hometown, while Tarleton's males are represented by easygoing Clark Darrow, "dark and lean" and "inclined to stoop," who has "spent the two years since he graduated from Georgia Tech in dozing round the lazy streets of his home town." It is not just for lack of ice that hockey is not Clark's sport; his less bruising pastimes are "hanging round" with girls, or "a few holes of golf, or a game of billiards, or the consumption of a quart of 'hard yella licker.'"

Along with Harry's admiration for Big Three athletes playing rough contact sports, he has a crude male admiration for big money and big moneymakers. "This is man's country, I tell you," he boasts. "Look at John J. Fishburn!"

Sally has no clue. "Don't you know?" Harry exclaims, shocked. "Greatest wheat man in the Northwest, and one of the greatest financiers in the country."

The bombastic superlatives, the boasting, the boorishness, the hypermasculinity, the money worship—all these enhance the charm of Clark Darrow's well-mannered indolence. "A part of me will always live in St. Paul which I think of as a tough and usually impolite city," Fitzgerald told a friend years later.[37] Destined for success, "Harry Bellamy had everything she wanted," Sally Carrol imagines, but he lacks qualities that grace and soften life. Clark Darrow's very weaknesses—"the living in the past, the lazy days and nights you have, and all your carelessness and generosity," as Sally Carrol enumerates—are preferable.

"Carelessness" here has the sense of *sans souci;* "generosity" that of unreflecting consideration and hospitality. Even years later, after his romance with Zelda and the South had waned, Fitzgerald admitted that "Southern manners are better—especially the rather punctilious deference to older people."[38]

There are early hints of Harry Bellamy's oafishness. On her first day in Minnesota he warns Sally Carrol not to criticize local worthies whom she might find guilty of "vulgar display."

"'Why,' said Sally Carrol, puzzled, 'did you s'pose I was goin' to make remarks about people?'" Her confusion arises not from the prospect of vulgarity but from the insinuation that she would be so ill-bred as to insult the locals. Never imagining such discourtesy, she "felt suddenly indignant—as though she had been unjustly spanked."

Harry's lumpishness soon descends to open rudeness, as he is prompted for no particular reason to "make remarks" about Sally Carrol's people: "They're sort of—sort of degenerates—not at all like the old Southerners," he blusters. "They've lived so long down there with all the colored people that they've gotten lazy and shiftless."

When she protests, a gentleman guilty of discourtesy would instantly apologize, but Harry churlishly persists: ". . . Of all the hangdog, ill-dressed, slovenly lot I ever saw, a bunch of small-town Southerners are the worst!"

The Bellamy women meanwhile are drab and charmless. At dinner they sit "in a haughty and expensive aloofness" while the men do the talking. Harry's sister-in-law Myra "seemed the essence of spiritless conventionality. Her conversation was so utterly devoid of personality that Sally Carrol, who came from a country where a certain amount of charm and assurance could be taken for granted in the women, was inclined to despise her." Harry's mother is "an egg with a cracked, veiny voice and . . . ungracious dumpiness of carriage."

As the mostly northern officers of Camp Sheridan enjoyed their evenings at Montgomery's country club, Fitzgerald could observe the contrast between their olive-drab masculine world and the girls lending color and charm to their off-duty hours. His South was a romantic land of dark verandas cloaked in moonvine, blue taffeta dresses, dances, soft sentiments, gracious manners, and the inimitable Zelda.

Early in her Minnesota visit Sally Carrol meets Roger Patton, a friend of Harry's family. Patton hardly figures in the plot and appears at length only in a part of the story Fitzgerald "didn't care particularly for." His role is to explicate Sally Carrol's emotional, intuitive response to the North.

From Philadelphia, with Big Three credentials (Harvard), Patton is a French professor at the local university. Though resident in Minnesota for ten years, he retains the detachment of a skeptical outsider. He and Sally Carrol, the other outsider, quickly form a sympathetic bond. Sensing her alienation, he offers his own ideas about Minnesota: "I used to have a theory about these people. I think they're freezing up . . . growing like Swedes—Ibsenesque, you know. Very gradually getting gloomy and melancholy. It's these long winters." Patton's theory recalls the germ of "The Ice Palace," when Fitzgerald and his Saint Paul friend "began talking about life in Sweden," and he wondered "if this climate doesn't make people rather hard and chill."

Sally Carrol not having read Ibsen, Patton explains: "Well, you find in his characters a certain brooding rigidity. They're righteous, narrow, and cheerless, without infinite possibilities for great sorrow or joy."

She suggests, more concretely, "Without smiles or tears?"

Patton agrees. "Exactly," he says. "That's my theory," and he applies it to a specific case: "Your future sister-in-law is half Swedish. Personally I like her, but my theory is. . . ." Sally Carrol has already pegged the "listless" Myra as "vaguely Scandinavian," and detecting her dislike, Patton hints his agreement. His commentary expands the story's emotional register; the South's warmth is not just a thermometer reading but a generosity of feeling. Sally's South may be leisurely, lazy, and slow, but Harry Bellamy's North betrays a January of the heart.

As they drive along snowy streets from the train station just after her arrival, she sees little boys "hitching sleds behind grocery wagons and automobiles." She exclaims, "I want to do that! Can we, Harry?" He scoffs, "That's for kids." Later, looking out the window she sees "two little boys makin' a snow man! Harry, do you reckon I can go out an' help 'em?"

Harry dismisses the idea. The spirit of childhood that might have lightened his heaviness has frozen. "Play" has yielded to aggressive, violent competitions like hockey and football for the youth and money-making for their fathers. By contrast, the favorite recreation of Sally Carrol's Tarleton friends of both sexes is swimming on hot days. Zelda was an avid swimmer: "If Zelda can't swim, she's miserable," Fitzgerald remarked shortly after their marriage.[39] "The Ice Palace" begins and ends with pool parties.

What matters is not the games and recreations themselves, but the ethos they embody. In characters like Harry and John J. Fishburn, "greatest wheat man in the Northwest," Sally Carrol's playful spontaneity encounters the leaden spirit of money- and power-seeking. The sympathies of "The Ice Palace" are never in doubt.

Soon after arriving at Harry's, Sally Carrol visits the library, a room once common in genteel homes. The Bellamys' library is a mildly pleasant room with handsomely bound books lining the shelves. "All the chairs had little lace squares where one's head should rest, the couch was just comfortable." The room was "neither attractive nor particularly otherwise. It was simply a room with a lot of fairly expensive things in it that all looked about fifteen years old."

Observing this emotionally barren room, Sally Carrol recalls her family's "battered old library at home, with her father's huge medical books, and the oil-paintings of her three great-uncles, and the old couch that had been mended up for forty-five years and was still luxurious to dream in." With its reassuring flavor of home, rich in family associations, the shabby Happer library carries the impress of Happers living and dead. The Bellamys' library, as generic as if dropped into the house at random, might be that of any affluent family anywhere. Against the Happers' "old couch . . . still luxurious to dream in," the Bellamy chairs with assigned squares for the placement of one's head suggest the home comforts of a dentist's chair.

Fitzgerald cherished few fond memories of a childhood home. When he was young the Fitzgeralds moved about often, from city to city and within cities from house to house. Matthew Bruccoli's *Some Sort of Epic Grandeur* lists ten different residences during his youth and suggests there were more; their itinerancy makes precise tabulation difficult.[40] Going off to a boarding school a thousand miles away, Fitzgerald suffered no evident homesickness.

It was Zelda who introduced him to affection for home and hometown, and though without such love himself, he could appreciate hers. The Sayres were no ideal family, and 6 Pleasant Avenue was crowded and like the Happer house possibly somewhat shabby; but the Sayres were anchored in the small, socially self-sufficient city of which they were prominent citizens, and together their austere father and indulgent mother created a stable home which Zelda loved.

When Camp Sheridan began winding down after the Armistice, "Seems almost like old times again," Zelda wrote to Fitzgerald in New York. "I wish you could get a glimpse of Montgomery like it really is—without the camp disturbing things so—and you'd know why I love it so."[41]

Impressed by her home-loving spirit, Fitzgerald bestowed her loyalties on the heroine of "The Ice Palace." One night during Sally Carrol's visit to Minnesota, Harry takes her to a vaudeville show. At the end, "the orchestra played 'Dixie' and Sally Carrol felt something stronger and more enduring than her tears and smiles of the day brim up inside her":

> To the spirited throb of the violins and the inspiring beat of the kettledrums her own old ghosts were marching by and on into the darkness, and as fifes whistled and sighed in the low encore they seemed so nearly out of sight that she could have waved good-by.
> "Away, away,
> Away down South in Dixie!"[42]

No one choked up, Fitzgerald perhaps reflected, when a band struck up "Hail Minnesota." The North does boast rousing music, however—which in the story's climactic scene reverberates darkly.

Earlier, Sally Carrol had led Harry through Tarleton's graveyard. On Fitzgerald's November 1919 return to Montgomery to resume his courtship, Zelda had taken him to Oakwood Cemetery, the city's largest and oldest, "a park-like place with its own neighborhoods of rich folks, not-so-rich folks, slaves, free blacks, Jews, Catholics and soldiers."[43] More than 750 Confederate soldiers lie buried in Oakwood, their graves marked by rows of plain upright slabs on a green hillside.

Zelda knew Oakwood well. An older brother who had died before she was born was buried there (her parents, another brother, and a sister would eventually join him). She certainly showed Fitzgerald the Confederate graves, and may also have conducted him to her brother's grave, but her visits to Oakwood were not always sentimental. Six months earlier she had ventured there at night, on a dare, ". . . trying to unlock a rusty iron vault built in the side of the hill. It's all washed and covered with weepy blue flowers that might have grown from dead eyes—sticky to touch with a sickening odor—The boys wanted to get in to test my nerve—to-night—I wanted to *feel* 'William Wreford, 1864.'"[44] There is no record of a William Wreford buried in Oakwood, but built into a bank and with steel doors welded shut, a large brick vault bears the legend, "Wreford 1866." Much vandalized over the years—perhaps by Zelda's "boys" among others—this is probably what she described in her letter to Fitzgerald. Designed to accommodate eight Wrefords, it holds only one.[45]

In "The Ice Palace," the Tarleton graveyard, "gray-white and golden-green under the cheerful late sun," is one of Sally Carrol's "favorite haunts." She first leads Harry to the grave of "Margery Lee"—perhaps, like "Sally Carrol," a double name. From Margery Lee's neglected grave, marked by "a tall, round headstone, freckled with dark spots of damp and half grown over with vines," Sally Carrol imagines her as "dark, I think; and she always wore her hair with a ribbon in it. . . ." For her, the graveyard is less about death than about imagining the once-living. Like the fallen leaves scattered about, the graves have "only the fragrance that their own shadowy memories could waken in living minds." Unable to speak for themselves, the dead wait for the living to reach out.

At Margery Lee's grave, Sally Carrol speculates, "I think perhaps a lot of men went away to war meanin' to come back to her"—Margery Lee had turned seventeen the year of Fort Sumter—"but maybe none of 'em ever did."

Such romantic fancies do not interest Harry. Searching the headstone's inscription for any indication of marriage, he reports, "There's nothing here to show"—but Sally Carrol brushes off this literal-minded observation. "How could there be anything there better than just 'Margery Lee' and that eloquent date?" In "The Jelly Bean," Fitzgerald would satirize Tarleton as "occasionally stirring in its slumbers and muttering something about a war that took place sometime, somewhere, and that everyone else has forgotten long ago." In Zelda he could forgive such nostalgia, and Sally Carrol's sentiments move even the dull Harry: "an unexpected lump came into his throat."

From Margery Lee's grave, Sally Carrol leads Harry to another spot, "where along the green turf were a thousand grayish-white crosses stretching in endless, ordered rows." "'Those are the Confederate dead,' said Sally

Carrol simply." Pointing out a row of graves marked "Unknown," she comments: "'These were just men, unimportant evidently or they wouldn't have been 'unknown'; but they died for the most beautiful thing in the world—the dead South. You see,' she continued, her voice still husky, her eyes glistening with tears, 'people have these dreams they fasten onto things, and I've always grown up with that dream.'" She continues with a eulogy for the vanished South, with its "past standards of noblesse oblige" and "courtliness and chivalry," now surviving only in attenuated form, "like the roses of an old garden dying all round us."

Romantic, imaginative, in love with a southern girl, the northerner Fitzgerald could appreciate these unreconstructed sentiments. Even the lumpish Harry expresses his sympathy not with the South, but with Sally Carrol's love for it: "I see through your precious eyes," he tells her, and "How you feel about it is beautiful to me."

In this, at least, he speaks for Fitzgerald, but presently, forgetting Sally Carrol's graveyard nostalgia, Harry begins chattering about her approaching visit to Minnesota. "It'll be slick," he lapses into collegiate slang. "There's a winter carnival on . . . skating and skiing and tobogganing and sleigh-riding, and all sorts of torchlight parades on snow-shoes."

"Will I be cold, Harry?" she interrupts his noisy boosterism. With this shiver of doubt she heads North to the ice palace.

A massive pile of high-stacked ice bricks, the palace thrills Harry: "It's beautiful. . . . My golly, it's beautiful, isn't it! . . . It's a hundred and seventy feet tall . . . covers six thousand square yards." Atop a hill, the palace by night is "outlined in vivid glaring green." If Tarleton's graveyard prompts reflection, the ice palace thrills with dazzle. Sally Carrol is moved by graves of the unknown and unimportant; Harry exults in novelty, splash, and glitter on elephantine scale.

Inside the ice palace's large hall, they witness another impressive spectacle, a torchlight procession of the local marching clubs:

. . . From outside drifted in the full-throated resonant chant of the marching clubs. It grew louder like some paean of a viking tribe traversing an ancient wild. . . . The volume of the voices grew; the great cavern was a phantasmagoria of torches waving in great banks of fire, of colors and the rhythm of soft-leather steps . . . platoon deployed in front of platoon until the whole procession made a solid flag of flame, and then from thousands of voices burst a mighty shout that filled the air like a crash of thunder, and sent the torches wavering.

The loud, flaring, martial, semi-barbaric show impresses and depresses Sally Carrol. "It was magnificent, it was tremendous! To Sally Carrol it was the North offering sacrifice on some mighty altar to the gray pagan God of Snow."

With the ceremonial exit of the marching clubs, the evening's formal entertainment ends, but the excited Harry forcibly urges one last amusement, dragging Sally Carrol "to see the labyrinths down-stairs before they turn the lights off!" These previously unmentioned labyrinths, not a feature of the ice palaces of the 1880s, had occurred to Fitzgerald impromptu. When writing in *The Editor* of Sally Carrol's approach to the ice palace, "of a sudden I began to get the picture of an ice labyrinth so I left the description of the palace and turned at once to the girl lost in the labyrinth."

Perhaps Sally Carrol's affinity with the long-dead Margery Lee sleeping in the mossy southern cemetery prompted the idea of Sally Carrol buried in the icy North. The story leads to the irony of a southern heroine, who loves "warmth and summer and Dixie," lost and frozen—almost—beneath ten thousand tons of ice.

From the beginning, Fitzgerald was steering "The Ice Palace" toward her recoil from the North. In *The Editor* he summarized the story's starting points:

1. The idea of this contrast [between Alabama and Minnesota].
2. The natural sequence of the girl [essentially, Zelda] visiting in the north.
3. The idea that some phase of the cold should prey on her mind.
4. That this phase should be an ice palace. . . .

Repetition of the inert "phase" suggests a still-missing element—a striking incident to dramatize the heroine's change of heart. Something would happen in the ice palace; just what, Fitzgerald was unsure. However it came to him, Sally Carrol's ordeal in the ice palace gave the story a decisive catastrophe and brought Sally Carrol herself to a revelation.

When the notion of ice labyrinth as grave had taken hold, Fitzgerald began inserting foreshadowing hints earlier in the story. The Tarleton graveyard scene, already written, became one anticipation. Then, traveling through Minnesota on the train—before the ice palace scenes in the story's time, but written later—Sally Carrol looks out on isolated farmhouses, imagines them as graves for the still-living, and "had an instant of chill compassion for the souls shut in there waiting for spring."

Riding on a horse-drawn sleigh toward the ice palace, she is oppressed by the heavy skies, snow, and north wind: "Sometimes at night it had seemed to her as though no one lived here—they had all gone long ago—leaving lighted houses to be covered in time by tombing heaps of sleet." Tombs carry her thoughts back to Tarleton's graveyard, and her own someday grave: "Oh, if there should be snow on her grave! To be beneath great piles of it all winter long, where even her headstone would be a light shadow against light shadows. Her grave—a grave that should be flower-strewn and washed with sun and rain." A little later, when Harry reports that the ice palace is the first "since eighty-five!" Sally Carrol's thoughts again revert to death: "Ice was a ghost, and this mansion of it was surely peopled by those shades of the eighties, with pale faces and blurred snow-filled hair."

Sledding to the palace, Sally Carrol had pitied the sleigh-horse: "'Oh, he's cold, Harry,' she said quickly."

"Who? The horse? Oh, no, he isn't. He likes it!" Harry responds, unaware that, in commiserating with the horse, Sally Carrol betrays her own feelings. Now, after the glare and hubbub of the marching clubs, Harry grabs her mittened hand and pulls her down into the labyrinth, boisterously shouting "Come on!"

Dragging her along, he has devised a prank: "Before she realized what he intended Harry had darted down one of the half-dozen glittering passages that opened into the room and was only a vague receding blot against the green shimmer." Playing hide-and-seek with his fiancée in an icy subterranean vault is Harry's idea of excellent fun. Baffled by a maze of corridors, turnings and blind alleys, Sally Carrol quickly becomes disoriented. Then the lights go out.

Her ordeal, Fitzgerald testified, was "the most exciting and stimulating to work out." His inventiveness in imagining the scene testifies to his enjoyment in the writing, but also to narrative skill beyond anything in *This Side of Paradise,* not yet even published.

Beneath the ice palace, bewildered and *in extremis,* Sally Carrol meets a familiar figure: Margery Lee, whose weathered gravestone had stirred her sympathy. "She was just as Sally Carrol had known she would be, with a young, white brow, and wide welcoming eyes, and a hoop-skirt of some soft material that was quite comforting to rest on." Sally Carrol had earlier conjured up Margery Lee from her southern grave; Margery Lee now succors Sally Carrol as she slips into an icy northern grave. The Tarleton graveyard scene had been written before Fitzgerald thought of the labyrinth; but though a late invention, Margery Lee's mystical appearance in the ice palace seems inevitable. An active imagination creates its own opportunities.

Sally Carrol is rescued from her tomb of ice not by Harry but by Roger Patton. Her earlier ambition "to go places and see people . . . to live where things happen on a big scale" has been ironically fulfilled. "'I'm going back home. Take me home . . . tomorrow!' she cried with delirious, unrestrained passion."

With this plea, born of fear and relief but also new self-awareness, Harry and the ice palace disappear like a bad dream on waking, and the story jumps to Tarleton, three months later. At home, "resting her chin on her arm," Sally Carrol gazes out sleepily while "the wealth of golden sunlight poured a quite enervating yet oddly comforting heat over the house where day long it faced the dusty stretch of road. . . ," which is just where she and the story had begun.

The Ice Palace" is the fanciful history of a young woman discovering where she belongs. As with the town mouse and country mouse, the moral is plain: despite the glamor of life "on a big scale," you're better off in your humble home.

There is irony in this wisdom as applied to Fitzgerald's own southern girl, though, for even as he wrote "The Ice Palace" he intended to carry Zelda off to where things happened on a prodigious scale. New York was where his Princeton friends had gravitated; where publishers, editors, and agents did business; where bootleg gin flowed freely. Neither Saint Paul nor Alabama was in his plans.

"I AM IN THE LAND OF AMBITION AND SUCCESS AND MY ONLY HOPE AND FAITH IS THAT MY DARLING HEART WILL BE WITH ME SOON," he had wired Zelda from New York soon after his discharge. She would better have heeded the lesson of Sally Carrol. "We belonged to two different worlds," Fitzgerald would later write of himself and Zelda. "She might have been happy with a kind simple man in a southern garden. She didn't have the strength for the big stage"—in which observation he was likely correct, while curiously overlooking his own crack-up on that stage.[46]

Though becoming a minor celebrity of the "jazz age," Zelda retained her love of Montgomery and the South. Praising Save Me the Waltz in 1932, Maxwell Perkins discerned correctly that "she is evidently passionately fond of Alabama, and that gets into the early part of the book."[47] During the 1930s, when they lived mostly apart, her letters to Fitzgerald frequently returned to her love of Montgomery, as if trying to recapture their early days there. "I found the old blind bugler from the Civil War that used to sell me candy when I was a child," she wrote from Montgomery in 1931, when he was in California. "I said 'Uncle Bob I used to buy your candy twenty-five years ago' and he said 'That's nothing new.'" A little later, "O dear, this beneficent weather—and a pink rose in the garden and the cat rolling a sun-beam over the grass and the nights like a child's prayer. I wish we were sharing the expansiveness of this benevolent country."[48]

In 1935, from a Baltimore psychiatric hospital, she recalled Fitzgerald's visit to Montgomery in fall 1919: "You remember the roses in Kinneys yard. . . . The wall was damp and mossy when we crossed the street and said we loved the south. I thought of the south and a happy past I'd never had and I thought I was part of the south. You said you loved this lovely land. The wistaria along the fence was green and the shade was cool and life was old. . . . it was a confederate, a romantic and nostalgic thought."[49] In such recollections one can detect even in the now-broken Zelda the sensibility and sentiments that fascinated Fitzgerald in 1918.

As that fascination faded in the 1920s, his romance with the South faded too. In the 1930s he became estranged from most of her family, who became for him "the South" (though most no longer lived there). Blaming the invalid Zelda for his own problems, in 1935 he blustered, like the oafish Harry of "The Ice Palace," "I hate southerners."[50]

But if his southern sympathies waned, the sensuality awakened by Zelda's South persisted. Six years later it would suffuse *The Great Gatsby,* making rich sensory experiences of drunken lawn parties on Long Island and even memories of December in Minnesota. It lingers still in his last fictional visit to the South, when early in *The Last Tycoon* several Hollywood characters drive through Tennessee countryside: "I could feel even in the darkness that the trees of the woodland were green—that it was all different from the dusty olive-tint of California. Somewhere we passed a Negro driving three cows ahead of him, and they mooed as he scatted them to the side of the road. They were real cows, with warm fresh, silky flanks. . . ." Perhaps he was recalling the image of twenty years earlier, when in "The Ice Palace" "a drove of low-moaning oxen were being urged along in front of a placid street-car."

"I suppose that poetry," the narrator of Fitzgerald's final Tarleton story reflects, "is a Northern man's dream of the South."

2

HONEYMOON YEARS

(1920–1924)

There'd be an orchestra—Bingo! Bango!—playing for us
to dance the tango.

—"THOUSAND-AND-FIRST SHIP"

Though in 1919 Fitzgerald burned with love for Zelda, her feelings were more equivocal. By July, four months after arriving in New York with high hopes, he had quit his job and returned to Saint Paul, with doubtful prospects and no Zelda.

Since his election to Princeton's Cottage Club in his sophomore year, four years earlier, he had flopped academically and dropped out. His classmates gave him five votes for "Prettiest," fifteen for "Thinks he is Wittiest," and zero for "Most Likely to Succeed." Somewhat absurdly, given his failure to graduate, "He will pursue graduate work in English at Harvard," he informed the *Bric-a-Brac*. After Princeton he had impressed no one as a junior infantry officer and "the army's worst aide de camp" (in his words), and missed the war in Europe.[1]

Breezing into New York after his discharge, expecting to set the city ablaze, he wired Zelda in Montgomery, "DARLING HEART AMBITION ENTHUSIASM AND CONFIDENCE I DECLARE EVERYTHING GLORIOUS THIS WORLD IS A GAME." But unable to find work as a journalist he fell into an advertising job while living in an uptown apartment where "I had one hundred and twenty-two rejections slips pinned in a frieze about my room," he later reported. His novel manuscript had meanwhile been rejected by Scribner's, twice, and two other publishers. His Princeton crowd were embarking on promising careers; he was getting nowhere.[2]

Then he lost Zelda, too. Wearying of their open-ended, long-distance engagement, she greeted him at Montgomery's Union Station one day in June, disengaged herself, and sent him back to New York.

Twenty months earlier, receiving his army commission, he had outfitted himself with that military essential, tailored uniforms from Brooks Brothers. (Twenty-three years later he would be buried in a new Brooks Brothers suit.) Now he wore shabby suits and padded the soles of worn-out shoes with cardboard—or so with Dickensian pathos he later claimed.

When he showed up at the door of 599 Summit Avenue, Saint Paul, with his trunk, woeful shoes, and dog-eared typescript of an unsalable novel, even his doting mother must have understood Zelda's doubts.

The next twelve months were Fitzgerald's *annus mirabilis,* the most dramatic and exciting year of his life. Retreating to the top floor of his parents' house, he rewrote his novel through the summer. Salvaging large chunks of the previous version, he changed the narrative from first- to third-person, added new material—the hero's girlfriend, carried over from the earlier draft, became a Zelda-like jilt—and cobbled it all into a disjointed, barely coherent, inconclusive, often silly—but energetic—narrative.

In September he sent off the typescript to Scribner's and two weeks later received an acceptance letter, kicking off an avalanche of good fortune. Becoming an author, even prospectively, for the distinguished house of Charles Scribner's Sons—publisher of Henry Adams, Robert Louis Stevenson, Theodore Roosevelt, Henry James, George Santayana, and Edith Wharton, with a handsome new headquarters and bookstore on Fifth Avenue—brought luster and marketability: "The offices of editors and publishers were open to me, impresarios begged plays, the movies panted for screen material."[3] After the frieze of rejection slips, he found magazines eager for his stories.

He acquired an agent and in November the *Saturday Evening Post* accepted "Head and Shoulders," the first of sixty-five stories he would eventually sell to the *Post.* Best remembered now for its Norman Rockwell covers, the *Post* between wars was the preeminent popular magazine in a golden age of print, when Americans turned pages rather than tapping screens. Serving a large public hungry for reading matter, especially fiction, magazines like the *Post, Redbook, Collier's, Scribner's, Metropolitan, Hearst's International, McCall's, Cosmopolitan,* and *Liberty* carried short fiction in every issue and sometimes novellas and novel serials. Prominent authors were happy to contribute.

When the *New Yorker* was established in 1925, its founding editor, Harold Ross, proclaimed an elitist agenda: *"The New Yorker* will be the magazine which is not edited for the old lady in Dubuque." The magazines to which Fitzgerald contributed were published for the millions, from Dubuque to Queens. The old lady in Iowa and other middle-American readers enjoyed a regular diet of well-crafted fiction. Like all periodicals they printed much uninspired pulp, but also carried on the vigorous vernacular tradition of Dickens and Mark Twain. Under George Horace Lorimer, editor during Fitzgerald's contributing years, the *Post* published stories by Willa Cather, Edith Wharton, Rudyard Kipling, Joseph Conrad, Stephen Crane, O. Henry, Theodore Dreiser, Ring Lardner, William Faulkner, and P. G. Wodehouse. During Lorimer's long editorial reign, from 1899 to 1936, the *Post*'s circulation rose to over three million, its pages were packed with advertising, and it paid writers well.

Years later, writing to his agent Harold Ober, Fitzgerald nostalgically recalled that "I was twenty-two [actually twenty-three] when I came to New York and found that you'd sold *Head and Shoulders* to the Post. I'd like to get a thrill like that again but I suppose its only once in a lifetime."[4] Soon such sales became commonplace; in the first six months of 1920, the *Post* published six of his stories (including "The Ice Palace"), its generous payments compensating for the dwindling thrill.

This Side of Paradise, published in March 1920, did not make Fitzgerald rich, but its jaunty tone ("verve," he later called it), up-to-date menu of collegiate characters and (especially) young women, and his own spruce good looks generated copy for the book columns and society paragraphs, then regular features in big-city dailies. He became a minor celebrity. It helped that he and Zelda, married a week after the novel appeared, photographed well. Perhaps inspired by her girlhood scrapbook of her Montgomery youth, he subscribed to a press-clipping service and began filling a scrapbook with hundreds of clippings about himself, from book reviews and full-length features to one-line mentions. In multiple volumes, the scrapbook survives at Princeton's Firestone Library, page after wearisome page of mostly puff and fluff.

Back in Saint Paul the previous September, unemployed after sending his typescript to Scribner's, he had taken "a job repairing car roofs at the Northern Pacific [Railroad] shops"—the only physical labor he would ever perform, and then only briefly. When the Scribner's acceptance letter arrived, he quit, "paid off my terrible small debts, bought a suit" (and presumably new shoes), and began a lifelong habit of spending money based on expectations rather than cash in hand. In 1919 he made, according to his ledger, $879 from his writing; early in 1920, flush from selling movie rights to "Head and Shoulders," he sent Zelda "a platinum and diamond wrist watch which cost six hundred dollars." His rising income kept up with expenditures, almost. In 1920 he earned $18,850.[5]

The only spot to enjoy oneself when young, healthy, prosperous, gregarious, newly married, and about to conquer the world was New York. Married in a brief ceremony at St. Patrick's, attended by neither Montgomery nor Saint Paul parents, he and Zelda honeymooned in the Biltmore, a luxury hotel overlooking Grand Central. Over the next four years they moved about restlessly, making a road trip to Montgomery, spending a spring in Europe and fifteen months in Saint Paul, departing again for Europe in the spring of 1924. Homeless, shifting about among hotels, apartments, and rented houses, they invariably gravitated to New York.

After nearly three years abroad, they returned to New York again. Fitzgerald would later recall his feelings "as the ship glided up the river": ". . . The city burst thunderously upon us in the early dusk—the white glacier by the Battery swooping down like a strand of a bridge to rise into 'uptown,' a miracle of foamy light suspended from the stars. A band started to play on deck, but the majesty of the city made the march trivial and tinkling. From that moment I knew that New York, however often I might leave it, was home."[6] He and Zelda actually resided in the city only once, but growing bored or discontented elsewhere they habitually drifted back, and with vast oceanic indifference New York re-swallowed them.

The first three or four years of their marriage were their champagne era. During that span he published two novels and about twenty stories, and earned $90,000. "I had a hell of a lot of fun when I was in my twenties and thirties," he would recall, though inaccurately with respect to much of his thirties.[7] But his mid-twenties had been a carnival ride.

Even then, however, he continued to brood on the great and moving experience of 1919. Two stories of the time reveal the tension between the rising, happily married young author and the wistful imagination "borne back ceaselessly into the past."

While other of Fitzgerald's early fantasies—"The Offshore Pirate," "The Diamond as Big as the Ritz," "The Curious Case of Benjamin Button"— are better known, "'O Russet Witch!'" most vividly captures the confidence and effervescence of these honeymoon years. Sending it to Ober, he called it "the best thing I ever wrote."[8] It began with a glance out the window.

After a honeymoon summer in Westport, Connecticut, on the shore of Long Island Sound, the Fitzgeralds moved into New York. The country life was not for them, especially with winter approaching. The city glittered and tempted, with theaters, fashionable hotels, restaurants, and speakeasies; the offices of Scribner's and Harold Ober were there, along with a circle of Princeton friends and literary types.

In October he and Zelda moved into an apartment at 38 West Fifty-Ninth Street, a few doors down from the Plaza Hotel and fronting Central Park. The heroine of "'O Russet Witch!'" lives "in a nice building with a white stone front, opposite the south side of Central Park. The back of her apartment faced the single window of the single room occupied by the single Mr. Grainger," the protagonist. Had Fitzgerald looked out the back window of his own Fifty-Ninth Street apartment he might have seen, across the area, Merlin Grainger gazing back, and Merlin in turn might have observed not just Fitzgerald, but the more interesting figure of Zelda.

A clerk in a bookshop, the Moonlight Quill, Merlin eventually becomes its owner (in the 1920s, there were almost as many bookshops as delicatessens in Manhattan).[9] "'O Russet Witch!'" follows him through a dreary life in which, outside slow-moving days in the bookshop, he marries a dull woman, picks up much the same dinner at the same delicatessen each evening on his way home to their stale walk-up, vacations in a boarding house on the New Jersey shore, and tells "the same jokes three or four times a year at the family table."

His drab existence is related with rich comic zest: "'O Russet Witch'" is the most high-spirited of all Fitzgerald's stories. A little later he explained, "I had just completed the first draft of my second novel [*The Beautiful and Damned*], and a natural reaction made me revel in a story wherein none of the characters need be taken seriously."[10] Liberated from the serious, his playful invention soared.

The story begins when, with Merlin straightening the bookshop shelves on a "particularly gloomy gray" day, a beautiful woman strides in. He recognizes her as a neighbor, after a fashion, for looking out his apartment window in the evenings he has frequently admired her across the way, a woman "dazzling and light, with a shimmering morass of russet waves to take the place of hair." With no idea who she is, Merlin fancifully names her "Caroline" and takes vicarious pleasure in her glamorous life as glimpsed through her lighted window.

The Moonlight Quill is illuminated by "a great squat lamp of crimson satin that, lighted through all the day, swung overhead." Entering the shop, "Caroline picked up a volume of poems lying loose upon a pile, fingered it absently with her slender white hand, and suddenly, with an easy gesture, tossed it upward toward the ceiling, where it disappeared in the crimson lamp and lodged there, seen through the illuminated silk as a dark, bulging rectangle. This pleased her—she broke into young, contagious laughter, in which Merlin found himself presently joining." Laughing together, they take turns launching book after book into the lamp until it crashes to the floor, and in glass-shattering abandon they proceed to destroy the rest of the shop and its stock, hurling books about with "a noise of smashing and ripping and tearing, mixed now and then with the tinkling of glass, the quick breathing of the two throwers, and the intermittent outbursts of laughter to which both of them periodically surrendered."

Caroline is, in short, a dreamlike liberation from inhibition and propriety. With their joyful book-flinging, she and Merlin mock the heavy authority of books, a small-scale storming of the literary Bastille. Even more valuable is her "contagious laughter"; she is the spirit of gaiety. Apart from her few appearances, we never see Merlin laugh.

She brings with her not just russet hair with purple shadows, but the entire spectrum. "'O Russet Witch!'" is Fitzgerald's most highly colored story, with at least seventy color references and the names of eighteen different colors—not counting that of Merlin's eventual wife, Olive, which Fitzgerald likely associated with army olive drab. In addition to its rainbow of hues, "'O Russet Witch!'" is rich in play of light—with "dazzling," "shimmering," "brilliance," "iridescent," "dripping" moonlight, "the crystalline sprinkling of broken glass," among others.

At the time of her visit to the Moonlight Quill, Caroline is nineteen, Merlin twenty-five. Though with her advent he had felt that "something very portentous in his life was about to occur," her visit has no perceptible effect on his life. A year and a half later, still clerking in the Moonlight Quill, he becomes engaged to Olive, the bookshop stenographer, even as he "laughed inwardly as he compared her to Caroline, or rather as he didn't compare her. There was no comparison."

As he proposes to Olive over a bottle of watered-down wine at a prosy little restaurant, Caroline bursts into his life again. Conspicuously festive and noisy, she disrupts another staid establishment:

> . . . A girl with russet, purple-shadowed hair mounted to her tabletop and began to dance thereon.
> "*Sacré nom de Dieu!* Come down off there!" cried the head-waiter. "Stop that music!"

The band ignores him, and "Caroline danced with grace and vivacity, her pink filmy dress swirling about her, her agile arms playing in supple, tenuous gestures along the smoky air," as other diners stand and applaud. Soon the room is "full of clapping and shouting" while the headwaiter remonstrates. An indignant Olive drags the reluctant Merlin away.

With this second incursion, it becomes apparent that the Russet Witch's appearances are more than just random interruptions of Merlin's dull life by an anarchic socialite, but rather a life ring tossed to a drowning victim of the dull and domestic. He fails to seize it.

Eight years after her second appearance, with Merlin long settled in his dispiriting marriage, Caroline appears yet again. Walking up Fifth Avenue with Olive and their son Arthur on Easter morning, he "perceived an open landaulet of deepest crimson, with handsome nickel trimmings, glide slowly up to the curb. . . . In it sat Caroline." Her appearance causes a sensation among the well-dressed crowd leaving nearby churches: "The crowd swelled. A row formed in back of the first, two more behind that. In the midst, an orchid rising from a black bouquet, sat Caroline enthroned in an open landaulet car, nodding and crying salutations and smiling with such true happiness that, of a sudden, a new relay of gentlemen had left their wives and consorts and were striding toward her." Again Merlin is caught up in the Witch's disruptive gaiety. Again Olive drags him away.

Three chances lost; there will be no fourth. Merlin will see the Russet Witch a final time, but only after thirty more years of dreariness, routine, and Olive. "'O Russet Witch'" summarizes those three decades in a few paragraphs. Contemplating the loss of youth, the twenty-four-year-old Fitzgerald saw no gain in the doubtful benefits of maturity, experience, children, serenity, or silver-haired wisdom—only a draining of vitality, enthusiasm, hope, intensity. In a rambling martial metaphor, Merlin's life falls into a dismal universal pattern of aging: "The years between thirty-five and sixty-five revolve before the passive mind as one unexplained, confusing merry-go-round. . . . For most men and women these thirty years are taken up with a gradual withdrawal from life, a retreat first from a front with many shelters, to a line with less . . . ending up at last in a solitary, desolate strong point that is not strong . . . as, by turns frightened and tired, we sit waiting for death." Perhaps Fitzgerald was thinking of his own aging father, who in 1920 turned sixty-seven. "At sixty-five," Merlin "distinctly doddered."

Forty years after her initial appearance, the Russet Witch returns to the Moonlight Quill. By the story's murky chronology she would now be fifty-nine, but to Merlin she appears "an old woman" with "webs of wrinkles," her eyes "dim, ill natured, and querulous." Nonetheless, terrorizing in succession her chauffeur, grandson, and stockbroker, she remains a firecracker, or as the Moonlight Quill's "lady clerk" Miss McCracken comments, "a spunky old piece."

Merlin now understands: the Russet Witch has been a warning apparition, like the Ghost of Christmas Future. "I see now that on a certain night when you danced upon a table-top," Merlin suggests, "you were nothing but my romantic yearning for a beautiful and perverse woman." To the editor of *Metropolitan* Fitzgerald commented, "As you can see the girl, of course, represents that inhibited attraction that all men show to a 'wild & beautiful woman.' The greyer a mans life is the more it comes out."[11]

A "beautiful," "perverse," "wild" woman points unmistakably to Zelda, with her witchlike name; as if to confirm it, Fitzgerald told *Metropolitan*'s illustrator that his sketch of the Witch dancing on the table "reminds me faintly of Zelda," herself an exuberant dancer.[12] Perhaps he understood Zelda as a challenge to match her daring and recklessness. The tabletop dance had come on the night Merlin proposed to Olive, and he now says to the Witch, "You were making an attempt at me. Olive's arms were closing about me and you wanted me to be free and keep my measure of youth and irresponsibility."

Then Merlin recalls the Witch's third appearance, thirty years earlier: "You shook me with that traffic tie-up. . . . The beauty and power you radiated! You became personified even to my wife, and she feared you. For weeks I wanted to slip out of the house at dark and forget the stuffiness of life with music and cocktails and a girl to make me young." But as Merlin sadly remarks, the tabletop dancing "came too late" to save him; and as for retaining his youth and irresponsibility—"I no longer knew how."

Originally meaning to suggest that the Witch's appearances were dreams, Fitzgerald at the last minute changed his mind. After her final appearance, the Moonlight Quill's lady clerk Miss McCracken, who has dropped out for many pages and forty years, abruptly reappears and informs Merlin that the Witch is an actual woman and journalistic celebrity, "Old Alicia Dare. Mrs. Thomas Allerdyce she is now, of course; has been these thirty years. . . . Why, surely, Mr. Grainger, you can't tell me that you've forgotten her, when for ten years she was the most notorious character in New York." Miss McCracken further reports that Alicia Dare had once figured scandalously as co-respondent in a well-publicized society divorce case.

The altered ending does not alter the moral. Shrinking from the Witch's invitation to live boldly, Merlin has wasted his life. "He was an old man now indeed, so old that it was impossible for him to dream of ever having been young, so old that the glamour was gone out of the world." Wisdom has come too late: "He had angered Providence by resisting too many temptations." With this endorsement of the reckless and festive, the story ends.

O Russet Witch!'" expressed not simply Fitzgerald's philosophy of the moment, but his sense of living in exciting times. Looking back to his return to New York in early 1920, he would claim to have foreseen the "the roaring twenties": ". . . A fresh picture of life in America began to form before my eyes. The uncertainties of 1919 were over—there seemed little doubt about what was going to happen—America was going on the greatest, gaudiest spree in history. . . . The whole golden boom was in the air—its splendid generosities, its outrageous corruptions and the tortuous death struggle of the old America in prohibition."[13] However accurate this recollection, he and Zelda threw themselves with abandon into the 1920s as he understood them. "Bliss was it in that dawn to be alive," he might have echoed Wordsworth, "But to be young was very heaven!" Youth was a cult, *carpe diem* a mandate.

But the cult had a term limit. Life ended at thirty—at least Youth did, essentially the same thing. When *This Side of Paradise* was published, Fitzgerald was creeping toward twenty-four. Approaching that age in *The Beautiful and Damned,* the heroine, Gloria, "was in an attractive but sincere panic about it. Six years to thirty!"

Before their marriage, Zelda had written to him, "We will just *have* to die when we're thirty."[14] A little later he described a typical married couple:

> Take a woman of thirty. . . . She acquires only the useless knowledge found in cheap movies, cheap novels, and the cheap memoirs of titled foreigners.
>
> By this time her husband has also become suspicious of anything gay or new. . . . At the family dinner on Sunday he occasionally gives her some fascinating statistics on party politics, some opinions from the morning's newspaper editorial.
>
> But after thirty, both husband and wife know in their hearts that the game is up.[15]

In Fitzgerald's 1923 play *The Vegetable,* the protagonist's nagging wife is portrayed in a series of photographs: "Look! This is the way she was [at nineteen] when she was after a husband. She might be worse. There's a certain young charm or something, but in the next picture you can see what five years of general housework have done to her. You wouldn't turn your eyes half a degree to watch her in the street. And that was taken six years ago—now she's thirty and already an old woman."[16] As his own thirtieth loomed, he gloomed. "I feel very old this winter," he told Ober in early 1925. "I'm twenty-eight." A year later, "You remember," he told Perkins, "I used to say I wanted to die at thirty—well, I'm now twenty-nine and the prospect is still welcome." In *Gatsby,* Nick Carraway mourns his thirtieth birthday.[17]

Until then, however, Fitzgerald claimed youth's entitlement not just to romance, mirth, and narcissism, but also to wisdom. Contemplating the World War's repercussions, he had seized on the idea of a liberated postwar generation. Freed from the dullness and stuffy mores of elders who had pushed Europe into a disastrous war and America into Prohibition, youth danced toward better days.

It was a simplistic but useful and adaptable notion, and he eagerly profited from it. "I'll not talk of flappers," he told an interviewer in 1923. "I can sell that sort of chatter."[18] On the strength of *This Side of Paradise,* newspapers and magazines found him a willing publicist for the postwar generation, and he wrote articles such as "What I Think and Feel at 25," "Imagination—and a Few Mothers," and "Girls Believe in Girls." As the titles suggest, he was willing to share his thoughts on topics about which he knew little or nothing, supplying the vacancy with clichés and facile dicta. His daughter was two years old when he wrote "'Wait Till You Have Children of Your Own!'"—a manifesto on parenting.

His glib opinions can be explained if not wholly excused by the simple market principle of giving magazines like *Ladies' Home Journal* and *Woman's Home Companion* what they wanted. But while he would later admit that he and Zelda had often been quoted in gossip columns "on a variety of subjects we knew nothing about," equally dubious commentary appeared under his own byline.[19]

His letters of these early years are full of plans, schemes, schedules, and confident opinions. He plunged into the literary world like a small child invited, or inviting himself, to play with the big kids. His swagger went beyond journalistic fluff. Having published a college novel and a half-dozen stories, he awarded himself high rank in contemporary letters, with authority to judge fellow writers and disparage the reading public.

A self-interview of spring 1920 preserves him in a state of high youthful egotism, and reprinting it without comment, the *New York Tribune*'s book columnist Heywood Broun added simply, "Having heard Mr. Fitzgerald, we are not entirely minded to abandon our notion that he is a rather complacent, somewhat pretentious and altogether self-conscious young man."[20]

In 1923 Fitzgerald airily dismissed American literature "between the Civil War and the World War" (which would include Emily Dickinson, *Huckleberry Finn*, Stephen Crane, Henry James, the early Edith Wharton, Theodore Dreiser, and Robert Frost) as a "junk heap."[21]

During this same era, he one day had lunch with George Horace Lorimer, the *Saturday Evening Post*'s editor. Another at the table recalled:

> Fitzgerald took the occasion to hold forth at length on the topic of crass commercialism in the editorial policy of American magazines. . . . Lorimer listened to him with polite but stony attention, asking an occasional question, offering no rebuttals. At length, Fitzgerald worked himself up to his peroration: "American magazines have always published the works of mediocrities and nobodies. They've taken no notice of real genius. It's a safe bet that nobody in this room ever heard of the most important American writer of the early 1900s. It may be fifty years before anybody, except a few of us, even knows that Frank Norris ever existed!"

At all this, Lorimer "nodded soberly."

"Then maybe I didn't go so far wrong after all," he observed, "when I bought 'The Pit' and 'The Octopus' from Frank Norris and serialized them both in the Post."[22]

Fitzgerald's tongue had undoubtedly been loosened by cocktails, but much in character, tipsy or sober, was his readiness to pontificate at a table of older and more accomplished men of letters.

G iven his glowing temperament and the gratifying success of *This Side of Paradise*, Fitzgerald's celebration of youth and even his presumption and pretensions were predictable and mostly harmless.

Other, less benign symptoms appeared, though. His election to Cottage Club in his sophomore spring at Princeton had marked the summit of his undergraduate career, and when *This Side of Paradise* was about to be published five years later he decided to greet its release not with his fiancée, still in Alabama; nor with his family; nor even in New York—but back at Princeton, where he took a room at Cottage to await the notable day. In some hazy way he perhaps imagined that his triumphant return would revive that glorious spring of 1915. His class of 1917 having long departed, however, some forever—twenty-one had died in the First World War—none of his contemporaries was still around, and the current generation of Cottage members must have wondered why this youthful old boy was hanging around.

A second return to Princeton the following month was more ominous. He and Zelda had been married only a few weeks, and this was probably her first visit to the campus. Some years later he described it: "We had been part of a rather gay party staged conspicuously in Harvey Firestone's car of robin's egg blue, and in the course of it I got an accidental black eye trying to stop a fight. This was magnified as an orgy. . . . I was suspended from my club [Cottage] for a couple of months."[23] The "rather gay party" and altercation throw doubt on his pacific intentions; earlier, writing to a friend and omitting the "accidental" black eye, he had described the party in more sensational terms: "We were there [Princeton] three days, Zelda and five men in Harvey Firestone's car, and not one of us drew a sober breath. . . . It was the damnedest party ever held in Princeton and everybody in the University will agree."[24] Since he was now married, a published novelist, and almost seven years beyond the first thrills of college drinking, such freshman boasting seems oddly puerile. Biographer Andrew Turnbull describes in vivid detail another drunken and raucous Princeton visit the following weekend, as well.[25]

The same undergraduate spirit governed the early years of the Fitzgeralds' married life, which can be summarized by the three *R*'s of rackety, restless, and rootless. Extracts from the 1920 diary of a Princeton friend in New York, Alexander McKaig, give a taste:

April 12 Called on Scott Fitz and his bride. . . . Both drinking heavily.

June 13 Visit Fitz at Westport [Connecticut]. . . . Terrible party. Fitz & Zelda fighting like mad. . . .

Sept. 15 In the evening, Zelda—drunk—having decided to leave Fitz

& having nearly been killed walking down RR tracks, blew in [to
McKaig's New York apartment]. . . . They continued their fight
while here. . . .

Oct. 21 Went up to Fitzgeralds [now in the Fifty-Ninth Street apart-
ment] to spend evening. They just recovering from an awful
party. . . .

Oct. 25 [Ziegfeld] Follies with Scott & Zelda. Fitz very cuckoo. Lost
purse with $50.00 & then after every one in place hunted for it,
found it. . . .

Dec. 11 Evening at Fitz. Fitz & I argued with Zelda about notoriety they
are getting through being so publicly and spectacularly drunk.
Zelda wants to live the life of an "extravagant."[26]

Ten years later, after her first breakdown, Zelda would in stream-of-
reminiscence style recall their early married days as a confusion of people,
places, drinking, and quarreling. Excerpts from a much longer document:

The strangeness and excitement of New York, of reporters and furry
smothered hotel lobbies . . . and much tea dancing and my eccentric behavior at Princeton. . . . There were always Ludlow and Townsend and
Alex [McKaig] and Billy Mackey and you and me. . . . There was Georges
appartment and his absinth cock-tails and Ruth Findlays gold hair in
his comb, and visits to the "Smart Set" and "Vanity Fair"—a collegiate
literary world puffed into wide proportions by the New York papers.
There were flowers and night clubs. . . . At West Port we quarreled over
morals once. . . . There was the road house where we bought gin. . . . We
swam in the depth of the night with George before we quarreled with
him and went to John Williams parties where there were actresses who
spoke French when they were drunk. . . . We moved to 59th Street. We
quarrelled and you broke the bathroom door and hurt my eye. We went
so much to the theatre that you took it off the income tax. . . . We had
Bourbon and Deviled Ham and Christmas at the Overmans and ate lots
at the Lafayette. . . .[27]

Fitzgerald's second novel, *The Beautiful and Damned*, reproduces the round of amusements and alcoholic conviviality chronicled by McKaig and Zelda. "My new novel," Fitzgerald informed Maxwell Perkins in August 1920, ". . . concerns the life of one Anthony Patch between his 25th and 33rd years. . . . How he and his beautiful young wife are wrecked on the shoals of dissipation. . . ."[28]

Amidst the revelry and dissipation, Fitzgerald remained productive. He could work with focus and intensity for long stretches. An early story of about nine thousand words, "The Camel's Back," was written in a single day of fourteen, nineteen, or twenty-one hours' straight writing, depending on which of three differing accounts one prefers.[29] He wrote *The Beautiful and Damned*, the longest of his four novels, between July 1920 and the following May. In 1920 and 1921 he also wrote ten short stories.

S pending lavishly and borrowing even at the height of his popularity and productivity, the Fitzgeralds during these early married years were unconsciously making fateful choices. Almost every letter to Perkins or Ober included a request for money. They never opened a savings account.

Zelda meanwhile grew bored. When he sequestered himself to write, she found little to do. "Went to Fitzgeralds," McKaig recorded in October 1920: "Usual problem there. What shall Zelda do?" A few days later: "Zelda increasingly restless—says frankly she simply wants to be amused and is only good for useless, pleasure-giving pursuits; great problem—what is she to do?"[30] She had no interest in domestic occupations or obligations; the dirty laundry piled up. She had grown up in a home with hired help, and the Fitzgeralds soon got into the habit of retaining servants. A comic figure in *The Beautiful and Damned*, the Japanese servant Tanalahaka—"Tana"—is based on a Japanese house servant of the same name whom they employed in Westport. In Zelda's autobiographical novel *Save Me the Waltz* he appears again, now as Tanka, "the Japanese butler" whom the newly married Knights "tried to do without till Alabama cut her hand on a can of baked beans and David sprained his painting wrist on the lawn mower."

A consequence of their restlessness, and one not adding to domestic tranquility, the Fitzgeralds were as nomadic as Bedouins. In the four years between their marriage and spring 1924, when they removed to Europe, they had eight or nine different addresses, not counting hotels in New York, Europe, and elsewhere, and a road trip to Montgomery.

McKaig records in October 1920 that the Fitzgeralds were deliberating a new idea: "Much taken with idea of having a baby."[31] The following February, Fitzgerald noted in his ledger, with precision, "Zelda becomes pregnant on 1st. Begins to realize it 14th." This was a natural and wholesome consequence of an affectionate marriage, but the idea may have been practical, too, with the thought that motherhood would give Zelda an interest and occupation.

With the baby due around Halloween, they set sail for Europe in May 1921 to visit England, France, and Italy, returning to New York in July. Almost instinctively seeking a homelike setting for the approaching birth, they traveled first to Montgomery to settle near the Sayres. "Needless to say," he had written in a letter to Edmund Wilson railing against Italy and France, "our idea of a year in Italy was well shattered & we sail for America on the 9th & thence to The 'Sahara of the Bozart' (Montgomery) for life."[32]

Settling in Montgomery "for life," with its penal ring, was probably facetious, but the plan was to stay at least until the baby was born. "Considering house in Montgomery," Fitzgerald's ledger notes, but not surprisingly Montgomery was hot in August, and two weeks after arriving they retreated to Saint Paul.

Again, the plan may have been to settle there, though almost immediately they began shifting about—from the summer-resort town Dellwood on White Bear Lake, to the Commodore Hotel in the city, where they seem to have been staying when their daughter Scottie was born in late October. Soon after they moved to a rented house on Goodrich Avenue from which Fitzgerald headed a letter to Perkins, "New Address/Permanent!"[33]

"Permanent" in this case meant about six months—for the Fitzgeralds, a long stretch. Their new role as parents failed to stabilize them. Zelda's maternal flame burned low; though fond of Scottie, she handed over the baby's care to a hired nurse. Nor did fatherhood alter Fitzgerald's undergraduate propensities; in February 1922, when Scottie was three months old, his ledger notes of himself and Zelda: "Both sick. Drinking." About the same time Zelda evidently became pregnant again, with the ledger containing a note,

"Zelda & her abortionist." A second child so quickly would be inconvenient, and she worried about her figure. A little earlier the ledger had noted, "Zelda's weight."

In June they moved yet again, from Goodrich Avenue to rooms at the Yacht Club on White Bear Lake for the summer, but in the fall, dreading another Minnesota winter, they abandoned Saint Paul altogether.

Montgomery had been boring, remote, and hot; Saint Paul boring, remote, and cold. Zelda would surely have preferred the heat, but the decision was for neither. "St. Paul is dull as hell," Fitzgerald complained, and "I am lonesome for New York"; and "the philistine pressure [in Saint Paul] is terrific. . . . I never knew how much I cared for New York."[34]

In September 1922, leaving Scottie in Saint Paul with his sister Annabel and the nurse, they "came to New York and rented a house when we were both tight," Zelda recalled.[35] The house was in Great Neck, on Long Island's north shore, twenty miles east of Manhattan and an easy train ride into the city—the train on which *Gatsby*'s Nick Carraway would commute from his bungalow in West Egg. In October, Zelda returned to Saint Paul to retrieve the baby.

Their eighteen months in Great Neck, the Fitzgeralds' longest continuous time together at one address, would provide him with rich material for *The Great Gatsby*. His tastes were urban and cosmopolitan; New York had glamor, money, fashion, sophistication, nervous energy. A few months after arriving he wrote to Cecilia Taylor: "Great Neck is a great place for celebrities—it being the habitat of Mae Murray, Frank Craven, Herbert Swope, Arthur Hopkins, Jane Cowl, Joseph Santley, Samuel Goldwyn, Ring Lardner, Fontayne Fox, "Tad" [Dorgan], Gene Buck, Donald Bryan, Tom Wise, Jack Hazard, General Pershing. It is most amusing after the dull healthy middle west. For instance at a party last night where we went were John McCormick, Hugh Walpole, F.P.A [Franklin Pierce Adams], Neysa Mcmien, Arthur William Brown, Rudolph Frimll & Deems Taylor."[36] And Great Neck was just a small sliver of the metropolis. Many of these names would have been as unknown to Cousin Ceci as to readers of a century later, but they provided the crowded, colorful scene lacking in Saint Paul.

Moving to New York was not a promising strategy for solvency, however. With the gay crowd and bootleg parties, the Fitzgeralds slid into a wandering, unfocused pursuit of novelty and amusement. Their freewheeling
spending forced him to scramble to stay ahead or catch up. The only time
during the Great Neck era when he seems not to have been short of money
was a month's visit with the Sayres in Montgomery, when he returned a
$1,000 advance to Ober. But six months later, back in Great Neck, "I have
got myself in a terrible mess," he informed Perkins: "I'm at the end of my
rope—as the immortal phrase goes. I owe the Scribner Company something
over $3,500.00. . . . If I don't in some way get $650 in the bank by Wedens-
day morning I'll have to pawn the furniture."[37] Yet Fitzgerald earned over
$28,000 that year.

Money was the least of his concerns, though, or should have been. More
ominous were Zelda's malaise and his own erratic habits and drinking.
Two years before his death he would complain to sixteen-year-old Scottie,
"When I was your age I lived with a great dream. The dream grew and I
learned how to speak of it and make people listen. Then the dream divided
one day when I decided to marry your mother after all, even though I knew
she was spoiled and meant no good to me. . . . I was a man divided—she
wanted me to work too much for *her* and not enough for my dream. She realized too late that work was dignity, and the only dignity. . . ."[38]

The accusation lacked both justice and self-awareness; Zelda might
have retorted, like *Tender Is the Night*'s Nicole scourging Dick Diver's self-
pity: "You're a coward! You've made a failure of your life, and you want
to blame it on me." Zelda had certainly been spoiled, but cosseted by his
mother and pampered by early success, Fitzgerald was even more so.

Most of his problems were self-inflicted. In all the consequential choices
the Fitzgeralds made in 1922 and the years following—the moving about,
partying, extravagance, drinking—he took the lead. Great Neck's celebrities meant nothing to Zelda, who would probably have been content with a
sober husband and stable home in a provincial burg like Montgomery. She
was close to her mother, revered her austere father, and loved flowers.

The return to New York ended any chance of sobriety. Fitzgerald in Saint
Paul had scarcely been a milk drinker; in June 1922 he apologized to Perkins
for the tardy submission of copy for *Tales of the Jazz Age:* "I'm sorry I've been

so slow on this—there's no particular excuse except liquor and of course that isn't any."[39] But in New York the partying was faster and gayer, the bootleg cocktails stronger.

Among his new acquaintances in Great Neck was Ring Lardner—baseball journalist, writer, wit, and dipsomaniac. Together they sometimes drank through the night. "Dear Kaly," Fitzgerald wrote to a Saint Paul friend, Oscar Kalman, after one all-night bout of fraternity-boy hilarity. "This is a letter from your two favorite authors. Ring & I got stewed together the other night & sat up till the next night without what he would laughingly refer to as a wink of sleep. About 5.30 [a.m.] I told him he should write you a letter." When the Fitzgeralds sailed for Europe after eighteen months, Lardner mourned, "Great Neck is like a cemetery since Scott and Zelda went. And I might say that as far as I'm concerned, it would have been more like one if they'd staid." A decade later Lardner died at 48.[40]

Zelda's troubles were already beginning. With Fitzgerald immured in his study over the garage or out drinking, with servants attending to household chores and Scottie's care, she was idle, without vocation or purpose, often lonely. Daisy Buchanan's detached mothering of her young daughter Pammy, glimpsed briefly in *The Great Gatsby,* may echo Zelda's with Scottie.

After two or three elective abortions she was ready for another child. In 1923 she had been asked, "Do you like large or small families?"

"Large ones," she replied. "Yes, quite large."

She would have no second child.[41]

After *The Beautiful and Damned* was published in early 1922, Fitzgerald decided to defer a third novel, throwing himself instead into writing a play. Drama was "my first love," he would admit.[42] A theatergoer since youth, he had written and acted in juvenile plays in Saint Paul, and at Princeton plunged into the Triangle Club's musical farces. Now the money and glamor of Broadway beckoned.

Theater bulked large in New York's allure. Of the twenty-two Great Neck celebrities named in his letter to his cousin Ceci, quoted above, over a third were theatrical. Visiting *Gatsby*'s parties with Nick Carraway we glimpse actresses, producers, and chorus girls; West Egg is "this unprecedented 'place' that Broadway had begotten upon a Long Island fishing village," and in the roll call of Gatsby's guests, "theatrical people" receive special mention.

Finishing *The Beautiful and Damned* the year before, "the story of a young couple who rapidly go to pieces," Fitzgerald described it as bitter, insolent, and pessimistic and predicted it would never be popular, a prophecy proving largely correct. By contrast, his play would be a light-hearted satire to create a splash and enrich himself. "I'm writing an awfully funny play that's going to make me rich forever," he told Perkins, and again, "After my play is produced I'll be rich forever and never have to bother you [for advances] again." To Ober: "My play is the funniest ever written & will make a fortune," and "the play is going to make me rich," he reminded him a few days later.[43]

Beginning on this funniest-ever play during their year in Saint Paul, he admired it extravagantly. "My play is a gem," he told Perkins, "a wonder," he told Ober, "the best American comedy to date & undoubtedly the best thing I have ever written," he assured Perkins six months later.[44] First titled *Gabriel's Trombone,* it became *Frost.* Perkins had reservations, but in April 1923 Scribner's published a reading version of *The Vegetable,* its final and inauspicious title.

Shortly before the curtain was to rise on untold wealth, however, he ran out of money. Begging a loan from Perkins, he broke away from the play long enough to write a story for the *Post.* While the vaunted play was a frothy farce, the quick potboiler story probed "still bleeding" memories.

A story of young love with a nominally happy ending, "'The Sensible Thing'" recounts Fitzgerald's frantic and despairing but ultimately successful courtship of Zelda in 1919. Though writing the story in a single day (according to his ledger), he had brooded on the experience for four years. Writing to Perkins, he remarked of "'The Sensible Thing,'" "Story about Zelda & me. All true," and rereading his early stories years later, Zelda "wanted to cry over the Sensible Thing."[45]

Parallels between life and story:

THE HERO

"'The Sensible Thing'": Young engineer with Irish surname (O'Kelly) working at an uncongenial, low-paying job (insurance) in a New York office near Times Square and living on the Upper West Side near the 137th Street subway station.

Fitzgerald: Young writer with Irish surname working at an uncongenial, low-paying job (advertising) in a New York office on 42nd Street near Times Square and living on the Upper West Side near the 125th Street subway station.

THE GIRL

"'The Sensible Thing'": Jonquil, from a town in "southern Tennessee" seven hundred miles from New York; popular with the local boys.

Zelda: From Montgomery, Alabama, one thousand miles from New York; popular with the local boys.

SCENE 1

"'The Sensible Thing'": O'Kelly receives a "nervous" letter from Jonquil, quits his job, and takes a train to Tennessee for the second time in two weeks to reassure her.

Fitzgerald: Receives "nervous" letters from Zelda, takes a train to Alabama three times in successive months to reassure her.

SCENE 2

"'The Sensible Thing'": When O'Kelly arrives, Jonquil breaks off their engagement. Disconsolate, he returns to New York, with no girl, no job, and no prospects.

Fitzgerald: When he arrives the third time, Zelda breaks off their engagement. Disconsolate, he returns to New York with no girl and no prospects, and quits his job.

SCENE 3

"'The Sensible Thing'": Eighteen months later, his prospects now bright after great success in an engineering expedition to Peru, O'Kelly returns to Tennessee to court Jonquil again.

Fitzgerald: Five months later, after retreating to Minnesota and writing a novel accepted by a prominent New York publisher, his prospects now bright, he returns to Alabama to court Zelda again.

ENDING

"'The Sensible Thing'": Jonquil and O'Kelly become reengaged.

Fitzgerald: Becomes reengaged to Zelda.

Though MIT graduate and skilled engineer, O'Kelly has like Fitzgerald the imagination of an artist and the ardor of a lover: "It had seemed romantic to George O'Kelly to change the sweep of rivers and the shape of mountains. . . . He loved steel, and there was always steel near him in his dreams. . . . Steel inexhaustible, to be made lovely and austere in his imaginative fire." No character of rectilinear feeling and slide-rule logic could know the ecstasies and miseries of love.

We first meet O'Kelly in New York, in the full flush of desire—excited, absorbed, preoccupied, frantic, his "mind over seven hundred miles away," with Jonquil in Tennessee. At lunch hour he races to catch a subway from Times Square to his uptown apartment to check the mail. Finding a letter waiting—"in sacred ink, on blessed paper"—he pores over it, "the commas, the blots, and the thumb-smudge on the margin—then he threw himself hopelessly upon his bed." Jonquil's letter betrays doubts.

It is a vivid, energetic, lighthearted sketch of a besotted young lover, essentially Fitzgerald himself in 1919, working, partying, and hobnobbing with friends in New York, but "haunted always by my other life—my drab room in the Bronx [actually Manhattan], my square foot of the subway, my fixation upon the day's letter from Alabama—would it come and what would it say?—my shabby suits, my poverty and love." After any outing, "I returned eagerly to my home on Claremont Avenue—home because there might be a letter waiting outside the door."[46]

So too O'Kelly, and finding at his apartment a "nervous" letter, he takes the next train to Tennessee: "He knew what 'nervous' meant—that she was emotionally depressed, that the prospect of marrying into a life of poverty and struggle was putting too much strain upon her love." Jonquil, like Zelda, has already decided to call off their engagement.

Just weeks after Zelda had disengaged them in 1919, Fitzgerald had inserted a broken engagement into *This Side of Paradise*. Amory Blaine has fallen for Rosalind, a metropolitan society vamp and debutante daughter of a wealthy New York family. Like Zelda she has the power to fascinate and hurt, and even while professing her love, Rosalind drops the penniless Amory.[47]

Unlike Rosalind, Zelda was unaccustomed to luxury and did not demand it. "Don't—please—accumulate a lot of furniture," she wrote as Fitzgerald made hopeful plans for her to join him in New York. "Really, Scott, I'd just as soon live *anywhere*—and can't we find a bed ready-made?"[48] Her standard was 6 Pleasant Avenue, Montgomery; all she demanded was moderate gentility. That the college dropout, unpublished scribbler, and advertising hack Scott Fitzgerald could support her comfortably, or ever would, seemed doubtful.

The lovers' breakup in "'The Sensible Thing'" parallels the version in *This Side of Paradise*. In both novel and story the girls have made their decision, take command of the situation, and dictate the breakup, sadly but firmly.

"He [Amory] has not been able to eat a mouthful in the last thirty-six hours." (*This Side of Paradise*)
". . . he [O'Kelly] had scarcely eaten a bite since he had left New York." ("'The Sensible Thing'")

"I got a raise—of two dollars a week." (Amory)
"I've been promoted—better salary." (O'Kelly)

"There have been times in the last month I'd have been completely yours if you'd said so." (Rosalind)

"If you'd been ready for me two months ago I'd have married you. . . ." (Jonquil)

"We've got to take our chance for happiness." (Amory)
"If you'll . . . take a chance with me. . . ." (O'Kelly)

"You'd better go." (Rosalind)
"You'd better go now." (Jonquil)

"I'm doing the wise thing, the only thing." (Rosalind)
". . . the sensible thing." (Jonquil)
"Perhaps after all this is the sensible thing." (Jonquil's mother)

The echoing phrases suggest the tenor and perhaps actual language of con-versations in June 1919.

Retreating to Saint Paul to rewrite his novel, Fitzgerald dreamed, anx-iously, of winning Zelda back. Choosing money over love, *This Side of Para-dise*'s Rosalind marries Amory's wealthy rival suitor. Heartbroken, mutter-ing self-consciously cynical wisdom, Amory straggles back to Princeton, moaning: "But—oh, Rosalind! Rosalind! . . ." Fitzgerald feared, with reason, that his courtship would conclude similarly.

Like Fitzgerald, O'Kelly is excitedly in love and near despair, but deter-mined to make a last effort. Returning to Tennessee after his triumphs in malarial Peru (probably confused with Panama), O'Kelly notices changes—first, in Jonquil. "For four long seasons every minute of his leisure had been crowded with anticipation of this hour"—but the voice greeting him on the telephone is "cool and unmoved . . . the voice of a stranger, unexcited, pleasantly glad to see him—that was all." Does her bland greeting reflect Zelda's when Fitzgerald returned to Montgomery to reclaim her? O'Kelly is dismayed by Jonquil's apathy: "He had thought of finding her married, en-gaged, in love—he had not thought that she would be unstirred at his return."

But the more profound change is in O'Kelly himself. The Carys' house is "smaller" and "shabbier than before—there was no cloud of magic hovering over its roof and issuing from windows of the upper floor." The sitting room is "only a room, and not the enchanted chamber where he had passed those poignant hours." Earlier, his fancy "had distorted and colored all these simple familiar things": what has shrunk is neither house nor sitting room, but his passion. The glow of his beloved has dimmed, and his cool clear-sighted detachment diminishes the lover himself.

A flat, depressing reunion with Jonquil follows, reaching its nadir with his bleak half-question, "You don't love me any more, do you?" and her blunt "No." And yet "he knew now that he still wanted this girl," and (anticipating Jay Gatsby) "he knew that the past sometimes comes back."

As he and Jonquil sit in awkward silence, Jonquil's mother gets them on their feet to take a walk: "I want you two to go and see the lady who has the chrysanthemums." There follows a scene so apparently (and literally) pedestrian, yet so circumstantial, that it probably reproduces an incident during his Montgomery visit of November 1919—especially as flowers are the catalyst, and Zelda and her mother loved flowers.

The excursion to the chrysanthemum garden strangely reawakens slumbering emotions. As Jonquil and O'Kelly walk along, he recognizes "with a sort of excitement" her shorter stride harmonizing with his longer one. The flowers are "extraordinarily beautiful," and wandering among them "was a trip back into the heart of summer"—a hint of warmer feelings returning.

"And then a curious thing happened." Nothing tangible happens, however; passing through a gate, "George stepped aside to let Jonquil pass," and she pauses to gaze at him. "It was not so much the look . . . as it was the moment of silence. . . . both took a short faintly accelerated breath" before passing into the second garden. "That was all." The quietly dramatic scene concludes with understated feeling: "The afternoon waned. They thanked the lady and walked home slowly, thoughtfully, side by side." In a silent nonevent, love has rekindled. Years later, Zelda reminded Fitzgerald of their long-ago visit in Montgomery to see "the roses in Kinneys yard."[49]

The actual reengagement of Jonquil and O'Kelly is managed through a series of double entendres as he narrates his Peruvian expedition while Jonquil echoes him, invitingly:

> . . . That had been his chance [O'Kelly explains, with Jonquil sitting on his lap], a chance for anybody but a fool, a marvellous chance—

"A chance for anybody but a fool?" she interrupted innocently.

"Even for a fool," he continued. "It was wonderful. Well, I wired New York—"

"And so," she interrupted again, "they wired that you ought to take a chance?"

As with their rupture, the reconciliation is engineered not by the engineer O'Kelly, but by Jonquil.

N ear the end of his life, when the *Post* had stopped buying his stories, Fitzgerald would credit his romance with Zelda for much of his earlier success as a story writer. "It's odd that my old talent for the short story vanished," he told her: "It was partly that times changed, editors changed, but part of it was tied up somehow with you and me—the happy ending. Of course every third story had some other ending but essentially I got my public with stories of young love."[50] But though "'The Sensible Thing'" breathes the "you and me" of Zelda and himself, its ending is happy only with a lowercase *h*.

It is not that Jonquil disappoints O'Kelly: "He had not remembered how beautiful she was, and he felt his face grow pale and his voice diminish to a poor sigh in his throat. . . . a spasm of fright went through him at her beauty's power of inflicting pain." Nor does he regret the outcome: ". . . she was something desirable and rare that he had fought for and made his own."

He mourns, rather, for his own diminished fervor. About to reclaim this rare and desirable girl, he feels strangely melancholy:

He and Jonquil were alone in the room which had seen the beginning of their love affair and the end. It seemed to him long ago and inexpressibly sad. On that sofa he had felt agony and grief such as he would never feel again. He would never be so weak or so tired and miserable and poor. Yet he knew that that boy of fifteen months before had had something, a trust, a warmth that was gone forever. . . . with his youth, life had carried away the freshness of his love.

Even as Jonquil "drew herself to him . . . her lips half open like a flower," O'Kelly's thoughts wander off: ". . . as he kissed her he knew that though he search through eternity he could never recapture those lost April hours"; "never again" would she be "an intangible whisper in the dusk, or on the breeze of night."

Back in 1919, soon after Fitzgerald's reengagement, Zelda had written, "And, Scott, Darlin' *don't* try so hard to convince yourself that we're very old people who've lost their most precious possession. . . . All the fire and sweetness—the emotional strength that we're capable of is growing—growing and just because sanity and wisdom are growing too and we're building our love-castle on a firm foundation, nothing is lost."[51] Had he confessed to diminished ardor? Zelda seems to be responding to some such complaint.

"That first abandon *couldn't* last," she continued, "but the things that went to make it are tremendously alive . . . so don't mourn for a poor little forlorn, wonderful memory when we've got each other." But the sorrow was deep within Fitzgerald. George O'Kelly's disillusion echoes Dexter Green's in "Winter Dreams," and anticipates Jay Gatsby's.

W hen in *This Side of Paradise* Rosalind tires of waiting for the penni- less Amory and breaks their engagement, he accuses: "You're afraid of taking two years' knocks with me." Fitzgerald, too, resented Zelda's re- luctance to risk marriage with a penniless writer, blithely expecting her to leave behind family, home, and beloved hometown to join him in New York with all-for-love abandon. His later mistress Sheilah Graham would quote him as saying, of Zelda's hesitation, "I would never love her as much."[52]

Zelda's sister Rosalind explained Zelda's reservations differently: "I do not believe that Zelda's hesitancy about marrying Scott was prompted by any mercenary motive, but rather that it was her uncertainty about the wis- dom of the step that restrained her. Scott already was a more than moder- ate drinker even in those days—he told us that he began drinking at 12, and thought it was funny!—and Zelda certainly felt some misgivings as to what life with him would be." By another account, Zelda's uncertainty and Fitz- gerald's poverty combine: a Montgomery friend reported her telling him in spring 1919 "that they were engaged, off and on, but that he wanted her to come to New York to marry him. Frankly, it all seemed such a gamble to her, she said, and besides Scott was without the necessary funds."[53]

Whatever her motives, Zelda's 1919 reluctance rankled. He would later recall trying "to make enough money in the advertising business to rent a stuffy apartment for two in the Bronx," adding, "The girl concerned had never seen New York but she was wise enough to be rather reluctant." Privately, though, he attributed her hesitancy not to wisdom but to calculation: a late 1930s entry in his notebooks comments that, "except for the sexual recklessness, Zelda was cagey about throwing in her lot with me before I was a money-maker."[54]

The alleged recklessness also bothered him. He and Zelda probably first made love during one of his two visits to Montgomery in January and early February 1920; by March she feared she might be pregnant.[55] She was not, but meanwhile he worried that he was not the first to share her bed: "There was an elaborate self-consciousness about our seduction which told of deep intuition that you were playing a role, though my one track mind didn't choose to notice it, and I should have guessed that it wasn't Paul Lagrand or anyone casual from your first story THE MAGNOLIA TREE—guessed there had been old emotional experience for you had learned to feel before I did."[56] In an unsent 1939 rant he wrote, ". . . by your own admission many years after (and for which I have never reproached you) you had been seduced and provincially outcast. I sensed this the night we slept together first for you're a poor bluffer and I loved you . . . for your beauty & defiant intelligence."[57]

Whatever Zelda's sexual history, he should not have been surprised. "Any girl who gets stewed in public," he wrote of her before their marriage, "who frankly enjoys and tells shocking stories, who smokes constantly and makes the remark that she has 'kissed thousands of men and intends to kiss thousands more,' cannot be considered beyond reproach even if above it."[58] Admiration for her Russet Witch audacity competed with a romantic idealism that shrank from casual sex, especially in the premarital résumé of his wife.

* * *

When Scribner's published *The Vegetable* it received overwhelmingly bad reviews, some derisory. Stage producers were reluctant to risk it, but a backer eventually turned up and a tryout was staged in Atlantic City in November 1923. In Zelda's words, "The show flopped as flat as one of Aunt Jemimas famous pancakes—Scott and Truex [Ernest Truex, the lead actor] and Harris [the producer] were terribly disappointed. . . . The first act went fine but Ernest says he has *never* had an experience on the stage like the second. . . . People were so obviously bored!" Fitzgerald himself admitted, "It was a colossal frost," punning on the name of the play's protagonist, Jerry Frost. "People left their seats and walked out, people rustled their programs and talked audibly in bored impatient whispers."[59]

Fitzgerald had been supremely confident; Edmund Wilson, a certified member of the intellectual elite, had praised the play as "marvellous—no doubt, the best American comedy ever written"; Maxwell Perkins had given his imprimatur; a veteran Broadway producer had thought it would be "*the* flapper play" and backed his opinion with his checkbook. But as occasionally happens, the experts had it wrong.[60]

The Vegetable has seldom been produced since, but a weary afternoon reading it vindicates the apathy of the opening-night audience. Fitzgerald described it as mixing "comedy and burlesque," but the comedy is silly and sophomoric, and as drama the play is devoid of either character or plot interest. "This drivel is supposed to be satire on the vanities and incapacities of public officials, but it affords nothing save the spectacle of a breezy charlatan—the author—engaged in stuffing his mental hollows with a shallow brand of humor," Ben Hecht, the Chicago journalist and later Hollywood screenwriter, wrote in disgust. Fitzgerald wrote nothing worse until, possibly, the Count of Darkness stories a decade later.[61]

With an orchestra, song, and Princeton boys in drag in a kick line, *The Vegetable* might have been a tolerable, if forgettable, undergraduate musical. For professional actors it could only have been painful. A decade later, listing "his outstanding impressions in the theater," Fitzgerald included "Ernest Truax's face when he was carrying through bravely in a flop of my own that opened cold in Atlantic City."[62]

Fitzgerald came to agree with the bored opening-night audience. The second act "was the biggest flop of all," and the third (and last) "was flat as a pancake," he echoed Zelda. ". . . The whole thing has already cost me about a year & a half of work so I'd rather let it drop. From Feb 1922 until Nov. 1923 I was almost constantly working & patching the damn thin[g] & I don't think I could bear to look at [it] anymore."[63]

Knowing "what colossal sums were earned on play royalties," he had calculated on making "about $100,000," removing all irksome restraints on spending. Before the Atlantic City trial, Zelda told a friend, she "had already spent the first weeks N.Y. royalty for a dress to wear to the opening night that could not be exchanged." Perhaps a Zelda-esque exaggeration, it would in any event have been typical of their domestic economy.[64]

The failure was sobering. A few months later Fitzgerald would tell Perkins: "It is only in the last four months that I've realized how much I've— well, almost *deteriorated* in the three years since I finished the Beautiful and Damned [in May 1921]. . . . If I'd spent this time reading or travelling or doing anything—even staying healthy—it'd be different but I spent it uselessly, niether in study nor in contemplation but only in drinking and raising hell generally." And to Ober, more succinctly, "I feel now as though I wasted 1922 & 1923."[65]

Beneath the turbulence, drinking, and hell-raising, however, *The Great Gatsby* was fermenting. Great Neck and New York would provide the stage props, characters, and crowd scenes—the swirling bootleg parties, the crooks, the parvenus, the drunks, the theater and movie people, the chorus girls, the valley of ashes, Gatsby's gleaming auto and large mansion on Long Island Sound. If not for the still-resonating emotions of 1919, though, all this would have been nothing more than 1920s period furniture.

3

THE GREAT GATSBY

(1925)

Inside of him remained . . . the memory of the girl.

—"FLIGHT AND PURSUIT"

Fitzgerald's third novel, published in April 1925, was startlingly, exponentially superior to his earlier two. Coming so soon after the inane *Vegetable, The Great Gatsby* was all the more astonishing.

As with most classics, perhaps, few at first recognized its virtuosity. Several reviewers praised it with enthusiasm; most, with qualification; some dismissed it as insignificant. The superbly self-assured H. L. Mencken, while praising "the charm and beauty of the writing," declared *Gatsby* "in form no more than a glorified anecdote, and not too probable at that"; found the characters "mere marionettes," with Gatsby a "clown" while "the other performers in the Totentanz [Dance of Death] are of a like, or even worse quality"; and scoffed, "The story is obviously unimportant."[1]

Sales languished. A first printing of 21,000 copies went off the shelves in the first few months, but a small second printing of 3,000 failed to sell out in Fitzgerald's lifetime. By contrast, 49,000 copies of *This Side of Paradise* had been printed five years earlier.[2]

The Fitzgeralds were sunning themselves in Capri when *Gatsby* appeared in the bookstores, and he waited anxiously for updates from New York. To Perkins, he worried, "The book comes out today, and I am overcome with fears and forebodings." Perkins wired back, candidly: "Sales situation doubtful."

Fitzgerald blamed slack sales on the title, "only fair, rather bad than good," and on "no important woman character," because "women controll the fiction market." Perkins, likely the better judge, thought the novel's brevity a marketing problem: *Gatsby* is only two-fifths as long as its predecessor, *The Beautiful and Damned.* "A great many of the [bookselling] trade have been very skeptical," Perkins wrote. ". . . One point is the small number of pages in the book" which "did in the end lead a couple of big distributors to reduce their orders immensely at the very last minute."[3]

Despite slow traffic in the bookstores, *Gatsby* turned into a moneymaker with the sale of dramatic and film rights. The stage production "put in my pocket seventeen or eighteen thousand without a stroke of work on my part," Fitzgerald gloated, and a film version contributed about the same.[4] With this bonanza, however, his finest achievement set on foot his decline.

L ife is brief and erratic; art endures, sometimes. Fitzgerald's own future years were troubled and relatively few; *Gatsby* would far outlive him.

In Willa Cather's 1915 novel *The Song of the Lark,* a small-town girl becomes an opera diva. When another character asks her old teacher, "What's her secret?" he "rumpled his hair irritably and shrugged his shoulders": "Her secret? It is every artist's secret . . . passion. That is all. It is an open secret, and perfectly safe. Like heroism, it is inimitable in cheap materials." *Gatsby*'s secret, too, begins with passion—the emotional turmoil of spring 1919. Of that time he later recalled, "in a haze of anxiety and unhappiness I passed the four most impressionable months of my life." *Gatsby*'s power to move us flows ultimately from that experience—passion in the sense of powerful desire, but also in its radical sense of suffering.[5]

But while those four impressionable months charged the novel with emotion, its writing was also energized by a passionate artistry. "I feel I have an enormous power in me now," he told Perkins while writing *Gatsby.* ". . . This book will be a consciously artistic achievement & must depend on that as the 1st books did not." Years later, he described *Gatsby* as "an attempt to show a man's life through some passionately regarded segment of it"— "passionate" referring not to the tale but to the telling.[6]

First conceiving of it as something like a biography of Jay Gatsby, he began writing the novel in June 1923 and worked on it haltingly for several months, then laid it aside when rehearsals for *The Vegetable* began. Only the following spring, after the play's failure and after repairing his finances by writing ten stories in five months—apart from "'The Sensible Thing,'" none among his best—did he return to the novel. "Much of what I wrote last summer was good," he told Perkins in April 1924, "but it was so interrupted that it was ragged & in approaching it from a new angle I've had to discard a lot of it. . . ."[7]

The "new angle" was the crucial breakthrough. Its nature comes to light in a letter Fitzgerald wrote to Willa Cather, whom he had never met.[8] As *Gatsby* was about to be published, he was troubled by a misgiving: a passage in its opening chapter echoed a passage in Cather's *A Lost Lady,* published eighteen months earlier. He was concerned that, learning of the similarity, she would suspect literary theft.

Professing himself "one of your greatest admirers," Fitzgerald wrote "to explain an instance of apparent plagiarism which some suspicious person may presently bring to your attention." He continued: "When I was in the middle of the first draft [of *Gatsby*] *A Lost Lady* was published and I read it with the greatest delight." Cather's "lost lady" is Marian Forrester—lovely, sparkling, exquisite, charming. As with *Gatsby*'s Daisy, we come to know her through the sensibility of a susceptible young man, and near the end of *A Lost Lady* this character, Niel, looks back on her "in her best days," years earlier: "Her eyes, when they laughed for a moment into one's own, seemed to promise a wild delight that he has not found in life. 'I know where it is,' they seemed to say. 'I could show you!'" Though apologizing for misquoting ("I have no copy by me"), Fitzgerald quoted almost verbatim.

He went on to explain that "a month or two before I had written into my own book a parallel and almost similar idea in the description of a woman's charm"—not "so clear, nor so beautiful, nor so moving as yours," he remarked modestly, "but the essential similarity was undoubtedly there."

The lines worrying him come when, visiting the Buchanans in East Egg, Nick sees Daisy for the first time in several years: "Her face was sad and lovely with bright things in it—bright eyes and a bright passionate mouth— but there was an excitement in her voice that men who had cared for her found difficult to forget: a singing compulsion, a whispered 'Listen,' a promise that she had done gay exciting things just a while since and that there were gay exciting things hovering in the next hour." To show this passage had been conceived before *A Lost Lady* appeared, Fitzgerald enclosed two holograph pages of *Gatsby*'s "first draft," containing separate attempts to suggest the "gay exciting things" in Daisy's voice.[9]

These are the only surviving pages from *Gatsby*'s earliest pencil drafts. As evidence of precedence they are inconclusive, but Cather graciously disclaimed suspicion. They apparently never corresponded again, nor ever met, but their brief exchange, itself a minor literary curiosity, has for *Gatsby*'s history a Rosetta Stone value.

The pages preserved by Cather represent the earliest phase of the novel's composition, in summer 1923, before the new angle. Containing between them about 270 words and scribbled with corrections, cancellations, circlings, and marginal comments, the two leaves are not consecutive. One describes Daisy alone, with no action; the other begins, "They stood up when dinner was announced," and observes Daisy and Jordan rising to move into the dining room. (In the draft the novel's Daisy is "Ada"; Jordan Baker, "Jordan Vance.")

Both pages attempt to capture the music of Daisy's voice. One, following a description of Ada's/Daisy's voice, continues: "About the rest of her Caraway felt ~~rather than~~ was aware of a diminishing of vitality. . . ." A sentence in the other "ur-Gatsby" page reads, "Her voice was dark and musical like her great eyes and [?] followed eyes and mouth and voice up and down their scale." The brackets indicate an uncertain word, possibly a name, perhaps "Nick." Both passages take the point of view of a character in the narrative, but through an omniscient voice outside it.

The uncertainty reveals Fitzgerald wrestling with a pivotal question: who could best narrate the story? The breakthrough came with a decision that for him was novel, for *Gatsby* all-important. Shifting from a detached narrator conveying Caraway's impressions, Fitzgerald elected to let Caraway speak for himself. With this shift the novel found its voice. *Gatsby* became an experiment in narration so successful that Fitzgerald could never repeat it.

In my younger and more vulnerable years," *Gatsby* famously begins, "my father gave me some advice. . . ." With five first-person pronouns, the opening sentence could hardly announce more emphatically that "I"—

whoever "I" is—will tell the story from a distinctly personal point of view. It will be Gatsby's history, but also "my" experience of Gatsby—hearing about him, meeting him, disapproving, sympathizing, befriending, and assisting; burying him and returning home with his ghost. At the end, with Gatsby in his grave, the "I" remains, "brooding" over his experience.

The shift of voice to a character within the novel involved more than just changing pronouns from "he" and "him" to "I" and "me." It meant constructing a story-telling personality. Several of Fitzgerald's earlier stories had begun in first-person, but after a page or two lapsed into third-person. Prior to 1925 he had written only one sustained first-person fiction, "*The Romantic Egotist,*" "a tedius, disconnected casserole" by his own admission, twice rejected by Scribner's.[10] Its successor, *This Side of Paradise,* retreated to third-person narration.

For precedents in first-person novels Fitzgerald could have turned to *Robinson Crusoe, Jane Eyre, Wuthering Heights,* or *Great Expectations* among English, for example, or *Moby-Dick* and *Huckleberry Finn* among American. He was better conversant with more recent novels, however, and two in particular influenced *Gatsby.*

Joseph Conrad's 1899 *Heart of Darkness,* the impressionistic tale of an English sailor, Marlow, recounts a voyage up the Congo toward a mystery figure deep in the jungle, Kurtz, of whom Marlow hears intriguing tales and rumors. His journey is both literal and metaphoric: as his rattletrap steamboat chugs into the heart of Africa, Marlow approaches a startling glimpse of savagery lurking within the ostensibly civilized. *Gatsby'*s Nick Carraway encounters a different jungle, metropolitan Long Island, but like Marlow after encountering Kurtz (echoed in Gatsby's actual surname, Gatz), Nick returns home sadder but wiser.

Another influence on *Gatsby,* less direct, was Cather's 1918 *My Ántonia,* a nostalgic novel of rural and small-town Nebraska. Fitzgerald had no interest in agrarian sentimentality, telling Perkins soon after *Gatsby* was published that "I suspect tragedy in the American country side because all the people capable of it move to the big towns at twenty," and a little later scoffing at novels about "*the Simple Inarticulate Farmer and his Hired Man Christy.* . . . As a matter of fact, the American peasant as 'real' material scarcely exists. . . . if [he] has any sensitivity whatsoever . . . he is in the towns before he's twenty," he repeated (although Fitzgerald in his entire life probably never met a farmer).[11]

As Cather's contribution to the novel of the inarticulate farmer, Fitzgerald continued, she "turns him Swede" in *My Ántonia* (confusing the Bohemian Ántonia with the Swedish Alexandra of *O Pioneers!*). But just after reading *My Ántonia* he had called it "a great book!" He "likes Willa Cather and that old woman, Edith Wharton," a friend reported later. "Willa the best [woman novelist] in U.S.A."[12]

My Ántonia's narrator, Jim Burden, grows up in a Midwest village; goes east to Harvard and thence to New York as an attorney with a railroad. Likewise, Nick Carraway is a transplanted midwesterner who has gone east to a Big Three university (Yale) and eventually to New York. Planning *My Ántonia,* Cather too had deliberated on a narrator. Its heroine was inspired by "the Bohemian hired girl of one of our [Nebraska] neighbors," she later told an interviewer. This girl, Annie Pavelka "was one of the truest artists I ever knew in the keenness and sensitiveness of her enjoyment" (anticipating Gatsby's "heightened sensitivity to the promises of life"). ". . . Annie fascinated me, and I always had it in mind to write a story about her."

"But from what point of view should I write it up?" she continued. ". . . I noticed that much of what I knew about Annie came from the talks I had with young men. She had a fascination for them. . . . and she meant a good deal to some of them. So I decided to make my observer a young man."[13] Rejecting a romance, she made Ántonia several years older than her narrator and established her feelings as those of a fond sister for a younger brother.

But it's unlikely that all the young men whom Annie Pavelka fascinated and to whom she "meant a good deal" were interested in her solely as a sisterly pal. Jim Burden infuses the novel's voice with stronger feeling—with the natural attraction a youth would feel for a warm, attractive, spirited girl. Jim dutifully observes and reports, but his interest in Ántonia goes further. One night, walking her home from a dance, "I told her she must kiss me good night."

She consents to this friendly leave-taking: "Why, sure, Jim."

But: "A moment later she drew her face away and whispered indignantly, 'Why, Jim! You know you ain't right to kiss me like that.'"

The sexual tension enriches the narrative; the impersonal reportage of a detached narrator would hardly convey Ántonia's magnetism as keenly as the recollections of a male admirer. Though never her lover, Jim is a poet of her charms, and his affection impregnates the novel's lyrical prose. Even his descriptions of the prairie landscape ripple with eroticism.

Considering narrative options for *The Great Gatsby,* Fitzgerald faced a similar issue. Needing to convey Gatsby's all-absorbing passion persuasively, he needed a heroine of magnetic allure. Nick's susceptibility to Daisy's charm in *Gatsby*'s opening chapter is prerequisite for what follows. The manuscript pages sent to Cather show Fitzgerald experimenting not with Gatsby, who hardly appears until the novel's third chapter, but with a technique for conveying Daisy's enchantment.

To sympathize with Gatsby, we too must sense her fascination. No mere catalog of features and freckles would suffice, and specifics about Daisy's appearance are in fact few; Jordan Baker is described more concretely. Fitzgerald's strategy for conveying Daisy's allure was selective and narrow; even in the early drafts he had decided to accentuate her voice—but how to convey the siren power of that "deathless song"? Like Cather searching for a point of view for *My Ántonia,* Fitzgerald concluded that the best person to describe the charms of a young woman was a young man—a point of view that came naturally to him anyway. Thus "Caraway" was born, though not yet as narrator.

As Daisy appears in the Cather pages, her voice became an immediate descriptive challenge: "The whispering of it 'listen' ~~to me now~~ of it richness of it which seem to proceed every word—the words changed their notes. The sentences were songs. There are no words to describe such voices but there is a promise of gay things in them of something magical done or yet to do." The testing of different phrases, a missing word, a cancellation and interlinear insertions all indicate a writer struggling with a first draft.

But even with the roughness smoothed away, the problem of perspective remained: to whom do these impressions belong? To "Caraway," we discover, but relayed through a disengaged narrator who provides such routine information as "They [including Caraway] stood up when dinner was announced."

Presently Caraway's perspective returns. "About the rest of her Caraway felt ~~rather than~~ was aware of a diminishing of vitality since he first knew her." Uncharacteristically vague ("About the rest of her . . . diminishing of vitality"), the sentence plods, with bland reminders that "Caraway felt" or "was aware of."

Fitzgerald had to rethink this approach. He intended, he told Perkins, to make *The Great Gatsby* "the very best I'm capable of," even "something better than I'm capable of," but this was not yet it.[14]

Replying to his letter about *A Lost Lady,* Cather would observe: "Everybody who has ever been swept away by personal charm tries in some way to express his wonder that the effect is so much greater than the cause,—and in the end we all fall back upon an old device and write about the effect and not the lovely creature who produced it."[15] The evocative power of music, too, descending into regions where words flounder, transcends its pedestrian cause in an organized series of tones. To suggest Daisy's seductive effect, Fitzgerald turned to this mysterious power. And it would not work to repeat, continually, "Nick felt" or "Nick thought." With the "new angle" of 1924, the novel's impersonal voice took on a personality—sympathetic, responsive, appreciative, critical.

From a biography of Gatsby, the novel became a narrative of Nick Carraway's summer as his neighbor and friend. Before meeting either Daisy or Gatsby, we learn much about Nick himself, and at the end, apart from the two Wilsons and Gatsby—all three dead—Nick is the most deeply affected character.

To make him the narrator, Fitzgerald discarded, as disturbing "the neatness of the plan," some 18,000 words, more than a third the length of *Gatsby* as published. From the excised pages he salvaged a 5,600-word short story, "Absolution." Narrated in third-person, "Absolution" takes the viewpoint of an eleven-year-old sensuous, dreamy, weak-fathered, ambitious North Dakota boy who in such characteristics resembles the briefly glimpsed youth of Jay Gatsby. Together, "Absolution" and the fragments sent to Cather suggest that Fitzgerald originally intended to narrate Gatsby's progress from boyhood to his affair twenty years later with "Ada," unhappily married to "an intensely strong vital man" prefiguring *Gatsby*'s Tom Buchanan.[16]

The "new angle" greatly compressed this chronology, from decades to a single summer. Though Gatsby's past is sketched in flashbacks, the main action occupies only his final three months. "Absolution," Fitzgerald remarked later, "was intended to be a picture of his early life, but . . . I cut it because I preferred to preserve the sense of mystery."[17]

As an experiment, *Gatsby*'s first-person narrator was facilitated by Nick Carraway's similarities to Fitzgerald himself. The Carraways "have been prominent, well-to-do people in this middle-western city for three generations," just as Fitzgerald represented the third Saint Paul generation of his mother's well-to-do family, the McQuillans. Fitzgerald's grandfather McQuillan founded a wholesale grocery business; Carraway's great uncle, a wholesale hardware business.

Financially and socially, wholesale was a stratum above retail: in a pre-supermarket era of neighborhood markets, the 1910 *Saint Paul City Directory* lists over four hundred retail grocers supplied by only nine wholesalers. The Carraway hardware business would have been similar: the man in the apron scooping nails did not graduate from Yale (as Nick's father did), and his son was unlikely to be a Yale classmate of Nick himself. Like Fitzgerald, Nick served as an army officer in the Great War and afterwards makes his way to New York.

Even the Carraways' grandiose legend of descent from the dukes of Bucchleuch draws on Fitzgerald family lore: a 1913 ledger entry, remarking on a visit to Fitzgerald's Maryland relations, notes, "Grandmother & the Duke of Buccleugh."

Yet despite these similarities, Nick is a fabricated personality. His family is still prominent and firmly established, the Fitzgeralds much less so. The Carraway hardware business prospers; the McQuillan grocery business was long defunct, and the Fitzgeralds lived on its dwindling legacy. When Nick moves to New York, "Father agreed to finance me for a year"; Fitzgerald in New York was on his own. Nick has grown up "in the Carraway house in a city where dwellings are still called through decades by a family's name," but there was no "Fitzgerald house" in Saint Paul. As Nick's father reminds him, "all the people in this world haven't had the advantages that you've had," and those unhappily disadvantaged included, to some extent, Fitzgerald himself.

Citing his father's reminder as an admonition to reserve judgment, Nick approaches his story accordingly, with traditional but forgiving moral standards anchored in genteel tastes and manners and heartland common sense and sobriety. The latter had some basis in Fitzgerald, or at least in his family; his grandfather McQuillan could not have built up his profitable grocery business from scratch without sober application. An 1877 obituary pasted into Fitzgerald's scrapbook extolled McQuillan's "clear head, sound judgment, good habits, strict honesty and willing hands."[18] Writing *Gatsby* at his desk in Antibes, Fitzgerald too maintained a clear head; only later would he need a bottle for "stimulus."

But while Nick at thirty assures us that "I have been drunk just twice in my life and the second time was that afternoon" (at the impromptu party in Tom Buchanan's love nest), Fitzgerald had begun drinking even before Princeton, continued to get "stewed" (a favorite term) thereafter, and at twenty-eight was sliding into alcoholism. A rambling letter to Princeton friend John Peale Bishop, for example, just before *Gatsby* was published, begins with a note across the top, "I am quite drunk"; proceeds to sketch a comic play about Woodrow Wilson which only another drunk Princetonian could appreciate; interjects a note, "Oh Christ! I'm sobering up!" and ends with a postscript, "I am quite drunk again."[19]

As most scenes in *Gatsby* involve drinking, however, a sober observer was desirable. At the first Gatsby party he attends, Nick recognizes no one and wanders about uncomfortably, "on my way to get roaring drunk from sheer embarrassment"—but doesn't. Spotting Jordan Baker he spends the evening with her and grows high, not drunk, on champagne. Only relatively sober could he coolly appreciate the nightmare comedy of the party's final incident, the confused, cacophonous scene of fuddled drunks whose car has run into a wall and lost a wheel.

Nick's assets as a narrator, though, go beyond temperance, discretion, and prudence, virtues we might respect without much liking him. The most ingratiating feature of his narrative voice is its self-effacing irony. His rectitude is tempered by humor: he makes fun of himself, even of his own sobriety. We trust his facts, but even more we appreciate his modesty—the absence of high self-opinion, self-importance, or vanity. When he tells us that "I am one of the few honest people that I have ever known," for example, we recognize a serious claim, but one qualified by characteristic self-mockery.

Fitzgerald's swagger, by contrast, flourished. "I think now that I'm much better than any of the young Americans *without exception*," he congratulated himself in 1925, whereas his distinguished elder Edith Wharton was only "a very distinguished grande dame who fought the good fight with bronze age weapons when there were very few people in the line at all"— that is, before the advent of Fitzgerald himself.[20] Smugness would not have made for a winning narrator.

Fitzgerald had recently experimented with first-person narration in three magazine articles. One was a travelogue recounting a road trip to Montgomery that he and Zelda had made in 1920. Beginning as a twenty-five-thousand-word article declined by high-paying magazines, a shorter version was eventually published as "The Cruise of the Rolling Junk," in a magazine for motorists.[21]

Groping for portentous meaning in the largely facetious "Cruise," one biographer detects in it Fitzgerald's "response to the underside of the Twenties that he found in the Main Streets of the South."[22] The article's only serious grievance, actually, is that several people insulted Zelda's flashy white knickerbocker suit. "The Cruise" is otherwise almost wholly comic, retailing successive crises, mostly mechanical, during their seven-day drive from Connecticut to Alabama long before the age of freeways. In Washington, DC, for example, a wheel falls off their car, an incident echoed in *The Great Gatsby*. Finally reaching Montgomery unannounced, they find the Sayres out of town and the house locked. This anticlimax was fiction, however; in fact they spent two weeks in Montgomery with the Sayres, sold the car, and took a train back to Connecticut.

"Technicccally it isn't a success," Fitzgerald wrote of "The Cruise of the Rolling Junk," but one element proved valuable.[23] Adopting a comic tone, he felt free to play the clown: "Anything mechanical from nail-hammering to applied dynamics is a great dark secret to me," he confesses, and the admission allows him to make himself the butt of much of the humor. In North Carolina, for example, their "Expenso" (actually a Marmon "Speedster") suffers a mechanical mishap. With rackety noises issuing from the undercarriage, they stop at a garage where "a tall young man driving a large and powerful Expenso, of the same type as ours," appears:

> Without exactly looking at the young man, I began to mope disconsolately around my own car, shaking the wheels sternly and picking bits of dust off the fender—in short, giving the impression that I was only waiting for something or somebody before beginning to perform some significant mechanical action. The young man, having parked his Expenso, strolled over to look at mine.
>
> "Trouble?" he demanded.
>
> "Nothing much," I answered grimly. "It's all broken inside, that's all."
>
> "Your wheel's coming off," he remarked dispassionately.
>
> "Oh, it's done that," I assured him. "It did that in Washington."
>
> "It's coming off again—from the inside."
>
> I smiled politely as though I had noticed it some time before. I took the wrench from the rear of the car and began to tighten the wheel.
>
> "It's coming off from the *inside*. No use tightening it there—you'll have to take it off."
>
> I was somewhat confused, as I had not been previously aware that a wheel could come off from the inside as well as just come off, but I snapped my fingers and remarked:
>
> "Of course. How stupid of me!"

The full account of this encounter is five times longer, Fitzgerald enjoying his comic role as mechanical incompetent.

It was a new voice for him—a self-effacing narrative "I." Perhaps influenced by silent-film comedians like Buster Keaton and Harold Lloyd, Fitzgerald narrates a series of mishaps as farce or slapstick in which all eventually turns out well. Though not a close pattern for Nick Carraway, the broad comedy was a rough draft of Nick's more refined humor.

Motor magazine ran "The Cruise" in three consecutive issues in early 1924, as Fitzgerald was returning to *Gatsby* after *The Vegetable* fiasco. A little later, the *Saturday Evening Post* carried two more comic articles. In the first, "How to Live on $36,000 a Year," Fitzgerald joked about his and Zelda's inability to live on what was then a handsome income. This article appeared in May 1924, as they sailed to Europe, and soon he wrote a companion piece, "How to Live on Practically Nothing a Year," based on their misadventures in France, where the dollar's strength reputedly made it possible for Americans to live on "practically nothing."

He wrote this second article in July, as he was also writing *Gatsby,* so that the humorous voice of the two "How to Live" articles was much in his mind as he crafted Nick Carraway's voice. In both articles the humor comes largely at the expense of Fitzgerald himself, who can't keep his expenses under control, who speaks atrocious pidgin French and is exploited by servants and tradesmen, who thinks a crowd gawking at two movie actors has gathered to gape at him, who makes detailed lists but can't add simple sums. "How to Live on $36,000 a Year" even ridicules a more serious folly, his golden hopes for *The Vegetable.*

These first-person 1924 articles were mostly comic. *Gatsby*'s plot, on the other hand, leads to three violent deaths, a rainy funeral, and Nick's disillusioned retreat to his midwestern home.

All the same, Nick is only occasionally somber and never cynical. Recoiling from *The Beautiful and Damned*'s acerbity, Fitzgerald made a deliberate effort to soften and brighten *Gatsby.* "I think it's about ten years better than anything I've done," he told a critic before publication. "All my harsh smartness has been kept ruthlessly out of it—it's the greatest weakness in my work. . . . I don't think this has a touch left."[24] Neither harsh nor smart, Nick's voice from the beginning is informal, conversational, lightly ironic, likeably humorous. He smiles at his own boast of good breeding ("as my father snobbishly suggested and I snobbishly repeat"); at his family's claim of descent from the Dukes of Buccleuch; at his own appearance ("I'm supposed to look like him [a great uncle] with special reference to the rather hard-boiled painting that hangs in Father's office"). Other than his claims to tolerance and honesty, themselves half-ironic, he has few pretensions.

Restlessness prompts him to leave the Midwest for the East to make money in "the bond business," but his tastes and needs are modest: "a weather beaten cardboard bungalow," a dog (who runs away), "an old Dodge and a Finnish woman who made my bed and cooked breakfast." In the city he lunches on "little pig sausages and mashed potatoes and coffee." Even his skirt-chasing is moderate, a brief affair with "a girl who lived in Jersey City and worked in the accounting department," and "I let it blow quietly away."

Most readers will appreciate Nick's moral sense, his solid midwestern ethos. His "provincial inexperience" is an asset. The family business, hardware, deals in durable, practical merchandise—hammers and hinges—for "hands-on" work like building and farming, not boutique goods, vanities, or financial speculations. He is embedded in family—grandfather and great uncle, "Father," and "all my aunts and uncles" are mentioned (though not his mother). He and his father, whose sage counsel he heeds, are "unusually communicative in a reserved way." The whole clan deliberates solemnly on his move to New York.

But though rooted in a conservative culture, Nick, true to his boasted tolerance, avoids quick or severe judgment; usually any explicit judgment at all. When in the opening chapter he sides with Daisy against the cheating Tom—"It seemed to me that the thing for Daisy to do was to rush out of the house, child in arms"—readers probably agree. Yet Tom is the only character Nick strongly dislikes, and even for Tom he makes allowances. He goes about with the "incurably dishonest" Jordan Baker, for whom he feels "a sort of tender curiosity," forgiving her cheating and lying on the curious grounds that "Dishonesty in a woman is a thing you never blame deeply." Though describing the party in Myrtle Wilson's apartment in lurid detail, he refrains from censure.

We can generally guess Nick's views and feelings; occasionally he makes them plain. The uninvited guests at Gatsby's parties conduct "themselves according the rules of behavior associated with amusement parks." Daisy's abandonment of Gatsby disappoints him. When the shameless sponge Klipspringer shirks Gatsby's funeral, Nick hangs up on him. But mostly he keeps his opinions to himself, like Doctor T. J. Eckleburg gazing over the wasteland without comment. Beneath Nick's even-tempered observation, however, lie the honorable certainties of "this middle western city" and the solid Carraway clan.

His moral code emerges without preaching. He mocks his own temperamental conservatism with a metaphor from his army days: "When I came back from the East last autumn I felt that I wanted the world to be in uniform and at a sort of moral attention forever." He is clear-sighted about Gatsby's sham grandeur, the anarchic West Egg partyers he catalogs, Tom Buchanan's tawdry love nest, Daisy's betrayal—yet he is no puritan. Wolfshiem—gambler, fixer, bootlegger, and racketeer—rather fascinates him; when Wolfshiem points out his human-molar cuff buttons, Nick blandly remarks, "That's a very interesting idea." The novel's sternest condemnation, for Tom and Daisy, is merely that they are "careless people," childlike and insulated by wealth, and Nick concludes even this mild censure by shaking hands with Tom. Explaining his motives for returning home at novel's end, he does not moralize, as commentators often do for him, but cites nightmare and nostalgia.

There is more to Nick's tolerance than simple live-and-let-live. Curiosity about people prompts his attentive sympathy. In one of *Gatsby*'s most well-imagined scenes, he describes the impromptu party in Tom Buchanan's Manhattan hideaway. Involved, almost captive, in smoky, drunken, violent confusion, Nick lets his thoughts wander outside, imagining himself a casual observer on the street below, glancing up at the lighted windows. "I was him too," Nick muses, "looking up and wondering. I was within and without, simultaneously enchanted and repelled by the inexhaustible variety of life." The double perspective is one of Nick's narrative virtues. Even standing back in distaste and disapproval, he observes closely and appreciatively.

Much of *Gatsby*'s appeal lies in its gallery of sharply etched characters, like Wolfshiem, Tom Buchanan, Jordan Baker, and Myrtle Wilson. Even minor, briefly glimpsed figures like Myrtle's sister Catherine, the effeminate photographer McKee with shaving cream on his cheek, and Gatsby's father, "very helpless and dismayed, bundled up in a long cheap ulster against the warm September day," contribute to the novel's "inexhaustible variety of life." Searching for themes and moralisms, earnest readers often fail to enjoy *Gatsby*'s vigorously realized characters. If one needs a theme, the inexhaustible variety of life would be a good start.

* * *

Nick Carraway's summer on Long Island leads him not to a lofty critique of the American Dream, but to a better understanding of himself. A conventional young man of his era and class, born into a midwestern mercantile family and attending prep school in the East and then Yale, Nick has a genteel but unpoetic background. He identifies himself on the first page as "a normal person." With characteristic humor, he mocks his ordinariness: "I was rather literary in college—one year I wrote a series of very solemn and obvious editorials for the 'Yale News.'" Now his ambition, equally pedestrian, is to become a "well-rounded" man while selling bonds.

He works at Probity Trust in lower Manhattan and regales his evenings with "a dozen volumes on banking and credit and investment securities." "Probity Trust" suggests Nick winking at his self-proclaimed honesty. But his conventionality enhances his credibility. Who would suspect a pontificating undergraduate journalist, now a Wall Street drudge, of poetic fancies? Jordan Baker avoids "clever shrewd men" but sees Nick as safe, a careful driver, someone for whom "divergence from a code" is unthinkable. (Only later, jilted and embittered, does she recant.)

His tepid amours conform. His romantic history seems confined to a dead-end dalliance with "an old friend" whom he had no interest in marrying and of whom his sharpest memory is "a faint mustache of perspiration" when playing tennis. She is displaced by Jordan Baker, with whom "I wasn't actually in love." When she, not he, "deliberately shifted our relations," inviting a more serious romance, "for a moment I thought I loved her. But I am slow thinking and full of interior rules that act as brakes on my desires." After jilting her he has a brief second thought, but even then finds himself only "half in love with her." By his own admission he is restrained, cautious, hesitating.

How could prudent Nick, heavy-footed on the emotional brakes, understand and sympathize with Gatsby—fevered, possessed and driven by love; or rather, by the memory of lost love?—a character with no brakes, and for whom there is no "half in love"?

There is more to Nick, however, than caution, restraint, and conventional background. Arriving in the novel's opening scene at the Buchanans' estate in old-money East Egg, he admires the grounds: "The lawn started at the beach and ran toward the front door for a quarter of a mile, jumping over sun-dials and brick walks and burning gardens—finally when it reached the house drifting up the side in bright vines as though from the momentum of its run. The front was broken by a line of French windows, glowing now with reflected gold, and wide open to the warm windy afternoon. . . ." What he gives us is not simply a pleasant lawn on a pleasant day, but an active, sensory, richly colored landscape in motion—running, jumping, drifting, windy; saturated with light and color in the green lawn, the bright vines, the windows glowing in the sinking sun; keenly tactile, with the burning gardens and warm breeze. Figures of speech abound—the lawn runs and hurdles from the shore, unable to stop itself at the house. The vigor, color, and fancy of the passage reveal high poetic energy.

Ushered into the house, Nick endows it too with motion, color, and sensory life: "We walked through a hallway into a bright rosy-colored space, fragilely bound into the house by French windows at either end. The windows were ajar and gleaming white against the fresh grass outside that seemed to grow a little way into the house. A breeze blew through the room, blew curtains in at one end and out the other like pale flags, twisting them up toward the frosted wedding cake of the ceiling—and then rippled over the wine-colored rug, making a shadow on it as wind does on the sea." With the colors—rose, gleaming white, and burgundy—comes a hint of fragrance and wine; the "frosted wedding cake" ceiling adds sweetness. A breeze stirs the curtains and rug; the green of the lawn encroaches, and a suggestion of the nearby Long Island Sound wafts in, as the rug stirs and darkens like a ruffled sea. Daisy and Jordan, "both in white," "their dresses . . . rippling and fluttering," float on the breeze. Under Nick's eye the room itself is alive.

Despite his prosaic résumé he exhibits a keen lyric impulse. Though he moils in bonds from nine to five, his imagination is fresh, vivid, sensuous, fanciful. Writing in April 1924 of his intentions in *Gatsby*, Fitzgerald told Perkins, "in my new novel I'm thrown directly on purely creative work . . . the sustained imagination of a sincere and yet radiant world."[25] From Nick we might have expected the sincerity, but the radiance surprises.

Years later Fitzgerald would mourn his own faded impressionability and a dulling sensibility to "the dramatic and glamorous": "I used to think that my sensory impression of the world came from outside. I used to actually believe that it was as objective as blue skies or a piece of music. Now

I know it was within, and emphatically cherish what little is left." *Gatsby's* vividly imagined world, drenched in sensory excitement, shows him at the height of his powers.[26]

An especially good example is the opulent opening of chapter 3, prologue to the first of Gatsby's parties that Nick attends. The paragraphs glow with rich imagery: "There was music from my neighbor's house through the summer nights. In his blue gardens men and girls came and went like moths among the whisperings and the champagne and the stars." Color, music ("yellow cocktail music"), whisperings, flutterings, sparkling wine, and starlight soak the scene in romance. The buffet table, perhaps no more glamorous in reality than that of any banquet-room wedding reception, assumes in Nick's eyes a seductive visual savor, "with glistening hors d'oeuvres, spiced baked hams crowded against salads of harlequin designs and pastry pigs and turkeys bewitched to a dark gold." Even the turkeys glow.

Apart from this cornucopia, food seems of no particular interest to Nick. What he *is* susceptible to, despite his lackluster romances, is women. He indulges in fantasies of walking along Fifth Avenue to "pick out romantic women from the crowd and imagine that in a few minutes I was going to enter their lives. . . ." For the one woman he actually does romance, the "clean, hard, limited" Jordan Baker, Nick feels not only "a tender curiosity," but moments of desire: "It was dark now and as we dipped under a little bridge I put my arm around Jordan's golden shoulder and drew her toward me," and "We passed a barrier of dark trees, and then the façade of Fifty-ninth Street, a block of delicate pale light, beamed into the Park. . . . I drew up the girl beside me, tightening my arms," and for the only time in the novel, they kiss.

If Daisy's voice enchants, Jordan's keynote is "jaunty," used in some form to describe her five times, and used for no one else. The novel's third important woman is neither enchanting nor jaunty but loud, vulgar, and voluptuous. Yet Myrtle Wilson's brazen charms also fascinate Nick: "She was in the middle thirties, and faintly stout, but she carried her surplus flesh sensuously as some women can. Her face . . . contained no facet or gleam of beauty but there was an immediately perceptible vitality about her as if the nerves of her body were continually smouldering. She smiled slowly and . . . shook hands with Tom, looking him flush in the eye. Then she wet her lips and spoke . . . in a soft, coarse voice." Though a good deal of this is impressionistic, Myrtle is sketched in greater physical detail than either of her two refined sister characters. "I'm sorry Myrtle is better than Daisy," Fitzgerald told Perkins, alluding to Myrtle's crude carnal presence, the "smouldering" sexuality complementing the "cruel" muscularity of her lover Tom Buchanan.[27] Physically, the two supporting characters come before us more sharply than Daisy and Gatsby.

Nonetheless, Daisy alone fascinates Nick. Only someone susceptible to her siren voice could possibly understand Jay Gatsby.

Fitzgerald vacillated over the novel's title. Though suggesting *The Great Gatsby* early on, he considered, reconsidered, wavered, and debated alternatives. *Under the Ash Heaps and Millionaires* was vetoed by Perkins; *Trimalchio* "was voted down by Zelda and everybody else," on the grounds that few would recognize the allusion or know how to pronounce "Trimalchio." *Gold-Hatted Gatsby, The High-bouncing Lover,* and *Under the Red White and Blue* were other candidates. Even after *The Great Gatsby* as title was final, Fitzgerald's doubts remained.[28]

One of his reservations was that "there's no emphasis even ironically on his [Gatsby's] greatness or lack of it."[29] Nonetheless, "great" points to the ambiguity of Gatsby's character and career. He is a "parvenu," "bootlegger-crook," "common swindler," protégé and partner of Meyer Wolfshiem, co-perpetrator of a deadly hit-and-run accident, and vulgarian in a pink suit—with all this, "great" seems risible. Even Nick's parting words, "You're worth the whole damn bunch put together," is modest tribute when the bunch itself is "a rotten crowd."

Yet "great" is not wholly inapt. Dead sober, intensely single-minded, Gatsby stands above the crowd, in "complete isolation" even at his own "overpopulated" parties. He is extraordinary in his "heightened sensitivity to the promises of life," "an extraordinary gift for hope, a romantic readiness." He aspires, dreams, desires, and quests on epic scale.

In our first glimpse of Gatsby, Nick is taking a bite of fresh air after returning home from dinner at the Buchanans,' when a figure emerges from the shadows of the neighboring lawn. Nick speculates that "it was Mr. Gatsby himself, come out to determine what share was his of our local heavens," and his neighborly impulse is to introduce himself. But the mystery figure "gave a sudden intimation that he was content to be alone," reaching out toward "a single green light, minute and far away, that might have been the end of a dock."

The well-known image captures Gatsby's essence: the dim far-off hope, the longing, the reaching out, the lonely fixation. For practical, heart-free Nick, it is a glimpse of compelling desire, soaring beyond hardware, Yale, and Probity Trust.

Eventually we learn more about Gatsby, from youth to death, not consecutively but in out-of-order disclosures. We do not hear of his North Dakota boyhood until the day before his funeral. In the novel's typescript most of Gatsby's history was packed into the next-to-last chapter, but Perkins suggested it be parceled out in smaller pieces throughout: "I thought you might find ways to let the truth of some of his claims like 'Oxford' and his army career come out bit by bit in the course of actual narrative." Fitzgerald at first demurred—Gatsby's "long narrative in Chap. VIII will be difficult to split up"—but then complied and generously credited Perkins: "Max, it amuses me when praise comes in on the 'structure' of the book—because it was you who fixed up the structure, not me."[30]

As glimpses of Gatsby's past drop into the flow of Nick's summer, the novel becomes a story of discovery, of Nick learning piecemeal about his enigmatic neighbor. He first hears scandal and rumor; then Gatsby himself narrates a condensed autobiography, mostly lies. Gatsby's association with Meyer Wolfshiem is suspicious. Not until almost halfway through, when Nick yields (for the only time) to another narrator, Jordan Baker, does he learn of Gatsby's past with Daisy, including the revelation that he had acquired his mansion in West Egg "so that Daisy would be just across the bay."

Chapter 6, however, takes us back even further, to Gatsby before Daisy, with Nick relating the story of Gatsby's youth and five years with Dan Cody. This was material Fitzgerald had transferred from the longer Gatsby history two chapters later, and in its new location it actually comes prematurely, for Gatsby "told me all this very much later"

As a teenager, Gatsby's "heart was in a constant, turbulent riot," Nick summarizes, and illustrates with a striking image: "The most fantastic and grotesque conceits haunted him in his bed at night. A universe of ineffable gaudiness spun itself out in his brain while the clock ticked on the wash-stand and the moon soaked with wet light his tangled clothes upon the floor." Like the moon shedding glamor on dirty laundry, Gatsby's imagination irradiates the commonplace, his gaudy, fantastic, grotesque visions leaving behind that relentless reminder of the mundane, the ticking clock.

In such images we apprehend Gatsby's "greatness," which has little to do with money or worldly ambition. "There was something gorgeous about him," Nick tells us at the outset, and that "something" is his high-flying aspiration, free of any moderation, unrestrained by legality, taste, or long odds. His youthful ambitions incline to "ineffable gaudiness," "a vast, vulgar and meretricious beauty," later manifested in pink and caramel-colored suits, sham castle, and "circus wagon" automobile.

Like Fitzgerald, Gatsby meets his destiny during his army days. With Daisy, his untethered visions—his extravagant fancies, his "fantastic and grotesque conceits"—crystallize in the "excitingly desirable" girl. The occasion is described in one of the novel's fine lyric passages, in which Nick imagines the transforming moment. Gatsby and Daisy Fay, the belle of Louisville, are strolling along a moonlit street on a cool autumn night full of "mysterious excitement." It is an hour of fulfillment, but also crisis. Until now, unattached and "alone," Gatsby's imagination has been free to roam.

But free only if alone. In falling for Daisy—marrying his floating dreams and ambitions to a single girl—he will "forever wed his unutterable visions to her perishable breath." When they kiss, "she blossomed for him like a flower and the incarnation was complete." The metaphor is explicitly theological: Gatsby's extravagant visions, romping "like the mind of God," become mysteriously incarnate in a mortal girl. For Gatsby, contemptuous of women, it is an ironic twist.

Even with his poetic fancies, a cautious, conventional bond salesman hardly seems a suitable narrator for such a transcendent moment. Not only are Nick and Gatsby temperamentally different, but between them yawns a class gap—Nick from a comfortably fixed mercantile family and Yale, Gatsby the son of "shiftless and unsuccessful farm people." Gatsby's higher education consists of five years of cruising about with the old roué

Dan Cody; Nick by contrast has absorbed the manners and tastes of America's patrician establishment. The Yale Club reprobated pink suits. Tom Buchanan's contemptuous "Mr. Nobody from Nowhere" is unapologetic snobbery—"I'll be damned if I know how you got within a mile of her [Daisy] unless you brought the groceries to the back door"—but Nick too regrets Gatsby's "rough-neck" quality and vulgarity. For all Tom's boorishness, Nick shares his class assumptions, and his summary censure of Gatsby—"I disapproved of him from beginning to end"—is more aesthetic than moral.

Nonetheless, the genteel Yalie becomes the parvenu Gatsby's only friend and sympathetic chronicler. Their affinity begins to emerge before they meet. In the opening scene, Nick drives his old Dodge—the only time he seems to go anywhere in it—to dinner with the Buchanans, "two old friends whom I scarcely knew at all." Daisy is his "second cousin once removed," a connection perhaps understood only by professional genealogists. He has met Daisy at least once, having visited the Buchanans some three years earlier, but tells us nothing about her before he arrives at their East Egg mansion, where he immediately focuses on her defining feature.

"She laughed, an absurd, charming little laugh," he remarks, and her first words are a hyperbolic greeting in an affected stutter, "I'm p-paralyzed with happiness." Vaguely introducing the other woman present, Daisy "hinted in a murmur" Jordan Baker's name, and Nick adds parenthetically: "I've heard it said that Daisy's murmur was only to make people lean toward her; an irrelevant criticism that made it no less charming."

Soon after, she "began asking questions in her low, thrilling voice. It was the kind of voice that the ear follows up and down as if each speech is an arrangement of notes that will never be played again," and Nick continues in another lyrical sentence to expound on the "excitement" in her voice.

Fascinated, he mentions Daisy's voice over and over, a dozen times in a short novel in which, apart from Jordan's Louisville retrospective, she appears in only four of nine chapters. Gatsby savors the rich vibrations of Daisy's song, and Jordan observes, "there's something in that voice of hers," but Nick has the most susceptible ear. Even Gatsby mentions her voice only once, prompted by Nick.[31]

We *see* Tom Buchanan's rippling muscles and arrogance, and Myrtle Wilson's crude vigor, but we see very little of Daisy, Nick's descriptions sticking almost entirely to her melodic voice. Struck by it, he begins to understand Gatsby's obsession even before meeting him. "Do you mean you're in love with Miss Baker?" Nick later asks Gatsby, and we might be tempted to ask Nick, in turn, Are you in love with Daisy? In their shared susceptibility to her, Nick and Gatsby constitute a freemasonry of two.

The turning point in Nick's attitude to Gatsby comes with Jordan Baker's reminiscence of her Louisville days, revealing that Nick's neighbor "Mr. Gatsby" was once Daisy's suitor. "It was a strange coincidence," Nick comments—but Jordan corrects him: "But it wasn't a coincidence at all. . . . Gatsby bought that house so that Daisy would be just across the bay." At this, Nick recalls his first sight of Gatsby, reaching toward the green light, and the curious gesture suddenly makes sense. "He's waited so long," Jordan explains, and now he simply wants Nick to "let him come over" while Daisy visits for tea. Having expected some "utterly fantastic" request, Nick sees that, in view of Gatsby's long, consuming quest, the favor asked is trivial.

"The modesty of the demand shook me," he remarks, and his sympathy goes out to Gatsby. The spurious chateau, flamboyant parties, flashy car, hydroplanes—all that "purposeless splendor"—have left Nick unimpressed, even contemptuous. So much vulgar ostentation and promiscuous hospitality—for what? Jordan provides the answer, and for Nick, Gatsby's lonely quest justifies the circus. Immediately he enlists in the plot to reconnect the one-time lovers.

I n a fine lyrical passage in the penultimate chapter, Nick narrates Gatsby's poignant visit to Louisville after the war, having lost Daisy to Tom while at Oxford. Nick's account ends with Gatsby leaving the city. He concludes his reconstruction of Gatsby's visit with the train drawing away from Louisville, ". . . the vanishing city where she had drawn her breath. He stretched out his hand desperately as if to snatch only a wisp of air, to save a fragment of the spot that she had made lovely for him. But it was all going by too fast now for his blurred eyes and he knew that he had lost that part of it, the freshest and the best, forever." Nick would have had to imagine Gatsby's feelings, but Fitzgerald himself could draw on memories of himself, jilted, leaving Montgomery on a train five years earlier.

That melancholy departure remained etched in his imagination. "The Sensible Thing" had described it, too, with George O'Kelly leaving Jonquil's Tennessee town after being jilted: "Past clanging street-crossings, gathering speed through wide suburban spaces toward the sunset. . . . This night's dusk would cover up forever the sun and the trees and the flowers and laughter of his young world." In Nick's tendency not simply to report but to enter into Gatsby's emotions, Gatsby, Nick, and Fitzgerald converge. Instinctively, Fitzgerald attributed his own emotions to his characters.

Reading the typescript, Perkins felt hazy about Gatsby's age. "I think for some reason or other," he commented, "a reader . . . gets an idea that Gatsby is a much older man than he is" (which is "a year or two over thirty").[32]

"It seems of almost mystical significance to me that you thot he was older," Fitzgerald responded; "the man I had in mind, half unconsciously, *was* older (a specific individual). . . ." This was William M. Fuller, a Great Neck resident accused, when his brokerage firm went bankrupt in June 1922, of running a "bucket shop." A long-running, well-publicized scandal, the "Fuller-McGee case" saw Fuller and his partner McGee tried four times, with both eventually serving a year in Sing Sing. In 1922 Fuller was about forty and a bachelor; during his months in Great Neck, Fitzgerald may have met or at least seen him at one or more of the parties he attended there.[33]

From a character originating in someone Fitzgerald knew slightly if at all, Gatsby evolved into someone he knew rather better—himself. Responding to criticism by John Peale Bishop, Fitzgerald admitted that "you are right about Gatsby being blurred and patchy. I never at any one time saw him clear myself—for he started as one man I knew and then changed into myself—the amalgam was never complete in my mind." Two years later, he echoed this: "Gatsby was never quite real to me. His original served for a good enough exterior until about the middle of the book he grew thin and I began to fill him with my own emotional life."[34]

Originating in the crooked high-rolling stockbroker of forty with a string of mistresses, Gatsby ends as a younger man on a quixotic quest, "the following of a grail." Rather than *The Great Gatsby* being "about money," it moves away from money. Daisy is the grail, money simply the means. "I feel far away from her," Gatsby laments after one of his parties. "It's hard to make her understand."

Nick replies, "You mean about the dance?"

Gatsby scoffs: "'The dance?' He dismissed all the dances he had given with a snap of his fingers. 'Old sport, the dance is unimportant.'" With this fillip he dismisses as trifling all the money he has made and squandered. Only Daisy matters.

In a 1932 essay, "My Lost City," Fitzgerald recalled looking for a room in New York in the winter of 1919, just arrived from Montgomery and the army. "I interviewed a blowsy landlady in Greenwich Village. She told me I could bring girls to the room, and the idea filled me with dismay. Why should I want to bring girls to my room?—I had a girl."[35] It was not a question of resisting temptation, but of fixation. "A girl" was *the* girl.

Fitzgerald bestowed on Gatsby the same riveted dedication. In a later-deleted passage in *Gatsby's* typescript, Gatsby resents Daisy's disruption of his ambitions. "I might be a great man if I could forget that once I lost Daisy. . . . I used to think wonderful things were going to happen to me, before I met her. And I knew it was a great mistake for a man like me to fall in love—and then one night I let myself go, and it was too late—." He is upset, sobs in fact, because Daisy wants simply to run away with Gatsby rather than formally renounce Tom and their three years of marriage. On reflection Fitzgerald probably thought Gatsby's lapse into tears mawkish, but the deleted passage suggests Fitzgerald's idea of Gatsby driven by a compelling, even unwilling passion.[36]

At his bacchanalian parties, with multitudes of attractive tipsy women and every opportunity for seduction, Gatsby remains sober and aloof: "Girls were swooning backward playfully into men's arms, even into groups knowing that someone would arrest their falls—but no one swooned backward on Gatsby and no French bobs touched Gatsby's shoulder and no singing quartets were formed with Gatsby's head for one link." Like Fitzgerald with the blowsy landlady, Gatsby is absorbed by *the* woman. The rest don't matter.

One of the novel's most curiously sensuous scenes features shirts. After their reunion in Nick's bungalow, Gatsby has led Daisy next door, with Nick tagging along, for a tour of his house, first the public rooms and then upstairs, "through period bedrooms swathed in rose and lavender silk and vivid with new flowers, through dressing rooms and poolrooms, and bathrooms with sunken baths," until they reach Gatsby's private quarters, where he opens

> two hulking patent cabinets which held his massed suits and dressing gowns and ties, and his shirts piled like bricks in stacks a dozen high. . . . He took out a pile of shirts and began throwing them, one by one before us, shirts of sheer linen and thick silk and fine flannel which lost their folds as they fell and covered the table in many-colored disarray. While we admired he brought more and the soft rich heap mounted higher—shirts with stripes and scrolls and plaids in coral and apple-green and lavender and faint orange with monograms of Indian blue.

At this kaleidoscopic spectacle,

> . . . suddenly with a strained sound Daisy bent her head into the shirts and began to cry stormily.
> "They're such beautiful shirts," she sobbed, her voice muffled in the thick folds. "It makes me sad because I've never seen such—such beautiful shirts before."

How should we read Daisy's "beautiful" for these garish shirts? Why does she weep "stormily"? Why weep at all?

Over the years, Daisy has received bad press. Fitzgerald himself admitted that "a tremendous fault" in the novel was "the lack of an emotional presentment of Daisy's attitude toward Gatsby after their reunion," and thought Myrtle Wilson's characterization superior. Commentators since have often depreciated Daisy in moral terms.[37]

By Nick's account, she is lovely, sophisticated, and charming, but ultimately weak and faithless. She vacillates at the Plaza, then lets Gatsby take the blame for Myrtle Wilson's death; she skips Gatsby's funeral and leaves town. In the opening chapter Nick pities her as a captive princess shackled to an unfaithful husband; in the final chapter he condemns both as fellow irresponsibles: ". . . they smashed up things and creatures and then retreated back into their money or their vast carelessness. . . ."

But this rant needs to be read in the context of Nick's disillusion and disgust with the entire East at this point, not just the Buchanans—who as he points out are not even Easterners. It would be better to think of Daisy, rather, as divided between two pasts. Gatsby's quest is hopeless, but straightforward—there is a single woman in his life. But Daisy has had a past not only with Gatsby, but with Tom too. "I did love him once," she cries to Gatsby, "—but I loved you too." She must choose between two pasts, but even more between two futures. Good fiction pushes beyond simplistic judgments to difficult, even intractable, dilemmas.

The rainbow of shirts expresses Gatsby's extravagant love, but Daisy's reaction should bend our sympathies to her as well. His harlequin exhibition recalls the novel's epigraph:

> Then wear the gold hat, if that will move her;
> If you can bounce high, bounce for her too. . . .

Gatsby expresses his passion not in words but in splendor and display, in tasteless free-spending, in carnivalesque parties with a glut of amusement-park partyers. Emptying his clothes cabinet, he declares his love in a poetry of shirts—not the starched white shirts of a bond trader, but shirts of bright color, sensuous texture, varied fabrics, loud patterns, flying through the air and piling up in a "soft rich heap." Their "many-colored" profusion and "disarray" speak of rich, unstinting, overflowing love. For all their gaudy excess, Daisy rightly understands them as an outpouring of adoration.

One early admirer of *The Great Gatsby* singled out the shirt passage for special praise. "I could go on for a long time quoting things that delight me," Roger Burlingame, a Scribner's editor, told Fitzgerald. "The beginning of Ch. II, for instance [the valley of ashes], & that gorgeous place where she cried into the shirts, & the night 'when we hunted through the great rooms for cigarettes.'"[38] In perceiving the power of such passages, Burlingame better understood Fitzgerald's genius than many since.

Burying her face in shirts, Daisy weeps in gratitude and sorrow, recognizing in them a consuming love, "five years of unwavering devotion," which she cannot reciprocate. Gatsby "had been full of the idea so long, dreamed it right through to the end, waited with his teeth set, so to speak, at an inconceivable pitch of intensity." If *The Great Gatsby* is "about" anything, it is about loving not wisely but too well, "living too long with a single dream." Gratefully and sadly, Daisy understands it.

W hen Gatsby's mentor, Meyer Wolfshiem, begs off Gatsby's funeral and Daisy slips out of town, Nick alone—critical still, but sympathetic; a moralist but not a prig—keeps vigil with Gatsby's body. In Conrad's *Heart of Darkness,* Marlow, though thoroughly disapproving, "remained loyal to Kurtz to the last, and even beyond. . . ." So too Nick, who finds himself "on Gatsby's side, and alone," feeling a "scornful solidarity between Gatsby and me against them all." Nick has inherited the loneliness of Gatsby's lonely passion.

One reason for Nick's bond with Gatsby is simple: Fitzgerald himself was both. Ambitious, extravagant, and exhibitionist, Fitzgerald was wistful and nostalgic, too, drawn back (like Nick) to "something—an elusive rhythm, a fragment of lost words, that I had heard somewhere a long time ago." He was of flashy West Egg and genteel Princeton; of electrified 1920s New York, "the racy, adventurous feel of it at night . . . the constant flicker of men and women and machines," but also of sedate Summit Avenue, Saint Paul, to which at the end Nick, though not Fitzgerald, retreats.

Nick's return brings his story full circle, for at the opening he had just arrived from his "middle-western city." His retreat now would seem to imply a future with the Carraway clan's hardware business; marriage not to a fast-set, cheating celebrity like Jordan Baker, but to the girl of the perspiration mustache, or someone like her; domesticity and a comfortable Summit Avenue home among Ordways, Herseys, and Schultzes, with summer cottage and country club on White Bear Lake and children at eastern prep schools or Miss This-or-That's, the boys going on to Yale.

In short, a return to the world of Nick's youth, much like Fitzgerald's. Nick to be sure has more to go back to; Fitzgerald's family had no prosperous wholesale business; his parents had by now retired to Washington, DC. But *Gatsby*'s fine passage recalling train rides home from prep school and college at Christmas echoes Fitzgerald's own strain of nostalgia. "That's my middle-west . . . ," Nick observes, "I am part of that. . . ."

Nowhere before "have you ever touched the warmth and living color of this Gatsby; or its beauty or its strange nostalgia or its amazing color," Roger

Burlingame told Fitzgerald when *Gatsby* was published: ". . . Someone once said that the thing that was common to all real works of art was a nostalgic quality, often indefinable, not specific. If that is so then The Great Gatsby is surely one because it makes me want to be back somewhere as much, I think as anything I've ever read." Fitzgerald replied, "That describes, better than I could have put it myself, whatever unifying emotion the book has, either in regard to the temperament of Gatsby himself or in my own mood while writing it."[39]

My Ántonia again provides a parallel. Like Nick, Cather's Jim Burden, having abandoned the Midwest for New York, returns at the end to Nebraska. Though only visiting, "Out there I felt at home again," Jim remarks, and "I had the sense of coming home to myself." Of Ántonia and himself he reflects, "Whatever we had missed, we possessed together the precious, the incommunicable past." Years later Fitzgerald would quote this sentence as the final words of his final essay.[40]

S ailing to Europe in May 1924, the Fitzgeralds had visited Paris and then settled on the Riviera for the summer, renting a villa near St. Raphael, where he worked steadily on the novel begun the year before. With little to occupy her, Zelda enjoyed sunbathing and swimming.

"We are living here in a sort of idyllic state among everything lovely imaginable in the way of Mediterranean delights," he wrote one correspondent, and to another, ". . . I think St. Raphael (where we are) is the lovliest spot I've ever seen. . . . We have bought a little Reynault car & Zelda & the Baby & the Governess swim every day on a sandy beach—in fact everything's idyllic and for the first time since I went to Saint Paul in 1921 . . . I'm perfectly happy."[41]

The idyll was short-lived. In an often cited but hazy episode, Zelda became involved with a French naval aviator, Edouard Jozan, in what was an innocent dalliance, summer romance, brief fling, or serious affair, depending on one's intuitions or imagination. Assertions, speculation, guessing, and fictional versions abound; verifiable facts are scarce.[42]

Jozan's name, misspelled, first appears in Fitzgerald's ledger for June 1924, without elaboration. The next month's entry begins, "The Big crisis—13th of July." As Fitzgerald was generally casual about dating, the precision and upper-case "B" suggest a dramatic event, probably a confrontation with Zelda, Jozan, or both. In October the ledger notes with apparent relief, "Last sight of Josanne."

By then marital harmony had been restored, or Fitzgerald chose to think so. In August the ledger reports "Good work on novel. Zelda and I close together," and the same month he told Perkins, "Its been a fair summer. I've been unhappy but my work hasn't suffered from it."[43]

But if forgiving, he did not forget. Later he would remind Zelda of "your heart betraying me," and recall "how I'd dragged the great Gatsby out of the pit of my stomach in a time of misery." Later yet he would refer to her "love for Josaune."[44]

Both Fitzgeralds would eventually write a story or novel chapter based on the affair. Biographers sometimes treat these fictions as straight reportage, but what they convey more accurately is how each later remembered the emotions of July 1924.

In Zelda's 1932 *Save Me the Waltz,* an episode inspired by the Jozan affair concludes with the unhappy Zelda figure, Alabama, consoled by a French acquaintance as the Jozan character Jacques departs for China: "I'm very sorry for you. . . . We had not thought it was so serious an affair—we had thought it was just an affair," and with Alabama grieving as she tears up his photo: "What was the use of keeping it? There wasn't a way to hold on to the summer . . . no hopes to be salvaged from a cheap French photograph. Whatever it was that she wanted from Jacques, Jacques took it with him to squander on the Chinese. You took what you wanted from life, if you could get it, and you did without the rest."

Fitzgerald's 1935 story "Image on the Heart," involving a Riviera triangle of American couple and French naval aviator, concludes with the couple uneasily reconciled and departing for Italy together, leaving France and the lover behind: ". . . as they curved down through Provence, they were silent for a while, each with a separate thought. His thought was that he would never know—what her thought was must be left unfathomed—and perhaps unfathomable in that obscure pool in the bottom of every woman's heart." Later, Fitzgerald would remark, "That September 1924, I knew something had happened that could never be repaired."[45]

How the incident affected *Gatsby,* if at all, is uncertain. The novel had been conceived and its "new angle" established months before Jozan appeared, and within a week of the "Big crisis" *Gatsby* was "almost done," Fitzgerald reported.[46]

By early September he had completed a full draft. It's unlikely that it greatly deviated from the plan laid down six months earlier and developed up to July. Yet the Jozan affair may have contributed to the nostalgic, melancholy disillusion of *Gatsby*'s final chapter.

The Great Gatsby was published on April 10, 1925—a signal moment in American letters and the summit of Fitzgerald's achievement. He was twenty-eight.

4

THE RIVIERA, THE ACTRESS, AND FOOTBALL

(1926–1927)

Something very lovely . . . that he had not found in life.

—"OFFSIDE PLAY"

I f graphed like the swings of the stock market, Fitzgerald's fortunes would show similar oscillations, with ascents growing fewer and declines more frequent and steeper after *The Great Gatsby*. Among the bad times, the two years following *Gatsby's* publication were nothing compared to Zelda's 1930 breakdown, his own crack-up in 1935, or a dismal 1939 which both began and ended with disappointment and alcoholic collapse. But though free of major calamities, the immediate post-*Gatsby* years were prologue to later misfortunes. Drifting in his vocation, falling into idleness and alcoholism, he would never recover his momentum as a novelist.

Sending *Gatsby's* corrected proofs to Scribner's in early 1925, he was understandably ready for a break. His ledger for the following months documents heavy sociability, with dozens of names and entries such as "Zelda painting, me drinking" (April); "1000 parties and no work" (June); and "Again 1000 parties and no work—until last ten days" (July).

July's ten days of work were devoted to one of his longest and finest stories, "The Rich Boy." He wrote little else, however, and for sixteen months— from February 1926 to June 1927, according to his ledger—nothing at all. When *Gatsby* was published he was young, healthy, confident, and ambitious, but the two years following were his least productive since Princeton.

In his ledger he candidly described his twenty-ninth year as "Drink, loafing & the Murphys," his thirtieth as "Futile, shameful useless. . . . Self disgust. Health gone."

A few months after finishing *Gatsby* he reported to Perkins, "The novel has begun."[1] But *Gatsby*'s successor soon stalled as he fell into more pleasant diversions and enthusiasms—in particular football, a young woman not his wife, and the Murphys mentioned in the ledger entry quoted above.

One detailed account of Fitzgerald in action during this period survives. Though exaggerated, it likely contains much truth. Ernest Hemingway's name, misspelled, first appears in his ledger in May 1925, twice, the second time recording a trip to "Lyon with Ernest." Hemingway's memoir of his Paris years, *A Moveable Feast,* devotes a chapter to the excursion.[2]

He and the Fitzgeralds had met after they arrived in Paris from wandering about Italy during the winter. Driving from Marseilles, they had abandoned their Renault in Lyon and finished the journey by train. According to Fitzgerald's ledger the car was "broken," but Hemingway claims it was abandoned because its cloth top had been damaged and Zelda had ordered it cut off: "His wife hated car tops, Scott told me." Then it began to rain.

Now the two men were traveling to Lyon to retrieve the stranded Renault. Fitzgerald described the adventure as "a slick drive through Burgundy."[3] Hemingway's version differed. By his account, Fitzgerald missed the train they had arranged to take together from Paris; disappeared; reappeared, already tipsy, at Hemingway's Lyon hotel before breakfast next morning; then after reclaiming the car and driving all day through rain, collapsed from too much wine; insisted he was dangerously ill with "congestion of the lungs"; quickly recovered when Hemingway took his temperature with a borrowed thermometer and told him, guessing, that it was normal; proceeded to narrate a long history of himself and Zelda, including a poignant account of the Jozan affair the year before; and finally passed out at dinner in the hotel restaurant and was carried back to his room and put to bed.

A Moveable Feast is seasoned with invention and spite, and Hemingway's antipathy to Zelda, fully reciprocated, runs through its chapters on Fitzgerald. Conversations recalled at thirty years' distance are rough reconstructions at best, but much of Hemingway's sketch aligns with other sources on Fitzgerald's addiction to and limited capacity for alcohol, his hypochondria, and his loquacity in his cups.

Hemingway concludes the account by claiming that, a day or two after the Lyon excursion, Fitzgerald brought him a copy of the just-published *Gatsby,* and after reading it, "I knew that no matter what Scott did, nor how preposterously he behaved, I must know it was like a sickness and be of any help I could to him and try to be a good friend." This pious resolve, however, was among Hemingway's fictions.

Though *Gatsby* was moving slowly off bookstore shelves during the spring of 1925, "I'm not depressed and intend to do about five short stories this summer," he told Harold Ober, but he was spared a summer of story writing by the sale of dramatic and film rights to *Gatsby.*[4] After his golden hopes for *The Vegetable,* it was ironically his novel which became the successful play, though he had nothing to do with adapting or producing it. With income from play and movie rolling in, he had no pressing need for money, and without that incentive there was none at all. In 1926 he wrote only two stories, both in the first two months of the year, with the second "one of the lowsiest stories I've ever written. Just *terrible!*"[5] In the following sixteen months he wrote no stories at all.

The Murphys with whom he drank and loafed were Gerald and Sara, wealthy Americans who made their villa in Antibes a hospitable retreat for expatriate American writers and artists. The Murphys would long fascinate Fitzgerald—Gerald as a model of good manners and social skills, Sara as a warm attractive woman with whom he fell about three-quarters in love (as did others, including Hemingway and Picasso). The Murphys were paragons of leisured, stylish living. Later he would recall his Riviera days with the Murphys in the summers of 1924, 1925, and 1926 as his happiest.

Hemingway, in a heavy-footed attempt to deflect blame, would in *A Moveable Feast* accuse the Murphys of abetting him in the breakup of his first marriage in 1926. This was perhaps unjust, but in encouraging him to separate from Hadley, Gerald Murphy, always glib in correspondence, openly toadied. In July, saluting the Hemingways together, "Dear Hadern," he had flattered effusively: "As for you two children: you grace the earth...."

You're close to what's elemental. Your values are hitched up to the universe. We're proud to know you," and so on. Two months later Murphy urged Hemingway to break with Hadley "cleanly and sharply. . . . Hadley and you, I feel, are out after two different kinds of truth in life. . . . Hadley is saving herself for some personal truth,—you are destined to enrich and remain where you are. . . . Your heart will never be at peace to live, work and enjoy unless you clean up and cut through."[6]

The Murphys' influence on Fitzgerald was more insidious. Hemingway later wrote of their hospitality, "That every day should be a fiesta seemed to me a wonderful discovery," but the pleasure-loving Fitzgerald was the more susceptible. "About five years ago," he would write in 1929, having met them in 1924, "I became interested in the insoluble problems of personal charm and have spent the intervening time on a novel that's going to interest nobody." His fascination clung to *Gatsby*'s successor even as it evolved over the years. In 1932 he projected a novel "in which the liesure class is at their truly most brilliant & glamorous such as Murphys." Two years later, *Tender Is the Night* opens with a Murphy-like couple sunbathing on a Riviera beach.[7]

Fitzgerald was dazzled by the limpid turquoise Mediterranean, cerulean skies, palmy beaches, balmy breezes, expatriate sociability, and otiose hedonism. "This is the loveliest piece of earth I've ever seen without excepting Oxford or Venice or Princeton or anywhere," he exulted in Hyères in May 1924, during their first Riviera stay. ". . . The moon is an absolutely *au fait* Mediteraenean moon with a blurred silver linnen cap & we're both a little tight and very happily drunk. . . ." When Hyères nonetheless "proved too hot for summer," they moved up the coast to St. Raphael, "the loveliest spot I've ever seen" and where the bathing was better. It was here that Zelda became involved with Edouard Jozan.[8]

She enjoyed the Riviera's sunbathing and swimming; Fitzgerald too liked the beaches, but even more the liquid, free-floating circle of expatriates centered on the Murphys, who lived and entertained at their picturesque Villa America during the Riviera's slow season. Their names appear in his ledger some thirty times, more than almost any other.

The following year, 1925, he wrote from Paris, "We leave for Antibes on August 4—Zelda and I in our car . . . nurse and baby by train. . . . God, I'm wild for the Riviera." Afterwards he reported:

There was no one at Antibes this summer except me, Zelda, the Valen-
tino, the Murphy's, Mistenguet, Rex Ingram, Dos Passos, Alice Terry, the
Mclieshes, Charlie Bracket, Maude Kahn, Esther Murphy, Marguerite
Namara, E. Phillips Openhiem, Mannes the violinist, Floyd Dell, Max
and Chrystal Eastman, ex-Premier Orlando, Etienne de Beaumont—
just a real place to rough it, an escape from all the world. But we had a
great time.

And the following summer: "We have rather a nice place here on the Rivierra between Antibes & Cannes and half the Americans I know have been
or are hereabouts this summer—Gerald Murphys, Archie Mclieshes, Marice
Hamilton, Deering Davis, the Wymans, Grace Moore, Ruth Goldbeck, Anita
Loos, John Emerson, Hemmingway, Picasso, Mistinguet, Ben Finney, Don
Stuart the Debt Commission & so many others I can't enumerate." He regretted their planned return to the States: ". . . I don't want to. I'd like to live
and die on the French Riviera," he told Perkins. Living in Juan-les-Pins, "in
a nice villa on my beloved Rivierra (between Cannes and Nice) I'm happier
than I've been for years."[9]

He was too content, at any rate, to rouse himself to work. As Tennyson's
lotos-eating mariners sing:

Surely, surely, slumber is more sweet than toil, the shore
Than labour in the deep mid-ocean, wind and wave and oar.

Substituting "pen" for "oar," Fitzgerald had joined them.

In a frequently reproduced photo of the Fitzgeralds *en famille,* they hold
hands and perform a sedate chorus-line dance kick in front of a large
Christmas tree. He wears a dapper three-piece suit, Zelda an unflattering
flapper dress, and four-year-old Scottie a frilly little-girl tunic.

The photo was taken during Christmas season 1925 in a sitting room in
the Fitzgeralds' furnished apartment at 14 Rue de Tilsitt in Paris, an expensive neighborhood near the Arc de Triomphe. A heavy chandelier hangs
above; heavy crown molding tops the walls; French doors give onto a nar-

row balcony overlooking the street. Beneath the elaborately decorated tree lies a tumble of unwrapped presents, mostly obscure in nature; behind are bookshelves lined with books, perhaps from Fitzgerald's own library (he later boasted of owning two thousand; Sheilah Graham would put the figure at twenty-four hundred). Carefully posed, the Fitzgeralds smile in the uneasy manner of unnaturally posed portraits. Scottie looks to be biting her lip as she smiles on command.

The photo is a rare glimpse of the domestic Fitzgeralds, apparently a happy family of transplanted Americans celebrating an American Christmas in their foreign home. But the appearance is misleading. In "the depths of one of my unholy depressions," Fitzgerald was drinking heavily and doing no work. Zelda was ill, "always sick," she later reminded him, and ". . . you were naturally more and more away."[10]

And if "home" implies even a semipermanent residence, 14 Rue de Tilsitt hardly qualified; the Fitzgeralds' lease ran only eight months, one of them actually spent on the Riviera. At the time of the photo they had been drifting about Europe for twenty months—Rome, Capri, the Riviera, London, Paris—and would continue drifting for another year before returning to the States in December 1926.

After two-and-a-half years abroad they may have thought it best, Zelda especially, to visit their aging parents. She herself had been in poor health and he, while enjoying himself, was accomplishing nothing. Four-fifths of his income that year had come from the *Gatsby* play and film, sources that were evaporating.

They spent the Christmas holidays with Zelda's family in Montgomery, but when early in January the Hollywood studio United Artists made a lucrative offer, he and Zelda headed west, leaving behind (as usual) Scottie, "accompanied by her governess."

It was the heyday of silent movies, and also their sunset. From small-town bijous to large urban palaces, over twenty thousand theaters catered to America's appetite for films; New York's Roxy Theater, opening in 1927, seated over six thousand. To keep the screens flickering the film industry, by now centered in Hollywood and dominated by a half-dozen large studios, turned out about eight hundred films a year. Capable scriptwriters were in demand and well paid.[11]

Fitzgerald's assignment was to draft "a fine modern college story for [actress] Constance Talmadge."[12] Staying in a bungalow on the grounds of the immense Ambassador Hotel, he and Zelda spent money with their usual abandon, partied with their usual exuberance, and hobnobbed in the Ambassador's Cocoanut Grove nightclub and elsewhere with Hollywood's gods, goddesses, and stragglers. His ledger for their two months in Hollywood is largely a list of names, more than thirty.

In the film proposal he wrote amidst these diversions, the Talmadge heroine receives a lipstick with uncanny power over males. "Everyone thinks the beginning or premise contains exceptionally fine material," producer John W. Considine Jr. wired Fitzgerald after he and Zelda had returned east, but candidly, "the rest of story is weak."[13] As most of Fitzgerald's payment was contingent on acceptance, the rejection was a blow.

He blamed Talmadge, with whom "he got into a row"—certainly possible, as the Fitzgeralds alienated others in Hollywood as well. But this explanation evaded the chief problem: the frothy story itself. "Total result—a great time & no work," he later summarized more honestly. He and Zelda returned east not enriched as he had confidently expected, but having spent "considerably more" than the $3,500 he earned.[14]

For him there was one consolation, however: seventeen-year-old Lois Moran. Like many young film actresses, Moran was promoted, managed, and chaperoned by an ambitious mother. The twice-widowed Gladys had taken her as an eleven-year-old from her native Pittsburgh to France, apparently to train her for a career as a dancer. Two French film roles came her way, however, and after making these pictures she and Gladys returned to the States, where Lois was given a leading role in the 1925 film *Stella Dallas*. A "tearjerker," the movie made a splash, and made Lois Moran.[15]

This first of her Hollywood films would prove the summit of her career. She made some thirty more, as many as seven a year, but none so successful. With the advent of talkies her career waned, but when Fitzgerald met her in January 1927 she was flying high—attractive and spirited, an accomplished and celebrated young actress.

Arriving in Hollywood, Fitzgerald found it "a tragic city of beautiful girls—

the girls who mop the floor are beautiful, the waitresses, the shop ladies," and a decade later he recalled that "the ladies all looked very beautiful to a man of thirty." Lois Moran was not among Hollywood's beauties. In *Stella Dallas,* the character she played, Stella's daughter, first appears as a ten-year-old, and Lois would retain the fresh looks of a healthy girl, a cute teenager. Her face was round, her chin prominent, her cheeks tending to plump, her nose slightly pointed. Even her fond biographer admits that, "endowed with a lithe, boyish figure and features that reflected her Irish heritage, she did not have the glamorous look prized by actresses of the time."[16]

A better wording would be "prized *in* actresses of the time." Lois's colleen looks could not compete with stunners like Carole Lombard, Hedy Lamarr, Marlene Dietrich, and Greta Garbo. Two years after *Stella Dallas,* a movie magazine would title an article "The Girl Without 'It': A Study of Lois Moran."[17] Outgrowing juvenile roles, she made her last feature film at twenty-two. In the 1950s she appeared in thirty episodes of a television series, *Waterfront,* playing the middle-aged wife of a tugboat captain.

Fitzgerald's first meeting with Moran probably took place at one of the many Hollywood parties and dinners to which he and Zelda were invited or showed up uninvited. Lois too was sociable. "To sum up the Hollywood (1927) period," she would recall, "we went to many parties, night-clubs, etc."[18] From the start she and Fitzgerald were mutually attracted.

The first mention of her in his ledger, among dozens of other names and lumped with her mother, is simply "Morans"; a little later the ledger notes, "Party at Lois." The shift from "Morans" to the singular, more personal "Lois" hints at their growing friendliness. She was bright, spoke fluent French, and was an avid reader. "A writer to me was the greatest thing in the world," she wrote later, though she seems to have read little of Fitzgerald's writing.[19]

He was attracted by her perky youth and flattered by her admiration. Thirty and feeling old, he remained youthfully handsome and slim, and she was attracted to older men (eventually marrying one more than twenty years her senior). A happy image of them together survives in her recollection of parties at the Morans' apartment on Mariposa Street, one of which would have been the ledger's "party at Lois." When the apartment overflowed with guests, "we'd go out into the hall, sit on the stairs and talk,"

Moran recalled. "Those brief talks are my loveliest memories of Scott. I can't remember a thing he said, but everything was right and everything was beautiful."[20]

That recollection dated from two decades later. A more immediate record of her feelings survives in a journal she kept sporadically. Beginning two months after Fitzgerald's departure from Hollywood and return east, eight entries spaced out over two years address an unnamed "you"—a "you" who has written her "a beautiful letter," who has recently taken a train east, who has sent her a story he had written, who travels to France in 1928, who seems to be having difficulty writing something. All this agrees with Fitzgerald in those years, and Lois is not known to have had other romantic interests at the time, certainly none aligning so closely with the "you" of the journal entries.[21]

In the first, written on an "eastbound train" in May 1927, she writes, "I've just climbed upstairs [an upper berth in a Pullman sleeper] and I'm thinking of you on your trip and of the beautiful letter you sent me—And thinking that very soon we will be near again—I don't *care* for you at all but . . . if one could put one's feelings into words, they wouldn't be dangerous. . . ."

Other entries are spoony and worshipful:

> Have been so incurably sentimental and romantic lately—Wept my heart out at "7th Heaven"—want to go to Honolulu. . . .
>
> I have never been able to tell you how enormously I love your work—Maybe I will when I am older and my opinion will mean something.
>
> I'm growing, dear—*Maybe* you will be pleased with me—And you will be pleased more two years hence—I certainly intend to be *someone* by that time.

Two years hence Lois would turn twenty-one, and perhaps a sexual hint lurks in this coming-of-age promise. Other entries are more explicit:

> I want you so badly!
>
> I'm so happy—feel so grown up—complete. I wish you were here. Will you like me as a woman?

Such expressions might suggest that they slept together, as her biographer dearly wishes, but the evidence is slender. She herself later asserted that at no time was she ever with Fitzgerald without her mother present.[22]

However innocent, his infatuation was a second strike against his marriage. "For eight years," he would later say of himself and Zelda, "we sufficed each other and then she fell in love with the French naval aviator. And then I fell in love with Lois Moran."[23]

At the time of Moran's first journal entry, heading east and "thinking that we will be near again," she was expressing not just a hope but a firm intention. Before returning to California she would see Fitzgerald twice.

On their return from Hollywood in March 1927, thinking to settle in a quiet location with fewer temptations than New York, but "within two hours' motor radius," the Fitzgeralds rented a house outside Wilmington, with grounds sloping down to the banks of the Delaware. Ellerslie was a large, high-ceilinged antebellum mansion, unfurnished and vastly oversized for a family of three. "The squareness of the rooms and the sweep of the columns were to bring us a judicious tranquillity," Zelda later noted ironically. But sociable, bibulous, and still recurrently sophomoric, Fitzgerald could not live quietly for long. Trips to New York soon began alternating with weekend house parties at Ellerslie.[24]

Accompanied by her mother, Lois Moran was "Guest of Honor" at the first of these. In his scrapbook Fitzgerald pasted snapshots of the weekend, Moran in a modest white high-collared dress, in one photo clinging to his arm as they stroll across the lawn; in another, standing close beside him. While other men wear dinner jackets, Fitzgerald is youthfully trim and dapper in white trousers and sport coat with a handkerchief spilling out of his breast pocket. With Lois and Mrs. Moran there, he was no doubt making a special effort at propriety and urbanity; to lend further respectability, he had invited his parents.[25]

It was the weekend of Lindbergh's flight to Paris. When news of his landing flashed back to the States, the Ellerslie guests celebrated. Fitzgerald's Princeton friend John Biggs recalled his arrival at the party:

All of them were sitting on the sea wall along the river. It was a bright moonlight night. . . . Lois Moran, to show how strong she was, picked up her stage mother [Gladys]; Charlie MacArthur then picked up the mothers of both Helen Hayes [MacArthur's wife, the actress] and Lois Moran; and I, to show how strong I was, picked all of them up, but I couldn't hold them and dropped one of them into the river. . . .

We stayed up until about five o'clock in the morning when the party broke up. . . .

Liquid spirits were plainly ample. The roistering Biggs would later serve as chief judge of the US Court of Appeals, Third Circuit.[26]

Soon after the party, the Fitzgeralds visited New York and stayed four nights at the Plaza, where their bill came to $275 (in an era when bank clerks made $1,500 a year, railway laborers less than $1,000). Sometime during this visit they joined Lois at a party for heavyweight champion Gene Tunney, where Moran would recall Fitzgerald clinging to Tunney's side so tenaciously that Zelda had difficulty pulling him away.[27] His reluctance to depart may have been owing more to Moran than to Tunney.

Zelda resented his infatuation. Returning by train from California, she had unstrapped the platinum and diamond wristwatch Fitzgerald had given her after their 1919 reengagement and flung it out a window. The immediate provocation might have been a facetious telegram from Lois, received en route: "HOLLYWOOD COMPLETELY DISRUPTED SINCE YOU LEFT BOOTLEG-GERS GONE OUT OF BUSINESS COTTON CLUB CLOSED ALL FLAGS AT HALF MAST . . . BOTTLES OF LOVE TO YOU BOTH."[28] The jocular hyperbole of the note, ostensibly "to you both," made its primary audience plain.

Zelda conducted herself with blameless civility to Lois, but would later reproach him: "In California [in 1927], though you would not allow me to go anywhere without you, you yourself engaged in flagrantly sentimental re-lations with a child. . . . We came east. . . . There was our first house-party and you and Lois. . . . You went to New York to see Lois. . . ."[29] He justified himself, unpersuasively:

A lot of money came in [in 1926] and I made [one] of those mistakes literary men make—I thought I was "a man of the world["]—that everybody liked and admired me for myself but I only liked a few people like Ernest [Hemingway] and Charlie McArthur and Gerald and Sara [Murphy] who were my peers. Time goes bye fast in those moods and nothing is ever done. I thought then that things came easily. . . . I woke up in Hollywood no longer my egotistic, certain self. . . . Anybody that could make me believe that [I was "a man of the world"], like Lois Moran did, was precious to me.[30]

While candid about his vanity and insecurity, he does not seem even in retrospect to think it odd that his pose of masculine worldliness needed propping up by the adulation of a teenage girl. Two years later he explained it differently, as "a sort of revenge" for Zelda's "affair with Edward Josaune in 1925" (actually 1924).[31]

He and Lois met several times over the next few years, but (as Fitzgerald reported) Moran "broke with him finally for he came to her dressing room drunk and jeopardized her career." When and where this might have happened are uncertain.[32] "Later meetings with Scott in the early '30s were tortured and miserable," she recalled; he was "bitter and unhappy and lost." When she married in 1935, he congratulated her in a partly nostalgic, partly recriminatory letter beginning: "I was touched that you all called me up on your wedding day, and it more than made up for the somewhat chilled receptions I had come to expect from your telephone," but concluding, "Anyhow, I love you tremendously always. . . ."[33]

When a brief but violently emotional affair some years later left him distraught, he would tell a confidante that "he had not felt this way about anyone for so many years that it hurt more than he remembered. He had only felt this way for his early girl [Ginevra King], for Zelda, and for Lois Moran."[34]

Moran was seventeen, Zelda's age when Fitzgerald had met her. Their wedding and his first and still greatest success, *This Side of Paradise,* now lay seven years behind. He was drinking heavily. Once striving and ambitious, he had just spent two years idling. He and Zelda remained interdependent, but she had moved beyond her sparkling role as the Russet Witch. Some of their juvenile Hollywood pranks in 1927 suggest the strain of keeping up their joint act as Jazz Age harlequins.

In some not-too-mysterious way, Lois Moran restored Fitzgerald's youth, or at least revived warm memories of youth. He would later complain that editors wanted nothing of him but stories of "young love," but there was good reason: his own youthful romances had been his greatest creative inspiration. Reawakening memories of those exciting days, Moran was a symptom of a growing nostalgia, and over the next several years memories of his infatuation with her would inspire half a dozen *Post* stories and launch *Tender Is the Night.*

I n *Gatsby,* we first encounter Tom Buchanan in riding boots and jodhpurs, but "not even the effeminate swank of his riding clothes could hide the enormous power of that body . . . a body capable of enormous leverage—a cruel body." Tom is now a horseman and polo player, but Nick recalls him as "one of the most powerful ends that ever played football in New Haven." It is *Gatsby*'s only mention of football, with negative suggestion and scarcely a hint of Fitzgerald's passion for the game.

His youth had coincided with the rise of college football from disorganized pioneering days in the late nineteenth century to dominance in college athletics and preeminence as a spectator sport. Despite fluctuating rules and despite or because of its violence, the new sport captured the popular fancy. Game attendance grew; newspapers took note and began reporting on college football. In 1903 Harvard Stadium, seating 42,000, was built. During Fitzgerald's second year at Princeton, Palmer Stadium was completed, seating 45,000. That same year, 1914, the Yale Bowl opened; seating over 70,000, it was the largest athletic stadium in the world. The first game played there, against Harvard, drew over 68,000.

"The Big Three"—Yale, Harvard, and Princeton—dominated football's early decades. From 1883 to 1892, their combined record was 299 wins and 25 losses, most of the wins by shutout, most of the losses to one another. As one historian of the game notes, "These were not just the three best teams in the country, they were really the only three good teams."[35] Yale dominated; during the first decade of the new century it won 94 games and lost only 6; the 1909 team, led by Fitzgerald hero Ted Coy, outscored its ten opponents 209–0. In the following decade Yale slumped, and Harvard during one stretch won 33 consecutive games.

This was football as Fitzgerald knew it as a boy. As Big-Three dominance suggests, it was initially a sport of the gentry, like crew or polo. Many of Saint Paul's ambitious families sent their sons east to prep school and college, and for the romantic young Fitzgerald the glamor of the East was reinforced by the glamor of Big Three football.

Most players were of average size and build. When Fitzgerald appeared at freshman tryouts at Princeton, he weighed just 138 pounds, but even the outstanding Princeton player of the era, Hobey Baker, weighed only 161. Notwithstanding the lack of beefiness, their football was a rough, occasionally brutal game. Padding was minimal or nonexistent; many disdained helmets, which until 1920 were optional.

Earlier, Harvard graduate Oliver Wendell Holmes Jr., the jurist, had celebrated football violence. "I rejoice," he proclaimed, "at every dangerous sport which I see pursued. . . . If once in a while in our rough riding a neck is broken, I regard it not as a waste but as a price well paid for the breeding of a race fit for headship and command."[36] Fitzgerald might have been less cavalier about broken necks, but he too felt that football injuries were a badge of manhood.

One well-documented 1913 game suggests the romance of football for him. During his freshman autumn, Princeton and Yale played in New Haven. It was the last game in Yale's old stadium, on a clear crisp day with "just enough sting in the November air to make costly furs becoming on pretty girls," the *New York Times* reported with long-vanished gallantry.[37]

On the field, however, "It was a bruising, desperately fought game." Though favoring Yale, the reporter distributed praise evenhandedly. By virtue of a field goal Yale led 3-0 until late in the third quarter, when Princeton "felt the depression of defeat hanging over them." In these gloomy circumstances, "'Hobey' Baker took all the responsibility of saving Princeton's name on his own shoulders." The reporter served up the drama with relish:

"Hobey" brushed his blond hair back from his perspiring, mud-stained forehead. He dropped back to the 43-yard line. Even Princeton men whispered: "He will never do it." The Yale stands screamed for somebody to smash through and block that kick. Baker was cool under fire, and his coolness and his nerve commanded silence. From that big gath-

ering of 35,000 no sound came. All eyes were glued on Baker. E. Trenk-
mann gave him a pretty pass. Baker dropped it to his toe, swung easily,
and the ball spinning end over end sailed high over the crossbars, and
Princeton's honor was safe.

That was Baker's first heroic moment. The second came near the end, when
a Yale halfback, ". . . Ainsworth, with his head bundled in bandages, gave the
crowd its greatest thrill in the last period. From the 40-yard line he broke
through the left wing of the Princeton team and rushed along on a wild trip
toward the Princeton goal. One by one he passed the Tiger tacklers. Three
different men hurled themselves at Ainsworth and he scampered by them
all. He tore along head down and with the ball clutched tightly under his
arm. The rabid crowd, fired to a point of frenzy, howled for a touchdown."

Only one man remained between Ainsworth and a touchdown—Hobey
Baker, of course. Hollywood could have devised no more suspenseful moment: "The Princeton Captain alone could save Princeton now. Baker set
himself like a panther, ready to spring. . . . For a moment it looked as if
Ainsworth was free to pass. But Baker threw himself at the galloping half
back. . . . when Baker struck him, he did not have power enough to push
him back, so Ainsworth fell over toward the Tiger goal line, just six yards
from the coveted chalk mark."[38]

Even with this dramatic tackle, Yale had four tries to go only six yards
for a touchdown. Now another Princeton player stepped up: "'Buzz' Law,
the Tiger punter, received a deep gash in the head early in the game. Yards
of bandages were wrapped around the cut and Law played on. Before long
the blood oozed through the bandages and more were applied, and still Law
played on, crashing into the Yale line every time he was called upon. . . ."

Yale backs were thrown back on their first three attempts. "The Princeton stands shook under the roar of the howling thousands," the *Times* reported. "'Hold 'em, Princeton, hold 'em,' they yelled." On fourth down, "as a
last resort, Yale tried a forward pass," which "went sailing straight for Car-
ter's outstretched hands, when Law leaped into the air and intercepted the
throw. Princeton was saved. Then Law went far back over his goal line and
punted out of danger." As at Thermopylae or the Alamo, the valor of the
overmatched seizes the imagination, at least Fitzgerald's. He was present

to see Baker's game-saving tackle and Law's game-saving interception, and never forgot them. Fifteen years later, strolling down the Champs Élysées, he unexpectedly recognized another pedestrian, "a slender, dark-haired young man with an indolent characteristic walk. . . . It was the romantic Buzz Law, whom I had last seen one cold fall twilight in 1913, kicking from behind his goal line with a bloody bandage round his head."[39]

He dreamed of performing such exploits himself for years:

> "Once upon a time" (I tell myself) "they needed a quarterback at Princeton, and they had nobody and were in despair. The head coach noticed me kicking and passing on the side of the field, and he cried, 'Who is *that* man?—why haven't we noticed *him* before?' . . .
>
> ". . . we go to the day of the Yale game. I weigh only one hundred and thirty-five, so they save me until the third quarter. . . ."[40]

Unlike Hemingway, with his penchant for individual sports—bullfighting, boxing, fishing, hunting—Fitzgerald loved one of the most crowded of team sports, but he admired not teamwork, but heroism.

A football story and poem are among his earliest surviving schoolboy works. Later, in *This Side of Paradise,* Amory Blaine—Hobey Baker's middle name was Amory—scores a presumably game-winning touchdown in a prep-school game: ". . . finally bruised and weary, but still elusive, circling an end, twisting, changing pace, straight-arming . . . falling behind the Groton goal with two men on his legs, in the only touchdown of the game" (though the game's outcome is not actually specified).

Amory's wounded head recalls Buzz Law's in the Yale Bowl: ". . . Amory at quarterback, exhorting in a wild despair, making impossible tackles, calling signals in a voice that had diminished to a hoarse, furious whisper, yet found time to revel in the blood-stained bandage around his head, and the straining, glorious heroism of plunging, crashing bodies and aching limbs." Up to a point, Fitzgerald's schoolboy fantasies were a creative asset.

On Amory's first evening at Princeton he watches the senior class march across campus singing "Old Nassau," "a white-clad phalanx" led by "Allenby, the football captain, slim and defiant, as if aware that the hopes of the college rested on him, that his hundred-and-sixty pounds were expected to dodge to victory through the heavy blue and crimson lines." The Princeton captain during Fitzgerald's freshman year was so magnificent in his eyes that in his ledger he noted as a highlight of October, "I meet Hobey Baker."

Much of Baker's appeal lay in "slim and defiant." By resourcefulness and pluck, the lighter warrior must overcome the "heavy" line of Yale. In *"The Romantic Egotist,"* an earlier version of *This Side of Paradise,* the narrator observes that his "Princeton sympathy" originated in Yale's superior strength. "I imagined the Princeton men as slight and keen and romantic," he recalls, "and the Yale men as brawny and brutal and powerful"—like *Gatsby*'s Tom Buchanan.[41]

Admitted to Princeton on his seventeenth birthday, Fitzgerald had wired his mother: "ADMITTED SEND FOOTBALL PADS AND SHOES IMMEDIATELY PLEASE."[42] He needed them only briefly, later recalling "the shoulder pads worn for one day on the Princeton freshman football field." One of his "juvenile regrets," he admitted, was "not being big enough (or good enough) to play football in college." Instead he redirected his Princeton ambitions to the Triangle Club, whose annual comic shows were better suited to a 138-pound youth with dramatic and literary flair but slender athletic ability.[43]

Despite his brief playing career, Princeton football remained a hobby sometimes verging on obsession. As a student he probably missed few if any home games and sometimes attended out-of-town games. His ledger reports "Dissapointing Yale game" in the new Yale Bowl his junior year. In his four undergraduate autumns, Princeton never defeated Yale, contributing to Tom Buchanan's role as heavy in *The Great Gatsby*.

During the decade after he left Princeton in 1917, football receded from Fitzgerald's life. Army duty kept him moving about; afterwards he was preoccupied with Zelda and his first novel. After his marriage he was diverted from football by years of wandering, half in Europe, along with two more novels, dozens of stories, an unsuccessful play, the birth of Scottie, and partying and dissipation. Even so, he returned to Princeton for games at least twice—against Yale in November 1920 and Notre Dame in October 1923. While abroad during three football seasons he tried to keep up, from Paris asking Perkins (a Harvard graduate), "Would you send me the N.Y. World with accounts of Harvard-Princeton and Yale-Princeton games?"[44] In 1925, in France, he noted "Following football" in his ledger.

Fitzgerald turned thirty in September 1926, while still in Europe. For years the dread day had yawned like an open grave. It was not simply another birthday: he had invested a treasury of enthusiasm in his now-vanished youth. When *Gatsby*'s Nick, turning thirty and gloomily foreseeing "a thinning brief-case of enthusiasm," returns to his midwestern hometown, it represents a nostalgic retreat but also a progress toward stability and adult responsibility. Turning thirty himself, Fitzgerald also looked back, but moving forward would prove problematic.

As his thirtieth birthday receded, he ransacked memories of his early youth, going further back even than Ginevra King and Zelda, and over the next few years he wrote more than a dozen stories inspired by those memories. Nine trace the progress of one Basil Duke Lee from Saint Paul to an eastern prep school and then a Big Three university, nominally Yale. Another five follow the romantic career of a Chicago debutante, partly inspired by memories of Ginevra. Another, "The Last of the Belles," returns to his army days in Montgomery.

None of these stories is strictly autobiographical, but their fancy and invention build on a foundation of remembered people, experiences, and feelings. In the Basil stories, for instance, Basil attends a tony Episcopalian New England prep school, "St. Regis," rather than Fitzgerald's no-prestige Newman in Hackensack. But Basil's mistakes and tribulations at St. Regis revisit Fitzgerald's at Newman, where he had quickly made himself unpopular.

Soon after his 1926 return from Europe, the retrospective mood also surfaced in his rejected story proposal for "Lipstick," the "modern college story." Most of its action occurs during prom week on the campus of "one of the oldest and most conservative of eastern universities, given over in large measure to the education of those who have had money for several generations"—unmistakably Princeton. ". . . Its grey Gothic architecture sprawls for miles over a green undulating campus—with here and there for variety, a hall that was old before the revolution began," alluding to Princeton's Nassau Hall.[45]

His nostalgia grew with visits to campus in 1927. Later he would claim that, after the university's hostility to *This Side of Paradise* in 1920, "for seven years I didn't go to Princeton." This was not literally true, for during those years he attended football games on campus, but football may have been the sole exception to his self-exile. "Then a magazine asked me for an article about" Princeton, and when I started to write it I found I really loved the place."[46]

His nostalgia was encouraged by Princeton's easy accessibility after thirty months abroad. Wilmington was two hours by train to Penn Station; along the way lay Princeton. "Getting settled," he recorded in his ledger in April 1927, but the Fitzgeralds seldom settled anywhere, and ledger entries log many sorties from Ellerslie.

In May and June that year he wrote the solicited essay on Princeton: "Only when you tried to tear part of your past out of your heart, as I once did, were you aware of its power of arousing a deep and imperishable love." Wrapping up, the essay grandly asserts that one will seek in vain "for any corner of the republic that preserves so much of what is fair, gracious, charming and honorable in American life."[47]

Much of "Princeton" is glib and prosaic. Only another old Princetonian could interest himself in its lengthy survey of eating clubs; and with nuggets like "The 'Nassau Literary Magazine' is the oldest college publication in America," Fitzgerald must have bored even himself. Halfway through the essay's four thousand words comes the only mention of academics, a short paragraph mostly disparaging the English Department.

Turning to football, however, the essay rises to mystical heights: "For at Princeton . . . football became, back in the nineties, a sort of symbol. Symbol of what? . . . Who knows? It became something at first satisfactory, then essential and beautiful. It became, long before the insatiable millions took it . . . to its heart, the most intense and dramatic spectacle since the Olympic games. The death of Johnny Poe with the Black Watch in Flanders starts the cymbals crashing for me, plucks the string of nervous violins as no adventure of the mind that Princeton ever offered."[48] As plainly as anything he wrote, the final sentence expresses the power of emotion over intellect ("adventure of the mind") in Fitzgerald's imagination. Soon after, he began writing a story bringing together his three current passions—football, Princeton, Lois Moran—in a confused heap.

Like his lagging novel, "The Bowl" proved knotty. While he would later talk about one-day stories and three-day stories, "The Bowl" took three months, its erratic progress documented in letters and telegrams to Harold Ober.[49]

In June 1927, telling Ober that "Princeton" had been sent off, he asked for an advance of $450; with the failure of "Lipstick" and despite the modest rent and advertised tranquility of Ellerslie, the Fitzgeralds were, as often, pressed for cash. A week later, he asked for another $1,000, and similar requests followed through the summer. The long-suffering Ober invariably complied.

On September 1, Fitzgerald wired: "WORKING ON A TWO PART SOPHISTICATED FOOTBALL STORY," hoping that the *Saturday Evening Post* could run it during the approaching football season, and requesting $500. A week later "The Bowl" was "ALMOST FINISHED"; could Ober wire another $500? A week later, "STORY FINISHED"; could Ober deposit another $500 in Fitzgerald's account?

But a week later, "CAN YOU DEPOSIT 300 THIS MORNING SOMEWHAT URGENT"—with no mention of the story. Though now late September, Ober replied that the *Post* would still consider the story for autumn publication if Fitzgerald could send along at least a part, even in rough form.

For several days there was no response; then "WAS CALLED UNAVOIDABLE TO NEW YORK AND STOPPED OFF IN PRINCETON TWO DAYS TO WATCH FOOTBALL PRACTICE AND SEE IF I COULD GET A LITTLE LIFE INTO THAT WHICH IS THE WEAK PART OF MY STORY. . . . WORKING AS FAST AS I CAN." He hoped to finish in three or four days. Three days later, however, "THE STORY IS JUST AN AWFUL MESS AND I CAN'T FINISH IT BY TOMMORROW."

During these weeks, Perkins visited Ellerslie. The house, "solid and high and yellow, has more quality of its own than almost any house I was ever in," he told Hemingway. "But Scott is in bad shape," he continued, ". . . perfectly O.K. physically, yet you feel as if he might have a breakdown nervously. But Zelda," he added," is in great shape in every way."[50]

With the *Post* waiting, Ober lending, and Fitzgerald floundering, delays and excuses continued through October and November until, on the day Princeton lost to Yale, "MY STORY HAS COLLAPSED" he wired Ober.[51] Finally, in early December he salvaged "The Bowl," no longer in two parts. "CAN

YOU DEPOSIT TWO HUNDRED AND FIFTY I WILL BE IN TOMORROW WITH FOOTBALL STORY WITHOUT FAIL," he wired. It had taken almost as long to write as *The Great Gatsby,* drafted mostly in a single summer. Reading "The Bowl" in typescript, Ober must have wondered why a relatively modest story had taken so long.

"The Bowl," though, provides a good snapshot of Fitzgerald in 1927, following his years in Europe and two months in Hollywood—his nostalgia, his enthusiasms, his infatuation with Lois Moran, and his struggle to cobble them together in a coherent story.

P rinceton and football were much on his mind that fall, his first football season in the States in four years. Ledger entries include "Trip to Princeton," "Several trips Princeton," "Football, . . . Cornell game [vs. Princeton]," "Football interest," and "$\triangle$ dance," presumably at Princeton. Meanwhile the ledger contains no mention of Zelda at all.

Visits to campus were a reunion with an old lover: "April came and the first real Princeton weather, the lazy green-and-gold afternoons and the bright thrilling nights haunted with the hour of senior singing," the narrator of "The Bowl" recalls. "I was happy. . . ." Fitzgerald's romance with Princeton was inseparable from football. "The Bowl" begins with the football-loving narrator rebuking a scholarly undergraduate for his indifference to football: "I suspect the originality of his judgment on what is beautiful, what is remarkable and what is fun."[52]

"Fun" was home-game weekends, with dates, dances, and revelry; "remarkable" was the spectacle of forty-seven thousand people filling Palmer Stadium to watch twenty-two undergraduates knocking heads. The most telling adjective, though, is "beautiful." Fitzgerald was moved by the spectacle and atmosphere of college football games, their appeal to the senses, their pull on the emotions, the drama of epic struggle on a green-turf battlefield through waning autumn afternoons, on which hung the fate not of nations, but at least of college pride. Fitzgerald's leading males ordinarily attended Yale (as in *Gatsby*) or even unglamorous Harvard (like *The Beautiful and Damned*'s Anthony Patch), but for "The Bowl" only Princeton would do.

The pregame rituals of the story's climactic Yale-Princeton game suggest sacred mysteries at the high altar: "The eleven little men [from high up in the Yale Bowl] who ran out on the field at last were like bewitched figures in another world, strange and infinitely romantic, blurred by a throbbing mist of people and sound. One aches with them intolerably, trembles with their excitement, but they have no traffic with us now, they are beyond help, consecrated and unreachable—vaguely holy." There is no irony in the religious language.

The narrator of "The Bowl," Jeff Deering, is a football devotee: "I reveled in football, as audience, amateur statistician and foiled participant—for I had played in prep school, and once there was a headline in the school newspaper: 'Deering and Mullins Star Against Taft in Stiff Game Saturday.'" Like Fitzgerald, Deering tries out for freshman football at Princeton, with similar results: ". . . When at Princeton the following fall," Deering reports, "I looked anxiously over the freshman candidates and saw the polite disregard with which they looked back at me, I realized that particular dream was over."

Again like Fitzgerald, Deering reaches the summit of his Princeton career in spring of his second year: "Sophomore year is the most dramatic at Princeton. . . . Life was very full for me. I made the board of the Princetonian [the campus newspaper] . . . and Dolly [his roommate] and I joined the upperclass club we'd always wanted to be in." Fitzgerald in his sophomore year had been chosen for the board of the *Tiger,* Princeton's humor magazine; elected secretary of the Triangle Club; and selected for Cottage, his first choice among the eating clubs.

If Deering as character resembles Fitzgerald, as narrator he resembles Nick Carraway. Both are privileged observers, Nick as Gatsby's neighbor and Daisy's cousin, Deering as roommate of the story's hero; both are sympathetic but not uncritical friends. Like Nick, Deering begins by talking of himself—in his case, about his love of football, his own brief tryout, and his roommate, Dolly.

Dolly is not "a star player," but "no team in the country could have spared using him." Like all Fitzgerald's football heroes, he is of moderate size, weighing "a little more than a hundred and sixty" (by the end he has dropped to one hundred fifty-three). More importantly, he is a leader: "Morally, he captained any team he played on."

Dolly has two football problems, however. Against Yale in the Yale Bowl in his sophomore year, he makes a brilliant play leading to Princeton's winning touchdown. But the huge yawning stadium dizzies him when he looks up to catch punts. Usually sure-handed, he panics and juggles several. Dolly's second problem is more general: he "fiercely and bitterly hated the game."

For Deering, who would "have given ten years of my life" to play Princeton football, Dolly's aversion is almost incomprehensible, but he tries to see it from Dolly's point of view: "He hated the long, dull periods of training, the element of personal conflict, the demand on his time, the monotony of the routine and the nervous apprehension of disaster just before the end." Strangely drawn nonetheless, Dolly plays again his junior year, though "From first to last, he hated it." Ahead lies his senior year and another dreaded season.

But at this point in the story, "the girl walked into it." She had actually appeared earlier, but needing to speed his hero through a football season without her, Fitzgerald dispatched her to Spain. When she returns, Dolly's real problems begin.

Vienna Thorne has "warmth and delicacy" in her features and the figure of "an exquisite, romanticized little ballerina." Only sixteen, she is sophisticated and cosmopolitan, a diplomat's daughter, accounting for her removal to Europe soon after meeting Dolly. On her return, "even prettier than she had been before," she and Dolly reconnect and quickly become engaged. Seeing Dolly "with youth and hope and beauty in his arms," Deering admires and envies. The lovely Vienna and football luminary Dolly, "one of the handsomest men I ever knew," make a striking couple.

They share more than good looks; Vienna also hates football, for good reason: her younger brother had died in a prep-school game. She persuades Dolly to abandon football his senior year.

Deering is unsympathetic. "Would you have taken this stand if it hadn't been for Vienna?" he accuses Dolly, insinuating her emasculating influence. There is no suggestion that Fitzgerald's attitude differs from Deering's. Football is a violent game; broken necks happen. With Princeton's honor at stake, there is no time for sentimentality about younger brothers.

There have been earlier hints that Vienna is the wrong girl for Dolly. Though weeping for her brother, she is a hard young woman. At sixteen, she harshly dismisses an unwanted suitor: "'I am not going to be lectured,' she said, her tone changing suddenly. 'I told you if you took another drink I was through with you. I'm a person of my word and I'd be enormously happy if you went away.'" At which rebuff the shattered suitor goes off to shoot himself. Hearing of it, she stares "rigidly" but expresses no compunction or regret.

She has another notable flaw. "Miss Thorne was sophisticated," Deering remarks. Though Fitzgerald had promised Ober a "sophisticated football story" without evident irony, "sophisticated" as applied to sixteen-year-old Vienna is ambiguous. Raised mostly in European capitals while trailing along with her "charming" diplomat father—"charming" also ambiguous—Vienna has acquired precocious cultural tastes, or at least pretentiously cultured friends. Deering meets a few: "All sorts of curious people used to drop in to see Vienna. I wouldn't mind them now—I'm more sophisticated—but then they seemed rather a blot on the summer. They were all slightly famous in one way or another, and it was up to you to find out how. There was a lot of talk. . . ." We later meet the same crowd at another party, where the guests "turned out chiefly to be importations from New York. The musicians, the playwrights, the vague supernumeraries of the arts . . . were here in force." Deering mocks the very circles Fitzgerald had frequented during his years in Europe among expatriate artists and writers. Despite the few he liked—Hemingway, the Murphys—many evidently struck him as dilettantes, poseurs, and café geniuses. Probably none was interested in football. He had just spent two months in Hollywood, too.

But the satire on Vienna's crowd is more than a passing shot at artsy types of high self-regard and small accomplishment. Their unforgivable sin is their disdain for football. They dismiss Dolly as "dull"—although, Deering adds, "He was better in his line than any of them were in theirs," and for Fitzgerald football was a nobler "line" than any the "vague supernumeraries" might pretend to. More than just a football story, "The Bowl" is an apologia for football—above all, Princeton football. Seducing Dolly from the team, Vienna commits *lèse-majesté;* a Yale fifth-columnist could do no worse. The radical conflict in the story lies not between Yale and Princeton, but between Vienna Thorne and Princeton. Deering's sympathies express Fitzgerald's and are never in doubt. "The girl" must go.

Following its unfriendly reaction to *This Side of Paradise,* Princeton had receded from Fitzgerald's fiction, but he continued to follow its football fortunes. He could be angry with "the black mass of faculty and alumni," with the *Princeton Alumni Weekly,* with the English Department, with Cottage Club, which suspended him after a rowdy visit in 1920. Princeton football, though, transcended small personalities and mean-spirited slights.

Dolly, too, cherishes Princeton football too much to make renunciation painless or permanent. Encouraged by Vienna and also breaking his ankle, he begins his senior year *hors de combat.* Princeton wins just one of its first four games; a bleak November looms. As the heirs of Johnny Poe, Hobey Baker, and Buzz Law sink into mediocrity, with a final-game drubbing by Yale looming, Dolly frets.

After yet another loss he collects newspaper accounts and studies them glumly. "He worried; that terrible sense of responsibility was at work." Princeton loses again. Afterwards his face is "smudgy and dirty as if he had been crying." When Vienna weeps, too, recalling her brother's death, Deering reports her sobs coolly.

At length, just before the all-important Yale game, Dolly resolves to rejoin the team. Vienna pleads: "Won't you do this for me—just this one little thing for me?" For Dolly, Deering, and Fitzgerald, Princeton football is no "little thing," but overlooking her misconception, Dolly replies simply, "I tried, but I can't."

"I think we're both wasting our time," Vienna snaps, "her expression . . . ruthless." While admiring Dolly's "constant cold sure aggression" on the field, Deering recoils from Vienna's cold hard will, in which she, not the football player Dolly, resembles *Gatsby*'s Tom Buchanan.

Even in homespun terms Dolly's argument expresses Fitzgerald's feelings about football. Football is "my stuff, don't you understand, Vienna?" Dolly pleads. "People have got to do their stuff." An English major might have recited Gerard Manley Hopkins:

> Each mortal thing does one thing and the same:
> Deals out that being indoors each one dwells;
> Selves—goes itself; *myself* it speaks and spells,
> Crying *What I do is me: for that I came.*[53]

"My stuff" makes the point well enough, though. Dolly's gift is football; it's what he does fiercely and well. More than hobby or recreation, it is a calling, a duty, a mission—*"for that I came."*

"I am the most ardent Princetonian there is," Fitzgerald would later proclaim, after an ale and two beers but without exaggeration. West Point's motto "Duty, Honor, Country" could hardly express his feelings better—substituting for "Country," "Princeton."[54]

"The Bowl" had begun with Dolly's "first big game," in the Yale Bowl his sophomore year. Two years later the story returns to New Haven. Seventy thousand crowd the Yale Bowl—apart from war, the world's largest stage for glory.

Dolly's first and only game of the season, it will be his last Princeton game ever. Besides his cracked ankle, he must cope with vertigo when fielding punts in the Yale Bowl. The game is supremely important. Harvard and Yale called their annual encounter "The Game," but for Princeton, Harvard was just another Saturday; Yale was *the* game.

Borrowing from the rapid-fire monologues of football-game radio broadcasts, a novelty in 1927, Deering's play-by-play narration names thirteen different Princeton players and describes a dozen or more plays: "Spears goes through center for three. A short pass, Samson to Tatnall, is completed, but for no gain. Harlan punts to Devereaux, who is downed in his tracks on the Yale forty-yard line . . ."—and so on. There is "color" commentary, too: "You could hear the tenseness growing all around you. . . . it was reflected in the excited movements of the cheer leaders and the uncontrollable patches of sound that leaped out of the crowd, catching up voices here and there and swelling to an undisciplined roar."

With this excited "live" reporting, Fitzgerald happily invented a football game, minute by minute—not just the action on the field but the emotions which sweep through the stadium and "rise to the intensity of wind and rain and thunder, and beat across the twilight from one side of the Bowl to the other like the agony of lost souls swinging across a gap in space." No passage in Fitzgerald better reveals his love of football drama.

Yale is the stronger team, but thanks to a splendid play by Dolly, Princeton rallies to tie the game. His view of the field blocked, Deering almost misses the great moment: "The air was full of hats, cushions, coats, and a deafening roar. Dolly Harlan . . . had picked a long pass from Kimball out of the air and, dragging a tackler, struggled five yards to the Yale goal." *This Side of Paradise*'s Amory Blaine had performed much the same feat in prep school. Some dreams of football heroics were timeless.

E ven with Dolly's game-saving touchdown, the story lacked an essential element, a heroine to replace Vienna Thorne—not a football-hating society girl, but one worthy of the staunch Dolly. Enter Lois Moran, thinly disguised as Daisy Cary. A young and rising film actress, Daisy first appears two-thirds into the story, briefly, and then drops out of sight until the climactic Yale game.

Despite Vienna's anger about Dolly's return to football, he somewhat cluelessly, it would seem, considers them still engaged, and arriving in New York after the Yale game, he goes directly to the Ritz to meet her. Since football had caused the breach and Dolly has now played his final game, a reconciliation seems possible. A woman of her word, as she declared earlier, Vienna stands firm. Having chosen football over her, Dolly is rebuffed and sent on his way.

The story might have ended on this bittersweet note, Dolly triumphant on the field but unhappy in love. For sentimental reasons if no other, though, Fitzgerald thought his hero deserved a new girl—not just a consolatory make-do, but an improvement. "The Bowl" matches eighteen-year-old Daisy not with a man a dozen years older, like Fitzgerald with Moran, but with an undergraduate closer to her own age. A married thirty-year-old's infatuation with a teenager must not complicate a story honoring Princeton football.

The girl's character, too, must match the hero's. None but the brave deserves the fair, but the fair must in turn deserve the brave. "The two basic stories of all times are Cinderella and Jack the Giant Killer," Fitzgerald observed in his notebook, "—the charm of women and the courage of men."[55] Daisy presumably has charm enough, but in a story turning on the gallantry of a wounded hero, Fitzgerald wanted to stress, rather, Lois Moran's work ethic.

Though sociable and enjoying a party, Moran was ambitious, hardworking, sober, and amenable to maternal management and chaperoning. Perhaps Fitzgerald recognized in her self-discipline and sobriety a model for himself. "You see, Fitzgerald wanted to be the greatest writer of his generation," his Princeton and Wilmington friend John Biggs recalled: ". . . But he didn't feel he was accomplishing this. . . . that's all he wanted to talk about—writing. He wasn't interested in politics, or religion, or anything else. Writing and literature were the things that interested him most. . . ."[56] They interested Moran, too, while her dedication to her acting career—added to her celebrity, vivacity, and youth—appealed to him.

Like Moran, Daisy Cary is a hardworking actress "just beginning to be famous." As she and Dolly chat after the Yale game, in which he played in pain, she speaks of a comparable experience, when

> . . . with a vile cold, she had had to fall into an open-air lagoon out in Hollywood the winter before.
>
> "Six times—with a fever of a hundred and two. But the production was costing ten thousand dollars a day."
>
> "Couldn't they use a double?" [Dolly asks].
>
> "They did whenever they could—I only fell in when it had to be done."

Daisy's anecdote alludes to the filming of a scene in *The Prince of Tempters* the year before, when Moran, despite a high fever, had jumped into a pool multiple times before the director was satisfied.[57]

Though movie actress and football hero, Daisy and Dolly are no *prima donnas*. "They were both workers," Deering reflects: "sick or well, there were things that Daisy also had to do." Turning implicitly to Vienna Thorne, "I compared [Daisy's] background of courage and independence and achievement, of politeness based upon the realities of cooperation, with that of most society girls I had known. There was no way in which she wasn't inestimably their superior." Deering scarcely knows Daisy, actually, and "the realities of cooperation" is mushy, but no matter: his remarks constitute Fitzgerald's tribute to Lois Moran.

"It seems to me," Dolly had told Vienna earlier, "that your friends talk a great deal. I've never heard so much jabber as I've listened to tonight"—the jabber of her artistic circle. "Is the idea of actually doing anything repulsive to you, Vienna?" he taunts.

Her friends are talkers; Daisy and Dolly, doers. "That's a marvelous girl," Dolly remarks of Daisy, a compliment Zelda would easily have recognized as referring to Lois Moran. No wonder Zelda began slipping into a manic pursuit of ballet in the year of "The Bowl."

Fitzgerald did not rate "The Bowl" highly. Deliberating several years later on stories for his final collection, *Taps at Reveille* (1935), he ranked it fifteenth of fifteen possibilities, and when *Taps* was eventually published with eighteen stories, "The Bowl" had disappeared altogether.

Yet his original plan for a two-part story suggests ambitious hopes. A two-part *Post* story would likely have stretched to fifteen thousand words or more, as long as the excellent 1926 "The Rich Boy" or the earlier "The Diamond as Big as the Ritz," one of his favorites, written with "real enthusiasm" in only three weeks.[58] Even as he encountered difficulties, he felt "The Bowl" worth a continued investment of time, with the *Post's* $3,500 story payment a compelling incentive, but he also wanted to honor football as a test of vocation and courage, as Hemingway had in *The Sun Also Rises* the year before used bullfighting to illustrate "grace under pressure."

Lois Moran, too, was a warm incentive, though her appearance in the story was probably impromptu. That Vienna Thorne was originally intended as heroine is likely: her name appears forty-nine times, Daisy's ten. Both *Post* illustrations depict Vienna. Daisy enters belatedly, appears only twice, briefly, speaks only six short lines, and is oddly missing from the story's romantic climax.

The labored composition and somewhat awkward construction of "The Bowl" testify to Fitzgerald's distractions, festivities, and drinking. After well-known actress Ina Claire attended an Ellerslie party, for example, Fitzgerald wrote next morning an "old fashioned time honored unacceptable unwelcome inevitable apology," beginning, "Whether I passed out or was even more offensive I don't know." To Gilbert Seldes, after a (violent?) altercation with Zelda: "I don't blame either of you for being disgusted with our public brawl the other day. . . . our difference of opinion, which had been going on for a miserable fortnight . . . before we came to New York and led to all the unpleasantness, is settled and forgotten." Zelda recalled a time when "Scott came home [to Ellerslie] drunk from Princeton and smashed my nose about some conflict of his own and my sister left the house and never forgave him, poor man."[59]

The drinking was nothing new, but now writing problems also obtruded. Whereas *Gatsby* circumvented difficulties like describing action the narrator can't have witnessed—by delegating several pages to Jordan Baker or by Nick's own fanciful imagining of Gatsby's past—"The Bowl" stumbles. Seated high in the Yale Bowl, for example, Deering observes Dolly down on the field through binoculars, but at halftime Deering remains in the stands while the narration without him somehow shifts to the Princeton locker room. At story's end Dolly is first jilted by Vienna, then welcomed into Daisy's arms; but with Deering a no-show at both encounters, we see neither.

E ven as he wrote "The Bowl," partly in her honor, Moran was a fading infatuation, a reminder of the earlier, greater passion. When he recalled her a few years later as "a lady who once played such an important rôle in my life," she had become a memory of a memory.[60]

Zelda would later describe Moran as "a young actress like a breakfast food that many men identified with whatever they missed from life," and Fitzgerald would characterize his love of football similarly.[61] In a 1937 football story, "Offside Play," a minor character named Gittings compiles imaginary teams of old Yale players with names beginning with a given letter (as in "Ketcham, Kelley, Kilpatrick, and so forth"). "Football's his passion," another character remarks. "He's a little crazy on the subject." Gittings was self-parody: Fitzgerald too was both a compulsive list-maker and crazy about football. For Gittings, "Every autumn the eleven young men who ran out on the football field of a crisp Saturday represented something very lovely to him that he had not found in life."[62]

So too for Fitzgerald. In "The Bowl" the heroine merits respect, but Princeton football inspires lyricism. It remained a lifelong love, awakening strong emotion when no woman could do the same. In 1934, he took thirteen-year-old Andrew Turnbull, then his neighbor and later his biographer, to a game at Princeton. "I remember the tears in his eyes," Turnbull recalled, "as he stood in the darkening stadium waving his hat and singing 'Old Nassau.'" Six years later, in his last living moments, Fitzgerald was eating a chocolate bar, reading the *Princeton Alumni Weekly,* and "making notes on the margin of an article about the Princeton football team."[63]

In the Darkest Hour

A Poignant Romance of Chaos and Leadership

ON a May afternoon in the Year of Our Lord 872 a young man rode a white Arabian horse down a steep slope into the Valley of the Loire, at a point fifty miles west of the city of Tours.

He was lost. He was following directions given him six weeks before in Cordova—directions that were based on a woman's memory of eighteen years before. Since then all this part of France had been ravaged and pillaged by band after band of Northmen surging into the estuary of the Loire with their small Viking galleys; and most of the landmarks Philippe's mother had given him had long disappeared.

He was broad and strong, and well-developed for his twenty years. His hair was tawny and waving; his mouth was firm; his eyes, of a somewhat cruel gray, were shrewd and bright. Though not of Moorish birth, he wore a pointed Oriental headpiece, cloth-covered to keep out the sun, and a travel-stained tunic bordered with gold and held together by a leather belt, from which swung a curved sword. More formidably, a mace was hooked to his saddle; and a light coat of fence-rings sewn upon leather was rolled like a blanket behind it.

During three days Philippe had not seen a human being—only half-burned farmhouses, inhabited here and there by ghostly ill-nourished pigs and poultry prowling among the ruins; now as he stopped to drink from a stream, he started as he saw a youth of his own age engaged in the same function on the other side not fifteen feet away. He was of a type that, for all the Christian

by F. Scott Fitzgerald

Fitzgerald's "most abysmal failure": *Redbook,* October 1934. (Scottie Fitzgerald on the Count of Darkness stories.) Courtesy of Hearst Communications.

Town & Country

SOCIETY · AND · COUNTRY · LIFE · ART · LITERATURE · RECREATION · TRAVEL

Arnold Genthe

Ginevra King, age nineteen: "She was the first girl I ever loved. . . . she ended up
by throwing me over with the most supreme boredom and indifference."
(Fitzgerald to Scottie, 1937.)

Fitzgerald met Zelda Sayre on the dance floor of the Montgomery Country Club
in July 1918: "No officer could have visited it three times without
falling in love." (*Save Me the Waltz.*)

Zelda's modest childhood home, 6 Pleasant Avenue, Montgomery.
For the besotted Fitzgerald of 1918–19, it had a "cloud of magic hovering over its roof
and issuing from the windows of the upper floor." ("'The Sensible Thing.'")
Courtesy of Scott and Zelda Fitzgerald Museum, Montgomery.

Zelda Sayre in 1920, the year she married Fitzgerald.

Saint Paul's ice palace, 1888: "On a tall hill outlined in vivid glaring green against the wintry sky stood the ice palace." ("The Ice Palace.")

Zelda and Scott Fitzgerald with guinea pig, about the time of *Gatsby*.
Estate of Honoria Murphy Donnelly / Licensed by VAGA
at Artists Rights Society (ARS), NY.

Lois Moran with Ronald Colman in *Stella Dallas*,
her first and greatest success in Hollywood.

The Yale Bowl moment that Fitzgerald never forgot, "the romantic Buzz Law . . .
one cold fall twilight in 1913, kicking from behind his goal line with
a bloody bandage round his head." ("Princeton.")

The Murphys sunning on Garoupe Beach, Antibes, 1920s:
Gerald *on left,* Sara *in foreground.* Estate of Honoria Murphy Donnelly /
Licensed by VAGA at Artists Rights Society (ARS), NY.

Scott, Scottie, and Zelda, Garoupe Beach on the Riviera, 1928,
"swimming and getting tanned and young and being near the sea."
(Fitzgerald to Zelda, 1930.) Estate of Honoria Murphy Donnelly /
Licensed by VAGA at Artists Rights Society (ARS), NY.

The Turnbulls on La Paix's veranda, 1890s. "I wanted to walk around and look at the trees, but Scott thought we ought to settle down to gin-rickeys." (Maxwell Perkins, visiting Fitzgerald at La Paix in 1932.) Courtesy of Maryland Center for History and Culture.

The two most important men in Fitzgerald's world: Maxwell Perkins and
Ernest Hemingway, Key West, 1935. Courtesy of Princeton University Library.

The Great Hall's thirty-six-foot stone fireplace at Asheville's Grove Park Inn, where Laura Guthrie met Fitzgerald while reading his palm.

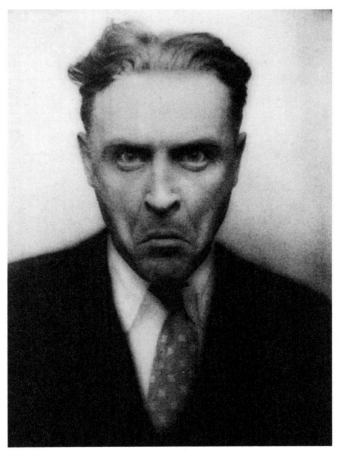

Fitzgerald "decided to make faces like a gorilla and make believe he was going to pounce on me. His face was most awfully contorted and there was actually a glint of madness in his eyes." (Laura Guthrie journal.) Courtesy of Princeton University Library.

Beatrice Dance: "Her cute little stuttering ways, and golden hair, and deep adoration . . . changed his plans." (Laura Guthrie journal.) From a private collection, with permission.

Fitzgerald and Sheilah Graham at his rented house in Encino, California, 1939–40.
The shadow taking the snapshot is probably that of Frances Kroll, Fitzgerald's secretary.
Courtesy of Princeton University Library.

With John O'Hara (*right*), 1940: possibly the last photograph of Fitzgerald.
Courtesy of Irvin Department of Rare Books and Special
Collections, University of South Carolina.

5

RESTLESSNESS AND HIGH SEAS

(1928–1929)

A hurricane was forming.
—"THE ROUGH CROSSING"

The Bowl" appeared in the *Saturday Evening Post* in January 1928, but Fitzgerald's fourth novel continued to languish. The previous spring he had noted in his ledger, "Working again," and that September, summarizing his thirty-first year, "Work begins again." "Work" meant the novel, but it limped along slowly if at all. He was much in need of renewed impetus, something that hurt like hell, like "tearing your first tragic love story out of your heart." It had to be an emotionally intense experience, not just an idea or a plot.

More than half his income in 1927 came from stories, barely 10 percent from his three novels. Almost 20 percent—$5,752.06 by his inscrutable accounting—came as an advance on the unwritten novel. Across the next three years, 1928 through 1930, over four-fifths of his income came from twenty-two stories he wrote for the *Post*. Other sums came from further advances from Scribner's and Zelda's writing. Of a total income of over $33,000 in 1930, royalties on his three novels amounted to $30.60.

Thanks to his *Post* stories these were prosperous years, but for Fitzgerald as novelist they were dismal. Publishing *A Farewell to Arms* to applause and profit in 1929, Hemingway passed him in both reputation and income, and during his lifetime Fitzgerald would never catch up. "I envy you like hell," he told Hemingway, "but would rather have it happen to you than to anyone else."[1] Only near-idolatrous admiration could have reconciled him to his protégé's rise as his own career sputtered.

Even as his novel lagged, however, he wrote some of his finest stories. In those about young Basil Duke Lee, young love was largely displaced by reminiscence. Half a dozen other stories, focusing on vaguely discontented men, younger women, and troubled marriages, reverted to the Lois Moran episode.

A few brief excerpts from the Moran-colored stories suggest their common elements. For example, the girl:

> "How old are you?"
> "Sixteen." (Jacob's Ladder")

> She was seventeen. ("The Love Boat")

> She was just eighteen. ("Magnetism")

> She was not more than eighteen. . . . ("The Rough Crossing")

> The girl—she was perhaps eighteen. . . . ("The Swimmers")

As with the heroine of "The Bowl," two of the young women are film actresses. The men's point of view governs the stories, however, and their ages also show a pattern:

> Jacob was thirty-three. ("Jacob's Ladder")

> Bill grew a little stout after thirty, as athletes will. ("The Love Boat")

> Hannaford was thirty. . . . ("Magnetism")

> She [the wife, not the girl] was twenty-six—five years younger than he. ("The Rough Crossing")

> In the offices of The Promissory Trust Company, Paris Branch, facing the square, an American man of thirty-five. . . . ("The Swimmers")

The only outlier is Tom Squires of "At Your Age," a relatively geriatric fifty.[2]

Plots and outcomes vary, but in each story, seeking to relive the high-pressure emotions of young love, the protagonist reaches out for renewed youth, a fresh start through a younger woman:

> . . . He kissed her good night.
>
> He rode away in a mood of exultation, living more deeply in her youth and future than he had lived in himself for years. ("Jacob's Ladder")

> Suddenly Bill had remembered the boat floating down the river and Mae Purley on the deck under the summer moon. The image became a symbol of his youth, his introduction to life. Not only did he remember the deep excitement of that night but felt it again, her face against his, the rush of air about them. . . . ("The Love Boat")

> George Hannaford was still absorbed in the thought of Helen Avery as he left the studio. . . . It had given him a tremendous pleasure, like the things that had happened to him during his first big success, before he was so "made" that there was scarcely anything better ahead; it was something to take out and look at—a new and still mysterious joy. ("Magnetism")

> The new intimacy of their definite engagement brought Tom a feeling of young happiness. . . . On gray March afternoons when she wandered familiarly in his apartment the warm sureties of his youth flooded back—ecstasy and poignancy, the mortal and the eternal posed in their immemorially tragic juxtaposition. . . . ("At Your Age")

Slouching through his early thirties, Fitzgerald longed for the intensity of twenty-two, the "feverishly enjoyed miseries" reawakened by Lois Moran, even as he recognized that his infatuation was itself a symptom of creeping age.

Though still finding seventeen- and eighteen-year-old girls attractive, he recognized the indecorum. With a thirty-or-more-year gap between hero and girl, "At Your Age" exaggerates the arithmetic of Fitzgerald's flirtation with Moran, but not his awareness of the age gap between them. There was, too, another impediment to dalliance: his marriage. In 1919 Zelda had been all in all, *the* emotion. Now with a second woman involved, matters became more complicated.

In a 1935 letter to Lois Moran, Fitzgerald would remind her of one of his 1920s stories: "I have a book of short stories called "Taps at Reveille" coming out in a few weeks and I thought of including that old piece 'Jacob's Ladder.' . . ."[3] As Moran knew, the story drew on their own romance. Written three months after his Hollywood interlude and shortly after he had seen Moran at Ellerslie and in New York, "Jacob's Ladder" features a girl who becomes a marquee film actress. Perhaps it was a shared joke that like Moran the heroine is Irish—but a tough working-class girl speaking heavy Brooklynese ("Eas' Hun'erd thuyty-thuyd"), much unlike the refined, bookish Moran.

E arly in 1929, the Fitzgeralds packed up and returned to Europe, intending to stay indefinitely. Abandoning their fitful attempt at domesticity, they had in effect decided on nomadic expatriatism. Even at Ellerslie they had remained footloose, spending five months of their two-year lease in France and moving out the minute the lease expired.

Both recognized the advantages of Ellerslie's square, Doric-columned solidity. After their five months in Paris in 1928, Fitzgerald conceded that "Ellerslie was better and worse. Unhappiness is less acute when one lives with a certain sober dignity"—sober only relative to Paris, however, where during that summer he had twice been jailed for drunken truculence. Zelda for her part had tried to make the oversized Ellerslie homelike: "I worked over Ellerslie incessantly and made it function."[4]

Fitzgerald, however, had no interest in home as a fixed location. Growing up, he had scarcely lived in any one house or apartment for more than a year or two. Trading recriminations with Zelda in 1930, he would complain of their "desolate menage" and "all the consequences of bad appartments through your lack of patience . . . bad servants, through your indifference." Unquestionably Zelda was no housekeeper or domestic manager, but her indifference owed much to his own rootlessness; they never owned a home of which she could take emotional ownership. Increasingly absorbed by ballet in the late 1920s, she lost all interest in home, but he was scarcely a counterinfluence. In 1930 she accused him, probably with justice, of "giving your absolute minimum of effort both to your work and to our mutual welfare with no hope or plans for the future save the vague caprices which drive you from one place to another."[5]

Zelda has been quoted as remarking that "I hate a room without an open suitcase in it—it seems so permanent," but this was a throwaway witticism; both Fitzgeralds later agreed that she would have been happier with a stable home and larger family. Her letters contain poignant hints. "It seems odd," she wrote as a patient at a Swiss clinic in 1930, "that we were once a warm little family—secure in a home—." Later, at Phipps Clinic in Baltimore, she reported that "Sunday we went to a museum and I saw some directoire wall lights with stars that would be perfect for the house that we'll never have—." Years later, after Fitzgerald's death, she recalled, "We moved a lot: always carrying the encyclopedia and accumulating books as we went," and "He made and spent a million dollars, . . . always on 'largesse' rather than comfort. We always lived in cheap hotels and made up the difference in nightclubs; in not having to apologize; and in a *great* deal of expensive and unpremeditated moving about."[6]

The index to Matthew Bruccoli's *Some Sort of Epic Grandeur* lists some eighteen residences for Fitzgerald and Zelda in the dozen years following their 1920 marriage, not including hotels, hospitals, and sanitariums. "Show Mr. and Mrs. F to Number —," a jointly authored article but mostly by Zelda, mentions some eighty hotels where they stayed during those same years.

Apart from chronic restlessness, other motives lured them to France. At Ellerslie "the financial strain was too much. Between Sept [1928] when we left Paris and March [1929] when we reached Nice we were living at the rate of forty thousand a year." Ellerslie's $150-a-month rent was only a small part of that; the prodigality lay elsewhere. "All big men have spent money freely," Fitzgerald boasted. Edmund Wilson, guest at an Ellerslie house party, remarked on Fitzgerald's "invincible compulsion to live like a millionaire." That their income in 1928 was only two-thirds of their expenses imposed no awkward check on spending. Returning from their summer sojourn in France, he brought back a Parisian cab driver, Philippe, as butler, chauffeur, and drinking companion, while also in tow came Scottie's French governess. "Most of their trouble, which may kill Scott in the end," Perkins observed, "comes from extravagance." They could leave Ellerslie behind, but their free spending, like their luggage, traveled with them.[7]

Meanwhile, Zelda had determined to become a professional *danseuse.* Pavlova had begun her training at ten; Zelda was twenty-seven, but her ambition grew into a mania. Commuting to Philadelphia for ballet lessons, she purchased for Ellerslie a "gigantic gilt mirror . . . surrounded by scrollwork and cherubs and wreaths in the best heavily decorated style" and hung it "in the front room beside her Victrola. She had run a ballet bar in front of it and practiced there all day," recalled John Biggs's wife, Anna. "She would sometimes dance the entire time that we were there—whether it was for dinner, for a long afternoon's talk, whatever." Biggs himself reported that Zelda "would start at six or seven o'clock in the morning and she had one tune she used to play constantly, 'The Parade of the Wooden Soldiers.' She would keep it up until ten o'clock at night when she would drop from sheer exhaustion."[8]

As her hopes of becoming a Pavlova from Alabama required European training, Zelda was eager to continue her ballet in France. During the 1928 Paris summer, she had taken lessons from Lubov Egorova, an ex-ballerina of the Ballets Russes, and returning to Paris in 1929 she resumed them.

Although her "incessant entheusisam and absorbtion in the ballet" annoyed him, Fitzgerald had his own motives for returning to France. The Delaware River was not the Mediterranean; Wilmington was not Paris. France offered the Murphys' moveable salon and camaraderie with Hemingway. Looking ahead, "somehow I felt happier," he recalled. "Another spring—I would see Ernest whom I had launched [with Scribner's]. Gerald & Sarah. . . ."

He craved activity and sociability. Ellerslie was boring—too sedate, far from metropolitan diversions, even farther from *la belle vie* of Riviera beaches and the Murphys' Antibes villa. In France, "At least life would be less drab," he anticipated, "there would be parties with people who offered something, conversations with people with something to say. Later swimming and getting tanned and young and being near the sea."[9]

S ailing from New York in March 1929, the Fitzgeralds made their seventh Atlantic crossing in eight years. The previous, westward on a Cunarder five months earlier, had been stormy. Sailing now on the Italian *Conte Bian-*

camano, Fitzgerald conceived a story set on a transatlantic liner but inspired by his Lois Moran involvement two years earlier. In "The Rough Crossing," literal and marital storms converge.

It opens with a young American couple, the Smiths, boarding a liner moored at a busy terminal in New York, the city looming behind, the ship itself bulking overhead. In this transitional, in-between place, "One is no longer so sure of anything"—one of several ironies and foreshadowings in the opening pages.

Adrian Smith is a successful playwright and minor celebrity, Eva "something precious to everyone who knew her." She is twenty-six, Zelda's age when Fitzgerald met Lois Moran, and like the Fitzgeralds then, the Smiths have been married seven years. The latter are sailing to France as a retreat from a crowded life in New York, attempting to reestablish their privacy and closeness. Once aboard, waiting for the ship to sail, they exult:

> "We're going!" he cried presently, and they both laughed in ecstasy. "We've escaped. They can't get us now."
>
> "Who?"
>
> He waved his hand vaguely at the civic tiara.
>
> "All those people out there. They'll come with their posses and their warrants and list of crimes we've committed, and ring the bell at our door on Park Avenue and ask for the Adrian Smiths, but what ho! the Adrian Smiths and their children and nurse are off for France."

The Smiths' cloying endearments—"darling," "my precious"—hint at marital malaise, though, as does Eva's wish to be told "what a good time we'll have, and how we'll be much better and happier, and very close always" and her resolve "never to say a mean thing to you again." "Let's not get to know anybody," she urges, "but just stay together."

Despite this vision of renewal and contentment, an abrupt turn to threatening weather interjects a dark note: "On a northern parallel of latitude a hurricane was forming. . . . This liner, leaving New York Sunday evening, would enter the zone of the storm Tuesday, and of the hurricane late Wednesday night."

By Tuesday, sure enough, Adrian and Eva, already bored, stop by the smoking room "for just a minute." The stop "was not in accord with their intentions—they had 'never wanted to see a cocktail again' after leaving America"—and the just-for-a-minute visit to the smoking room proves fateful, for both Smiths end up drinking heavily, especially Eva, and both form sentimental attachments. Adrian has been on the lookout since embarking: "His antennae were already out, feeling over this new world" of the ship. Very quickly he had noticed "a dark little beauty with the fine crystal gloss over her that, in brunettes, takes the place of a blonde's bright glow." She is seventeen or eighteen, Adrian thirty-one.

Were she simply attractive, nothing might have come of his interest in the little beauty, Betsy D'Amido, but she eagerly returns his interest. When she first notices him, her eyes "lingered for an instant with a little start," and a later chat explains her surprise. In the smoking room,

> . . . Miss D'Amido changed seats with one of the men and placed her radiant self at Adrian's side, looking at him with manifest admiration.
>
> "I fell in love with you the minute I saw you," she said, audibly and without self-consciousness; "so I'll take all the blame for butting in. I've seen your play four times."

Adrian is flattered, as Fitzgerald had been by Lois Moran, a snapshot of whom at Ellerslie shows her standing close beside him and gazing up with adoration.

When her party of young people relocate from their table to join the Smiths, their boldness startles Adrian, but after Miss D'Amido places herself beside him, he mellows: "The deference with which she ignored the young men and bent her politeness on him was somehow very touching. A little glow went over him; he was having rather more than a pleasant time."

Observing Miss D'Amido's play for her husband, Eva is having less than a pleasant time. For her jealousy Fitzgerald need have looked no further than Zelda's contempt for his puppyish enthusiasm for Lois Moran. When Adrian informs Eva that they will be joining Miss D'Amido's friends at the ship's costume party, she replies, "Oh, the younger set. And you just having the time of your life—with a child"—anticipating Zelda's 1930 crack about "flagrantly sentimental relations with a child," a remark he had probably already heard.[10] Just as Zelda had thrown her diamond and platinum watch, a gift from Fitzgerald, out a train window, Eva will soon toss her pearl neck-lace, a gift from Adrian, into the Atlantic.

Eva too forms a friendship with a fellow passenger, as Adrian observes with concern: "To his surprise and discomfort she seemed on intimate and even sentimental terms with Butterworth, and he wondered if this was a form of revenge for his attention to Betsy D'Amido." In Fitzgerald's ledger entry for their 1929 crossing, "Conte Biancamano" is followed by a terse en-try, "Zelda's Beau." Perhaps answering his "sentimental relations" with Lois Moran, she had indulged in a shipboard flirtation.

But while reciprocity might explain Eva's flirtation with the "flat-faced" Butterworth, it can't excuse Adrian, who allows himself to be seduced sim-ply because Betsy D'Amido is young, attractive, and eager. "Allows" under-states the case, for after seven years of marriage Adrian is open to, even restless for, romance. Betsy is a novelty, her freshness exciting, her admi-ration gratifying.

As often, the charms of women and exhilaration of romance evoke Fitz-gerald's lyricism, and Adrian's infatuation with Betsy hints at Fitzgerald's own remembered feelings:

> At a table near them Adrian saw the pretty girl [Betsy] who had stared at him on the deck the first night. Again he was fascinated by her love-liness; there was no mist upon the brilliant gloss that gleamed through the smoky confusion of the room.

> Adrian and Miss D'Amido played their first match [of deck tennis]. She was deft and graceful. . . . There was even more warmth behind her ivory skin than there had been the day before. . . . She was already the pretty girl of the voyage, the cynosure of starved ship's eyes.

> He could not remember when anything had felt so young and fresh as her lips. The rain lay, like tears shed for him, upon the softly shining por-celain cheeks. She was all new and immaculate, and her eyes were wild.

> Her youth seemed to flow into him, bearing him up into a delicate, ro-mantic ecstasy that transcended passion. He couldn't relinquish it; he had discovered something that he had thought was lost with his own youth forever.

Excited by her youth and freshness, Adrian enjoys her sensuously—her gloss and gleam, her warmth, the touch of her lips, the rain on her cheeks, the porcelain and ivory of her skin, her graceful movements on the court. He detects wildness in her eyes, freshness in her lips, tears in raindrops. Desire seizes him, his blood "beating through him in wild tumult."

Like Fitzgerald with Moran, Adrian is intoxicated by the remembered excitement of youth. The days of romantic poignancy lay behind—*Gatsby*'s "freshest and the best," echoed in "The Rough Crossing" when, flinging her necklace into the sea, Eva "knew that with it went the freshest, fairest part of her life." The brief shift to her point of view perhaps hints at a recognition that for Zelda, too, the years had brought disappointment.[11]

The story's climax coincides with the fury of the storm. Exhausted, hung over, distraught and angry, Eva petulantly tells Adrian that she wants to divorce, leaves their cabin on the pretext of visiting their children across the passageway, but instead, "in the midst of the wildest hurricane on the North Atlantic in ten years," makes her way to the open boat deck.

Discovering that she has not in fact visited the children, Adrian sets out in search. Tracking her to the boat deck,

> . . . high over his head, over the very boat, he saw a gigantic, glittering white wave, and in the split second that it balanced there he became conscious of Eva, standing beside a ventilator twenty feet away. Pushing out from the stanchion, he lunged desperately toward her, just as the wave broke with a smashing roar. For a moment the rushing water was five feet deep, sweeping with enormous force towards the side, and then a human body was washed against him, and frantically he clutched it and was swept with it back toward the rail. He felt his body bump against it, but desperately he held on to his burden; then, as the ship rocked slowly back, the two of them, still joined by his fierce grip, were rolled out exhausted on the wet planks.

As Adrian clings to Eva, fighting the backwash, Betsy D'Amido has shrunk to insignificance. His flirtation and Eva's with Butterworth have been shipboard diversions; in crisis, the Smiths cling together. Together they will survive life's storms, or together drown. Eva's earlier wish, "Let's . . . just stay together" is literally realized, as nearly washed overboard, they remain "still joined by his fierce grip."

Abruptly the story jumps ahead two days, resuming with the Smiths in a compartment on the boat train to Paris: after storm and discord, a quiet family vignette. Their children appear for the first time; one even speaks. Eva dismisses Butterworth as a sponge and deadbeat, and Adrian's flame for Betsy D'Amido has flickered out too. Betsy has been traveling, it turns out, to meet a previously unmentioned fiancé:

> A pale and wan girl, passing along the corridor, recognized them and put her head through the doorway.
> "How do you feel?"
> "Awful."
> "Me, too," agreed Miss D'Amido. "I'm vainly hoping my fiancé will recognize me at the Gare du Nord. . . ."
> She passed gracefully along the corridor and out of their life.

Their flirtation extinguished, Betsy and Adrian part as casual acquaintances, and the Smiths' rough crossing seems just "an incredibly awful nightmare."

Adrian's fling is forgiven, apparently, along with Eva's flirtation and deep-sixing of her pearls. "Darling, there are better pearls in Paris," Adrian offers. (Fitzgerald, too, had replaced Zelda's angrily discarded watch.) Buffeted by heavy weather but still seaworthy, the Smiths' marriage weathers the storm.

Maybe. "Adrian," Eva suggests at the end, "let's never get to know anyone else, but just stay together always—just we two." A cozy sentiment, but we've heard it before, almost verbatim—just after Adrian's first glimpse of Betsy D'Amido. Does another Betsy lurk in his future?

In four of the six stories glancing at the Lois Moran episode, the hero is married: in three of the four, the marriage survives.[12] Though obliging the general preference for happy endings, these concluding reconciliations may also have reflected Fitzgerald's sentiments about his own marriage. Five years later, _Tender Is the Night_'s Dick Diver would dismiss his affair with

the young actress Rosemary as "less an infatuation than a romantic memory. Nicole was his girl—too often he was sick at heart about her, yet she was
his girl." For Fitzgerald, Zelda remained "his girl."

W hile "The Bowl" celebrates Princeton football and honors Lois Moran,
       and "The Rough Crossing" comments obliquely on the disruptive in-
fluence of the latter, a third story of these years stands as a gravestone over
the earlier and greater passion of 1918–19.

Fitzgerald wrote "The Last of the Belles" exactly a decade after the end
of the First World War, but its proximate origins lay in a visit to Montgomery
he and Zelda made after returning from Europe in December 1926. Landing
in New York, they had visited Fitzgerald's parents in Washington and then
gone on to Alabama for Christmas with the Sayres.

In the first three years of their marriage they had returned to Montgomery four times, but by 1926 it had been almost four years since their
last visit. In the meantime *The Vegetable* had flopped, they had spent two
and half years in Europe, *The Great Gatsby* had been written and published,
Zelda had been ill, they had spent large sums of money, and Fitzgerald had
begun writing a fourth novel which, he breezily informed a reporter on
landing in New York, "he hopes to publish in a few months."

In Montgomery the sputtering novel, nowhere near publication, sat on
the shelf. "During their visit to this city," a Montgomery paper reported, the
Fitzgeralds were "central figures of a series of delightful entertainments."
Zelda, "known before her marriage . . . throughout the length and breadth
of Alabama as the inimitable Zelda Sayre," was still a local celebrity, and the
Fitzgeralds did a circuit of her old friends and schoolmates.[13]

During the activity and moving about of the next eighteen months, Fitzgerald's impressions of the Montgomery visit lay dormant. Summer 1928
marked ten years since he had met and fallen in love with Zelda, however,
and as a compulsive record-keeper he would have noted the anniversary.
If he had forgotten, his ledger contained reminders: the initial mention of
"Zelda" in July 1918, for example, and "fell in love" two months later. Looking back, he could not fail to recognize how much of his life, for better and
worse, had flowed from those two terse entries.

In "The Last of the Belles" he returned to Tarleton, his fictional Montgomery, for a third and final time. As "Babylon Revisited" would be haunted by memories of expatriate Paris in the 1920s, "The Last of the Belles" is Montgomery Revisited, a reimmersion in the past. Few of Fitzgerald's stories contain more autobiographical detail—locations, incidents, names. His ledger provides a key to some; lurking unrecognized are probably others, known only to Fitzgerald and Zelda and now buried with them in a Maryland churchyard.

The story's early scenes predate the action of "The Ice Palace." It is 1918, and Tarleton girls are enjoying an influx of army officers encamped outside town. Like Fitzgerald in 1918, the story's narrator, Andy, is a northerner, Big Three graduate, and junior infantry officer just arrived at a camp outside a small southern city. Both have come from a posting in Atlanta—Camp Gordon for Fitzgerald and presumably Andy as well.

Soon after Fitzgerald reported to Montgomery's Camp Sheridan, Ginevra King wrote to announce her engagement. "Ginevra married," he recorded in his ledger in July (though the wedding was actually in September). Similarly, Andy arrives in Tarleton "empty-hearted," for "up North" the girl "I had loved for three years was getting married." Like Andy, who "saw the clippings and newspaper photographs," Fitzgerald pasted in his scrapbook a gushing newspaper account of Ginevra's wedding at Chicago's tony St. Chrysostom's.

As if Ginevra's marriage, though a wrench, had liberated him, three days later Fitzgerald "Fell in love on 7th." Shaking off his despondency, Andy quickly falls for the southern vamp Ailie Calhoun. She and Andy are introduced by "a nice fellow named Bill Knowles," who is courting Ailie and takes Andy to meet her.[14] As they arrive at her home there is a brief mix-up:

> When we came up the walk a girl in a white dress tumbled out of the front door, crying, "I'm so sorry I'm late!" and seeing us, added: "Why, I thought I heard you come ten minutes—"
>
> She broke off as a chair creaked and another man, an aviator from Camp Harry Lee, emerged from the obscurity of the veranda.

A tense confrontation follows, and Ailie sends the unhappy flyer off into the night. The scene probably recalls a Montgomery incident involving not Zelda but May Steiner, the first Montgomery girl mentioned in Fitzgerald's ledger, who seems to have encountered a similar congestion of suitors. The month after his arrival, Fitzgerald's ledger records, "May and I on the porch. Her visiting bows" [that is, beaux].

Noticing soon after their introduction that Andy's "guns are all crooked"—the infantry collar device of crossed rifles—Ailie straightens them. Immediately following Fitzgerald's September ledger entry "Fell in love" are the words, "My collar." Had Zelda straightened his own collar "guns"? In *Save Me the Waltz,* the heroine Alabama "through the summer . . . collected soldiers' insignia," and her favorite among the officers is "a blond lieutenant with one missing insignia . . . lost in the battle of Alabama"—that is, the officers' competition for herself.

The many specifics in "The Last of the Belles" corresponding to Fitzgerald's months in Montgomery suggest that, while writing the story, he consulted his 1918 ledger entries. In July, for example, the ledger lists "Swimming, Watermelons, The Country Club," while the December entry mentions "The grand Theatre"—Montgomery's vaudeville theater. Andy and Ailie likewise spend a Sunday afternoon "at a semiprivate swimming pool in the country" and go "to the vaudeville and to the country club on Saturday nights, where she seldom took ten consecutive steps with one man, and she took me to barbecues and rowdy watermelon parties."

But beyond such details, "Belles" represents a revisiting of hopeful days and nights a decade earlier—warm fragrant evenings, dances at the ramshackle country club, porch swings on vine-covered verandas, falling for the exciting young Zelda.

Like *Gatsby*'s Nick, Andy of "The Last of the Belles" tells his story as the close observer of a romantic triangle. Sharing quarters with fellow officer Earl Schoen, Andy becomes a friendly confidant of Ailie, whom Andy's Harvard friend Knowles and Schoen are both rushing. Schoen is rough, uneducated, and "bumptious," a street-car conductor in civilian life, who courts Ailie with crude gusto.

The genteel Andy too courts Ailie, briefly and unsuccessfully. The object of everyone's wooing, she is the textbook belle, "the Southern type in all its purity," a magnet to the northern officers. Unable to choose among them, she ends up marrying none. In the years following she is reported to have become engaged at least twice, but six years later Andy finds her unmarried still.

Having missed her moment and no longer in the first bloom of youth, Ailie has now accelerated her style to keep up with the 1920s: "The modulations of pride, the vocal hints that she knew the secrets of a brighter, finer ante-bellum day, were gone from her voice; there was no time for them now as it rambled on in the half-laughing, half-desperate banter of the newer South." In short, she has been left behind, "her wild animation . . . an admission of defeat." Though she claims to be engaged yet again, Andy has doubts which she shares, except that "she couldn't afford to let herself have doubts."

Soon after arriving in Montgomery, Fitzgerald had addressed a seventy-four-line rhyming verse letter, clever and allusive, to May Steiner, "a fresh sort of thing from a man you've just met." Its doggerel displays him in playful spirits:

> . . . I turn to you, May, for advice. . . . take my chance
> Throw my hand down and weep, give up hope of advance.
> Will you tell me, since you were a kid on a bike,
> WHAT SORT OF A KIND OF A MAN DO YOU LIKE?

and closing,

> I hope I can call—Hear what nerve the man's got. . . .
> Good-bye Oh MAGNIFICENT. . . .
> Faithfully, Scott[15]

A July 1918 ledger entry begins "May Stiener. Zelda," while the August entry reverses them: "Zelda and May." Their names continue to alternate, and when the ledger records "Fell in love" in September, it is not at first clear which of the two he meant; the October entry begins with "May Stiener" and makes no mention of Zelda. In his multivolume scrapbook Fitzgerald pasted a photo of "The fair May," later torn out, perhaps by a jealous Zelda.[16]

Like Ailie Calhoun, May Steiner was nineteen in the summer of 1918. Details about her are scarce, but after her wartime flirtations she remained

single until marrying a Birmingham lawyer in 1928. Perhaps during the Fitzgeralds' 1926 Christmas stay in Montgomery they saw or heard of May and
wondered if somehow "she had guessed wrong, missed out somewhere."
She long outlived both Fitzgeralds, and until her death in 1970 she alone
could have said whether the heroine of "The Last of the Belles" glanced at
her youthful self.

While "Belles" focuses largely on the incongruous romance of Ailie
and Schoen, in the final pages Andy himself, until now chiefly an observer, moves to the center and speaks of himself. His shift from mostly un-
involved narrator to nostalgic, disappointed character has been foreshad-
owed when a wartime dance at Tarleton's country club awakens him to the
urgency of the passing moment: "The three-piece orchestra was playing
After You've Gone, in a poignant incomplete way that I can hear yet, as if
each bar were trickling off a precious minute of that time." "After You've
Gone" was a song of 1918; early recordings survive, carrying one back to
country-club dances in Montgomery a century ago.

The song triggers Andy's fear of golden moments sliding away, their ir-
recoverable romance lost forever. "I knew then that I had grown to love Tarleton, and I glanced about half in panic to see if some face wouldn't come
in for me out of that warm, singing, outer darkness that yielded up couple
after couple in organdie and olive drab." From the unpredictable dictates of
army duty, landing him in a hot, backward little southern city unknown to
Harvard, comes one of Andy's "great and moving experiences."

"There'll come a time, now don't forget it / There'll come a time when
you regret it," "After You've Gone" laments. ". . . After you've gone, after
you've gone away . . . away." Not Tarleton but Andy himself is departing,
but as the officers and Tarleton girls dance until midnight, with romance,
promise, and hope slipping away with each minute, he mourns: "It was a
time of youth and war, and there was never so much love around."

His regret grows, later, at a small farewell dinner at the officers' mess,
comprising himself with Sally Carrol Happer (of "The Ice Palace"), Earl
Schoen with Ailie Calhoun, and a third officer and his date. It is Andy's last
night in Tarleton before leaving to embark for France and the war, or so he
thinks, and he is again moved by melancholy.

The dinner may recall an actual dinner at Camp Sheridan when Fitz-gerald was aide-de-camp to Brigadier General James E. Ryan. Years later Zelda remembered ". . . an expansive Alabama night a long long time ago when you envited me to dine and I had never dined before but had always just 'had supper.' The general was away. The night was soft and gray and the trees were feathery in the lamp light and the dim recesses of the pine forest were fragrant with the past, and you said you would come back from no matter where you are."[17] As he recalls his own farewell dinner, Andy's prose shifts from workaday narrative to evocative detail. The passage is worth quoting at length as a valedictory to hopeful youth, "taps" to the days of ecstasy:

> . . . I can still feel that last night vividly, the candlelight that flickered over the rough boards of the mess shack, over the frayed paper decorations left from the supply company's party, the sad mandolin down a company street that kept picking My Indiana Home out of the universal nostalgia of the departing summer. The three girls lost in this mysterious men's city felt something, too—a bewitched impermanence as though they were on a magic carpet that had lighted on the Southern countryside, and any moment the wind would lift it and waft it away. We toasted ourselves and the South. Then we left our napkins and empty glasses and a little of the past on the table, and hand in hand went out into the moonlight itself. Taps had been played; there was no sound but the far-away whinny of a horse, and a loud persistent snore at which we laughed, and the leathery snap of a sentry coming to port over by the guardhouse.

Earl Schoen is still around, but "Belles" has become Andy's story, sliding into ruminations on time passing, "the freshest and the best" receding:

> We drove through pine woods heavy with lichen and Spanish moss, and between the fallow cotton fields along a road white as the rim of the world. We parked under the broken shadow of a mill where there was the sound of running water and restive squawky birds and over everything a brightness that tried to filter in anywhere—into the lost n——cabins, the automobile, the fastnesses of the heart. The South sang to

us—I wonder if they remember. I remember—the cool pale faces, the
somnolent amorous eyes and the voices. . . .

"Remember" here denotes more than mental retrieval of the date of Lindbergh's flight or the score of last year's Yale-Princeton game. Earlier we've
been casually told that all "this was fifteen years ago," but only at this point,
as Andy recalls that final dinner at the officers' mess, do we understand that
nothing since has moved him so profoundly.[18]

Following the dinner, the story jumps to the postwar return of Ailie Calhoun's two chief suitors. Knowles comes and goes, rejected, in a single sentence. Schoen without the dignity of his officer's uniform has dwindled into
a store-window mannequin draped in vulgarity: "His hat was green, with a
radical feather; his suit was slashed and braided in a grotesque fashion. . . ."
Seeing him and the belle Ailie together, badly mismatched, "I don't think
I've ever been so sorry for a couple in my life," Andy commiserates.

Six years pass. Andy would be twenty-nine now. His postwar life has
been bleak, incoherent, empty: ". . . I finished at Harvard Law and built
commercial airplanes and backed a pavement block that went gritty under
trucks." He remains unmarried and unattached.

Memories of Tarleton and Ailie Calhoun, though faded, remain fragrant, "something that blew a little in my mind on warm nights when I
remembered the magnolia flowers." But his nostalgia sharply reawakens
when "a girl seen at twilight in a small Indiana station started me thinking
about going South. The girl, in stiff pink organdie, threw her arms about a
man who got off our train and hurried him to a waiting car, and I felt a sort
of pang." Lovers meeting on a train platform at dusk, never to be seen again,
pierce Andy with a poignant awareness of loneliness. Neither wife nor lover
waits for him anywhere.

Perhaps the pink organdie dress has recalled Tarleton's wartime dances
with "couple after couple in organdie and olive drab." From the Indiana station Andy's thoughts flash back over years and miles "into the lost midsum-
mer world of my early twenties, where time had stood still and charming
girls, dimly seen like the past itself, still loitered along the dusky streets."

"But it was months later," he remarks, "that I sent off a wire to Ailie, and
immediately followed it to Tarleton." Andy has been out of touch with her

except for Christmas cards and a secondhand report that, like Sally Carrol Happer in "The Ice Palace," she had become engaged to a northerner, "gone North to visit his family, and then broken it off."

Thus Andy knows, at least, that Ailie remains unmarried and "lovely as ever."

M eeting again, they have much in common. Ailie's best days had come during the war; Andy's life since has been busy but barren. Though six years earlier he had been mourning a lost love, he mentions no romance since. Ailie's life meanwhile has been noisy and crowded, like the "rowdy party" to which she takes Andy during his visit, but evidently little more. Both are aware of a diminished present. Guessing that she "had guessed wrong, missed out somewhere," Andy might be describing himself.

He finds Ailie changed, feverishly trying to adapt herself to "a new generation . . . with less dignity than the ones I had known." But that night, "tossing about my bed in the hotel," he understands ". . . what was the matter, what had always been the matter—I was deeply and incurably in love with her. In spite of every incompatibility, she was still, she would always be to me, the most attractive girl I had ever known."[19] Fitzgerald's points of incompatibility with Zelda had become evident, but he clung to memories of the "Most Attractive" girl in Sidney Lanier High School's class of 1918.

Ailie too looks back to earlier days with regret, wondering if rejecting Earl Schoen had been a mistake. When Andy asks if she has heard from him, she replies:

> "No." She was serious for a moment. "I often think of him. He was the—" She hesitated.
>
> "Go on."
>
> "I was going to say the man I loved most, but that wouldn't be true. I never exactly loved him, or I'd have married him any old how, wouldn't I?"

But when Andy assures her that marrying Schoen would have been "impossible," she agrees only "uncertainly."

Andy and Ailie seem to meet each other's need, and with him willing to risk the unspecified incompatibilities, marriage and a happy ending seem possible. But she draws back, "almost frightened": "Oh, no, I couldn't marry you. . . . I don't love you that way at all. . . . I never did. . . . next month I'm going to marry another man"—previously unmentioned—adding, "You know I couldn't ever marry a Northern man."

Tamely acquiescing, Andy replies, "All right," and abruptly asks her to accompany him to the site of the old army camp. Ailie assures him that it has been dismantled and abandoned. "You won't find a single thing, darling," she tells him. "The contractors took it all down."

Andy nonetheless directs the taxi driver to drive out to the camp and there tromps around in the brush, looking for "where I used to live." What he seeks is not his old barracks but his lost past, the romance and promise of 1918. "The taxi driver regarded me indulgently while I stumbled here and there in the knee-deep underbrush," Andy recalls, "looking for my youth in a clapboard or a strip of roofing or a rusty tomato can." No image in Fitzgerald's fiction, not even *Gatsby*'s green light, expresses his nostalgia more poignantly than the rusty tomato can.

Sifting in the weeds, Andy is uncertain that he is even searching in the right area. "All I could be sure of," he concludes, "was this place that had once been so full of life and effort was gone, as if it had never existed, and that in another month Ailie would be gone, and the South would be empty for me forever." "The Last of the Belles" grieves for that vanished world and vanished mood, Montgomery in 1918, the South of "The Ice Palace," "a living poetry of youth, warmth, charming girls, and romance."

Now for Fitzgerald youth was gone, romance was gone, his marriage was laboring in rough seas. Even his once-blazing career was flickering.

6

A NOVEL STALLS, ZELDA CRASHES

(1930)

Have we done so much wrong that we should deserve all this?

—"ONE TRIP ABROAD" TYPESCRIPT

Meanwhile the novel-in-progress dragged along. Four years had passed since *Gatsby*.

The problem was not that Fitzgerald had "exhausted all his store of experience," as he later told H. L. Mencken. Since the days of Camp Sheridan and courting Zelda, his life had been filled with people, travel, incident, and accomplishment—authorship, marriage, celebrity, money, fatherhood, literary and speakeasy New York, the Riviera, the Murphys, expatriate Paris, Hemingway, Hollywood, Alabama, Lois Moran, football. At Ellerslie they had even given domesticity a try. What he had exhausted was the emotionally intense experiences that infused his early writing.

Before *Gatsby* was even in bookstores he had begun revolving ideas for its successor. "I've got a new novel to write—title and all, that'll take about a year," he jauntily (and "a bit stewed") informed Perkins in December 1924. The prediction was optimistic but not implausible; he had published his first three novels within five years.[1]

When *Gatsby* was published the following spring he issued a more modest forecast, telling Mencken that "I expect to spend about two years on my next novel," adding with bravado that "it will have the most amazing form ever invented." Two months later, "The novel has begun." Titled *Our Type,* it was "about several things, one of which is an intellectual murder on the

Leopold-Loeb idea." Also, "Incidently it is about Zelda & me & the hysterias of last May & June [1925] in Paris."[2]

These cheery reports encouraged Perkins, but troubling hints soon appeared. In August Fitzgerald informed John Peale Bishop that "I am beginning a new novel next month on the Rivierra"—though a month earlier he had told Perkins it was already underway. Whether begun in July or September 1925, by October it was still in low gear: "The novel progresses slowly & carefully with much destroying & revision," he reported. About the same time he informed another correspondent that "My new novel is marvellous," a boast he qualified by adding, "I'm in the first chapter."[3]

To different correspondents he gave different reports on the novel's progress, but as months and then years went, a clear pattern emerged:

December 1925: "The book is wonderful . . . but the end seems far away. . . . My novel should be finished next fall."

January 1926: "Its begun but I'm putting it aside for a month or so like I did *Gatsby* and it won't be done before the end of the year."

April 1926: "The novel is about one fourth done. . . ."

May 1926: "My book is *wonderful.* I don't think it'll be interrupted again. I expect to reach New York about Dec. 10th with the ms. under my arm."

June 1926: "The novel, in abeyance during Zelda's operation [an appendectomy] now goes on apace. . . . I hope to have it done in January."

August 1926: "I'll be home with the finished manuscript of my book about mid-December."

December 1926: "I go back [to America] with my novel still unfinished and with less health & not much more money than when I came, but . . . happy about the amount of my book that I've already written."

January 1927: "I CAN FINISH NOVEL BY MAY FIRST BUT WOULD LIKE UNTIL JUNE FIRST IF POSSIBLE."

January 1927: "Expect to finish novel before April 1st."

April 1927: "My novel to be finished July 1st."

October 1927: "No work this summer but lots this fall. Hope to finish
the novel by 1st December."

June 1928: "TWO MORE CHAPTERS FINISHED ALL COMPLETED
AUGUST."[4]

As these updates were scattered among various correspondents, the pattern of promise and postponement would not have been apparent to most,
but Perkins could scarcely have missed it. Sitting in his Scribner's office on
Fifth Avenue with his hat on, a Perkins idiosyncrasy, he must often have
pushed it back to scratch his head thoughtfully on receipt of Fitzgerald's
latest bulletin.

He began to worry and gently prod. Two years after *Gatsby,* "I do not
want to harass you about your book, which might be bad for it," he wrote
when the Fitzgeralds moved into Ellerslie: "But if we could by any possibility have the title, and some text, and enough of an idea to make an effective
wrap, by the middle of April, we could get out a dummy. . . . It may though,
be impossible, and . . . all these things are insignificant along side of writing the book undisturbed by mfg. [manufacturing] questions."[5] The title *Our
Type* had evidently been discarded.

By the following January, Perkins was more concerned. When Fitzgerald claimed to have gone on the wagon, Perkins congratulated him but then
turned to the work-in-progress. "We feel no anxiety whatever about the
novel," he wrote reassuringly—but "I have worried a little about the length
of time elapsing between that and 'The Great Gatsby.'" A few weeks later
he prodded again, with a hint of impatience: "We can surely count on your
novel for the fall [1928], can't we? It must be very nearly finished now."[6]

But when in April 1928 the Fitzgeralds sailed to France for the summer,
Perkins would have read with jaded eye the optimistic bulletins from Paris:
"I'm working hard as hell," and "The novel goes fine . . . quite wonderful . . .
will be done *sure* in September."[7] From his ledger, however:

June: . . . Carried home from Ritz, disagreable concierges.

July: Bricks again [a cabaret], another story, Opera, Battlefields,
    Rhiems, Hadley Hemmingway Drinking & general unpleasant-
    ness, Bathroom, first trip jail. . . .

Aug: Jed Kiley [a drinking friend of Hemingway], Zelli's [a nightclub],
    Buzz Law, Vient de Paraitre [a play], Grand Guignol [a Paris theater
    known for horror shows], La Baule [a seaside resort in Brittany],
    Auto Trip, Cary Ross & dive in Lido [a Paris nightclub with a
    marble swimming pool], second trip jail. . . .

Later, in an indignant "j'accuse," Zelda recalled that summer in Paris: "We
lived in the rue Vaugirard. You were constantly drunk. You didn't work and
were dragged home at night by taxi-drivers when you came home at all. . . .
You were literally eternally drunk the whole summer. . . . You brought
drunken undergraduates in to meals when you came home for them, and
it made you angry that I didn't care any more."[8] In Zelda's *Save Me the Waltz*,
the Knights' "household [in Paris] fell into a mass of dissatisfaction without
an authority to harmonize its elements. . . . The life at home was simply an
existence of individuals in proximity; it had no basis of common interest."

Zelda's implicit standard for men was her father. Her Montgomery
contemporary Sara Mayfield, whose father was a fellow justice on the Alabama Supreme Court, recalled that Judge Sayre's "conduct was impeccable;
he never smoked, and drank only an occasional mint julep or eggnog; his
personal habits were Spartan, even austere."[9] Despite her quondam "flapper" rebelliousness, the troubled Zelda, now sliding into her ballet mania,
badly needed husbandly strength. In *Save Me the Waltz*, written soon after
Judge Sayre's death, the heroine explains that "it's very difficult to be two
simple people at once, one who wants to have a law to itself and the other
who wants to keep all the nice old things and be loved and safe and protected." Both Fitzgerald and her father loved her, but "safe and protected"
is plainly a yearning for her father, "an infallible source of wisdom, a bed
of sureness."

After the wasted Paris summer of 1928 the Fitzgeralds returned to the
States, he "in a blaze of work & liquor." The liquor was bootleg; the work,
stories for the *Post*. He wrote seven in 1928, six in the Basil Duke Lee series

inspired by his youth. Reinstalled at Ellerslie in September, he returned to the halting novel. By now it had gone through several titles, from *Our Type* to *The World's Fair* to *The Boy Who Killed His Mother*. When in late November 1928 he sent Perkins the first two chapters, it was nameless.

The long-delayed chapters were rough, Fitzgerald admitted, the first "good," but the second "has caused me more trouble than anything in the book. . . . I am far from satisfied with it even now, but won't go into its obvious faults." Perkins praised the chapters with restraint, and urged, "Send on others as soon as you can." Fitzgerald promised two more "about the 1st of December."[10]

The first of December came and went, Christmas passed, January and February rolled by—the promised chapters failed to materialize. Abandoning Ellerslie for good in early March 1929, the Fitzgeralds returned to Europe, to remain (it turned out) for the next two-and-a-half years. He left behind an apologetic note to Perkins: "I am sneaking away like a thief without leaving the chapters—there is a weeks work to straighten them out & in the confusion of influenza & leaving, I haven't been able to do it. I'll do it on the boat & send it from Genoa."[11] "Influenza" was a euphemism for a drinking binge and its consequences.

*T*ender *Is the Night*'s nine-year gestation is well documented. As a young PhD candidate in the late 1950s, the (later) dean of Fitzgerald studies Matthew Bruccoli spent seven months in Princeton's Firestone Library sorting through seven cartons of loose, chaotically disorganized drafts, "roughly 3500 pages of holograph manuscript and typescript—plus galley proof, page proof, and tearsheets," of what eventually became *Tender Is the Night*: "A given box includes parts of several drafts; and the parts range from notes on scraps of paper to fragmentary scenes to complete chapters. . . . Fitzgerald sometimes changed his pagination system in the middle of a scene. Some sequences of writing were used in various spots and consequently bear multiple sets of paginations." "Fitzgerald was not a methodical worker," Bruccoli concludes with understatement. He himself was heroically methodical. Sorting through the sea of paper, he was able to distinguish 199 "differentiable" units of material ranging from brief memoranda to one-hundred-page typescripts. Overall, he detected eighteen stages of development and at least seven titles between the earliest draft and published novel.[12]

Initially it was to be something like *Crime and Punishment* on the Côte d'Azur, revolving about "an intellectual murder on the Leopold-Loeb idea." Leopold and Loeb's 1924 murder of Bobby Franks in Chicago and their subsequent trial and conviction had been widely publicized. The novel soon shifted to a new murderer, however, "that girl who shot her mother on the Pacific coast last year." This was sixteen-year-old Dorothy Ellingson of San Francisco, who, annoyed by remonstrances about her late-hour nightclubbing, "in a fit of temper" killed her mother with a single shot from a .45 caliber pistol and then, leaving the corpse to cool, went off to another party. The murders and murderers had little in common, and with "Zelda & me & the hysteria of last May & June [1925] in Paris" thrown in, Fitzgerald was evidently unsure what the novel was even about.[13]

The matricide idea, supplanting Leopold-Loeb, would inject a "highly sensational" element into a novel otherwise dependent on his own disjointed experience of late, especially his months on the Riviera. Though the novel underwent many changes during its tortuous evolution, the Riviera remained the setting of the opening chapter, and he would later regret allowing the action to move away—to Paris, Switzerland, Rome, and elsewhere. Certain novels, he argued, "can only be written at the moment and when one is full of the idea—as 'Tender' should have been written in its original conception, all laid on the Riviera."[14] More than a picturesque setting, the Riviera was somehow essential.

What was missing was any deep passion, commitment, or "hurt." He basked on the Riviera's sun-baked beaches and enjoyed its blue sea and skies, vinous leisure, and Murphy hospitality—but balmy pleasures were not fictional engines. More promising, perhaps, might have been Zelda's Jozan affair, but it would be another decade before he would write about that, and then only in a story.[15]

Instead, early drafts follow one Francis Melarky, a young American drifting about Europe with his mother while back in the States his disgraced father languishes in prison. Apart from an opening chapter set in Rome, the action is on the Riviera. Melarky eventually disappeared, but the first draft's atmospheric description of a Riviera beach survived intact for nine years, appearing at length as the opening scene of *Tender Is the Night*.

Discontented and hot-tempered, Melarky in an argument with his mother hurls a shoe across the room, shattering a window. Accidentally bumped by a random passerby, he assaults the innocent offender. In Rome he provokes a violent altercation with a taxi driver and, after being arrested and freed, proceeds to slug a police detective, earning himself a beating and night in jail. (This fracas also appears in *Tender Is the Night*, transferred to a wholly different character.)

While Melarky wishes to pursue a career in filmmaking, his mother disapproves and obstructs. As indicated by *The Boy Who Killed His Mother*, he would eventually have murdered her. Perkins thought that with the matricide plot Fitzgerald "was attempting the impossible."[16] He nonetheless clung to the unpromising idea for about five years, completing four chapters.

On top of sociability and drinking, the windfall from stage and film rights to *The Great Gatsby* blunted his commitment, especially when the novel bogged down. Entire years passed in which the novel lay dormant. In his study of its composition, Bruccoli concludes that in 1927, 1928, and half of 1929 Fitzgerald did no work at all on it.[17]

Hearing from Perkins in 1928 that Fitzgerald "has made no progress with his novel for a long time," Hemingway responded, "I'm terribly sorry to hear about Scott. . . . I wish he would finish his novel or throw it away and write a new one. I think he has just gotten stuck and does not believe in it any more himself. . . ."[18]

Fitzgerald may almost have taken the advice literally. One story has it that sometime in the summer of 1928 or 1929, on the Riviera, "Sara and Gerald watched, as Scott destroyed the seventh draft" of the novel. "'He took it out in a rowboat,' Gerald reported, 'and he tore it up, page by page, and scattered it over the Mediterranean.'"[19]

W ith his second wife, Pauline, along with her sister and two young children, Hemingway arrived in Paris in April 1929, soon after the Fitzgeralds. Until Hemingway returned to Key West the following January, he and Fitzgerald saw each other more often than they would again, and when wandering separately from Paris during the summer they corresponded.

Meeting four years earlier, Fitzgerald had been at the apex of his reputation and powers, Hemingway a young unknown who had written a few promising stories. Now Hemingway was making final revisions to *A Farewell to Arms,* soon to begin running as a serial in *Scribner's Magazine.* Its book publication in September would catapult him to celebrity.

As the early chapters of *Farewell* began appearing in *Scribner's,* Hemingway lent a typescript of the rest to Fitzgerald, who responded with nine handwritten pages of commentary and advice. Though concluding with "A beautiful book it is!" he suggested "cut" or "cutting" nine times; used words like "gassy," "dull" (three times), "glib" (twice), and "slow" (twice); and remarked of one passage of tedious repetitions, "You're a little hypnotized by yourself here."[20]

Nothing was more likely to annoy the prickly Hemingway. His private response was a coarse retort scribbled on the last page of Fitzgerald's comments, and Fitzgerald's ledger notes in June: "Ernest's for dinner. Certain coldness." Hemingway later told Fitzgerald, "you don't know any more about when a book is a good book or what makes a book bad than ever. . . . you are like a brilliant mathematician who loves mathematics truly and always gets the wrong answers to the problems."[21]

Eager and admiring on Fitzgerald's side, patronizing and occasionally contemptuous on Hemingway's, their friendship survived the *Farewell* awkwardness, at least nominally, but it was just as well that Hemingway left Paris for a summer of Spanish bullfights while the Fitzgeralds settled on the Riviera. "It's been gay here," Fitzgerald wrote Hemingway from Cannes in August, "but we are, thank God, desperately unpopular and not invited anywhere."[22] The ledger clarifies: "Being drunk & snubbed."

Nonetheless Fitzgerald assured Hemingway that "I've been working like hell, better than for four years, and now am confident of getting old faithful [the novel] off before the all-American [football] teams are picked." Though annoyed by Fitzgerald's reference to his "nervous bitterness" in a murky landlord issue, Hemingway expressed fulsome delight in his progress: "I'm damned glad you are going well. . . . I cant tell you how glad I am you are getting the book done. . . . I'm gladder than I can ever let you know that it is going finely. . . ."[23]

For all the glad-talk, Hemingway remained skeptical. "Of course all this may be premature," he observed, "and you may not be finishing your book but only putting me on the list of friends to receive the more glowing reports"—which was the case.

Then he went on to analyze Fitzgerald's difficulties. Chief among them, he asserted, was a laudatory review of *The Great Gatsby* by the critic Gilbert Seldes.[24] "After that," Hemingway asserted, "you became self conscious about it and knew you must write a masterpiece." But setting out to write a masterpiece was inhibiting: writers "can only write as well as they can going on the system that if this one when done isn't a Masterpiece maybe the next one will be." He also blamed Fitzgerald for giving "the juice" to his *Post* stories, leaving only "dregs" for his novels.

Replying promptly, Fitzgerald candidly added: "Your analysis of my inability to get my serious work done is too kind in that it leaves out dissipation. . . ." As two paragraphs earlier he had described in detail his routine of getting drunk every night and alienating everyone around him, the admission was almost superfluous.[25]

But there was an additional difficulty, glanced at by Hemingway's "juice" remark. If by that he meant the impetus of strong feeling, Fitzgerald had little juice for Francis Melarky or the matricide plot.

He was drawing on a diminishing store of compelling experience, and knew it. "It is possible," he told Hemingway, "that the 5 yrs between my leaving the army & finishing *Gatsby* 1919–1924 which included 3 novels, about 50 popular stories & a play & numerous articles & movies may have taken all I had to say too early, adding that all the time we were living at top speed in the gayest worlds we could find. This *au fond* is what really worries me."[26] It was a fair summary of the situation.

Hemingway himself provided a useful contrast. After *The Sun Also Rises* had been published in 1926 and he had collected and revised stories for *Men Without Women,* he began working on a second novel, about a boy named Jimmy Breen. By October 1927 the novel was going well; Hemingway had written nine chapters, he reported, and by the following March he claimed to have written twenty-two. But by then it was sputtering. Sending Maxwell Perkins a long list of excuses and speaking of the novel in past tense (it "was supposed to be a sort of modern Tom Jones"), he admitted that "there is a *very very* good chance that I don't know enough to write that yet. . . ."[27]

Just as Fitzgerald had lost interest in Francis Melarky, Hemingway had lost interest in Jimmy Breen. The difference was that Hemingway had meanwhile embarked on a new project, a novel "that I thought was only a story but that goes on and goes *wonderfully*." In this new novel he returned to his 1918 months in wartime Italy, his own greatest and most moving experience. He had now, "suddenly, a great kick out of the war and all the things and places and it has been going very well." Returning to those potent memories, he found himself remembering not only things and places but also his first romance, with Red Cross nurse Agnes von Kurowsky.[28]

She remained for Hemingway the eternally regretted woman. "Years later in Paris," now married and a father, "he told Lincoln Steffens that if Ag came back, he'd have to leave Hadley and Bumby and follow her."[29] In "The Snows of Kilimanjaro" (1936), the dying writer recalls "the first one, the one who had left him. . . . what she had done could never matter since he knew he could not cure himself of loving her." He retained Agnes's letters through four decades and four marriages, until his death.

In six months he had finished a draft of this novel of war and love, *A Farewell to Arms*. Setting it aside for a time before revising, he mentioned again the "kick" it gave him: "I want to make sure that I leave it alone long enough so that I can find the places where I get the kick when writing it and neglect to convey it to the reader."[30] That "kick," or "juice," the stimulus of revisiting a deep experience, was what Fitzgerald lacked.

A bout this time he was struck by a new idea. "I am working night & day on novel from new angle that I think will solve previous difficulties," he told Perkins.[31] With the new angle, Melarky himself was jettisoned. Replacing him was Lew Kelly, Hollywood's second most successful film director. The Kelly draft echoes "The Rough Crossing," the story of the playwright, his wife, and the young vamp who lures the playwright into a flirtation. The new angle features a similar shipboard trio: Kelly, his wife Nicole, and a young woman on the make, Rosemary, a film actress.

For *Gatsby* a new angle had proved a breakthrough, but not for *Tender Is the Night*. Though Fitzgerald soon abandoned the Kelly version, however, its central elements persisted. Melarky the unmarried misfit had been replaced by a mature, married hero; the matricide plot had disappeared. But the distinguished man, attractive wife, and young actress would remain, as would the names "Nicole" and "Rosemary," in a romantic triangle dominating the opening third of *Tender Is the Night*.

Only two chapters of the Kelly version survive. For unknown reasons Fitzgerald returned to the Melarky plot. But at this point, further progress was interrupted.

I n December 1929, a Montgomery newspaper reported that the Fitzgeralds, "who had planned to return to the United States during December, and who were to have arrived for a short visit during Christmas to Judge and Mrs. A. D. Sayre, have taken an apartment in Paris, and have deferred their return until Spring."[32] It was a fatefully unhappy decision.

In February 1930, they left Paris and traveled to Algeria as tourists "doing" Arab North Africa. "It was a trying winter and to forget bad times we went to Algiers," Fitzgerald wrote. A posed three-by-five-inch photo pasted in his scrapbook shows them mounted on side-by-side camels against a backdrop of date palms; Zelda astride, Fitzgerald sidesaddle and dressed in natty suit and tie and fedora, as if strolling down Fifth Avenue. In a pair of snapshots, each stands alone on a bleak expanse of dunes, Zelda captioned "Lost in the Sahara"; he, "Looking for a mirage." In another snapshot, Zelda, bundled in a fur coat, stands on a cliffside overlook above the gorge at Constantine. It is labeled, "Have I *got* to go down?" Despite the camels, dunes, gorge, and jocular captions, Fitzgerald would later complain of Zelda's ballet "poisoning a trip to Africa."[33]

Back in Paris, she began behaving oddly. In his ledger, usually rich with names and sparse on incident, several terse entries are ominous. On April 13, "Strange Sunday walk"; a little later, "Bishop incident," probably alluding to an evening Zelda also recalled as "the night we had dinner with John Bishop and went to the fair afterwards which left me in hysterics."[34] In April the ledger reports, "Zelda quit [ballet] school & began again."

With their marriage strained, Fitzgerald drinking, and herself consumed by ballet, Zelda was sliding into a breakdown. Later she described her sensations:

> In Paris, before I realized that I was sick, there was a new significance to everything: stations and streets and façades of buildings—colors were infinite, part of the air, and not restricted by the lines that encompassed them and lines were free of the masses they held. There was music that beat behind my forehead and other music that fell into my stomach from a high parabola. . . . Then the world became embryonic in Africa—and there was no need for communication . . . a detachment as if I was on the other side of a black gauze—a fearless small feeling, and then the end at Easter. . . .[35]

Later yet she explained: "Suddenly last spring I began to see all red while I worked or I saw no colors—I could not bear to look out of windows, for sometimes I saw humanity as a bottle of ants."[36]

Three days after Easter, "weak and tired" (Fitzgerald's ledger notes), she was admitted to a Paris hospital. She would be in and out of hospitals and sanitariums the rest of her life.

L ife ended for me when Zelda and I crashed," Fitzgerald remarked later, with some hyperbole.[37] Zelda's collapse did, though, mark the midpoint of his career. The 1920s had brought accomplishment, reputation, high living, and a close if not tranquil marriage. Living with what Hemingway called the "festival conception of life," the Fitzgeralds had been "everything to each other. All human relationships. We were sister and brother, mother and son, father and daughter, husband and wife."[38] By 1930 the *Saturday Evening Post* was paying $4,000 for his stories. The following year his income rose to its peak.

But the flood tide had begun to ebb and now, decisively, their personal jazz age, "our decade of prosperity," ended.[39] For the present, *Post* stories paid the bills, but the income once squandered on extravagance would in future be engrossed by medical and sanitarium expenses for Zelda and schooling and care for Scottie. The fraying marriage would unravel as it gradually grew apparent that Zelda would never wholly recover, nor be able to function again as wife or mother.

Fitzgerald meanwhile would grow more addicted to drink, and his income would wane as the *Post* and other magazines coped with hard times and as his story-writing knack declined. The novel-in-progress, his great hope for resuscitating his finances and restoring his reputation, would do neither. At the end he would be scraping by in Hollywood on crumbs of screenwriting work and comic sketches for *Esquire.*

In April 1930 he could not have foreseen any of this, of course, and during the next several years, as Zelda struggled with schizophrenia and he with radically changed circumstances and a stagnating novel, he would write several of his finest stories. One in particular dramatizes, analyzes, and mourns the step-by-step disintegration of a fortunate, happily married young couple. The parallel was obvious.

When he wrote "One Trip Abroad" in summer 1930, Zelda had been ill for three months and was now a patient at Prangins clinic in Switzerland. Her illness was an incomplete story, its outcome shrouded. Reflecting a crisis not recollected in tranquility but still in doubt, "One Trip Abroad" speaks with unusual immediacy.

Its fictions interweave with the Fitzgeralds' history. Intelligent, genteel, artistic, attractive, and unworldly, the story's young couple, Nelson and Nicole Kelly, resemble the newly wed, newly flush Fitzgeralds of 1920. Its five settings correspond to sites the Fitzgeralds had visited and in some cases resided during their wanderings: North Africa, Sorrento, Monte Carlo, Paris, Switzerland.

But in imagining the Kellys, Fitzgerald had in mind a second couple as well. Expatriate refugees from a family business, comfortably set up with family money, elegantly leisured and artsy, Nelson and Nicole unmistakably resemble the Murphys. Like Gerald, Nelson has taken up painting. The Murphys were wealthier, more urbane, and more stable than the Fitzgeralds, but both couples enjoyed *la bonne vie* on the French Mediterranean, and the Kellys share this predilection: "They loved the Riviera in full summer with many friends there and the nights open and full of music." When they must depart, Nicole grieves: "What a pity—this lovely blue sea, this happy time."

When not on the Riviera the Fitzgeralds and Murphys were usually in Paris, where the Murphys spent the winter months and Gerald maintained a second studio. Retreating from Monte Carlo, the story's Kellys likewise go to Paris, where "Nelson began to paint again; he had a studio, and they visited the studios of Brancusi and Leger and Deschamps." Like Murphy, whose painting moved "beyond precisionism to cubism and finally to sophisticated surrealism," Nelson evidently paints in high modernist style.[40]

Fitzgerald would admit to a wish to become "a man of the world" like Gerald, and allude to him as a man "who had come to dictate my relations with other people when these relations were successful: how to do, what to say. . . . this man had seen the game, analyzed it and beaten it, and his word was good enough for me." Observing Gerald's social skills "always confused me and made me want to go out and get drunk," Fitzgerald claimed, oddly; perhaps the drunken antics which sometimes alienated the Murphys stemmed from trying to capture Sara's attention.[41]

But despite Gerald's foppishness and their somewhat precious cult of "living well," the Murphys were sober, responsible citizens and fond parents. Older than the Fitzgeralds (Sara, five years older than Gerald, was seventeen years older than Zelda), they possessed a maturity and adult ethos the Fitzgeralds as a couple would never achieve. The Murphys' daughter Honoria later related a story told by her father "of how they were all dancing at Juan-les-Pins. Just as they were leaving they crossed the dance floor, as you have to sometimes to leave a place. And Scott just plunked himself right down in the middle of the dance floor making believe he'd fallen. . . . And my father apparently turned to him and said, 'We're not at Princeton and I'm not your roommate. Get up, Scott.' And he got up."[42] Though later losing their two young sons, the Murphys never crashed.

As later in *Tender Is the Night,* the couple of "One Trip Abroad" begin as the Murphys and end as the Fitzgeralds. Broken in health at the end, Nicole "wonders why, of all those who sought pleasure over the face of Europe, this misfortune should have come to them." In a canceled passage she asks, more defensively, "Have we done so much wrong that we should deserve all this?" Fitzgerald may have wondered the same.

With a swarm of locusts darkening the sky over an open tour bus, "One Trip Abroad" abruptly drops us into the action, the who, where, and why unknown. Soon we discover that the bus is carrying tourists to "the little oasis town of Bou Saada" in North Africa. At the locusts' approach the women shriek and duck for cover, but the swarm passes overhead harmlessly and the travelers joke about the non-incident. Yet a sky "black with locusts" recalls the traditional reputation of locusts as devastating ravagers. Afterwards Nicole remarks with light hyperbole, "We survived that plague," but if not the plague itself, the locusts augur plague.

Two fellow travelers also presage ill. In a burst of conviviality following the swarm's passage, the Kellys fall into conversation with a somewhat older couple, the Mileses—snobbish, sophisticated, jaded, "bored with themselves," foraging for novelty—who see the young, fresh, naive Kellys as an easy mark. Birds of ill omen, the Mileses will appear three times, each marking a further step in the Kellys' decline.

The Mileses quickly become catalysts for the first fissure in the Kellys' extended honeymoon. The latter ". . . were in their twenties, and there was still a pleasant touch of bride and groom upon them. A handsome couple; the man rather intense and sensitive, the girl arrestingly light of hue in eyes and hair, her face without shadows, its living freshness modulated by a lovely confident calm." Nicole regrets that meeting the Mileses has opened the prospect of further sociability: "In the eight months of their marriage she had been so very happy that it seemed like spoiling something." Until now she and Nelson have stayed aloof, content to enjoy each other and earnestly improve themselves. Crossing the Atlantic, "they seriously studied French, and Nelson worked on business contingent on his recent inheritance of half a million dollars. Also he painted a picture of a smokestack."[43]

At dinner with the Mileses in Bou Saâda, Mrs. Miles patronizes the Kellys with worldly wisdom. Mr. Miles's contribution is to propose an after-dinner entertainment: "They tell me there's a great show here. . . . The Ouled Naïls. The concierge says they're some kind of tribe of girls who come down from the mountains and learn to be dancers. . . ." Accordingly, the Kellys allow themselves to be taken to this spectacle, though "Nicole regretted that she and Nelson were not strolling alone through the ever-lower, ever-softer, ever-brighter night." Much unlike the ever-brighter night and her wish to climb "to the top of a low hill where a white mosque shone clear as a planet

through the night," the Café of the Ouled Naïls is a cave-like nightclub pop-
ulated by titillated trippers ogling young girls performing erotic dances. As
a moral emblem, the Kellys' descent from the clear night outside into the
smoke-filled den needs no gloss.

Worse follows. During an indecisive pause in the show some depart and
"there was a whispering in the air." Nicole inquires, and Nelson's response
is hesitating and euphemistic: "Why, I believe—it appears that for a consideration the Ouled Naïls dance in more or less—ah—Oriental style—in very
little except jewelry." To Nicole's visible uneasiness, Mr. Miles, a glib Satan,
responds, "We're all staying," and provides specious justification.

Nicole rises to leave. "I'll wait outside."[44]

At this critical point Nelson vacillates, first urging Nicole to remain—
"After all, Mrs. Miles is staying"—then reluctantly following her out, then
abandoning her to return to the Mileses and the louche dancing: "I'll only
stay a minute. I want to see what it's like." The incident exposes Nelson as
waffling, lacking in chivalry and judgment, strangely prurient: why would
a man with an attractive young wife be interested in the nude dancing of
fourteen-year-old girls?

The Kellys quarrel but soon reconcile, the scene ending with the warm
image of Nicole "asleep upon his shoulder" later that night. But with the incident of the Ouled Naïls the Kellys' descent begins, almost imperceptibly: a
minor rift, soon patched up. In a story thick with omens, however, the slight
breach forebodes worse. A canceled passage in the typescript echoes *The Great
Gatsby*: "And there was some freshness gone that would come back no more."

Fiction allowed Fitzgerald a detachment he often lacked in contemplating his marriage. As "One Trip Abroad" generally takes Nicole's point of
view, our sympathies follow the wife. And notably, the husband shares with
Fitzgerald a problem leading to the story's second incident.

At first the Kellys drink moderately. Two bottles of champagne shared
with the Mileses at dinner affect them: "Neither of them [the Kellys] was accustomed to so much," and the Ouled Naïls contretemps follows.

From Algeria the Kellys travel to Italy where, in a Sorrento hotel pop-
ulated by elderly English, Nelson's drinking precipitates an embarrassing

public altercation. Their half-baked artistic avocations—his painting and her singing—yield little gratification, and hotel life grows tedious: "Could people be content to talk eternally about the weather, promenade the same walks, face the same variant of macaroni at dinner month after month?"

"An ancient and enormous mechanical piano" sits in the hotel salon, never used. "It is not the habitude to play the instrument in the evening," the Italian manager explains. "The clients are each one quiet on his or her table." Restless and bored, Nelson switches on the piano, an impulsive disruption of after-dinner calm that triggers a heated conflict with an elderly British couple outraged by "American cheek."

Before the player-piano incident the Kellys had washed down dinner with a flask of *vin de Capri*. Pot-valiant, Nelson grows bellicose while Nicole plays a conciliatory role: "Nicole hurried after Nelson, urging him to let the matter pass," and "'Don't get in an argument,' Nicole whispered. 'They're old.'" Aggressive, unmannerly, half-drunk, resembling Fitzgerald at his worst, Nelson persists. As "the speed and volume of the instrument tripled . . . in a wild pandemonium of sound," the piano itself becomes an image of Fitzgerald on a bender. "Scott is the soul of honor when sober," Hemingway remarked, "and completely irresponsible when drunk. . . . no more responsible than an insane man."[45]

T he story's third incident occurs after a large luncheon party that leaves at least one of the guests "faintly flushed on liqueurs."

Two years have passed, and the Kellys are settled in Monte Carlo. No longer innocent and earnest, they have sunk into a leisurely hedonism, with their own villa and a circle of wealthy, worldly fellow expatriates. Like the Mileses they have become snobbish, with "a large acquaintance among the spring and summer crowd—a crowd which, naturally, did not include people on charted trips or the shore parties from Mediterranean cruises; these latter had become for them 'tourists.'" As conscientious tourists themselves earlier, the Kellys had been startled by Mrs. Miles's disdain for tourists; now they have been assimilated into the Mileses' sophisticated crowd. The Mileses are in fact among the guests at Nicole's luncheon. The Kellys are *becoming* the Mileses.

The innocent partner in the Ouled Naïls incident and the calm voice in the Sorrento dispute, Nicole has become a less attractive character. Her singing lessons apparently abandoned, her life is devoted to idleness and amusements. On the day of the Monte Carlo incident we see her sleeping late; then playing golf; then meeting a male admirer with whom she is commencing a flirtation. "At one she was having a dozen charming people to luncheon," and she and Nelson are booked as dinner guests that evening on a yacht anchored in the harbor.

She has been swallowed up by money, *chic,* vanity, self-complacency, and snobbery, many of which are betrayed in her self-congratulatory musing: "I'm young and good-looking, and my name is often in the paper as having been here and there, but really I don't care about shi-shi. I think it's all awfully silly, but if you do want to see people, you might as well see the chic, amusing ones; and if people call you a snob, it's envy, and they know it and everybody knows it." Flirtation has become a leading diversion: ". . . She had two men in love with her, and she felt sad for one of them. . . . At 10:30 she was meeting a third man, who was just beginning to be in love with her 'in a harmless way.'" The quotation marks point to the irony of harmless dalliances, perhaps glancing at Zelda's with Edouard Jozan. Nicole's pity for one admirer hints that she might favor him with "harmless" consolation.

Regardless of how serious her flirtations, there is no doubt about Nelson's: overhearing him exchanging endearments with "an exquisite young French-woman," Nicole is shocked. Her startled response is to heave a vase of flowers, missing him and striking the lover. Stunned, "her hand slowly rising to cover the side of her face," the mistress verges on a stage swoon: "'*C'est liquide,*' gasped Noel in a whisper. '*Est-ce que c'est le sang?*'" It is actually water from the vase—a comic note punctuating the corruption of a once fresh and loving couple.

The "why" of the Kellys' disintegration emerges plainly in the Monte Carlo episode. Both are idle. Back in Sorrento "their vitality made them restless, for as yet his painting had no direction and her singing no immediate prospect of becoming serious." Monte Carlo has hardly solved their lack of occupation. Drifting, and with ample funds to indulge themselves, the unanchored Kellys are vulnerable.

Fitzgerald himself had a very certain vocation, and without a handsome legacy like Nelson's he needed to earn a living. Idleness should not have been his problem, yet often was. Hemingway's first wife, Hadley, who knew the Fitzgeralds well in 1925 and 1926, would later testify that they "were inconvenient friends. They would call on the Hemingways at four o'clock in the morning, and we had a baby and didn't appreciate it very much." Hemingway himself, setting sail for France in spring 1929, wrote Perkins: "Please dont under any circumstances give Scott our Paris home address—Last time he was in Paris he got us kicked out of one apt. and in trouble all the time (Insulted the landlord—pee-ed on the front porch—tried to break down the door at 3–4 and 5 a.m etc.). . . . When I heard he was going to Paris, it gave me the horrors." "When Scott wrote I don't know," Hadley wondered.[46]

For long periods he wrote little or nothing. His ledger details hundreds of distractions, and its annual summaries include such comments as, for his thirty-first year, "A lot of fun"; for his thirty-third, "No Real Progress in any way." He was capable of intensive work for short spells but lacked steady application for an ambitious novel. Somewhat like Samuel Johnson's fellow collegian who failed to become a philosopher because "cheerfulness was always breaking in," Fitzgerald wanted to be a great writer, but pleasure-seeking kept breaking in.[47] His appetite for company and amusement increased with domestic discontent, and vice versa. Beginning as a magic circle of two, "sufficient to each other"—"Just me for you, and you for me . . . alone," as the 1925 song goes—the Kellys have become bored with each other and hungry for crowds and diversion.

After the Ouled Naïls quarrel is patched up, the narrator comments: "It was a love match . . . and it could stand a great deal. She and Nelson had passed lonely youths, and now they wanted the taste and smell of the living world; for the present they were finding it in each other."

Not for long, however. After the Sorrento player-piano incident, the Kellys "were through with being alone." As models for boredom and discontent, a craving for distraction and escape, Fitzgerald need have looked no further than Zelda's now-manic ballet and his own dipsomania.

Though initially reluctant to mingle, the Kellys move to progressively more crowded and fashionable spots. The story's climactic incident occurs in Paris, where they have relocated from Monte Carlo and determined on social retrenchment. For "self-preservation," they withdraw from three-quarters of their previous crowd, the bottom three drawers—unsavories like the Mileses—and confine themselves to "Society" in the top-drawer sense.

Their new exclusivity augments their popularity, ironically, and within a more exalted circle they continue to dine out and entertain. Though resuming his painting, Nelson also keeps drinking, and hoping to encourage a more "serious and responsible attitude," Nicole decides to make him a father. Their catastrophe, a double blow, drops on them soon after she gives birth. Nelson is tricked into footing the large bill for a fancy society ball aboard a canalboat on the Seine. Three weeks postpartum, Nicole attends the ball against her doctor's advice, bringing about the theft of her heirloom jewels as well as the loss of her health.

The particulars are narrated circumstantially, but the causes are simple and evident. The Kellys are bored and corrupted by social climbing, while Nelson, his judgment clouded by drink, is duped by his bottle companion, a parasite exploiting their money and snobbery.

If fatherhood fails to make Nelson more responsible, motherhood seems at first to improve Nicole, but her maternal contentment is brief. Invited to the canalboat ball to be hosted by one of "the ancient noblesse," the Marquis de la Clos d'Hirondelle—the parasite's brother-in-law—Nicole slips back into her snobbery. "Her old idea, that if one had to see people they might as well be the best, was carried out in being invited to the De la Clos d'Hirondelles." The sponge dazzles her with vague promises about the approaching gala, and "great names swam before her eyes." Torn between her doctor's prohibition and her eagerness to attend the ball and be admired, she yields to vanity: "At the last minute the pale green evening dress from Callets, draped across a chair in her bedroom, decided her. She went."

The Fitzgeralds were not tuft-hunters. Zelda was no snob, and he, though drawn to leisured wealth like the Murphys', had no interest in titled Europeans. Too Princeton-genteel to mingle comfortably in bohemian circles, he was too mid-American to pursue the ancient noblesse. Indifferent to marquises, he preferred the rough and equally mid-American Hemingway.

Yet much in the Kellys' history echoes the Fitzgeralds'. Nicole's collapse is partly emotional: distress at the loss of her jewels superadded to fragile health: "I've lost my jewels and I'm sick, sick!" Before finding Nelson fight-ing "for life against jaundice" in a Swiss hospital, we have heard nothing about his health. His jaundice, perhaps a consequence of drink, hints at a creeping moral jaundice as well. The Kellys have sunk hand in hand.

N elson has spent his first weeks of fatherhood idling and tippling with the live-in sponge; ignoring medical advice, Nicole rushes off to an *haut monde* extravaganza. It would be unjust to accuse the Fitzgeralds of compa-rable irresponsibility, but they were undeniably easily distracted parents. When Zelda's health collapsed, Scottie was eight. Her care had been largely relegated to nurses and governesses. When she had been very young, her parents had partied, drunk, and flitted about; Scottie never knew a stable home and was seldom allowed to curtail their pleasures. While they had "a great time" in Hollywood in 1927, Scottie remained back east. Later, Fitz-gerald floundered in a sea of gin while Zelda grew preoccupied by ballet. In a long accusatory, self-pitying summary of the previous six years of their marriage that Fitzgerald addressed to Zelda in a Swiss sanitarium, Heming-way is mentioned six times, Scottie once, parenthetically.

Fitzgerald later described Scottie as "simply a carefully chaperoned waif." Andrew Turnbull, a Baltimore neighbor for eighteen months in the early 1930s, came to know her well and observed, "Scottie had put up with a great deal during her itinerant girlhood. On the Riviera a wit had remarked that she wasn't a child at all but a little widow of forty, though in the back-ground there had always been a nurse who threw an island of order around her. . . ."[48] After their deaths, Scottie loyally defended her parents, asserting, "The fact that I spent a lot of time with nurses instead of with my parents does not strike me as being the deprivation it seems to appear to certain people," but she admitted that, when staying with Zelda's sister Rosalind and her husband Newman Smith in 1930 and 1931, she found their stable household a relief: ". . . When I was with them I always felt very safe and secure. . . . in fact, at one point, when things were not going well with my fa-ther, wishing they had adopted me! . . . It was a delightful time and curiously enough, I really didn't miss my parents, who were in Switzerland." Perhaps it was not entirely curious.[49]

Only with Zelda's 1930 breakdown did Fitzgerald seem fully to recognize that his young daughter needed attention and nurture, and not until "Babylon Revisited," written later that year, does a sentiment of parental love or responsibility for a child appear with any force in his fiction. In the tragedy of Zelda's shattered life, his awakened awareness of Scottie was perhaps the single consolation.

The Kellys of "One Trip Abroad" reach their nadir in Switzerland where, in one of Fitzgerald's most quoted lines, "very few things begin, but many things end." Together they convalesce at a rest hotel on Lake Geneva.

"There've been too many people in our lives," Nelson analyzes their misfortunes. "We've never been able to resist people." Nicole agrees: "If we could ever be alone—really alone—we could make up some kind of life for ourselves." Pleading for a return to their old happiness, a renewal of themselves and their marriage, she urges: "We'll try, won't we, Nelson?" and: "'We can have it all again,' she whispered. 'Can't we try, Nelson?'" and: "Why did we lose peace and love and health, one after the other? If we knew, if there was anybody to tell us, I believe we could try. I'd try so hard." But there is unconscious irony in Nicole's hope that "if there was anybody to tell us" what had gone wrong the Kellys might restore their happy marriage. Someone *is* telling them.

Early in the story they had been attracted to a young couple resembling themselves. "They did look nice," Nelson remarks, and Nicole agrees "emphatically": "Charming . . . the girl and man, both. I'm almost sure I've met the girl somewhere before." That evening at the Ouled Naïls club, the wife of the unknown couple, like Nicole, walks out on the nude dancing, confirming their affinity.

Two years later the same couple show up in a Monte Carlo café. "They've changed," Nelson observes. "I suppose we have, too, but not so much. They're harder-looking and he looks dissipated. . . . The girl is *tout ce qu'il y a de chic,* as they say, but there's a hard look in her face too."

By now, with Nicole growing vain, complacent, and worldly and Nelson with a paramour and drinking problem, much the same might be said of the Kellys. Presently there is a ruckus at the other couple's table: "Something strident and violent had happened across the café; a woman screamed and the people at one table were all on their feet, surging back and forth. . . . for just a moment the Kellys saw the face of the girl they had been watching, pale now, and distorted with anger." Nicole, "panic-stricken," drags Nelson away, recognizing in the wife's outburst a replay of her own vase-throwing fury a few hours earlier.

With the help of Fitzgerald's stage-managing we, but not the Kellys, have tumbled to the meaning of the shadow couple. As alter egos, or doubles, or doppelgängers, they play an unusual role in Fitzgerald's fiction, which seldom employs the ghostly, weird, or supernatural. Even "One Trip Abroad" contains nothing inarguably eerie; the other couple's intermittent appearances might be simple coincidence. The heightened coloring of the final scene, however, hints that something otherworldly is afoot.

Sitting in the lounge of their Swiss rest hotel during a violent thunderstorm, "amid tumult and chaos and darkness," the Kellys again spy "the couple, first seen in Algiers, who had crossed their path several times since. . . . It seemed like destiny that at last here in this desolate place they should know them. . . ." The Kellys will soon come to know them too well.

Observed more carefully, the shadow couple betray continuing degeneracy. In the wife, Nicole sees ". . . an inquisitive face . . . possibly calculating; the eyes, intelligent enough, but with no peace in them," which "swept over people in a single quick glance as though estimating their value. 'Terrible egoist,' Nicole thought, with a certain distaste. For the rest, the cheeks were wan, and there were little pouches of ill health under the eyes; these combining with a certain flabbiness of arms and legs to give an impression of unwholesomeness." Meanwhile Nelson scrutinizes the husband: "I ran into the man in the bar, and . . . got a good look at his face in the mirror. . . . His face is so weak and self-indulgent that it's almost mean—the kind of face that needs half a dozen drinks really to open the eyes and stiffen the mouth up to normal." Recoiling from these marks of snobbery and dissipation, the Kellys avoid the couple, who reciprocate: "'I don't think they want to know us any more than we do them,' Nicole laughed."

The storm blows over, and as it retreats the Kellys wander out into the garden, while "the moon lifted itself and the lake brightened; the music and the far-away lights were like hope, like the enchanted distance from which children see things." The shadow pair, too, stroll through the garden. Then "suddenly, with a final intensity, the west flared with pale white lightning. Nelson and Nicole turned, and simultaneously the other couple turned, while for an instant the night was as bright as day. Then darkness and a last low peal of thunder, and from Nicole a sharp, terrified cry."

With the lightning bolt has come a terrible revelation:

> "Did you see?" she cried in a whisper. "Did you see them?"
> "Yes!"
> "They're us! They're us! Don't you see?"

With this shock of recognition the story ends: the Kellys have achieved the Delphic wisdom, "Know thyself." The shadow couple disappears. "Looking around after a moment, Nelson and Nicole saw that they were alone together in the tranquil moonlight."

But as the narrator has warned earlier, "Life is progressive, no matter what our intentions"—"progressive" not as "improving" but simply "moving on." At story's end the Kellys' fate remains uncertain. So too, in summer 1930, the Fitzgeralds'.

7

THE VINE-CURTAINED VERANDA
MEETS THE JAZZ AGE

(1931–1934)

Not always a progress, nor a search for new horizons.

—"MORE THAN JUST A HOUSE"

W ith Zelda's breakdown, her health and Scottie's care became
Fitzgerald's paramount concerns, and paying for both became a
heavy anxiety. His fourth novel, now five years in the planning,
writing, rewriting, stalling, and restarting, stopped altogether.

Zelda's illness radically altered his priorities, finances, and living situation. That his difficulties humbled him is less certain. Later, after reading
his 1936 "Crack-Up" articles, the sensible, candid Sara Murphy chastised:
"I did indeed read your trilogy in Esquire. . . . Do you *really* mean to say
you honestly thought "life was something you dominated if you were any
good"? Even if you meant your *own* life it is arrogant enough—but life? Well
if you thought *that,*—out of College, married, a father, travelled, seen life,
etc. etc.—I give up. . . . there are several very loose stones in your basement,
rocking the house." In the first of the "Crack-Up" articles Fitzgerald had described his self-assurance—in Sara's terms, arrogance—as lasting up to 1935.
But if after Zelda's 1930 slide into schizophrenia he thought he could dom-
inate life, Sara Murphy was correct in suspecting a slippery foundation.[1]

The challenge after 1930 was to prevent life from dominating *him*. With
a moribund novel, uncontrolled drinking, diminished *brio,* and responsi-
bilities and expenses for an ill wife and young daughter, he was ill-equipped
to confront the friend-turned-enemy, life.

From the beginning he had been able to extract story material from recent experience, and his stories of the early 1930s often spring from his altered circumstances. Staying in hotels near Zelda during her months in a Swiss sanitarium, he wrote an anecdotal tale about guests at a Swiss hotel, "The Hotel Child," a superbly written story. Feuding with Zelda's sister Rosalind, who justifiably saw him as contributing to Zelda's collapse, he wrote "Babylon Revisited," turning on a widower's battle with his sister-in-law.

The Fitzgeralds' plan on returning to the States in 1931 was to settle in Zelda's childhood hometown and live quietly near the Sayres. Arriving in Montgomery in September, they rented a large shingled Craftsman-inspired house on Felder Avenue, with a mounted moose head inside and spacious landscaped grounds; bought a car; played golf and tennis; visited with local friends; attended a play. He enrolled Scottie in school, followed college football, went to an Auburn game, played more tennis and golf, took walks. Predictably, though, he missed metropolitan diversions. "Life dull," he noted in his ledger, though two years later he would recall "the nine months before Zelda's second breakdown," including their five Montgomery months, as "the happiest of my life."[2]

After Christmas, "Zelda feels bad with asthma," his ledger notes in January 1932, and he took her to St. Petersburg for the sea air. There she developed eczema and a return of psychotic symptoms: "Unsuccessful walks . . . fishing trip & Zelda sicker, outbreak [of eczema], the trip back & liquor incident, Zelda increasingly sick." In February he took her to Baltimore, where she was admitted to Johns Hopkins's Phipps Psychiatric Clinic.

Returning to Montgomery, he "arrived home in depression." From Phipps, Zelda wrote, "It seemed very sad to see you going off in your new shoes alone. Little human vanities are somehow the most poignant things in people you love . . . the little things about people are always so touching."[3] Even in her delusive states she had periods of insight and eloquence.

When the Felder Avenue lease ran out at the end of March, Fitzgerald moved with Scottie to Baltimore. The house at 819 Felder (renumbered 919) still stands, now the Scott and Zelda Fitzgerald Museum, claiming in promotional literature, "This would be the last home that the Fitzgeralds lived in as a family." The claim is not quite accurate: they would also live together as a family in Baltimore, in a house Zelda one day set on fire.

D ictated by her illness, the move to Baltimore was a sentimental home-
coming for Fitzgerald. Though he had never lived there, he harbored
a strong family nostalgia for Maryland. His father (who had died the year
before and was buried in Maryland) had regaled him as a boy with stories of
his own boyhood in rural Montgomery County, especially tales of the Civil
War. Memories of those stories carried Fitzgerald back to his family's roots
in Maryland's green preindustrial past.

In "The Cruise of the Rolling Junk," his account of the road trip to Alabama he and Zelda had taken as newlyweds a dozen years earlier, he wrote:

> Then through Maryland, loveliest of states, the white-fenced rolling
> land. This was the state of Charles Carroll of Carrollton, of colonial An-
> napolis in its flowered brocades. Even now every lawn seemed to be
> the lawn of a manor, every village lane was a horse market that echoed
> with jokes from London coffee houses and the rich ring of spurs from St
> James Street—jokes and spurs more glamorous perhaps to the provin-
> cial beaux and belles for having reached them three months old. Here
> my great-grandfather's great-grandfather was born—and my father too
> on a farm near Rockville called Glenmary. . . .

After lunch together in 1932, H. L. Mencken noted in his diary that "Fitzgerald is related to various old Maryland families, including that of Francis
Scott Key. During his stay in Baltimore he has gone into southern Maryland
to visit the tombs of his ancestors."[4]

Three years later Fitzgerald wrote that "Baltimore is warm but pleasant—I love it more than I thought—it is so rich with memories—it is nice to
look up the street & see the statue of my great uncle, & to know Poe is buried
here and that many ancestors of mine have walked in the old town by the
bay. I belong here, where everything is civilized and gay and rotted and polite." The great-uncle was actually his distant ancestral cousin Francis Scott
Key, memorialized by a large monument in downtown Baltimore. "And I
wouldn't mind a bit," Fitzgerald continued, "if in a few years Zelda & I could
snuggle up together under a stone in some old graveyard here."[5]

His stories soon acquired Maryland settings and situations. Several
months after arriving and shortly after being treated for an "intestinal flu"

in the Johns Hopkins Hospital, he wrote "One Interne," a doctor-nurse romance set in a Baltimore hospital. A little later "On Schedule," turning on his penchant for schedules, outlines, and lists, reflected his life as a single parent, setting the hero in a house inspired by the aging fifteen-room house in which Fitzgerald was then living, just north of Baltimore.

When the Fitzgeralds moved into this house, La Paix, in May 1932, Perkins hoped it would prove a calm, landlocked anchorage: "Scott and Zelda seem to be settling down in Baltimore, and I hope they will stick to it, and be compelled to be quiet." A shingled two-and-a-half-story frame house with gables, chimneys, oriel bays, an eyebrow dormer, and step-out third-story porch, all with cavalier indifference to symmetry and uniformity, La Paix was set in an oak copse on sloping ground, with a pond. A sweeping gravel drive led to the entrance. "Scott and Zelda are living about forty minutes out from Baltimore in a house on a big place that is filled with wonderful old trees," Perkins told Hemingway after a visit in July 1932. "I wanted to walk around and look at the trees, but Scott thought we ought to settle down to gin-rickeys." Ten wide steps led up to a veranda extending across the front and turning the corner on both sides. Ellerslie had been neoclassical, rectilinear, heavy; La Paix was fanciful, quirky, slightly gothic. "It was really a fine sort of melancholy place," Perkins commented.[6]

The house was owned by a cultivated Baltimore family, the Turnbulls. Bayard Turnbull was a musician, French scholar, and architect. His sister Grace Hill Turnbull was a writer, traveler, temperance crusader, classicist, artist, and sculptor. In 1891 their wealthy parents had endowed the Percy Turnbull Memorial Lectureship of Poetry at the Johns Hopkins University, which still sponsors annual lectures by distinguished and not-so-distinguished academics and poets.

Bayard's wife, Margaret, was the daughter of a prominent Presbyterian minister in Philadelphia; her sister, like Bayard's, was a well-known artist, the painter Elizabeth Sparhawk-Jones. The Turnbulls had two daughters and a son, Andrew, and lived in Trimbush, a new house designed by Bayard and sitting on the same twenty-six acres as La Paix. In early 1933, while living at La Paix, Fitzgerald spent an evening at Trimbush with T. S. Eliot, that year's Turnbull lecturer.[7]

While he and Bayard Turnbull remained on formal terms, Fitzgerald became friendly with Margaret. Nine years older, cultivated and literary, she had a master's degree in history from the University of Pennsylvania and before marrying had contemplated a writing career. Years later, addressing her abandonment of professional ambitions, she remarked, "I found fulfillment enough with my family and house, and I have always loved and appreciated my freedom and tried to make good use of it." The freedom was partly a benefit of the Turnbulls' money—the new, meticulously crafted Trimbush, designed by Bayard, employed a full-time maid and a full-time gardener.[8]

Fitzgerald admired Trimbush's orderly stability, so different from his and Zelda's ménage. In a later "metaphysical" letter to Margaret expounding on "the inevitable fatalism that creeps into all womanhood," he broke off from his tirade to thank her for inviting Scottie to Trimbush while he was summering in North Carolina: "You have been good to her. I like it when she goes to your house and gets a sense of the continuity of life that her own choppy existence hasn't given her. I want her to be pretty hard but if she has to be a *condottiere* to a certain extent, I like her to know that all people don't."[9] Trimbush had scarcely noticed the Jazz Age passing by. La Paix brought Fitzgerald into contact with a well-ordered, domestically rooted household which, rootless himself since leaving Saint Paul twenty years earlier, he had seldom encountered since.

"Zelda comes home gradually," he recorded in his ledger soon after he and Scottie moved into La Paix, but her health remained fragile and "Zelda up & down" he summarized the following year. He himself was mostly down. Money anxieties grew worse; his income in both 1932 and 1933 sank to less than half that of 1931. His response to stress and disappointment was the bottle. "Unfortunately, Fitzgerald is a heavy drinker," Mencken observed, "and most of his experience has been got in bars. . . . He is a charming fellow, and when sober makes an excellent companion. Unfortunately liquor sets him wild and he is apt, when drunk, to knock over a dinner table, or run his automobile into a bank building."[10] Malcolm Cowley visited La Paix in the spring of 1933 and recalled: "Scott said to me, 'I'm on the wagon, but I got you a pint of whiskey from my bootlegger; I'm on water.' So we talked, or mostly *he* talked, and every once in a while he'd go out to the kitchen to get another glass of water. His talk became more belligerent, sometimes incoherent, until finally he said, 'You know, that water I've been drinking all evening—it's half grain alcohol.'"[11] Theodora Gager, a private nurse hired to control his drinking at La Paix, recalled his insomnia and nocturnal wanderings, a mania for having his hair washed, fussiness about his soft-boiled eggs, and a habit of reading the encyclopedia. Zelda "didn't like me, and I didn't like her," Gager remarked candidly. "I was a nurse and she didn't like nurses."[12]

On the other hand, Fitzgerald's secretary during his Baltimore years, Isobel Owens, remembered Zelda as "a very kind, generous, thoughtful person, so polite it hurt, and grateful for anything you did for her. I enjoyed being around her." Fitzgerald himself was less enjoyable, especially when drinking. "He thought nothing of calling up at midnight and asking about something or other, a check or a bill he wanted," Owens recalled. Her secretarial pay was twelve dollars a month, but for watching after or hosting Scottie, as she often did, she was uncompensated.[13]

The Turnbulls' son Andrew and his younger sister Eleanor bracketed Scottie in age, became her playmates, and came to know the Fitzgeralds well. Years later, in two *New Yorker* essays and then a 1962 biography, Andrew would give vivid glimpses of Fitzgerald during the eighteen months he, Scottie, and sometimes Zelda were neighbors. His romanticized recollections, through the eyes of an impressionable twelve-year-old, reveal Fitzgerald in a less-known domestic and paternal role. The Fitzgerald of Andrew Turnbull's recollections is not the celebrity novelist of the early 1920s or carousing expatriate of the later 1920s, but an impresario of children's games and activities—organizing and directing family theatricals, talking Princeton football and coaching Andrew, buying a .22 pistol and teaching the children to shoot, giving Andrew boxing lessons and arranging and refereeing a match between him and another boy.

Fitzgerald had little expertise in pistols, quarterbacking, or pugilism but, with a strong pedagogic strain, he loved to plan, organize, and direct. An amateur student of military history, he enjoyed playing field marshal with his little troop of children: "He had brought back from Europe an elaborate collection of lead soldiers and figures and scenery—knights, grenadiers, peasants, farm animals, even Gallic slaves . . . and one day, having spread these treasures on the dining room table, he assigned Scottie, Eleanor, and me different locales to reconstruct. When we were finished, he strode into the room with that Napoleonic decisiveness of his and pondered the results with folded arms."[14]

At the start of the school year in 1933, when Scottie began attending Bryn Mawr, a Baltimore school for girls, he organized a carpooling scheme with the Turnbulls. "How would this plan seem to you?" he suggested to Mrs. Turnbull, "for the school trek, beginning Thursday":

You to take Thursday and Friday; then:

Our week, your week, our week, your week, your week

Our week, " " " " " " "

etc.

—This arrangement because this year your children have the far mileage to cover.[15]

He had purchased an automobile in Alabama, "a second-hand Pierce-Arrow, long, blue, and very heavy," Andrew Turnbull recalled. "For all the faded plushiness of its interior, it seemed magnificent beside our own Model A Fords. We children would roam around the back seat of the Pierce while Fitzgerald sat up front with his colored chauffeur, Aquilla. . . ."[16] Clutching at gentility, he employed Aquilla as cook and butler as well as chauffeur.

His ledger mentions many of the activities that Andrew Turnbull remembered:

Games with children. (August 1932)

Andrew & Scotty to Navy Game. (October 1932)

The childrens plays. Skating. (December 1932)

Children boxing. (April 1933)

Football for Andrew. Shooting gallery. (September 1933)

But all was not children's games. Even as he entertained the children and worked on his novel, he was drinking heavily and often at odds with Zelda.

1st Hopkins [hospital] with intestinal flu. (August 1932)

Servant troubles—the Keatings. (September 1932)

Aquilla & his misdeeds. . . . (October 1932)

Drinking increased. Things go not so well. (December 1932)

Scotty's lessons bad. Quarrels with her. (January 1933)

Quarrel Ernest. Always the furnace. (February 1933)

In June 1933, burning old clothes in a disused fireplace, Zelda set a second-floor room in La Paix on fire. Firemen extinguished it promptly. Asking the Turnbulls to postpone repairs until he had finished his novel, Fitzgerald continued to write amidst the soot.[17] On returning in December from an unhappy holiday in Bermuda, the Fitzgeralds left La Paix.

E arlier, though, the house had inspired one of Fitzgerald's final *Post* stories. Part romance, part fairy tale, part meditation on changing times, "More Than Just a House" drags retrograde La Paix into the Jazz Age.

The romance is that of Lew Lowrie, who falls in love with La Paix, or as the story has it, the Gunthers' house. A conventional young man "on his way up" and "getting into the swing of the thing," Lew is a child of the early twentieth century. At story's beginning he "had his eye on a very modern bachelor apartment full of wrought-iron swinging gates." Later we learn that "he had occupied a twelve-room apartment in New York" and "rented a summer mansion on Long Island." We never learn the source of his prosperity, but with money, grandiose housing, "six new suits of clothes," Broadway first nights, cocktails, and dinner parties, Lew is living the American Dream, Manhattan style. Except for remaining sober and single, he resembles Fitzgerald during his flush years in the 1920s.

By quick thinking and deft action Lew has saved the life of a young woman, Amanda Gunther, and in gratitude her family invites him to their homestead in Maryland's rural Carroll County, where as if in a time warp the Gunthers remain in the 1880s. Lew quickly falls for Amanda, oldest of three daughters and "the beauty," but his attraction to her is inseparable from his fascination with the Gunthers' way of life. To Lew—urban, ambitious, successful, up-to-date, unattached to anyone or anywhere—the old-fashioned family is a revelation.

"With its decorative balconies outside the windows, its fickle gables, its gold-lettered, Swiss-chalet mottoes, the bulging projections of its many bays," with wide vine-covered veranda, grass tennis court, and "tangled, out-of-hand garden," the Gunther house is La Paix dropped into a drowsing backwater, peopled by leisurely out-of-touch, out-of-date rural gentry. On his first visit, "Lew's taste was changed in regard to architecture and interior decoration," but the house's influence goes further.

Accustomed to cocktail parties with canapés and *au courant* chat, Lew discovers that "at the Gunther house they served tea, hot or iced, sugar buns, gingerbread and hot rolls at half-past four." Amanda complains that "father won't allow a radio, and not even a phone till last summer." (Fitzgerald in 1934: "I forbid a radio in the house.")[18] Mr. Gunther collects apostle spoons, a novelty item in Shakespeare's England. Despite the loose shutters, sticking drawers, erratic hot water, iced tea and gingerbread, apostle spoons and radio ban—the conventional, up-to-date Lew falls in love with the counter-modern Gunthers.

Perhaps tacitly alluding to the rowdy parties Jay Gatsby hosted and Fitzgerald himself attended on Long Island, "More Than Just a House" visits a dance at the Gunthers':

> The harvest dance took place in an L-shaped space formed by the clearing of three rooms. Thirty young people were there, and a dozen of their elders, but there was no crowding, for the big windows were opened to the veranda and the guests danced against the wide, illimitable night. A country orchestra alternated with the phonograph, there was mildly calculated cider punch, and an air of safety beside the open bookshelves of the library and the oil portraits of the living room, as though this were one of an endless series of dances that had taken place here in the past and would take place again.

This dance takes place three years after Gatsby's parties, but Lew's grandfather might have attended roughly the same event fifty years earlier. ". . .
Designed for reading long Victorian novels around an open fire of the evening," the Gunther house stands apart from Jazz Age noise and rush. Ge-
nerically modern young Lew is enchanted. Later, as years go by, "his spirit,
warped by loneliness and grown gypsy with change, turned back persistently to this house."

Four years later, much at the Gunthers' has changed: the harvest parties are over, a telephone jangles, the house is rotting, the daughters have
fled or retreated into loveless solitude. Even so, in the years following, Lew
"thought of them often.' Visiting four years later yet, he finds the house col-
lapsing, the family almost extinct. The Gunthers' day has passed. And yet
"The Gunthers were part of him. . . . If the memory of them became extinct,
then something in himself became extinct also."

At forty-one, Fitzgerald would reflect on his 1920s self: ". . . As a restless
and ambitious man, I was never disposed to accept the present but always
striving to change it, better it, or even sometimes destroy it. There were always far horizons that were more golden, bluer skies somewhere."[19] But as
Lew Lowrie discovers, "life is not always a progress, nor a search for new
horizons, nor a going away."

T he story as fairy tale features the three Gunther daughters. Lew courts
each, successively. Amanda, the eldest, already engaged when he meets
her in 1925, marries and ends up in Manhattan, "super–Park Avenue and very
busy having Park Avenue babies." Jean also flees to New York and becomes
a Gatsbyesque reveler, as Lew discovers four years later. Returning to the
Gunthers' four years later yet, 1933, he finds Bess, the youngest, alone and
destitute, camped out in the now dilapidated, mortgaged, denuded house.

While her sisters have abandoned rural Maryland and rushed off to the
city, Bess has stayed behind to nurse their aging parents. Only twenty-four,
she has been "growing old" with the burden of the old homestead, her se-
nile father, and "hanging on to the past." Earlier she had called herself the
family Cinderella, but a better analogy might be Cordelia, youngest and truest of King Lear's three daughters. By the time of Lew's final visit both par-

ents are dead and Bess remains, alone and impoverished in the crumbling house stripped of furniture, books, and pictures.

Though wholly out of touch for four years, an hour after Lew's arrival he and Bess leave the house together to marry.

It is a pragmatic union. She can give him what, for all his worldly success, he lacks. ". . . I'm a sort of a home girl," she confesses, and "the kind of person that's forever." Lonely and "starved for a home," Lew needs what only a home girl can provide. He in turn proffers his ample means but also a greater gift—an awakening. Against Amanda the beauty and Jean the *chic,* Bess has been the wallflower, or thinks herself so: "I seem to lack the S.A. my sisters had."[20] Kid sister, daughter, nurse, homebody, she is a stranger to sexual love: "I'm not used to being loved. I wouldn't know what to do; I never got the trick of it."

When Lew first takes her hand, she recoils. "Not even used to being touched," she admits—but then, "Yes, touch me like that," she says. "Touch my cheek. I want to be touched; I want to be held." Only a lover can awaken her to her own desirability. Reflecting that "the love in her was all incrusted with the sacrificial years," Lew introduces her to sexual affection. With Bess's awakening from her long hibernation, Fitzgerald perhaps had in mind another fairy-tale—"Sleeping Beauty."

"More Than Just a House" proposes no return to settees on the veranda and pre-radio quiet. That past was gone as surely as the Gunther house was sliding off its foundations. But, once an eager and noisy advocate of youth and the Jazz Age, Fitzgerald had grown more reflective, and the story's ending does not gloat over the passing of the old order. Rather, in the marriage of Lew and Bess, go-ahead future marries venerable past.

With the question of marriage settled, Lew jests, "Suppose we begin by setting fire to this house." Instead, he leads her away "across the paralyzed door of the ice house, the rusting tin gutters, the loose-swinging shutter, the cracked cement of the front walk, the burned place of last year's rubbish back of the tennis court." As he backs "through the clogging weeds of the garden, Lew looked at the house over his shoulder" and remarks, "Next week or so we'll decide what to do about that." The sun is setting, and "a bright sunset—the creep of rosy light that played across the blue fenders of the car and across their crazily happy faces moved across the house too." The story ends with tempered optimism. "We'll survive, you and I," Lew assures Bess; perhaps the old house will too, renewed and repopulated.

But the ending acknowledges that life moderates expectations. As Robert Frost's oven bird mourns the vanished spring, "The question that he frames in all but words / Is what to make of a diminished thing." The festive days of "'O Russet Witch'" were over. Never to return were "the good gone times," in Zelda's words, "when we still believed in summer hotels and the philosophies of popular songs."[21]

Z elda begins to weaken & goes to Hopkins," Fitzgerald's 1934 ledger begins—a bad start to a bad year. For the past eighteen months, she had spent much of her time at La Paix. In February, he took her to a sanitarium in Beacon, New York, on the Hudson.

Craig House was the Plaza Hotel of sanitariums, "as luxurious and expensive an establishment as you will find in the country," *Fortune* magazine gushed. "Minimum rates are $150 a week, maximum four or five times that much. What do you get for this considerable outlay?" it wondered rhetorically:

> You get the run of a large and beautifully landscaped estate sprawled over the rolling hills above Beacon, New York. Its lawns and big gardens, famous among U.S. horticulturists, look down on the Hudson River. . . . There are several employees to every patient—almost a hundred nurses, a score of men working on the grounds, six doctors, dozens of cooks, waitresses, chauffeurs, etc. Each of the fifty-odd patients has his own nurse, who eats with him at a table for two, who plays golf or pool or cards with him, who takes him to the movies in Beacon or driving in one of the eight Cadillac limousines maintained for the patients. . . . Besides the golf course, there is an indoor and an outdoor swimming pool, a stable with six riding horses, tennis courts, a baseball field.[22]

That Fitzgerald sought premier accommodation and therapy for Zelda speaks to his solicitude, possibly also to guilty misgivings; perhaps, as well, to a hankering for the style of the Murphys. But the "Villa America" days were gone, too; the Murphys themselves were back in the States now, with Gerald working to revive the family business.

With Zelda in Craig House, Fitzgerald assumed willy-nilly the sole care of a teenage daughter—in October 1934, Scotty turned thirteen. Quick to exploit the situation, he projected a series of stories about a widower and his daughter Gwen. After publishing two, the *Saturday Evening Post* lost interest.

At La Paix, however, he had reconceived his fourth novel. Soon after relocating to Baltimore he had discussed with Mencken the novel-not-in-progress. "He has not published a novel for six years," Mencken observed in his diary. "He told me that he had dropped out deliberately, on the ground that he needed time to think things out anew. He began to write at 22, and had quickly exhausted all his store of experience. In the later twenties he found that his books were beginning to run thin, and so he decided to stop writing serious novels for a while and try to accumulate new experience."[23]

New experience had now arrived, unhappily in the form of Zelda's collapse. Though recycling characters and scenes from earlier drafts, the "phantom novel," as Fitzgerald called it, discarded matricide and turned back, inevitably, to himself and Zelda. Its hero became a brilliant doctor of psychiatry, a specialty first swimming into Fitzgerald's awareness with her breakdown. The plot would follow the doctor's deterioration, not unlike Fitzgerald's decline into a novelist who couldn't finish a novel, while his wife Nicole gradually recovers from schizophrenia.[24]

Resurrected by Zelda's collapse, the rejuvenated story grew absorbing. "I have lived so long within the circle of this book and with these characters," he told Perkins, "that often it seems to me that the real world does not exist but that only these characters exist, . . . their glees and woes are just as exactly important to me as what happens in life." He hoped the novel would reestablish him in the top rank of contemporary writers, alongside his idol Hemingway; more pragmatically, he hoped its profits would cover his debts, pay for Zelda's care and Scotty's schooling, and with the sale of film and dramatic rights relieve him of all financial stress. He revised assiduously; perhaps over-revised. "Almost every part of it now has been revised and thought out from three to six times."[25]

In point-by-point letters of advice and demands, he harassed Perkins:

I want to talk to you about advertising when I see you. . . . There will be other points when I see you in October. . . ." (September 1933)

I am saying this now and will remind you later. . . . the book form of the novel should be set up *from the corrected proof of the serial.* . . . Now as to the blurbs. . . . (October 1933)

What do you think of the idea of using twenty-four of those wood-cuts, which illustrate the serial, as head and tail pieces for chapters in the book? . . . Don't forget my suggestion that the jacket flap should carry an implication that though the book starts in a lyrical way . . . I would prefer the binding to be uniform with my other books. . . . (January 1934)

Please don't forget the indentation of title and author on the front cover. . . . In advertising the book some important points are . . . *don't* sidetrack these advertising points. (February 1934)

. . . I wish you could get some word to the printers that they should not interfere with my use of italics. . . . Now, about advertising. . . . (March 1934)[26]

Perkins's heart must have sunk as these *dictats* appeared on his desk. After nine years' absence from Scribner's list, though, Fitzgerald could ill afford nonchalance: "The book is my whole life now and I can't help this perfectionist attitude."[27]

Anxious about the book, about money, about Zelda, he remained shackled to gin. "I wish to Christ I could see him sober," Hemingway remarked about this time. Perkins read a draft in October 1933: "I went down to Baltimore and tried to read the manuscript [t]here in an extremely unfinished and chaotic form, with Scott handing me Tom Collinses every few minutes. . . ." Fitzgerald himself later lamented, "I would give anything if I hadn't had to write Part III of 'Tender is the Night' entirely on stimulant. If I had one more crack at it cold sober I believe it might have made a great difference."[28]

After running as a serial in *Scribner's Magazine,* the "very dilatory successor to 'The Great Gatsby'" was published in April 1934. "I believe that Scott will be completely reinstated, if not more, by his 'Tender Is the Night,'"

Perkins told Hemingway. ". . . I believe when he gets through with revising the first quarter for the book, he will have a genuine masterpiece in its kind." The wider response, though, was disappointing. Princeton mentors Edmund Wilson and John Peale Bishop offered only qualified praise. The friend whose approval Fitzgerald most coveted said nothing at all. "Did you like the book?" he pleaded with Hemingway. "For God's sake drop me a line and tell me one way or another."[29]

"I liked it and I didn't like it," Hemingway replied. "It started off with that marvelous description of Sara and Gerald [Murphy]. . . . Then you started fooling with them . . . changing them into other people. . . ." To Perkins, Hemingway complained (amidst much more) that *Tender Is the Night* "takes a strong woman like Sara, a regular pioneer mother, and first arbitrarily makes her into a psychopathic case and then makes her into Zelda, then back into Sara, and finally into nothing." *Esquire* editor Arnold Gingrich substantially agreed: "*Tender* grew confused—instead of one story it became a mixture of two confusedly intertwined. . . . [Fitzgerald's] life and Zelda's and her growing mental trouble got mixed up in the plot, together with the Murphys, his growing disillusionment and the story of Rosemary—and he never got it all unraveled." John O'Hara would observe that "Scott wrote the life" of the Murphys, "but not the lives. . . . Scott was always writing about the life. Sooner or later all his characters came back to being Fitzgerald characters in a Fitzgerald world."[30]

From the novel's long gestation and shifting focus emerged a long opening narration of scenes eight years after the story's actual beginning, inconsistent points of view, obscure time lapses, an ill-motivated disintegration of the hero, and over-labored prose—Hemingway called it (privately) a "Christmas-tree ornament" novel. While *Tender Is the Night* has its champions, they may be wishing for a Fitzgerald of epic scope, a Tolstoy or a Dickens. Fitzgerald's strength lay, rather, in lyric scale—in *Gatsby*'s discrete, superbly crafted chapters and rich poetic bursts, and in his best short stories. *Tender*'s individual scenes sometimes display this gift, and if its Riviera characters verge on triviality, Nicole Diver is an exception, throwing Daisy Buchanan in the shade. But even the loyal Perkins remarked that Fitzgerald "was too, too long in getting the book written, and he could not bear to exclude all of the superfluous material which he had gathered up in those years." Fitzgerald himself admitted that *Tender*'s "romantic introduction . . . was too long and too elaborated largely because of the fact that it had been written over a series of years with varying plans." Planning its successor five years later, he would adopt as model the concentrated form of *Gatsby,* half as long as *Tender.*[31]

Bookstore sales lagged. The indifferent reception was one hammer blow too many. Fitzgerald sank into deeper depression and heavier drinking.

From Craig House, Zelda sent wifely, encouraging letters, as if he and not she were the invalid. Despite the country-club amenities, she grew worse, however. In May, asking Perkins for a loan, Fitzgerald explained, "MUST GET ZELDA OUT OF HOCK AT THAT EXORBITANT CLINIC AND ENTER HER HERE IN REASONABLE PLACE."[32] "Here" was Baltimore, where in May, "in Katatonic State," she entered Sheppard Pratt, a psychiatric hospital.

With this latest "push," the third, four years after her first breakdown, it became evident that she would never wholly recover. As a scheme of co-habitation, the Fitzgeralds' marriage had ended; they never again lived together. Though remaining loyal to memories of their happier days together and to supporting Zelda financially, he had become *de facto* a widower. Beginning with "Babylon Revisited," the Absent Wife—dead, ill, or divorced—became a staple in his stories.

There was another worry. His once-reliable and lucrative market for stories, the *Saturday Evening Post,* was slipping away.

In 1931, he had published eight stories in the *Post;* then in

1932: six

1933: four

1934: three

1935: one.

Various factors contributed. In 1932 and 1933 he had been writing *Tender Is the Night;* in 1934, revising stories for *Taps at Reveille.* Zelda's health was a constant anxiety.

But the problem had deeper causes. "I wrote young & and I wrote a lot & the pot takes longer to fill up now," he admitted as early as 1930. He found stories of young love increasingly difficult, as the troubles of the early 1930s dulled his keen memories of the early romances. "It was easier when I was young and believed in things and hoped that life might be a happy matter," he wrote in 1935. The term "emotional bankruptcy" is sometimes applied to these years. Fitzgerald employed it as the title of a story, but also used it of himself—discouraging an amorous woman, for example: "I told her over and over that I was emotionally bankrupt."[33]

In 1937 he admitted that "for the present and for over 3 years the creative side of me has been dead as hell." In this state of depletion he drafted his "Count of Darkness" stories, intending to assemble them as a novel. "This is my only plan," he admitted to Perkins. ". . . This goose is beginning to be pretty thoroughly plucked I am afraid." The Count himself was modeled, improbably but somehow predictably, on Hemingway. Fitzgerald thought "the new Marxian analysis" might illuminate the Count's ninth-century world, but the stories' medievalism actually reverted to his childhood: "My first story, written at the age of twelve, was called 'Elavo,'" he told an interviewer, "a novel in verse about knights and Norman strongholds, drawbridges, seneschals, donjon keeps and such. . . ."[34]

He told Perkins that he had become "so fascinated with the medieval series that my problem is making them into proper butcher's cuts for monthly consumption." Less fascinated, the *Post* declined them. Ober politely observed, "I think we have to remember that you have made a reputation for writing a very modern story. . . . when a reader picks up a magazine with one of your stories in it and finds a story about the ninth century he is going to be shocked." *Redbook* accepted them doubtfully.[35]

Anxious and depressed, Fitzgerald resorted to two immemorial solaces. Two months after *Tender Is the Night* was published, H. L. Mencken noted, "The case of F. Scott Fitzgerald becomes distressing. He is boozing in a wild manner, and has become a nuisance."[36] The other consolation was women. "Women and liquor take up so much time and get you into so much trouble," he lamented in 1935, speaking from experience.[37]

The Fitzgeralds' marriage, a union of two festive, fanciful, flighty temperaments, had seldom been tranquil, but as with the young Kellys of "One

Trip Abroad," "it was a love match . . . and it could stand a great deal." With the exception of mild flirtations and Lois Moran, Fitzgerald had been a one-woman man since 1918.

Now Zelda's absence from his daily life and his bed created a void. No one could replace her entirely: "I gave her all the youth and freshness that was in me," and over the years she had become integral to himself, an indelible "hereness" within him. In 1935 Fitzgerald would write of a visit to Zelda in Sheppard Pratt, "It was wonderful to sit with her head on my shoulder for hours and feel as I always have, even now, closer to her than to any other human being."[38] He had no vocation for celibacy, however.

Years later, John O'Hara recollected an evening with Fitzgerald, Dorothy Parker, and O'Hara's ex-wife Helen in New York, soon after Zelda entered Craig House: "Very late, on the way to Helen's apartment, Scott was making heavy passes at Helen and she was not fighting him off. . . . Scott followed her into the foyer as far as the elevator, then she left him. He was assisted by the doorman. Meanwhile Dottie had said to me, 'He's awful, why didn't you punch him?'"[39] Helen was simply a flirtation of opportunity, but Fitzgerald rushed others more persistently.

In July 1934, with Zelda at Sheppard Pratt, he and Perkins made a weekend visit to Perkins's good friend Elizabeth Lemmon at her family's estate in Virginia's then-rural and lovely Loudoun County. In August, Fitzgerald returned alone for a weekend, and in September visited again.

The youngest of eight daughters, Lemmon had grown up in Baltimore, but after her father's death she and her mother had relocated to Welbourne, in her mother's family since 1819. Three years older than Fitzgerald, the attractive, vivacious Lemmon was unmarried. She spent much of her time in Baltimore, where she still had family, and where sometime earlier Perkins had introduced her to Fitzgerald.

Though hopeful that Fitzgerald could pull himself together, Perkins by now regarded him as almost a charity case. "I had a bad time with Scott that last night," he told Lemmon in October 1934. "I can't seem to help him. . . ." She had already been enlisted in Perkins's rescue campaign, evidently, for when earlier Fitzgerald claimed that "he had not tasted a drop for four weeks," Perkins wrote to her, "I hope Scott can pull this off.—If he does it will be largely because he knew you."[40]

Hard of hearing, Perkins periodically traveled to Baltimore to visit an otologist at Johns Hopkins. When in July 1934 he told Lemmon he would be coming down to see his physician, she encouraged him to visit Welbourne and bring along his two most problematic novelists, Fitzgerald and Thomas Wolfe.

Perkins was reluctant: "You want to have Tom Wolfe & Scott play, & I want to have them work," he responded. Wolfe was writing *Of Time and the River* while Fitzgerald was revising stories for *Taps at Reveille,* and "neither of them is doing it rightly." "As for Scott," Perkins added, "he's easily beguiled from work to drink & if I had got him that would have been the sure result."[41]

Quietly in love with Lemmon in a reserved New England way, Perkins had assured her that "there is no one I so dislike to displease as you," and it was no idle compliment. Relenting, he invited the two writers. Wolfe declined, but Lemmon met Perkins and Fitzgerald in Washington and drove them out to Welbourne. Perkins may have reasoned that a day or two with a gracious hostess in an antebellum mansion in bucolic countryside might help lift Fitzgerald from depression and drinking in steamy Baltimore.

Surrounded by Civil War battlefields, once visited by Confederate legends Jeb Stuart and John Mosby, and preserving a savor of the old South, Welbourne had much to interest Fitzgerald. "It seems to me more detached than any place I have ever visited in the Union except a few remote towns in Alabama and Georgia . . . before radio came," he told Perkins, calling it a "novel and stimulating atmosphere" and mentioning "the spacious grace of that house."[42]

Lemmon herself was also interesting. First meeting her a dozen years earlier, Perkins had recalled (in Latin) the *Aeneid*'s description of Venus in disguise: ". . . and in her tread she was revealed a very goddess." With "small Latin" like Shakespeare, Fitzgerald expressed his own admiration more plainly: "I thought Elizabeth Lemon was charming—I wonder why the hell she never married."[43]

Soon afterwards he wrote a story inspired by Welbourne, for which the *Post* paid him $3,000. His visits were otherwise unprofitable: the house's hospitality and romantic history failed to sober him. On a later visit he passed out drunk, and back in Baltimore continued drinking.

Sailing from France to attend his father's funeral in Maryland in early 1931, with Zelda still at Prangins, Fitzgerald had met and become fascinated by a young New Yorker of "wild wit," Bert Barr (actually Mrs. Bertha Weinberg Goldstein). They may have slept together on the liner, for one of his notes to her while underway describes an early morning departure from her stateroom, "tottering, I might say weaving from your palatial suite—what I mean is I am sober, de-alcoholized, de-nicotinized and still adore you." She saved his notes and letters, often alcohol inspired.[44]

The affair continued with several further trysts, the last an unhappy rendezvous in Paris. In a letter to "Darling Mickey Mouse" and signed "Your Krazy Cat," he lamented, "It was too bad about us this time—we met like two crazyy people, both cross & worried & exhausted & as we're both somewhat spoiled we took to rows & solved nothing," but "I hope . . . that you'll try to remember the best & not the worst of that bad time." After this debacle, ending with "a hotel keeper's wife shrieking curses through the telephone," the affair cooled until they corresponded again in spring 1935.[45]

Claiming then that "twice in the last three years I've tried to get in touch with you when in New York," he promised that next time "I will faithfully give you a call and see if I can round you up." In July, planning a New York visit, he "hoped his Jewish girl friend would be out of town but she probably wouldn't." Nonetheless he agreed to meet her, later telling Perkins that he "went to N.Y. to see a woman I'm very fond of. . . . she'd given up the wk. end at the last minute to meet me & it was impossible to leave her to see you."[46] The woman was presumably Bert Barr, and after their reunion Fitzgerald worried that he might have contracted syphilis.

He had not, from her or anyone else, but there was also a second candidate, Margaret Case Harriman, a regular contributor to the *New Yorker* and daughter of Frank Case, owner of the Algonquin Hotel. Later reporting with characteristic lack of reticence that he had slept with Harriman twice, he added, "She was a 'quickie,' had had three husbands and several lovers. She *made* me, did everything herself. . . ." Harriman's attentions drove him from the Algonquin: "Just what has happened will not surprise you, but it fills me with a profound disgust," he wrote to his confidante Laura Guthrie. "I have become involved again & am moving to another hotel. . . . Don't women have anything more to do than to sit around and make love & drink beer?"[47]

This "flying visit to New York" in July 1935 was busy, for he took an interest in two other women as well: ". . . I went on a week end party where Elissa Landi was and also Anne [Honeycutt], head of R.K.O. and I paid her attention." He asked Honeycutt "for a date one evening but she didn't go as she was interested in another man that she intends to marry."[48]

Landi, despite a string of romantic involvements, was legally unattached, having recently divorced her English barrister husband. She was now en route to France to make a film. A well-known stage and movie actress, she had an exotic history stretching from Venice to Vienna, Montreal, Vancouver, Smyrna, London, and most recently Hollywood. Coming to America in 1930 and making a splash as Catherine Barclay in a New York stage production of *A Farewell to Arms,* she was recruited by Fox Films. She spoke German, Italian, and French and had published four novels; she was an excellent equestrian, skilled on the piano and organ, a lover of Wagnerian opera. Thirty years old, she had "bronze-gold hair and gray-green eyes," aristocratic poise, and Hollywood looks and figure.[49]

Fitzgerald took note. Writing to Scottie from New York, he said nothing of Ann Honeycutt, Bert Barr, or Margaret Harriman, but mentioned that he "spent yesterday afternoon with, of all people, Elissa Landi. She sailed for Europe last night. She is very nice." She remained in his thoughts: a letter to Scottie a week later mentions that "My correspondence is now limited to five people: Elissa Landi, Mrs. Roosevelt, Aquilla . . ."—a throwaway sentence with the sole point of mentioning Landi again.[50]

Scottie was thirteen, a teenybopper in the colloquial of a later era, and a regular moviegoer. In the early 1930s Landi had appeared in more than a dozen Hollywood films, and Fitzgerald drops her name as one Scottie would know from visits to the local bijou. But the fascinating Elissa Landi was one of the few women he met in the 1930s whom he did not claim as lover or would-be lover.[51]

E arly in February 1935, "half crazy with illness and worry," Fitzgerald pulled Scottie from school in Baltimore and took her with him to Tryon, North Carolina, south of Asheville. There he checked into Oak Hall, a sprawling three-story frame hotel with spacious grounds and a long veranda overlooking Tryon's main street.

Nora Flynn, youngest of Virginia's celebrated Langhorne sisters, had recently settled with her husband in Tryon. Notoriously spendthrift, untruthful, and sexually reckless, she was a woman of irresistible charm and likeability, "the most loved member of the entire family, without any doubt," a niece would later pay tribute. "You couldn't help love Aunt Nora. She was the funniest woman that ever lived, I think."[52]

Following two older sisters across the Atlantic, Nora had not allowed marriage to an English architect to foreclose other affections. She had "a heart like a hotel," she is reported to have remarked of herself, and another niece recalled that "Nora couldn't have a man in the room with her without that man falling in love with her."[53] In 1914, mother of two, she eloped with one such admirer, and they traveled about the country together before her father, "Chillie" Langhorne, tracked her down and restored her to her husband.

Sixteen years later she eloped again, with the same man. This time, resisting family efforts to reclaim her, she divorced the long-patient architect and married her once and once-again lover, Maurice "Lefty" Flynn.

Lefty too had a colorful history. He had played football and baseball at Yale until, as the *New York Times* exclaimed in a front-page headline, "YALE BARS WEDDED ATHLETE. 'Lefty' Flynn, Who Married a Chorus Girl, Cannot Return to College." Lefty and the chorus girl had met at a skating rink two days earlier. "Flynn is the most valuable all-around athlete at Yale," the *Times* observed, warning gloomily, "His loss will be a heavy blow to Yale's chances in football, baseball, and track athletics next season."[54] During the First World War, Lefty served as a naval aviator, and afterwards, recruited by Hollywood, acted in some forty silent films. His marriage to the chorus girl was brief, and by 1930 he had married and divorced twice more.

He had a fine deep voice, played the guitar, and performed comic routines with gusto. Just prior to his expulsion he had toured with Yale's musical clubs during the Christmas break, performing in ten cities from Syracuse to Denver. "'Lefty' Flynn, the athletic star," the *Times* noted, "had a screamingly funny baseball sketch, wherein he played audience, batter, pitcher, catcher, and groundkeeper." Nora too was an extraordinary performer, "a genius," a niece recalled; "she could mimic, she was brilliantly inventive, she sang better than anyone, but she could never finish the song." She played guitar, ukulele, and mandolin; together she and Lefty made a spirited minstrel act. Eloping the first time, they wandered off "singing and playing ukeleles in the moonlight and behaving like teenagers."[55]

They married in 1931. At the wedding, "A zealous photographer who sought to photograph bride & groom was knocked out by husky Mr. Flynn."[56] Settling outside Tryon, the Flynns entertained the local gentry first at a rented house and then at Little Orchard Farm, a gift from Nora's wealthy sister Nancy, Lady Astor. Tryon lies amid horse country, and both Flynns were good riders. Fitzgerald was immediately attracted to the scintillating, witty, flirtatious, uninhibited, irrepressible Nora. She appears ten or more times in his *Notebooks:* "Nora's gay, brave, stimulating, 'tighten up your belt, baby, let's get going. To any Pole,'" in one entry; in another, "It was fine hearing Nora say that she never looked behind." Perhaps she reminded him of the young Zelda.[57]

Nora was interested in Fitzgerald, too—as a celebrated writer, an amusing addition to her Tryon salon, and an alcoholic. As a Christian Scientist she abstained from drink and had struggled to cure Lefty of alcoholism. The Flynns' was a dry house. As he had for Perkins and Elizabeth Lemmon, Fitzgerald became for Nora a reclamation project, and he quickly fell under her sway. The following year he wrote to a friend who had asked if he knew her, "Indeed, I do know Lefty and Nora Flynn. . . . During the mood of depression that I seem to have fallen into about a year ago she was a saint to me; took care of Scottie for a month one time under the most peculiar circumstances, and is altogether, in my opinion, one of the world's most delightful women. But if you know her, there is no need to tell you that."[58] The peculiar circumstances were an alcoholic breakdown and admission to Tryon's St. Luke's hospital for withdrawal.

His ledger reports, "Went on wagon for all liquor & alcohol on Thursday [February] 7th (or Wed. 6th)"—only three or four days after his arrival in Tryon. Discharged from St. Luke's, he recognized that to enjoy Nora Flynn's hospitality he would have to forgo drink. Later he recalled how "Everything seemed so strange, that month, because I drank nothing and saw everything and everybody with such clarity. . . . The entire soberness was something new for me."[59]

With his new sobriety, his chief resort in Tryon apart from Oak Hall, the Flynns', and St. Luke's was the main-street drugstore and soda fountain,

Misseldine's, to which he addressed a short ode, one of his more successful verses—on a Misseldine's napkin, it is said. Perhaps the poem was inspired by Nora, with her genius for improvisation. Returning to Baltimore at the end of the month, he told Perkins, "I've been on the absolute wagon for a month, not even beer or wine, and feel fine."[60] His ledger indicates that it had been less than a month, but it seemed a promising start.

In his 1936 article "The Crack-Up," he wrote admiringly of the ebullient Nora as "a person whose life makes other people's lives seem like death—even this time, when she was cast in the usually unappealing role of Job's comforter":

> "Instead of being so sorry for yourself, listen—" she said. (She always says "Listen," because she thinks while she talks—*really* thinks.) So she said, "Listen. Suppose this wasn't a crack in you—suppose it was a crack in the Grand Canyon."
>
> "The crack's in me," I said heroically.
>
> "Listen! The world only exists in your eyes—your conception of it. You can make it as big or as small as you want to. And you're trying to be a puny little individual. By God, if I ever cracked I'd try to make the world crack with me. Listen! The world only exists through your apprehension of it, and so it's much better to say that it's not you that's cracked—it's the Grand Canyon."
>
> . . . She spoke, then, of old woes of her own, that seemed, in the telling, to have been more dolorous than mine, and how she had met them, over-ridden them, beaten them.[61]

Besides her sparkling company and sobering influence, Nora like Elizabeth Lemmon gave him a more tangible gift. Her tale of old woes impressed him enough that he jotted down notes and promptly worked them up into "The Intimate Strangers," for which *McCall's* paid $3,000.

Filled in with much invented detail, the story follows the Flynns' history in recognizable outline. The action is simplified, the infidelities lightened though not wholly scrubbed. There is no evasion of Nora's rash and adulterous first elopement with Lefty, but his own three earlier marriages are compressed into one, and by the time of the story's second elopement, hero

and heroine are both widowed, their marriage an "elopement" only in defy-
ing the heroine's in-laws. The point of view is entirely that of "Sara," a thinly
disguised Nora, and its sympathies go with her as well: not surprisingly, as
Nora was his principal source. An exuberant, impulsive personality, Sara is
also sensitive and affectionate.

"Killian," her husband, is more problematic. Plainly a depiction of Lefty
to those who knew him, Killian offended at least one of the Flynns' neighbors,
Harman Vanderhoef, whom Fitzgerald had known at Princeton. Shortly
after "The Intimate Strangers" appeared in *McCall's,* Fitzgerald visited the
Vanderhoefs and was mortified to be told that the story "made Lefty a complete moron." In an "almost threatening" manner, Vanderhoef informed
Fitzgerald "that he would thank him not to do them [the Vanderhoefs] that
way in any story."[62]

"Moron" overstates the case, but the Lefty/Killian character is undoubtedly erratic and irresponsible. When Sara and Killian, now free to marry,
come together again fourteen years after their earlier elopement, what might
have been a happy ending is marred first by Killian showing up drunk at
their reunion, and after they marry, by repeated unexplained disappear-
ances. It's unclear whether Killian's sprees reflected Lefty Flynn's habits;
he had supposedly been cured of alcoholism. Harman Vanderhoef thought
the portrait unjust, but Nora would have known better. Fitzgerald protested
to the Vanderhoefs that when he had lunched with the Flynns earlier that
same afternoon "they had not acted as [though] they were anything but
pleased with the story."[63] Perhaps Lefty was more forgiving than Harman
Vanderhoef.

Though recounting the Flynns' saga, "The Intimate Strangers" also
draws on Fitzgerald's own situation. Loving Killian and believing herself
the woman he loves and has always loved, Sara is naturally disheartened by
his periodic benders: "If he would only say more—what made him go?—if
there was only something between them beyond the old electrical attraction. They lived lately in the growing silence. . . ."

Killian, it turns out, loves another woman—his late wife, Dorothy. When
Sara finds him one day keeping vigil at Dorothy's grave, he confesses: "I love
you so much now that I can tell you this—that I wasn't really in love with
you when we ran away together." She is stunned to discover that she does

not and never will monopolize his affections, that half his heart lies buried with Dorothy. Whether Killian's bereavement accounts for his "wild times" is uncertain, as he is said to have gone on similar sprees while married to Dorothy.

Killian's lingering grief for Dorothy echoes no known anguish of Lefty Flynn, who left behind each of his earlier wives without perceptible regret. As his third marriage ended, *Photoplay,* a film-fan magazine, reported: "After one grand row with his wife, Viola Dana [a film actress], Lefty Flynn packed his trunks and disappeared from Hollywood"—a mysterious departure resembling one of Killian's. "Even Viola didn't know where he was, until Lefty turned up as a ranch owner in Craig, Colo. Viola isn't following him. . . ."[64] Within two years Lefty and Nora had reconnected.

But Fitzgerald did not need Lefty Flynn to understand mourning for a lost wife. Though living like an untethered bachelor, assessing every woman he met as a potential liaison, he continued to grieve for Zelda. "A part of me," he would write, "will always pity her with a sort of deep ache that is never absent from my mind for more than a few hours: an ache for the beautiful child that I loved and with whom I was happy as I shall never be again."[65] Through all the dissipation and failures of the 1930s, he retained his loyalty to their shared past.

8

CRACK-UP DRAMA

(1935–1936)

He and the beer and Beatrice were having rendez-vous.

—LAURA GUTHRIE JOURNAL

I n Princeton's Firestone Library, an extraordinary personal journal draws an intimate portrait of Fitzgerald during the summer of 1935. The 150-page single-spaced typescript follows him closely, day by day, often hour by hour. Most Fitzgerald scholars are aware of it; few have read it through, fewer still have mined it. It has never been and may never be published, but next to Fitzgerald's own writing and correspondence, this chronicle is the most valuable single source for any period of his life.[1]

In some ways it resembles Boswell's *Life of Johnson;* in other ways Restoration comedy, with rake, errant wife, cuckolding, and bedroom intrigue; from another angle it is the sad story of a once-brilliant writer descending to gin and despair. Guthrie's circumstantial and candid journal captures Fitzgerald at low ebb, the year of his notorious crack-up.

For that reason, biographers generally sidestep the journal or acknowledge it with reluctance, preferring Fitzgerald's own crafted account of his crack-up, three articles published in *Esquire* in early 1936. But Guthrie's circumstantial and honest record puts no gloss on his disintegration. If we knew nothing else about him in the three years between *Tender Is the Night* and his departure for Hollywood in mid-1937, the journal of Laura Guthrie would tell us enough.

James Boswell after a conversational evening with Samuel Johnson would return to his London lodgings and jot down all Johnson had said,

verbatim. Laura Guthrie possessed similar traits of observing, listening, remembering, and prompt note-taking. And just as Boswell's admiration was
qualified by awareness of Johnson's quirks, dictatorial opinions, and rough
manners, Guthrie grew familiar with Fitzgerald's problems and flaws even
as she remained loyal and, with reservations, fond.

At first, in fact, she was infatuated.

Three years earlier Guthrie had left New York with symptoms of tuberculosis, leaving behind her husband Bill and young son, and settled in
Asheville, where she would spend the rest of her life. In 1935 she was living
in a garage apartment off Macon Street, near the Grove Park Inn, a land-
mark resort outside the city. In heavy rains her apartment leaked in eight
places, and after an ice truck damaged a bridge on her lane, automobiles
could reach her door only by a roundabout route. She herself had no car.
Bill continued to send checks to support her, but by 1935 they were moving
toward divorce. Her only other income came from casual typing jobs and
reading palms for guests at the Grove Park, at fifty cents a reading.

How she came by her palm-reading skill is uncertain. A graduate of Columbia's School of Journalism, she had traveled as a young woman through
Europe, spoke French, and had written an account of months spent in czar-
ist Russia with her father, a Methodist minister and secretary of the International YMCA. A journal entry suggests that a Russian aristocrat had
courted her. She had chaperoned a celebrated young Armenian refugee,
Aurora Mardiganian, from Fresno to San Francisco to New York, after Aurora had portrayed herself in a Hollywood film based on her memoir of
Turkish atrocities.

Guthrie attempted with little success to sell stories to magazines, and
often published verse (with titles like "White Clouds" and "Asheville Rhodo-
dendron Festival") in the *Asheville Citizen-Times*. She was more proficient as
a palm reader. Dressed in a red gypsy costume and practicing her art at the
Grove Park, she met Fitzgerald.

He too was there for his health. "I am thinking about closing up shop
here and going to North Carolina for a real physical rest as I am God
damned tired of being half sick and half well," he had written Perkins from

Baltimore, and later elaborated: "As to the health business, I was given what amounted to a death sentence about 3 months ago"—which would have been April 1935—referring to a diagnosis of active tuberculosis.[2] His article "The Crack-Up" also mentions this "blow," as prelude to his collapse.

His Baltimore physician sent him to Asheville, referring him to Dr. Paul Ringer, a pulmonologist. With its mountain air and relatively cool summers, Asheville was considered salubrious for consumptives. America's first tuberculosis sanitarium had been established there sixty years earlier, and the city had since become a well-known health resort. In 1935 Dr. Ringer, also Guthrie's doctor, was one of some twenty tuberculosis specialists in Asheville.

Rather than checking into a sanitarium or taking a room in a modest hotel, Fitzgerald though in debt took two adjoining rooms at the high-end Grove Park, self-advertised "Finest Resort Hotel in the World." "I am here resting, very bored & rather uninspired by my surroundings," he reported to a Baltimore friend, "but here I stay another month by Doctor's orders."[3] He grew a moustache. Laura Guthrie first noticed him one evening "sprawled in a rocker, one leg over the arm," idly watching a conventioneers' dance. She was struck by his bleached-out, ill-looking face.

The next night he was persuaded to have his palm read. Although the readings were ostensibly blind and he identified himself as "Mr. Johnson," the hotel hostess had forewarned Guthrie of his identity. Guthrie was accustomed to dealing with convention junketers and their wives; on this particular night there was a conference of the US Fourth Judicial Circuit. She had read none of Fitzgerald's novels but recognized his name and was starstruck in the presence of a well-known writer.

"I took his hand and it was all wet and shaky," she recalled. "I presume he had had too many beers, but I did not know it at the time." She herself was almost shaky with awe. "I was thrilled with his hand and plunged right in to his most unusual and profitable career." She could hardly have been more dazzled by a date with Clark Gable. Fitzgerald "listened with his wide open grayish green eyes growing deeper and deeper. They are soulful and most expressive eyes," she gushed. "I was so thrilled to have such hands in mine that I gave him all I had. . . ." Her reading elicited his boasting confirmation of its accuracy—until it struck him that her insights were perhaps rather too accurate. Had the hostess fed her information? he asked.

She denied it, but even in a beery haze Fitzgerald "saw that I was fooling." She was undisturbed. "He seemed to think he might have hurt me by the question, he is so sensitive. . . ." In her registry of clients, Fitzgerald entered his correct name but gave his birth year as the current year, 1935. Prompting him to correct it, she discovered that at thirty-eight he was four years younger than she.

Despite evident symptoms of ill health or tipsiness or both, Guthrie was lovestruck. When a few days later he invited her on short notice to dinner, to discuss (he said) a story he had just written about fortune-telling, "I would certainly be too thrilled for words," she replied, instantly dropping another engagement. When he arrived at her apartment she was in a flurry of preparation. "It was the fastest dressing I ever did and I felt only half put together"—she "did not have my stringy hair up" yet, and just as the agitated Gatsby nearly knocks a clock off the mantle during his reunion with Daisy, "in my excitement I knocked over the lamp on my table but it did not fall off."

Fitzgerald praised her fulsomely. "He said that I just poured myself into a dress and he did think this royal blue was most becoming to me. Told me to eat enough dinner so to keep that nice body of mine going." The flattery delighted her. Still working on her hair as they taxied to the Grove Park, she discovered she had forgotten lipstick. They could procure some at the hotel, he replied, and as he leaned over to examine her lips, "it was the most natural thing in the world when he just kissed me very gently! It seemed quite inevitable and foreordained."

During dinner the gallantry continued. "He drank his ale and loved me with his eyes, and then with his lips for he said, 'I love you Laura,'" and presently insisted, "I do love you, Laura, and I have only said that to three women in my life." Though recognizing this wheedling as nonsense, she was fascinated and attracted. "It is a haunting feeling that is infatuation," she reflected, looking back: "It was very painful. . . . I was nearly crazy some of the time with thots [her regular shortcut spelling] of him, and knowing that nothing could come of it, that in fact nothing could be more unsuitable, and yet helpless in the grip of this overpowering emotion. I have been infatuated before, but nothing like this. . . ."

During the first dizzying fortnight, she wrote a little poem, "You and I":

I can't take this love so lightly
Emulating you,
For my whole soul's stirred and trembling,
Feeling life anew. . . .

—and so on—poor enough verse, but genuine feeling.

Even on their first evening together, though, she noticed disturbing traits. "He was not eating any dinner at all and just kept on drinking beer and also ale which is stronger and which he had cached away in his second room." Later ordered to fetch some papers off a cluttered work table in his rooms, she couldn't locate them: "He is extremely dictatorial and expects to be obeyed at once—and well." Any possibility of seduction after their cozy dinner ended when, sodden, he fell asleep on the couch. "Soon he was snoring heavily and I thot that it was time for me to go"—which she did.

Though smitten, she was not seeking an affair. He would later complain that "I have never known anyone like you—pushing sex away from you and feeling so strongly inhibited that it paralyzes me." She in turn wondered about married women on the make: "All these tales of how women seek out men and want to make them perform. . . . I wonder what women want of it—it is bad enough to have a husband without a lot of lovers, it seems to me."

Apart from her red gypsy costume, Guthrie did not turn heads: "my best friend could not say in the dark even that I am beautiful." She had been living alone for three years, earning a meager living. Though not without friends, she led a wearying life. "I went down [to the Inn] at nine and told hands in the lobby until 1 a.m. Walked home alone at 1." This had been a good night; she earned $5.50.

Meanwhile, Fitzgerald sold his fortune-telling story, "Fate in Her Hands," for $3,000. Little wonder that rushed by an attentive, amusing, clever, free-spending man—a celebrated writer, no less—she responded warmly and gratefully. Glamor and novelty had arrived to brighten a strait, lonely life.

Uninhibited in his revelations, mostly exaggerations, Fitzgerald boasted of flings with twenty women. In his younger days he had won the fascinating Zelda and flirted with young starlet Lois Moran. Now as he sank into beer and debt, his women were no longer belles or actresses, but bored wives and lonely divorcées.

Laura Guthrie was one of them. But though susceptible, she also knew she had been handed a rare opportunity. Just as *The Great Gatsby* chronicles Nick Carraway's memorable summer with Jay Gatsby, Guthrie's journal is that of a sympathetic but critical observer spending a summer with a tragic character.

A lready "bored and disgusted" with his drinking, Guthrie abandoned her infatuation when Fitzgerald shifted his attentions: "I lose interest in a man the moment I know he likes another woman it seems." Their friendship continued along different lines, however, as she became his companion, audience, confidante, secretary, head-scratcher, nurse, co-conspirator, and chronicler.

In many of these roles she resembled a patient mother dealing with a difficult teenage son; perhaps in some oblique manner Fitzgerald replaced her son Bobby, in New York with her estranged husband. Her loyalty withstood severe testing. When Fitzgerald departed Asheville in September she was delighted to see him leave and hoped he would never return, and yet putting him on the train to Baltimore she handed him an affectionate poem of farewell.

During the summer she jotted down daily memoranda and periodically collected them and typed up a fuller narrative. When she once allowed him to read some of her earlier diaries, he began to worry. "Do you put all names right [that is, without pseudonym] in your diary? . . . It is dangerous business. . . . You ought to disguise names—especially those of national importance"—apparently meaning his own. He was denied access to her current diaries, but one day she slipped up: "I had the above remarks and all those for Sept. 7 in abbreviated form on a paper that I had written when I came home at night, and Scott saw it the next day, as I had neglected to hide it. It evidently gave him a qualm and a fear. . . ."

She was a sympathetic, tolerant ear. Within days Fitzgerald was discussing the history of his marital "sex life," and during the summer at least three others confided their intimate woes to her. She could hold her tongue, and simple listening was one of her chief gifts to Fitzgerald, whose natural loquacity was well lubricated. Sometimes his remarks had substance; sometimes they were braggadocio or foolery; she wrote all down, regardless. Her transcriptions speak with the recognizable accent of his voice and views.

Guthrie was superstitious and, despite her experience and education, sometimes credulous; occasionally she seems to have misunderstood what he said. She found him uproariously funny at first, but gives dubious examples. One night, for instance, he was "in a very playful mood and suggested that we go into the underbrush and kill each other or do some cutting of some kind, and then he tried to think up some Hearst headlines! I helped and we had quite a gay time laughing."

This drollery came at five in the morning, after three hours and many beers at an Asheville nightclub. Another time, playing on Guthrie's palm-reading, "He was exceedingly funny. . . . He extemporized famously and she [Mrs. Reeves, the Grove Park hostess] and I had to laugh and laugh. When some beef steak came to the table he told me to read the lines on that and said, 'You don't have to worry about this line, because you are dead already.'"

His talk was largely monologic, and she refrained from interruption. "Part of your great charm is in your silence," he complimented, but even reticence could be hazardous: he sometimes demanded vocal assent. "You are so silent always," he chastised, and she commented in her journal, "The reason I keep so silent is that my thoughts would startle and displease him terribly, and so it is better to say nothing." An alternative to silence was a noncommittal "Oh," but he detected this dodge: "He says my conversation frequently has 'Oh,' in about twenty different cadences (sometimes I don't dare make comments on what he says for fear of saying the wrong thing, and 'oh' can be interpreted any way)."

Fitzgerald did not welcome contradiction, and Guthrie sacrificed self-assertion for peace. She was not without her own views, however, often expressed in parenthetical interpolations, as in the passage just quoted. Or, "Scott has promised himself that he will not touch strong drink, either wine or whiskey again—and so is keeping his conscience (and how elastic it must be) quiet by just drinking beer continually."

Again: "He said that 40 was the best age for enjoyment of life. (He is only 38 tho, and does not seem to be enjoying life even a little bit unless he is full of beer.)"

On one of his resolves: "'But I've got to be different, there are some things I cannot do any more.' (I guess he meant whoring around the countryside.)"

". . . He said . . . he was beginning to kill himself with work. To me it seemed more like he was killing himself with drink but if he wants to call it work, I will not speak up!"

And more on drinking: "'I have always been a hard worker. I worked hard and played hard.' (I thought yes, and drank hard.)"

Drinking is a major theme in Guthrie's journal.

She herself drank little and was impressed and appalled by his consumption. At dinner she observed him drink beer after beer, as "a child would gorge himself on jujubes." On a day trip to visit the Flynns in Tryon, he had already drunk three beers before picking her up at eight in the morning, and drank two more en route. He was anxious that Nora not notice, but "I did not see how this was to be avoided," Guthrie comments, "since he was literally saturated with it." Sure enough, at luncheon "the others at the table knew that he was not himself. Although," she added, "this self is the only one that I know to date," and she had known him almost two weeks by then. Ten days later yet, "I have never really known him at all when he was completely sober."

Even after seeing him almost daily for two months, however, never entirely sober, she failed to recognize alcoholism. Apparently, so did he: "From various things he says and from reading his stories I see that for years he has been addicted to drink at least spasmodically. So now it has the better of him and in his heart he is terribly afraid that he will become an alcoholic for he speaks of this frequently." His beer consumption astonished the Grove Park staff. The chambermaids reported one day collecting thirty-one empty bottles from his room. Guthrie herself reported his consumption "as high as 37 bottles in one day. It seems incredible, but it is so." In August he tried for a time to wean himself from beer, but soon "was drinking heavily again—beer and ale both (as many as 30 or more cans a day)." Packing up for him before he left Asheville, she and the bell captain, Ulysses, had to maneuver around "about 150 beer bottles!" on the floor. "Empty of course."

He variously excused or justified his drinking. It was a mark of genius: "Every genius has a very weak streak, some terrible weakness that gets him in the end!" he insisted. "He rather fancies Edgar Allen Poe," Guthrie notes, "because he had the romantic death of drinking himself into t.b. and final demise." And "Jack London, Ring Lardner both drank themselves to death," he claimed. "Dickens died at 58 but drink did not get him until the last 15 years!" (Drink never "got" Dickens, however.)

Or beer was a salutary alternative to liquor. "Getting off a whiskey jag would be a terrible nerve-racking affair—I'd have to have a doctor and per-haps nurse and sedative. Cutting down on beer is not so hard." Or drink-ing was a demonic compulsion: "He talked of it [his "beer jag"] as tho the beer were alive and forcing him to take it, as tho he had little control of himself."

And, he asserted, drink enhanced his writing: "Drink heightens feeling. . . . when I drink it heightens emotion and I put it in a story." Yet during his beer "cure" in Asheville, Guthrie observed him fuddled when narrating even simple anecdotes: "He starts a story that really would be interesting if he could remember it, but he stops suddenly and says, 'Oh, I'll tell you all that some other time—it's too long and complicated.' In reality his mind is too hazy to deal with it at all clearly."

Predictably, drinking often left him fuzzy and dizzy:

"He bewailed the fact that he had fallen into this beer jag and was in a fog so much of the time."

"The next day . . . Scott phoned to say he was in a daze (he had been for some time). . . ."

"He said he was pretty drunk and doesn't remember everything that happened."

"He could not dance after awhile as the beer [six bottles] made him dizzy."

"Did I see you yesterday or the day before? Yesterday was a haze."

"I was in a fog the whole evening."

He once explained, oddly: "I don't lose myself when I drink. I just get slowed down and logy and stupid." He sometimes mumbled and slurred his words. At one point Guthrie's journal records him saying, ". . . when I wrote

???(BearandDan??) I worried. . . ." Possibly he was trying to enunciate "The Beautiful and Damned."

He smoked incessantly and hazardously: "He is always burning himself—also sheets, bed spreads and his clothes. He will drop a cigarette into the cuff of his trousers and they will burn. And many a time we hunted the floor and waste basket over to find out where the thick smoke was coming from. He always keeps two tubes of Unguentine on hand to put on the burns." With its rooms carpeted with "French rugs made at Aubusson, France," the Grove Park cannot have been pleased.

But despite an occasional smoker's cough, most of his ailments, real and imagined, were drink-related. He slept badly, lacked appetite, grew soft, and suffered from eczema. "He said that the beer he drank this morning has made him sea sick!" Guthrie reported. "Also he is beginning to break out in welts that itch. This all and the trembling are getting worse." Later, "his eczema is terrible, and gets worse the more he drinks." In August he reported, "I am still swollen up like a barrel but have reduced my consumption to nine bottles today. My spots are fading. . . ."[4]

His alcoholic moods ranged from exhibitionist antics to carping to truculence. He often grew weepy. Dictating a brief testimonial to Mark Twain, "he got very emotional. . . . In fact tears rolled down his cheeks." Pacing "in his dressing gown, most unkempt," drinking beer and dictating a radio script advocating peace, "He wept several times as he thot how sad war was." Trying to revise a muddled story, "he came to some of the incomprehensible stuff and it made him cry. He cries more easily than anyone I have ever seen anyhow."

Or he might grow belligerent. Once, enraged at a taxi driver who overcharged him for a fare to the Grove Park, he "felt it would be nice to go back to the square [Asheville's Pack Square] and see if he could find the man and beat him up." Guthrie pacified him. "As far as I know, Scott did not get into a fight with anyone all the time he was here drunk," she reported as a fact worthy of note.

Even knowing that his addiction to alcohol was multiplying and deepening his woes, he could not free himself from, as he admitted elsewhere, "my insane indulgence in drink." In July he admitted that "I'm such a wreck physically, that I expect the heart, liver and lungs to collapse again at a moment's notice—six weeks of late hours, beer, and talk, talk, talk." Over the summer he grew worse. In September, missing a deadline, he went back to spirits, "with the idea," Guthrie noted, "that he had to finish the story and that he could not do it on beer, even if he took 30 or so cans a day, and so he would have to have strong help—first whiskey and then gin." His final break-down in Asheville came with this reversion to gin.[5]

I n late June, Fitzgerald left Asheville for a ten-day visit to Baltimore and New York. Though recovered from infatuation, Guthrie had continued to keep him company whenever he demanded, and his frequent summonses were cutting into her palm-reading income. "I began to wonder," she wrote, "how I could earn my living if I was going to keep him from being lonesome now, and thot that there was no reason why he couldn't let me do his typing instead of that unattractive person at the Asheville Hotel." When he returned in early July, Guthrie replaced the unattractive person as his typist and secretary.

This arrangement at least made her attendance on him a (poorly) paid position. He regularly and recklessly overtipped waiters and cab drivers, but was not an overgenerous employer. At least two of her paychecks bounced.

She excelled as neither stenographer nor typist, but as steady companion and prop she became indispensable. For the next three months she saw him almost daily and often nightly, and much of the journal simply quotes or paraphrases his table talk. Drinking and talking always went together. If there is truth *in vino* (which, however, Fitzgerald seems not to have drunk that summer), in his case it lay less in factual accuracy than in telltale clues—the posing, the exaggeration, the boasting, the fantasies.

Since childhood he had been a talker and performer, and he not only talked to Guthrie but frequently performed. Early in their acquaintance, his uninhibited fancies amused her: "He is a law unto himself and he says the most outrageous things, both true and untrue," she commented at one point, and again: "He surely does say the most outrageous things that I ever heard anyone say. And in a proper, strict city like this [Asheville] it is different from a big city or foreign places." But Asheville's conservative mores

and her own calmer temperament made the perfect foil for his antic behavior: "On the way down the hill he commanded the taxi driver to back up
to a little white house. He told me that here was where a doctor lived who
performed necessary operations! He said we better go in, and told the taxi
driver that I was his wife! I could only say that he was absolutely crazy and
that we better go along before we woke the people up. But he was enjoying
his fancy idea and there we sat for ages."

Though tolerant, Guthrie began to tire of sophomoric buffoonery. Late
one night at her apartment, after he had been drinking heavily and she was
desperate for his departure, he finally called a taxi, but "even now he was not
going but decided to make faces like a gorilla and make believe he was going to pounce on me. His face was most awfully contorted and there was
actually a glint of madness in his eyes. I lent myself to the play and crowded
back against the wall in terror, and this pleased him for he thot he was putting on a marvelous act, as indeed he was." At length the impatient taxi
driver sounded his horn and Fitzgerald reluctantly departed, "to my weary
delight," she commented. "I think it was about three a.m."

Mostly, however, he just talked. "He ordered supper tho he surely did
not eat much. He talked a blue streak tho." She quickly noticed his favorite
subject: "He likes to talk about himself." One night as they arrived at a nightclub at two in the morning, "The orchestra was just leaving but it did not
matter. . . . Some others, loth to go home, made music on the piano and various instruments, and we just sat and talked and talked. He did most of it."

Over the summer the novelty of his loquacity faded. When he once acknowledged his verbosity, she responded too candidly: "When he told me
that he talked too much and that I was patient to listen I said that sometimes
he might talk for two hours but then would come such a sentence of bright
and shining truth that it was worth waiting for." Despite her praise of the occasional golden sentence, he was wounded by the suggestion that it might
be preceded by two hours of tiresome monologue.

"I am so egotistical," he candidly admitted, "that I talk of myself and feel
superior and don't need compliments." In addition to drinking and egotism,
though, simple loneliness drove his talk. Guthrie soon noticed and often
mentioned his craving for company: "I feel that Scott is about the loneliest
person in the world that I know. . . . He is completely alone because no per-

sons are near to him, and he has no religion to comfort him. He makes me think of a lost soul, wandering in purgatory—sometimes hell." She had rescued him from solitude: "He said that he had been so lonesome here in the hotel[,] for for two weeks no one but the elevator boy spoke to him." For the next three months she dedicated herself to the role of sympathetic auditor. On one occasion, after staying with him for thirteen hours as he labored on a story and she typed his handwritten drafts, she said she could stay no longer. It was one in the morning. "He seemed hurt as a child, as tho I were deserting him," and had Guthrie summon the night clerk to keep him company. "He's got to have a human being there to talk to."

Though sporadically grateful, he was demanding and peremptory, and Guthrie tired of "his imperativeness and suddenness." He expected her to be available at all hours and, when summoned, to report for duty or be ready to be picked up promptly. Summonses usually came by telephone, but not always. Once, kept up late tending to his affairs, "I went to bed [after midnight] and was having awful dreams but at 5:30 when a taxi drew up I knew at once who it was. Scott threw stones up at my window screen and I went down and he asked if I wouldn't hurry up and dress and come back for breakfast with him."

Another morning, "Scott phoned the 22nd at 8.30 and I was so tired and he commanded me to come over at once. I was dizzy and went back to bed and he called later on and when I said I was too dizzy he insisted on coming over at once and said I needed a doctor. Of course all I needed was a little real rest and to be left alone." Their joint working hours were irregular. "Scott came at 10.30 [a.m.] on Aug. 28th and for an hour talked of inconsequential things, and then suddenly realizing that we had any amt. of work to get thru . . . got to work." Late starts followed late nights: "At 10 p.m. he began to give me a long lecture on Karl Marx and then said I did not seem to be listening (I was dead tired) and so told me to go home. And I was delighted to escape."

Lonely and insomniac, "Scott loves to linger and linger over a table drinking and talking," she remarked, learning his habits. At a nightclub outside Asheville, "it got to be 1:30 and Scott begged me to stay a little while longer. . . . He says he cannot sleep at night and so he just begged me to stay. . . . I said I was dead tired and that I had to get up and type in the morning, too, and even at that he is so selfish in some matters, that he just begged me to stay awhile longer with him." She got home at 3:30, and "in the morning I had a beastly headache." For her secretarial work she was at least compensated; her social duties were unpaid. ". . . When I worked at the Inn," she observed, "never an evening passed but what I had some money earned in my pocket. While of course all this night life with him is supposed to be its own reward."

In September, after a long evening of dinner, a stop for beer, a movie, another stop for beer, and finally return to Guthrie's apartment, Fitzgerald devised a parlor game, ranking the mental ages of friends and famous people: "He drew a long diagram of the ages he thot they were. . . . He was really quite drunk and just kept on and on interminably and I was dying to go to bed but had to seem to be interested because he is the most demanding man—in the matter of requiring your undivided attention and vivid interest." It was this same evening that he favored her with his gorilla imitation.

The year before, Hemingway had told Fitzgerald that "a long time ago you stopped listening except to the answers to your own questions. . . . That's what dries a writer up . . . not listening."[6]

G uthrie's tolerance was tried by not only Fitzgerald's drinking and talking, but also his abrasiveness. "He is utterly intolerant of anyone else's opinion unless it coincides with his, and he acts as tho he thot you were crazy for differing with him." His pretensions could grate: "He was in a talkative mood but also a critical one, and said, 'How much do you know about Emmanuel Kant—or the Renaissance?'"—though he himself certainly knew little about either.

He could be insulting. Early on, he uncharacteristically asked Guthrie "to do a little talking now, saying that he did not know anything of my life and experiences. So I began and told him a lot," but his attention soon wandered. "'A singularly uninteresting life,' he pronounced it later, adding that several times he had been tempted to ask me to stop the recital but didn't have the heart to." Other instances:

I . . . was trying to comfort him, when he burst forth with, "How do you think that your peanut of a brain can possibly help or advise one like mine!"

"You have the loudest voice, man or woman's that I ever heard. You should belong to a circus."

"You must take care of yourself," he said. "Your bad breath shows that something is wrong."

He gave me one blow when he told me that my religion was bogus, that I did not regard it as real.

All these comments she swallowed without resentment, except the last. A follower of a vaguely Christian sect called Unity Church, Guthrie wrote that, "If it is bogus, then I am too. I believe it and try to practice it."

She might have been less willing to endure Fitzgerald's demands and criticism had he not continually stroked her with flattery. "Every time he says anything nice to me, I feel so pleased!" she admitted, and recorded compliments:

He said something perfectly lovely to me. . . . "There's something fine in you, perhaps finer than I've found in anyone else I know."

"You are a man's woman."

"You have such a lovely texture of skin, so smooth, like cool snow."

"You are physically attractive to me." He said this many times. And also that I was very graceful and never made an ungraceful move. . . . Also she [Zelda] and I have the most perfect shaped legs he has seen.

"Some day you will fall completely in love. And you will be all in all to him. He will be lucky for you have so much to give. You know you are really a passionate woman. You have so much vitality."

"You have such a virginal quality, Laura. . . . I love the way you use your hands. They are so graceful. The Lord gave you a beautiful body."

It is difficult to gauge how much of this was genuine, how much tipsy unction, how much calculated.

Though susceptible to his blandishments, she learned that he switched on his charm almost reflexively for women. "He admits that he likes women and I suppose that he has a method of approach that has many times proved to be successful," she commented. Another time, "You dance well," he told her in the Vanderbilt Hotel ballroom. "But," she observed, "he tells everyone these things."

"Zelda, you and Nora would all have made good whores," he told Guthrie. ". . . You would have been the kind of a woman who would support a man on her earnings." Turning this impertinence into flattery, he continued: "There is such a small dividing line between the two roads, good and bad. After the divergence there is the great difference. The chance of birth made you good." But Guthrie had heard it before; coolly, she noted that it was "the remark that I guess he makes to all women."

He boasted frequently, his braggadocio mixing egotism, desire to impress, drunken bluster, and grasping for vanished glory. Some of his assertions, unless Guthrie misunderstood, were simple "stretchers." "He has made $19,000 in three months," she reported in June, but for all of 1935 his ledger records an income of less than $17,000, much of it coming after June. For short stories, he boasted, "the Sat. Eve. Post was paying him $5000 apiece for some time," but his ledger records no more than $4,000.

Guthrie reports him "crying out like a nervous woman to the [taxi] driver every time anyone crosses the street in front of the car or when the car goes too fast," and to justify his timidity he solemnly explained "that when in Princeton a foursome of men were coming back from N.Y.C. and hit a post and two were killed and he was knocked insensible. . . . He carried the dead bodies into a house and one died in his arms."

"That was a terrible thing of course," Guthrie innocently commented, "and must have conditioned him for the rest of time." But nothing like this had happened; the harrowing anecdote was an enhanced version of an invented incident in *This Side of Paradise*.[7]

Another boast was his friendship with Hemingway, as if this were a distinction, though Hemingway had many undistinguished friends. "He keeps referring to his best friend, Ernest Hemingway. He said, 'He is the best damn writer in the U.S.A. today.'" To which Fitzgerald added, pathetically, "I am good too." Although they had seen each other only twice in five years, "We are Damon and Pythias," he informed her. So out of touch was he with his purported best friend that he told Guthrie that Hemingway was currently in Tahiti, when he was actually devastating game fish off Bimini.[8]

Ironies abound in his adulation for "his best friend" and "best damn writer" Hemingway, whose best writing was well behind him, who was too jealous of other writers to be good friends with any, whose feelings about Fitzgerald ranged from pity to contempt, and who would soon openly mock him in "The Snows of Kilimanjaro" and posthumously in *A Moveable Feast.* "Not *really* friends since '26," Fitzgerald later acknowledged.[9]

There was some truth to the Hemingway talk; in Paris they had been friendly. Some of Fitzgerald's other boasts were simply nostalgic fantasies. "He likes to remember foot ball and how he played it and was once a hero. . . ." But the nostalgia went beyond athletic glory to flights of vainglory:

> "I am part of the race consciousness. I have influenced the language and youth. . . . I have a very large vocabulary. I have torn up thousands of words in stories. . . . that's why I command the prices I do, baby."
>
> "You can be one of the best psychologists in the world [he told Guthrie]. You can occupy a lonely eminence—for it *is* lonely, being a big shot."
>
> "I can't imagine anyone defying me in the really big things. I *must* rule." [Guthrie] said: "Napoleon was like that wasn't he?" A bright sudden smile of agreement, "He was indeed." Scott likes to think of the similarity between them.
>
> "All the small writers look up to me. I am a top notcher. I am the maitre.—I don't know any man who has a better mind than I have."

Even the struggling palm reader had her doubts. "They've been saying for years that Scott Fitzgerald was through," he once remarked, defiantly. "Well," she reflected, "I guess sometimes he thinks that one of these days they will be right."

* * *

Another ubiquitous theme in Guthrie's journal is women. "I have always been woman crazy, God knows," he told Mencken, and to Guthrie he remarked, "I like women. . . . Women give me something," to which she added parenthetically, "I should say that they did—most of his stories for example."[10]

He sometimes explored large ideas about the sexes. "He talked a long while on women," she reported on one monologue, "and how they were not gaining anything in the battle of the sexes for men still had the upper hand and were fighting the women now, tho he approves intellectually of the equality of the sexes . . ." and so on.

His views on sexual equality were erratic, however. He might sometimes sound like an earnest feminist: "I think women are now trying for truth—to recognize and express it more than ever before in history. This is the NEW woman." But a week later, "Women are all alike—all nations. They have just the functions of being good wives, mothers, mistresses—all wise women conform to the men's lead." Or again, "He was telling us how superior men were to women, all hanging from the top branch of the universal, while women pended from the branches. . . ." ("It was hard to follow," Guthrie observed.)

He was, however, only sporadically philosophical; his deeper interest in women was personal and sexual. To Guthrie he related his amorous adventures in detail and quantity. "When he told me that he had had twenty women I guess he meant about 100 at least," she wrote admiringly after one story-telling session, though later lowering her estimate: "He says he has only had twenty, but I am sure it is twice that." The actual number, though unknowable, was almost certainly lower than twenty. He named at various times at least a dozen women eager to become his paramour, but the evidence for most is inconclusive, nonexistent, or adverse.

As a young man he had been handsome, slender, well-groomed, and dapper—Guthrie estimated that he had two hundred ties in his closet. He was clever and lively company, prosperous, a literary star and, for added allure, slightly notorious. But until his flirtation with Lois Moran in 1927 he had been faithful to Zelda, and probably continued so until 1931, after her breakdown.

By then, however, he was no longer a debonair first-nighter. His drinking had become a habit and a crutch; he had fallen into debt; his celebrity glamor was waning. Physically inactive since football days, he had grown sedentary, while his beer diet sapped his energy and added pounds. Guthrie routinely walked the half-mile between her apartment and the Grove Park, even late at night; Fitzgerald took taxis everywhere. Once, leaving an Asheville restaurant he hailed a cab to take them to a movie theater two-and-a-half blocks away. "He does not like to walk at all," Guthrie observed, "and says that he has been forbidden to, but since he only had a tonsil operation I believe that he is getting lazy and wants to ride and not exert himself at all."

His awareness of declining vitality and attractions prompted the wishful notion that women found him irresistible. Among his self-reported amours, Guthrie's journal tells

> . . . how he slept with some Montgomery Ala. girl two nights before her marriage (she was 27) and when she walked up the aisle she winked at him. She had told him that she hoped she would have his child. "All these women seem to want to have your child," [Guthrie] said. "Yes, practically all have. . . ."
>
> . . . of Eve leGallienne and how she is a lesbian . . . Scott met her in Paris and they were riding in the rumble seat of a friend's car and he began to make love to her. She responded warmly and both seemed to be very passionate, but when he begged her to meet him that evening where they could perform she refused. . . . He said he was taking plenty of chances for Zelda was there and yet he was willing to if she would. However she kept on refusing.
>
> . . . [Mrs. Hamilton Basso] was taller, pretty and dressed in a sport suit. . . . she tried to "make" him when he and the Bassos went to the Castle [a nightclub] to drink after the dinner party was over.

("I wonder if Scott always knows what he is talking about," Guthrie commented. ". . . I don't believe the woman tried to 'make' him at all.")

> . . . that Dorothy Gish [a well-known film actress] had tried to "make" him in the days when he was perfectly true to Zelda. She had come to his room in a hotel . . . and he came in and found D. on his bed and they petted some but he did not fall. Tho it seems that she wanted him to very much. . . .

Another prominent actress who tried to seduce him—with Lois Moran, this made three alleged Hollywood girlfriends—was Norma Shearer, whom he met in 1931, the year after she had won the Academy Award for Best Actress: "He told me all about how he went to Hollywood and met Norma Shearer and they fell for each other at once. She even brought her baby to his office [at MGM] for him to admire and her husband [MGM producer Irving Thalberg] happened to be in the building for some reason and came there and found them." After Thalberg's death in 1936, however, Fitzgerald would write, "I liked the guy enormously," but "He had an idea that his wife and I were playing around, which was absolute nonsense. . . ."[11]

At first crediting his stories, Guthrie grew skeptical. After one such tale she observed that "he had to bolster up his pride again and must have known that he was not an attractive object when he got so [drunk] that he did not know what he was saying."[12]

Another victim of his sexual magnetism, he claimed, was Maxwell Perkins's friend Elizabeth Lemmon. "He got very tired of his Va. virgin but tried to let her down easy, and she pursued him with letters and phones and demands," Guthrie reported, though knowing nothing of Lemmon and by now familiar with his tales of conquest.

Perkins's correspondence with Lemmon, however, reveals that her solicitude for Fitzgerald was essentially social work to oblige Perkins. "Scott is under forty, & if he's finished with alcohol he might do greater things than he has ever thought of," he wrote to her hopefully. "I knew you had not consciously or directly influenced Scott but you were a revelation to him & did unconsciously."

Writing in sympathy to Perkins's widow after his death in 1947, Lemmon recalled that "Max poured strength into people and made them stand on their own feet," and then for an example turned to someone much in need of strength: "Even poor Scott sobered up and tried to put on a show when Max came to Baltimore, and to this day I don't know if Max actually saw through him—but those efforts kept Scott going—and Max accepted them as though they were genuine—perhaps they were, perhaps Max reached the truth in him as he did in everyone."[13] She had seen "poor Scott" when not on best behavior for Perkins. Describing one of his visits to Welbourne, Fitzgerald admitted that "I went down and behaved myself well on all occasions but one, when I did my usual act, which is—to seem perfectly all right up to five minutes before collapse and then to go completely black." He added hopefully, "The strain on Elizabeth was nul."[14] A houseguest passing out drunk seems unlikely to have charmed her, though.

In Fitzgerald's 1934 story "Her Last Case," the heroine is a traveling nurse who arrives at an old Virginia estate inspired by Welbourne to care for a troubled alcoholic who admits, "I seem to be something of a wreck." The nurse's role perhaps glances at Lemmon's, as Perkins's delegated hostess-therapist for his troubled novelist. When the story concludes with the nurse falling in love with her reformed patient, though, it slides into pure fiction.

W hen Fitzgerald and Guthrie became acquainted in June 1935, however, his talk was all of Nora Flynn. One morning he took Guthrie to luncheon at the Flynns' in Tryon, and en route divulged that Nora was in love with him.

"They had an affair this year back in Jan. I think, anyhow it did not reach consummation," Guthrie duly recorded, "and so she is still interested!" In fact, Nora was eager to run off with him, "far away—anywhere, except she does not want to 'hurt Lefty.' But Scott says she would go in a minute if he would take her." However, "the love he did have for her is now ashes, while she is more determined than ever!" The exclamation marks reveal Guthrie's enjoyment of the drama of the dying romance, the lady's heartbreak. "He said that Nora was becoming a bother to him, she should realize that it was a flame and died, and not try now to stir up the embers."

Though at this point still infatuated herself, Guthrie grew doubtful. Nora took her aside and "hoped I could do something for him," and listening to her lecture Fitzgerald about his drinking, she found it "hard to believe that she was really trying to persuade Scott to go away with her." It was curious, too, that though he claimed to be evading Nora's advances, it was he who had telephoned and invited himself for lunch. Later Guthrie observed him "looking at her with such longing eyes!"

Earnest in her efforts to wean him from drink but at the same time naturally flirtatious, Nora Flynn dazzled the lonely Fitzgerald. She was, in Guthrie's words, "very full of life and vigor and charm." Margaret Culkin Banning, a writer, Tryon resident, and friend of the Flynns, would later comment: "Nora Flynn was a good influence in keeping him sober, by stimulating him with her gay companionship. . . . her dislike—which was total—of alcohol derived from the fact that Lefty was a reformed alcoholic and she wanted to keep him from going back to the bottle." (Banning did not take to Fitzgerald himself: "I never saw the glamor that had surrounded him a few years before. . . . But what I saw in person was a pasty-faced man who didn't look healthy and wanted almost too desperately to sell what he wrote.")[15]

Zelda met Nora Flynn the following year. "He loved her I think," Zelda remarked after Fitzgerald's death, "not clandestinely, but she was one of several women he always needed around him to stimulate him & to turn to when he got low—& needed a lift. Sara Murphy was that way too."[16]

The Flynns' friend and neighbor Mrs. Vanderhoef thought Nora a tease: "Mrs. Vanderhof told me [Guthrie] on the porch that it was the talk of the place how he had been crazy about Nora, but that Nora was just fooling and leading him on to show that she could win men and get all the attention that she used to. Mrs. V. seemed rather condemnatory about Nora, and thot that she should not have acted so to Scott, whom they all seem to think had it 'bad.'" As Nora's niece noted, to see her was to love her. Fitzgerald's insistent talk of Nora Flynn suggests that he did indeed have it "bad." Her name occurs some sixty times in Guthrie's journal.

Mrs. Vanderhoef herself, the Flynns' neighbor just quoted, also fell for him, he claimed: "About Issy [Isabel Vanderhoef] he said to me [Guthrie] later, 'She loves me. She must love me for she rubbed my head for three hours!' I got no details and asked for none."

The following year, 1936, Marjorie Kinnan Rawlings, another Scribner's author, at Perkins's urging paid a visit to Fitzgerald. He was again at the Grove Park, while she was staying in a mountain cabin several hours from Asheville.

They shared a congenial bibulous afternoon and evening. He informed her that Hemingway "had had his testicles shot off during the first World War, in Italy, and an Italian surgeon had grafted on a new set. 'It must have worked,' Scott said, 'because he had children after that.'"[17]

Laura Guthrie had withdrawn as his companion and confidante, and he was now attended by a nurse whose chief task was to control his drinking. "His previous nurse," Fitzgerald told Rawlings, "had been his mistress, but she had been 'afraid of getting pregnant,'" and, annoyed by this anxiety, he had dismissed her.[18]

Rawlings's report of this alleged conquest corroborates Guthrie's accounts of his amorous tales, and Rawlings's other observations also echo Guthrie's journal. "He had less reticence than anyone I have ever known," Rawlings reported. ". . . He talked like a machine gun, mostly about himself, and I was glad to listen."[19]

A year or two later, chatting with Perkins in New York, she mentioned her day with Fitzgerald. "You know, it's odd," she added. "Scott and I got along famously, but I never heard from him since my visit."

"Max smiled his wry smile," Rawlings recalled. He had known Fitzgerald for almost twenty years. "Scott, you know," he said, "thinks every woman is in love with him."[20]

While Laura Guthrie's journal is a day-by-day chronicle of Fitzgerald's 1935 summer, it also evolves into a dramatic story with heroine, romance, and poignant ending.

Beatrice Dance, thirty-two, was staying at the Grove Park with her unmarried sister Eleanor. One of the few Fitzgerald biographers to interest himself in Beatrice was French scholar André Le Vot, who with a romantic flair like Fitzgerald's describes her as "a blond Southern beauty" with "charm and breeding that were only accentuated by an oddly British lisp."[21]

Unfortunately these details are mostly wrong. Though "handsome" and svelte, Beatrice was "the first woman I ever loved who was not beautiful," Fitzgerald remarked, and Guthrie reported: "The song they liked together was 'Lovely to look at,' and he paid the orchestra to play it. . . . About the 'Lovely to look at' he said, 'And she (Beatrice) wasn't lovely to look at at all.'"

Nor did she have "an oddly British lisp." She had a slight stutter, mentioned multiple times in Guthrie's journal and also in a letter Fitzgerald wrote to Beatrice, mentioning "your voice with the lovely pathetic little 'peep' at the crescendo of the stutter." He once asked her to read aloud his tribute to Mark Twain, which mentioned *Huckleberry Finn:* "So she took the paper and read "H-H-H-" in her little stutter. She simply could not get Huckleberry out, and said despairingly, 'I am so excited I can't do my 'h's' tonight.' . . . He had told me before, 'B's stuttering is so cute.'" Her chief charm was not the cute stutter, however, but "her great passion."[22]

She and Eleanor arrived at the Grove Park shortly after Guthrie had read Fitzgerald's palm. Eleanor had bad nerves and came to Asheville to convalesce; Beatrice came along as companion, leaving behind her husband, Dupré ("Hop"), a West Point graduate but now a stockbroker, and nine-year-old daughter Tulah. A Bryn Mawr graduate from a wealthy and prominent San Antonio family, Beatrice (like her mother and grandmother) had been queen of the city's annual Fiesta—San Antonio's highest social honor. She had married Hop with hesitation, but they had now been married eleven years.[23]

In no hurry to return home, Beatrice and Eleanor remained in Asheville more than two months. Bored, lonely, and on the lookout, Fitzgerald quickly spotted and befriended them. They first appear in Guthrie's journal when she noticed him one evening "talking to two young women from Texas, the married one, Mrs. Danse being the one he liked." Later, summoned to join him on the hotel porch, Guthrie "went flying out there and he was with the girls sipping beer!" Seeing how matters stood and already weary of his "guzzling," she promptly dropped her infatuation.

Not so Beatrice. To Hop in San Antonio she wrote, "Two weeks yesterday since we left—and such nice weeks too except for missing you." After discussing a new automobile delivered to them in Asheville, Beatrice continued, "We plan to take some trips to nearby points of interest this week however we had an experience that has put us off our sleeping schedule":

> Saturday night we met Scott Fitzgerald and since then we have had to sleep all day to compensate for the loss of it at night. . . . He is really a most pathetic, charming and gentle person—so completely a neurotic that it is easy to understand his books after knowing him. I believe he writes most of the night and sleeps all day. Saturday evening Mrs. Reeves introduced us and as [far as] I know he has not spoken to

more than three people beside us in the Inn. He is terribly lonely and evidentally wants companionship—for we sat on the porch and listened to him until one thirty Saturday then he insisted that we stop by his room for his new book "Tender is the Night"—which he gave to Eleanor and autographed—also he let us take his scrap book,—press notices— reviews of his books and personal letters,—the most charming I have ever read. . . .

What Beatrice did not mention, but Guthrie's journal does, was that, when Beatrice later went to Fitzgerald's rooms to return the scrapbook, "they had had quite a loving party. He said that she is a very passionate woman, probably a nymphomaniac but that they had just fooled around and she was a good woman, and he didn't want to break up her faithfulness to her husband."

The faithfulness soon tottered, though. "Goodbye darling—I love you so dearly," she closed her letter to Hop, but her thoughts were riveted on the renowned writer:

He is now thirty eight and a man of really great personal charm, if only he were not so desperate and driving himself so. I believe he has recently been very ill and certainly is well on the way to being so again. Last night he called at dinner and asked us to go to a movie, we accepted but the movie was poor, he didn't want to stay so we left and went to a funny little supper club on top of a mountain . . . had some beer, talked and came home but Mr. Fitzgerald still wanted to talk—so the night wore on and while it was an interesting experience, two nights, so late, were not good for my patient [Eleanor]. . . . I feel so terribly sorry for him and had no idea that he is as important a person among American writers as it seems from the countless reviews both favorable and unfavorable.

She concluded, "Everyone here seems to feel he is a particularly tragic person."

She herself, though, had been "quite through transfixed with a deadly dart."[24] A tragedy, or at least tragicomedy, was brewing. Fitzgerald's beer-flavored talk is unreliable, but as confidante, advisor, and crying towel, the level-headed Laura Guthrie witnessed and participated in what followed.

A full account would be exhausting. ". . . I wish I had all my notes written down here in finished form for it is a regular novel before I get through with it," she later observed. Along the way:

Beatrice infatuated, Fitzgerald indifferent. "Neither she [Beatrice] nor her sister, certainly not the sister, were very interesting. Of course it is handy having her right there and no doubt she is much enamored of him and the thot that she is having a love affair with a famous author."

A dramatic bedroom tryst, Beatrice clinging to her virtue. "Tho she was quite willing to be loved she refused the completion."

A comic scene: Beatrice suddenly returns to his room, now ready to surrender—only to be greeted by a now-incapable Fitzgerald. "He was very passionate . . . and so decided that this was an awful state to be in and he would do something about it. He did—and then a knock came on the door and Mrs. Dance arrived. She had prepared herself to make the great sacrifice! 'I have changed my mind,' she said. And he with a great show of virtue . . . 'And I have changed my mind, too.'"

Fleeing the pursuing women, Fitzgerald goes off to Baltimore. "He was also running from Mrs. Dance for the poor girl is completely crazy about him now. . . ."

Returning to Asheville, he intends to jettison Beatrice. "He was sorry he had had so much to do with them before for they were just two unsophisticated little Texas girls, and didn't have anything for him."

Beatrice's ardor conquers. "That has happened that I did not want to have happen," [he told Guthrie]. . . . I avoided her a lot, going out thru the barber shop. SHE did it all and kept coming to my room."

Reluctantly, he indulges her. "Beatrice loves me but I don't love her. . . . Beatrice stayed in my room all last night. We had a bath together. She is nice. I like her."

As Hop approaches from Texas, Fitzgerald falls in love. "He told me all about what a terrible night [the two lovers] had had last night as her husband, Hop, was to arrive this morning. . . . He told her that this was farewell. . . . he said [to Guthrie] with tears that it was terrible for he found now that he did love her [Beatrice]. . . ."

More comedy: Fitzgerald lays plans to repel an assault. "If Hop should come and knock at the door, I would have my dressing gown all ready and throw it over his head and knock him down and attack him before he could do anything. . . . I would have to act first and fast."

Not Hop but Beatrice knocks at the door. "When she came to his room she fell into his arms and stayed there and they did not even think of locking the door. And there her husband was on the [Grove Park] golf links but might have come in from suspicion of rain."

Terrified, Fitzgerald flees Asheville. "We had looked at a map the day before and decided on [North Carolina's] Lake Lure. . . . he is getting into a terrible state now, what with the beer and passion, and yes, fear."

Again he prepares for battle. ". . . Scott before he went to bed at night [at Lake Lure], would arrange the beer bottles in such a way that he could reach one and swing it at any one coming into the room. He had resolved to knock Hop out at once. . . ."

Bored at Lake Lure, he sneaks back through Asheville en route to New York. ". . . Scott told me to get him six cans of that ale to have on the train. . . . He was unshaven, unpressed, and shaking terribly."

Hop departs; Fitzgerald returns and takes rooms in the downtown Vanderbilt Hotel to avoid Beatrice, but "He was expecting to have one more interview with B. that a.m. and end everything! . . . Her cute little stuttering ways, and golden hair, and deep adoration, coupled with the many beers that he had, changed his plans."

While the lovers spend the night together at the Vanderbilt, Hop telephones Beatrice's empty room at the Grove Park. The inn operator consults

Guthrie. "It was well that I knew where they were . . . as he [Hop] had been calling the Inn for some time. I immediately called the Vanderbilt and when I told Scott what had happened he . . . had Beatrice call Hop from there and she talked nearly an hour, kidding him!'"

Meanwhile, Eleanor the sister joins the drama. "She . . . had beer and luminol both and got into such a state that she went to sleep on the golf links and this morning was awakened by three bell boys and a woman coming to carry her in! . . . it was for her breaking health and mind that the girls came here. . . .'"

Comic interlude: wheedling Eleanor, Fitzgerald bumbles into trouble. "He . . . had tried to get Eleanor to trust him and had put his arm around her and said pleasant things. . . . she resented the whole thing and told Bea that he tried to make love to her and felt her breast."

Hop returns from San Antonio. "As Bea cried over the phone and had done so the night before also, Hop got so excited that he insisted he was coming on with the doctor [Eleanor's San Antonio physician], by airplane."

Fitzgerald again prepares for battle. ". . . S. was so sure that Hop would fight that he had some very sharp beer can openers on his table to attack or protect himself with if Hop did fight."

In Hop's presence, the lovers kiss farewell. "He came over to Beatrice's bed and asked in a thrilling voice, 'May I kiss you good night?' 'Of course,' she said with a radiant upward look and he bent and kissed her cheek."

Hop catches on. "I saw a dark and terrible look come over Hop's face. . . . Scott and I went, and with a vicious bang, Hop shut the door after us and noisily turned the key in the lock."

Hop carries Beatrice back to San Antonio. "Scott was awfully upset . . . threw himself on his bed with his head in his arms and cried. . . .

'This is leaving an awful wound, with bleeding parts. But it doesn't matter—nothing matters.' And he sobbed aloud. . . ."

In an undated note to Hop, Beatrice pleaded, "My own little boy, forgive me, forgive me for what I have done. I love you so much and am so heartbroken. I want to be a good wife and to make you happy. For the thousandth time let's try again." Back in San Antonio she entered Nix Hospital with a nervous breakdown.

Rather gratified by the wholesale misery, Fitzgerald groaned, "There are four people broken now because of this affair. Beatrice, Hop, Eleanor and myself"—to which Guthrie added, "I felt like saying that there would be five, if he didn't soon let me get some rest and peace."[25]

She knew his histrionic bent. Parting from Beatrice when Hop arrived in Asheville on his first visit, "Scott was more shaken and white and trembling than I have ever seen him, and he was in misery . . . and enjoying his misery in a way and deep in his mind thinking that it would make a corking good story one day if he could just bear up long enough to write it!" Later reflecting on the "turmoil and near tragedy," Guthrie observed, "Of course the drama had to do with Scott; he is born to drama and if it doesn't come in the course of events he has to, seems impelled to, do things that bring the drama."

Perkins saw possible benefits: "Scott is still in Asheville & I gather he's been having some kind of what's called a love affair. . . . I don't like the idea, but it won't hurt his writing or his health, like gin. Might even help."

The fling with Beatrice Dance might and perhaps should have inspired a story or even a novel, a Fitzgerald updating of *Madame Bovary*. "Some day darling Beatrice I will write something about you 'that the world will not willingly let die,'" Fitzgerald promised after they parted, "but that time isn't yet."[26] It never came. Instead, he sat down to write his three "Crack-Up" articles, which wholly ignore her.

Beatrice left Asheville on August 8, and "except for one brief time after she went," Guthrie reported, "he was not sober all the weeks between then and when he had to go to the hospital on Sept. 13." Switching from beer to gin in early September, he fell apart: " My nerves," Guthrie wrote, "trying to deal with an alcoholic, were near exhaustion. He begged me, 'Oh, don't leave me L., don't desert me now. Stick with me.' This was when his second story ["Image on the Heart"] was under construction, and he must have known how disgusted I was with him, and tired, for he would not let me go home at night because he was afraid to be alone." Urgently summoned several days later, Guthrie found him frantic over a letter requesting revisions to his radio script on peace: ". . . Snarling with rage, Scott tore and wrinkled the letter into a ball and threw it at the wastebasket," missing.

> "Then he began tc cry," Guthrie wrote, "and I looked at his dirty un-
> shaven face and felt absolutely disgusted with him. . . ."
> [He was] surely in the worst condition I have ever seen a man in or
> ever hope to. . . . the exema had become so bad since he went on the gin
> a week before, that it itched unmercifully and was like a raw wound. . . .
> Horribly bloodshot eyes and thin drawn lips, even a distorted look to his
> face made me realize that he couldn't last much longer. . . .
> "My nerves are going," he said. "I am going to break."

Desperate to finish on gin a story that had stalled on beer, he "futilely tried to correct some of the story I had typed the day before."

"'This is my last story,' Scott said, and began to weep." Guthrie was beyond sympathy. Earlier, when he implored, "You've got to bear with me because of the condition I am in," she commented: "And I felt like saying, what kind of a condition do you think I am in! Dealing day and night with a practically crazy drunk, and trying to complete a story sensibly meanwhile!"

Scripting his approaching deathbed, he pleaded, "If I die will you be by my bed? I don't want my mother. . . . Promise me—*you'll* be there." The appeal left her cold: "Scott was dramatizing everything of course."

Two years earlier he had described himself as "an overextended, imaginative, functioning man using alcohol as a stimulus or a temporary *aisment*."[27] "Functioning" no longer applied. Dr. Ringer arrived and suggested a psychiatric sanitarium. Fitzgerald objecting, Ringer sent him to Asheville's Mission Hospital. Like Nick Carraway left to arrange Gatsby's funeral, Guthrie was left to pack up Fitzgerald's hotel room and get him to Mission. "I did think that someone else should have had some of the responsibility of getting him there . . . but the thot of really getting rid of him was so strong that it kept me going, thru the next difficult hours."

Seeing him installed in a hospital bed and attended by two nurses, she was exultant. "I left and felt like a kid out of school, wanted to run and sing for my responsibility was over and I felt that nothing could ever happen to get me to put my head in this noose again."

He had suffered three earlier collapses, he reported. "The second time," he told Guthrie, "I broke down on the street [in Baltimore] and began to yell—thought a taxi was chasing me. . . . This is my fourth break but I got it in time. In just one more day I would have been at the yelling stage." Actually Guthrie, not he, had summoned Dr. Ringer.

D ischarged after a week in Mission Hospital, Fitzgerald left Asheville. Guthrie saw him off at the station. When he mentioned seeing her again, "I said nothing, he must know in his heart that I do not want him back here."[28] Scottie, who had spent the spring and summer at camp and with the Obers in Scarsdale, also returned to Baltimore, reuniting the little family in the same city, though Zelda remained at Sheppard Pratt.

Fitzgerald buckled to work, claiming that he put in "14 straight days at about 9 hrs a day. . . . I'm trying to make up for last July and August. Not since 1926 when I was rich and loafed have I done so little work in a year."[29] Soon, though, he "was beginning to cough again in Baltimore with the multiplicity of events, also to drink & get irrasticable with everyone around me," and also he had been rented "an appartment *next to a pianist,* & with clapboard walls!" Breaking his lease and returning to North Carolina, he checked into Skylands, "a $2.00 a day hotel" in Hendersonville, where for a week (he claimed) he washed his own clothes and ate "20 cent meals twice a day."[30]

Nora Flynn recalled visiting him there: "After leaving here [Tryon] he went off to that frightful hotel in Hendersonville, drunk & ill. And lay there thinking about himself, as usual. He never was interested in anything or anyone but himself. It was such a horrid place—I can still see it—with collar buttons on the bureau, and neck ties hanging from the light chain, and dirty pajamas strewn all over."[31]

Here he wrote an "emergency *Esquire* article." Apart from *The Great Gatsby,* this desperate piece and its two sequels, lumped together as the "Crack-Up" essays, may be Fitzgerald's best known writing.[32] An apparently *de profundis* memoir, they describe and analyze his recent breakdown in Asheville. Fitzgerald thought them similar in mood to the "great poems of lamentation."[33] Biographers have treated them as honest, even courageous attempts to plumb an anguished soul. The earliest, Arthur Mizener, found the articles "a serious attempt to get at his own state of mind," elaborating his breakdown "with clinical minuteness." In Fitzgerald's reference to his "dark night of the soul," Mizener noted the allusion to St. John of the Cross.[34]

The sympathetic Andrew Turnbull saw "The Crack-Up" as "a post-mortem" on Fitzgerald's "nervous and psychological breakdown," commendable for its "casual nakedness and candor." He too detected a religious note, finding it "the work of a lapsed Catholic, for whom confession was a rhythm of the soul."[35] Henry Dan Piper thought the articles "some of the finest prose of his career," with the first, "The Crack-Up," "essentially a confessional essay" showing Fitzgerald "engaged in an act of self-absolution."[36] For Matthew Bruccoli, the "Crack-Up" articles were "frightening exercises in self-dissection and come as close as a man can come to exposing the painful truths about himself. . . . the sheer brilliance of the writing often distracts the reader from the terror of these essays."[37] Biographer David Brown finds that the trilogy "took the temperature equally of its author, his country, and his times."[38]

Something like a scholarly consensus has descended on the "Crack-Up" articles. It may be pertinent to suggest counterevidence. Desperate for quick money but milked dry of story ideas, Fitzgerald turned to material both proprietary and close at hand, his own disintegration the summer just past. With more time he might have written a story about a long submergence in alcohol, as he would do several years later in "The Lost Decade." The next best thing was a confessional dramatization, written hastily in the knowledge that Arnold Gingrich of *Esquire* would accept almost anything he wrote.

Far from brilliantly written, the articles are littered with the clichés and tired metaphors of slipshod writing—"the dead hand of the past," "up to the hilt," "a place in the sun," "not a pretty picture," "a certain family resemblance," "burning the candle at both ends," "sleight of hand," "beady-eyed men"—and filled with vagueness, obscurity, facile generalizing, non sequiturs, and padding (a random diatribe against Hollywood, for example).

Laura Guthrie would have recognized the articles' self-dramatizing. In the last, "Handle with Care," Fitzgerald presents himself as disillusioned and hard-boiled but still essentially sentimental—the Humphrey Bogart of *Casablanca*. But Guthrie would have been astonished to learn that his crack-up somehow came of an excessive humanity, leading to his decision to "cease any attempts to be a person—to be kind, just or generous." Though dutifully supporting Zelda and Scottie, Fitzgerald had no particular reputation for kindness and was less generous than extravagant. ("He literally throws money at servants, orchestra players and dancers or taxi drivers etc." Guthrie commented.)

The "Crack-Up" articles have been called, cogently, "a curious literary exercise," in their time "considered confessional but by our standards . . . evasive."[39] They give the misleading impression, for instance, that apart from the friendly encouragement of Nora Flynn (unnamed), Fitzgerald suffered alone in a wilderness of despair, giving no hint that during his dark-night-of-the-soul ordeal he enjoyed the demonstrative adoration of Beatrice Dance.[40] There is no hint either of the other woman in his life that summer, the loyal underpaid Guthrie. For the three articles *Esquire* paid him $750; his parting gift to Guthrie was a three-dollar book. ("I would have preferred to have the money and then some!")

Some facts are simply falsified. Under oath, his account of his Princeton career might be indictable as perjury. The most flagrant imposture, though, lies in the assertion that his breakdown was unrelated to drinking. Contrasting his crack-up with that related in a reformed alcoholic's recent memoir, Fitzgerald claimed that he himself "was not so entangled, having at the time [of his crack-up] not having tasted so much as a glass of beer for six months."[41]

By the testimony of his own ledger the claim is exaggerated. Judging by the "Crack-Up" articles' vague chronology and Laura Guthrie's journal, he "cracked like an old plate" sometime in June 1935, while his ledger reports him "on wagon for all liquor & alcohol" beginning only in February.[42] "All" alcohol did not for Fitzgerald include beer and ale, moreover. How long, if ever, he was beer-free is uncertain, but by the time Laura Guthrie met him in early June he was "saturated," and remained so all summer. In all likelihood the crack-up was mostly a case of acute beer poisoning.

E   leanor, an innocent casualty of her sister's summer romance, would not have recognized the Byronic Fitzgerald of the "Crack-Up" articles. *Her* Fitzgerald was ". . . a very weak person, a drowning person and he was reaching for a straw to hold him, and so he grabbed Beatrice. But she would do him no good for she could not stay with him—Eleanor said that someone would have to keep on helping him if he was to be saved. . . . she had nothing against Scott but felt sorry for him but thot he was weak and selfish." Guthrie saw her point. "I thot this over," she remarked, "and it seemed very good to me. I wondered if I were going to be the next straw."

Hemingway was contemptuous of the "Crack-Up" articles. Fitzgerald "seems to almost take a pride in his shamelessness of defeat," he told Perkins. "The Esquire pieces seem to me to be so miserable."[43] Writing to Fitzgerald himself earlier, Hemingway had in his usual blustering manner tried to be encouraging. Fitzgerald was too concerned with writing for money, too anxious to please critics, had ruined himself by marrying Zelda, "and, of course you're a rummy," he remarked (with much else) in a long letter. Then he added, optimistically:

> . . . But, Scott, good writers always come back. Always. You are twice as good now as you were at the time you think you were so marvellous [with *Gatsby*]. . . . All you need to do is write truly and not care about what the fate of it is.
>
> Go on and write.[44]

N   onetheless, Fitzgerald's troubles continued. The *Post* was rejecting his stories, and "there are collection agencies at the door every day—rent unpaid, school unpaid, sanitarium unpaid & not a vestige of credit left [in] Baltimore," he told Ober in spring 1936.[45] In April he had Zelda transferred from Baltimore's Sheppard Pratt to a sanitarium in Asheville; two months later he followed, checking into the Grove Park for a second summer. Drained of interest in young love, however, he floundered in a search for new avenues. "Every single story since *Phillipe* I in the Spring of 1934 two years ago I've had to write over," he told Ober, listing ten stories and his "Crack-Up" articles. "It simply doubles my work."[46] Ober still had difficulty selling them.

In early October, Thomas Wolfe, an Asheville native, wrote to his brother: "There is a poor, desperate, unhappy man staying at the Grove Park Inn. He is a man of great talent but he is throwing it away on drink and worry over his misfortunes. . . . His name, I forgot to say, is Scott Fitzgerald, and a New York paper has just published a miserable interview with him—it was a lousy trick, a rotten . . . piece of journalism, going to see a man in that condition, gaining his confidence, and then betraying him."[47]

The "miserable interview" had come about when a journalist for the *New York Post* showed up in Asheville to gather material for an article noting Fitzgerald's fortieth birthday, September 24, 1936. Primed by *Esquire*'s "Crack-Up" essays, the reporter coolly jotted down Fitzgerald's "long, rambling, disjointed talk," observed his "jittery jumping off and onto his bed, his restless pacing, his trembling hands, his twitching face . . . his frequent trips to a highboy, in a drawer of which lay a bottle," and quoted him: "'A series of things happened to papa,' he said with mock brightness. 'So papa got depressed and started drinking a little.'" Though mockingly satiric, the article differed little in substance from Laura Guthrie's earlier observations, except that Fitzgerald was drinking gin rather than beer. *Time Magazine* ran a note summarizing the *Post* article. Fitzgerald was shocked, humiliated, outraged: "If I ever see [the reporter again,] what will happen will be very swift and sudden."[48]

Drowning in debt, he boarded a train for California in early July 1937, rescued from penury by a six-month screenwriting contract with MGM. Hollywood would be his last stop.

9

FITZGERALD'S LAST CHAPTER

HOLLYWOOD (1937–1940)

The last tired effort of a man who once did something finer and better.
—FITZGERALD TO HIS DAUGHTER

Hollywood film studios, like novels, packaged life's messiness into coherent, satisfying narratives, and as Fitzgerald rode the westbound Sunset Limited for his third attempt in the movie business, he was aware of the dramatic potential of what would be his last and longest Hollywood sojourn.

Writing on the train to Scottie, he reviewed the earlier two: "The third Hollywood venture. Two failures behind me though one no fault of mine." The three ventures were spaced at five-year intervals, "the first just ten years ago," when he and Zelda had partied energetically and alienated people, and his fascination with Lois Moran trumped "Lipstick," his story proposal. He had been "confidant to the point of conciet," he admitted, believing "that *with no effort on my part* I was a sort of magician with words. . . . Total result— a great time & no work."[1] Also no profit, as "Lipstick" was rejected.

Blaming himself for the initial failure, he blamed someone else for the next, in 1931. Though he conceded that he was then "beginning to drink more than I ought to," the culprit this time was "a bastard named de Sano, since a suicide," who "gyped" him "out of command. I wrote the picture & he changed as I wrote. . . . Result—a bad script."[2]

Nonetheless he was optimistic now, plotting a strategy of politicking and pugnacity: "I want to profit by these two experiences—I must be very tactful but keep my hand on the wheel from the start—find out the key man among the bosses and the most malleable among the collaborators—then fight the rest tooth and nail until, in fact or in effect, I'm alone on the picture. That's the only way I can do my best work." But imagining that he could overturn MGM's established and profitable screenwriting system was not a good start.

H is contract was generous. He owed Ober, Perkins, and Scribner's some $40,000, and with heavy continuing expenses for Scottie and Zelda he could scarcely hope to settle his debts by writing fiction. Thanks to MGM's munificence he was out of debt within his first eighteen months in Hollywood. It was no mystery why writers were drawn there.

Though driven by exigency, he initially enjoyed the experience. A pleasant sprawl of sunshine, palm trees, and moviemaking, Hollywood had become the capital of American popular entertainment. Each week eighty million Americans, three-fifths of the population, watched a film at their local theater. Fitzgerald arrived in the midst of film's two golden decades, between the early talkies and television, an era when movies were more literate and leading actors and actresses enjoyed a long-vanished prestige—the era of Clark Gable and Carole Lombard, Humphrey Bogart, Greta Garbo, Gary Cooper, Claudette Colbert, Cary Grant, Marlene Dietrich. Glamour crowded the Trocadero at night and next morning rubbed shoulders with ordinary mortals at the Schwab's drugstore on Sunset Boulevard.

The urbane Princetonian was as star-dazzled as any shop clerk or typist. Soon after arriving, Fitzgerald wrote Harold Ober's wife, Anne, with whom Scottie was staying, a cheerful name-dropping letter: ". . . I have seen Hollywood—talked with [Robert] Taylor, dined with [Fredric] March, danced with Ginger Rogers . . . been in Rosalind Russel's dressing room, wise-cracked with [Robert] Montgomery, drunk (gingerale) with Zukor and Lasky [founders of Paramount Pictures], lunched alone with Maureen O'Sullivan, watched [Joan] Crawford act. . . ."[3]

The work was congenial. Handed stories to convert into screenplays, he had no need to mine his own exhausted experience and emotions. Working under bosses and deadlines curtailed his self-indulgence. "I think I'm through drinking for good now," he wrote to Baltimore friends, "but it's

a help this first year to have the sense that you are under observation—
everyone *is* in this town, and it wouldn't help this budding young career
to be identified with John Barleycorn." Four or five months later he complained of the drawbacks of studio screenwriting, but not about the writing itself—"It is nervous work but I like it, save for the damn waiting & the
time-killing conferences." At Christmas he told Anne Ober, "I love it here.
It's nice work if you can get it. . . . I'm delighted with screen credit and really
hopeful of a hit. . . ." The credit was for a film titled *Three Comrades,* his first
major MGM assignment.[4]

Turning out fifty feature films a year, MGM was the preeminent Holly-
wood studio—the biggest, richest, most star-studded. Studio head Louis B.
Mayer was the highest-paid man in America, and MGM owned the services
of many of the most celebrated actors and actresses: Garbo, Gable, Hedy
Lamarr, Joan Crawford, Myrna Loy, Norma Shearer, William Powell, Judy
Garland, Mickey Rooney, Katherine Hepburn, Spencer Tracy, and Jimmy
Stewart, among others. In 1939 it would release two now-legendary films,
The Wizard of Oz and (with Mayer's son-in-law David O. Selznick) *Gone with
the Wind.* In January that year, as his MGM contract was expiring, Fitzgerald
worked briefly on "polishing" the latter's script.

Earlier, he had outlined the ladder to screenwriting success: "Screen
Credit 1st, a Hit 2nd and the Academy Award 3rd."[5] Had he reached the third
or even second rung, he might never have bothered to write another novel,
but he never got past the first. One reason is adumbrated in his remark to
Scottie about fighting tooth and nail until "in fact or in effect, I'm alone on
the picture." He naturally regarded writing as a solitary craft; except for a
few joint articles with Zelda, he had been doing it that way for twenty years.
But Hollywood scriptwriting was an industrial process moving from synopsis to treatment to a screenplay revised or rewritten again and again by a
succession of writers or script doctors, usually working in teams. He never
adapted.

Initially all went well. He spent his first months in Hollywood writing
a screenplay for *Three Comrades,* completing a draft in October. Then to his
annoyance he was assigned a collaborator, Edward E. Paramore, whom had
known in New York in the early 1920s. "I like Ted immensely," he had written ironically to Edmund Wilson at the time. "He is a little too much the successful Eli to live comfortably in his mind's bed-chamber but I like him im-

mensely."[6] Soon after, Fitzgerald introduced a character named Frederick E. Paramore into *The Beautiful and Damned*. A tedious social worker, prig, and teetotaler, the novel's Paramore in a brief appearance is seduced into taking a cocktail, becomes "perceptibly drunk," demonstrates his condition "by simulating funny-paper staggers," and exits "crawling rapidly toward the kitchen on his hands and knees."

Now they were yoked together. By 1937 Paramore had been a Hollywood screenwriter for eight years, and while Fitzgerald was hoping to earn his first credit, Paramore already had twenty. Accustomed to independence, Fitzgerald regarded his script as a proprietary work of art. A veteran screenwriter, Paramore regarded it as novice work, a rough draft needing overhaul.

Glancing at it, Paramore "blandly informed me," Fitzgerald wrote bitterly, "that you were going to write the whole thing over yourself, kindly including my best scenes. . . ."[7] To add to the misunderstanding, Fitzgerald had been either drunk or hung over when they met to discuss the script: "We got off to a bad start and I think you are under certain misapprehensions founded more on my state of mind and body last Friday than upon the real situation." Seeing their joint project not as a collaboration but a contest for control, he had plunged into battle, "tooth and nail"—a battle he was unlikely to win.

Two weeks later he wrote of Paramore more benignly to Scottie: "An old friend, Ted Paramore, has joined me on the picture in fixing up much of the movie construction, at which I am still a semi-amateur, though I won't be that much longer."[8] Evidently they had reached a *détente*. The bulk of his outrage would be reserved for the producer of *Three Comrades,* Joseph Mankiewicz.

As producer, Mankiewicz had final say. Fitzgerald may have chafed at submitting his work to a younger man, as close in age to Scottie as to himself. Worse yet, Mankiewicz like Paramore was a practiced screenwriter with almost twenty credits. To Fitzgerald's distress, he too set about rewriting *Three Comrades.*

Fitzgerald's anguish illustrates his difficulty adjusting to screenwriting. When Mankiewicz sent back his "third batch" of revisions, Fitzgerald greeted them with "mixed feelings," remarking that "my own type of writing doesn't survive being written over so thoroughly and there are certain pages out of which the rhythm has vanished." But to Mankiewicz the rhythm of

Fitzgerald's "own type of writing" was irrelevant; MGM was not publishing a novel. Despite his annoyance, Fitzgerald restrained his anger, commenting only that "I think that sometimes you've changed without improving."[9]

Then Mankiewicz, or "Monkeybitch" as Fitzgerald preferred, sent along his next batch of changes. Fitzgerald was appalled: "To say I'm disillusioned is putting it mildly," he began, prefacing four typed pages of detailed objections to Mankiewicz's changes: "For nineteen years, with two years out for sickness, I've written best-selling entertainment, and my dialogue is supposedly right up at the top. But I learn from the script that you've suddenly decided that it isn't good dialogue and you can take a few hours off and do much better." He concluded with a sad plea: "Oh, Joe, can't producers ever be wrong? I'm a good writer, honest—I thought you were going to play fair."[10]

His complaint was again beside the point: a writer's wounded sensibility would scarcely trouble a workaday producer trying to cobble together a profitable film. *Three Comrades* "will be the most colossal disappointment of Metro's year," Fitzgerald predicted, perhaps hopefully. "The producer wrote it over. The censors hacked at it. . . . So what we have left has very little to do with the script on which people still congratulate me."[11] (*Three Comrades* earned a handsome profit, however.)

Years later, Mankiewicz offered his version of the dispute: "I didn't count on Scott for dialogue. There could be no greater disservice done him than to have actors read his novels aloud as if they were plays. . . . In a novel the dialogue enters through the mind. The reader endows it with a certain quality. Dialogue spoken from the stage enters through the ear rather than the mind. It has an immediate emotional impact. Scott's dialogue lacked bite, color, rhythm."[12] Both cited "rhythm," but plainly meaning different things. "If I go down at all in literary history, in a footnote," Mankiewicz later observed, "it will be as the swine who rewrote F. Scott Fitzgerald."[13]

As a difficult collaborator on this first major assignment, Fitzgerald damaged himself. One can understand why he and Mankiewicz did not work together again. "Joe Mankiewicz asked me to come back and work with him," Fitzgerald later claimed, "but our relations were so definitely unpleasant after he decided to rewrite 'Three Comrades' himself that I don't think I could do it." Less tactfully, he classified Mankiewicz as "ignorant and vulgar."[14]

He alienated others as well. During his two earlier Hollywood ventures he had indulged in exhibitionist embarrassments, one of them observed by

MGM's head of production, Irving Thalberg, who had little use for drunks.[15] Now, chastened by adversity and eager to stay in favor, he had resolved on sobriety. But his difficulties with Paramore and Mankiewicz on *Three Comrades* exposed another frailty, one Guthrie had noted earlier: an aggressive self-assurance. "My tendency," he admitted, "was to get myself into a constant struggle with the producers about how I wanted a picture to be. Naturally, I made some enemies."[16]

When after eighteen months MGM dropped his contract, Fitzgerald became a freelance screenwriter. During the next two years he picked up occasional assignments but never again worked full-time for a studio. When his first agent found little work for him, he switched to another, Leland Hayward, at whose request he produced a survey of his screenwriting experience, checkered with the names of ill-disposed producers. In addition to Mankiewicz there was Bernie Hyman, for example, who

> . . . quite definitely doesn't like me. . . . Hunt [Stromberg] and I reached a dead end on "The Women." We wore each other out. . . . My relations with [John] Stahl were just a little too difficult so there's no use trying anything there. . . . Wanger is out absolutely. . . . Sam Wood and I had always gotten along before, but during this week that I worked there [United Artists] on "Raffles" everything got a little strained and I don't think that he would welcome me as a collaborator. . . . I think that Dave [Selznick] is probably under the impression that I am a novelist first and can't get the idea as to what pictures are about.[17]

He had accumulated these antagonists and skeptics in little over two years.

When Hayward too had difficulty finding work for him, Fitzgerald suspected conspiracy. ". . . There is a kind of cabal that goes on between producers around a backgammon table," he had been told, "and I have an idea that some such sinister finger is upon me. . . . I have a strong intuition that all is not well with my reputation and I'd like to know what is being said or not said." This seems mildly paranoid, but Fitzgerald had no doubt been pegged as an uncomfortable collaborator. ". . . In certain quarters," he confessed, "I am considered a lame duck or hard to get along with. Or even that I drink. . . ."[18]

His Hollywood sobriety had lasted only three months, if that. In October 1937, in a semi-comic, wholly irresponsible episode, he went on a binge drunk before and during a flying visit to Chicago, made a fool, nuisance, and hazard of himself and, still drunk, was denied permission to board a return flight. Finally back in Los Angeles, he absented himself from MGM, pleading illness, put himself under treatment for withdrawal, and dropped out of circulation for a week. An established pattern of controlled drinking interrupted by sprees and medically supervised withdrawal continued in Hollywood. Facing stress or disappointment, he could not resist the bottle.

When his MGM contract lapsed, he was discouraged and anxious. "I wanted to quit for a while," he told Hayward, "health bad and I was depressed about the Metro business."[19] "Health bad" meant heavy drinking. Almost immediately, however, he was hired to write a screenplay for a film about the Dartmouth Winter Carnival. Though not a long-term contract, it was an excellent opportunity; at $1,500 a week, the assignment paid even more than MGM's $1,250, and he stood to gain a screen credit.

Teamed with him was a young Dartmouth graduate with good Hollywood connections, Budd Schulberg. As they flew east together in early February to reconnoiter the 1939 Carnival for material and ideas, Schulberg offered to share a bottle of champagne. What followed, for Fitzgerald, was a week-long drunk in New York and Hanover, followed by a week in a New York hospital.

Outliving Fitzgerald by almost seventy years, Schulberg would give multiple accounts of this disastrous week, the fullest in his 1950 novel *The Disenchanted*.[20] Its portrait of Fitzgerald resembles Guthrie's. When drinking, the Fitzgerald character, "Manley Halliday," talks about himself endlessly, boasts, and reminisces:

> "... Ever seen anybody drink himself sober, Shep? I did once, over at the Lido, ever tell you how I. ..."
> ... "Yes," Shep said, "I'm sure you did. I think you must've told me every goddam thing you've done since you were three."

Like Guthrie's Fitzgerald, Halliday punctuates his talk with the vocative "baby" ("We gotta stick together, baby. We're in this together, baby").[21] When drunk he alternates between weepiness and truculence: during his sodden week he provokes several fistfights.

And like Fitzgerald at Dartmouth, Halliday is summarily fired by the film's producer and sent back to New York. There—unshaved, sleepless, hung over, draped in the rumpled clothes he had worn night and day for a week, and refused accommodation at a succession of hotels—Fitzgerald finally had himself delivered to Doctors Hospital for another course of withdrawal.

Schulberg too was fired, but his youth and connections earned him a reprieve. Rehired, he earned a screen credit for *Winter Carnival.* A credit for Fitzgerald might have revived his foundering screenwriting career.

Instead, two months later he was back in Doctors Hospital after another bender. This time it had begun in California, where he assaulted his mistress Sheilah Graham in a struggle for a handgun, and continued back east, where he flew to pick up Zelda from her Asheville sanitarium for a holiday in Cuba. In Cuba he was beaten up at a cockfight, trying to rescue the bird, while he cradled it in his arms, shouting 'You sons of bitches.'" It continued in New York, where he "was in a fight with a waiter" at the Algonquin "and tried to throw him down the stairs," and then assaulted a taxi driver, earning himself a black eye. "It was a sucker blow," Fitzgerald complained, though the match with a sober cabby was probably an uneven contest. Eventually he was taken to Bellevue and finally Doctors Hospital for another drying-out week. Zelda returned to Asheville on her own. "Your eye was most distressing," she commiserated.[22]

Worse than his eye was another consequence. His altercation with the cab driver had resulted from a fare to Harold Ober's home in Scarsdale. For years Ober had acted as his banker, extending hundreds of interest-free advances against stories yet to be sold, or yet to be written, while patiently tolerating his erratic conduct. Thanking a friend for her assistance during the latest binge, Fitzgerald offered that "if there was any damage take care of it either directly with me or with Harold Ober with whom I have a running account and who I am afraid, after twenty years, will not be very much shocked by any of my enormities."[23]

If not shocked, Ober took note. Closely following the Winter Carnival collapse, the latest fiasco persuaded him that Fitzgerald was finished as a writer. His drinking was uncontrollable, his stories increasingly difficult to sell to high-paying magazines. Fitzgerald attributed his latest binge to "an attempt to keep up my strength for an effort of which I was not capable," but

Ober was doubtful: Fitzgerald had been more or less drunk for a decade. Feeling pressed for funds, with two sons bound for Harvard, he shut down further advances.[24]

Ober's decision left Fitzgerald "flabbergasted"—stunned, baffled, resentful. "I think something to do with it is the fact that almost every time I have come to New York lately I have just taken Zelda somewhere and have gone on more or less of a binge," he explained to Perkins, as if Ober were unreasonable to object to the undergraduate benders of his forty-year-old client.[25]

For years Fitzgerald had presumed on Ober's tolerance and generosity. With Fitzgerald in California and Scottie in school back east, Ober and his wife Anne had made their comfortable home in Westchester County the homeless girl's refuge during school breaks and summers. Since 1935 she had spent a few scattered weeks with her father and many months with the Obers, and after Ober cut off Fitzgerald's credit they continued to harbor her. When she learned of her father's death in Hollywood eighteen months later, Scottie was staying with the Obers and had not seen her father for well over a year.[26]

F ollowing this second 1939 breakdown, he withdrew from circulation for three months. To Perkins, requesting a loan, he cabled, "HAVE BEEN WRITING IN BED WITH TUBERCULOSIS UNDER DOCTORS NURSES CARE [SINCE] ARRIVING WEST." To *Esquire*'s editor Arnold Gingrich, "BEEN SICK IN BED FOUR MONTHS." Requesting a loan from Gerald Murphy, he cabled, "WAS TAKEN ILL OUT HERE LAST APRIL AND CONFINED TO BED FIVE MONTHS." Murphy immediately wired, "MONEY READY WHERE SHALL I SEND IT[?]," but when Fitzgerald in follow-up letters harped on his medical woes, Murphy—long acquainted with Fitzgerald's drinking problem and having lost two young sons to disease—responded sharply, "Don't think me without heart:—but just as you—so have I—seen much illness around me."[27]

Directing his Hollywood agent to list him as temporarily unavailable, Fitzgerald lounged in a pleasant rented house in rural Encino where free from studio employment he began plotting a fifth novel. When he announced himself once again available to the studios, few offers appeared:

"Swanie [H. N. Swanson, his first agent] turned down a dozen jobs for me when I was sick in bed—but there just haven't been any since the [lung] cavity began to heal." His expenses continued unabated, and in October he wrote to his landlady, "Things are still so very uncertain with me" that he could afford to pay only a half-month's rent. He began marketing an unwritten novel, hoping to persuade *Collier's* to serialize it and in the meantime provide an advance.[28]

In April he had hired a secretary, a displaced young New Yorker named Frances Kroll, to type up his handwritten drafts and manage clerical and domestic chores, and for the next twenty months she faithfully served him as secretary, companion, and factotum. She quickly discovered that her new employer was not a consumptive but an alcoholic:

> The first thing I learned was that the water tumbler on his night stand was to be left alone. I had made an attempt to freshen it and he took the glass from me. The sweetish odor was not stale water, as I thought, but gin. . . .
>
> Next I learned that the "fever" that kept him in bed was really an alcoholic haze through which he was aimlessly drifting. . . .[29]

Kroll paid his bills and balanced his checkbook, ordered his groceries and sundries and sometimes picked them up from the market on her way to work: "The cigarettes that he chain-smoked were filtered Raleighs. [He bought a toaster for her with Raleigh coupons.] He ordered the gin—Gordon's—secretly, and managed to have it delivered from the small convenience market at the foot of Amestoy Avenue when I wasn't around. It was part of his deceptive game of 'not drinking.'" Despite the "not drinking," Kroll was tasked with disposing of empty gin bottles to prevent Fitzgerald's landlord from noticing them overflowing the trash barrels. Loading them into burlap sacks, she dropped them into ravines along the Sepulveda Canyon road, a clandestine operation figuring in one of his last stories, "Pat Hobby's College Days." "If it is of any interest to you," he informed Ober during this time, "I haven't had a drink in two months. . . ."[30]

His days were leisurely, with late starts, little regularity, and no urgency, Kroll recalled: "There were days when I arrived and he was not ready. I

waited around. . . . I would walk out into the garden, landscaped with beds
of rose bushes. . . . On fair days, I would sit on the grass and enjoy the sun,
or leaf through a newspaper. After awhile, Scott would come out wearing a
terry cloth bathrobe over a sweater, over pajamas. We'd stroll about, then
go in for some lunch."[31] He talked about the projected novel, planned and
plotted it, outlined it, jotted down pages of notes. Actual writing lagged. By
September, though not ready to submit even a short sample for another two
months, he had compiled sixty pages of notes and outlines for a novel of
Gatsby's length. "Part of the delay in getting down to real work was procras-
tination," Kroll concluded, "and part was just physical exhaustion."

In late September, he sent a synopsis to *Collier's*. Its fiction editor, Kenneth Littauer, declined to commit himself until seeing the first fifteen thousand words "in more or less finished form." Fitzgerald haggled over terms
and the writing went slowly until, eager for reassurance and cash, in November he sent Littauer not the requested fifteen thousand words, but the
shorter first chapter.

Littauer cabled, "FIRST SIX THOUSAND PRETTY CRYPTIC THEREFORE
DISAPPOINTING. . . . CAN WE DEFER VERDICT UNTIL FURTHER DEVELOP-
MENT OF STORY? IF IT HAS TO BE NOW IT HAS TO BE NO." Fitzgerald re-
sponded snippily: "NO HARD FEELINGS THERE HAS NEVER BEEN AN EDITOR
WITH PANTS ON SINCE GEORGE LORIMER"—an inapt cut, as Littauer had
been awarded France's Croix de Guerre and the American Distinguished
Service Cross for valor in World War 1.[32]

But Littauer got off lightly. Someone in skirts and closer at hand suffered Fitzgerald's raging disappointment.

He had met Sheilah Graham in July 1937, soon after arriving in Hollywood. She was Ukrainian Jewish and English, from a working-class
London family. Ambitious, enterprising, attractive, hardworking, shrewd,
and not over-scrupulous, she had climbed from Stepney Green poverty to
become a chorus girl, then journalist; in 1933 she had ventured to America.
In just two years she found her way to an enviable post as syndicated Hollywood gossip-writer for the North American Newspaper Alliance, her column soon distributed to sixty-five newspapers.

It helped that she had been sleeping with the syndicate's general manager, John Wheeler. When she met Fitzgerald she had just legally extracted herself from marriage to an Englishman twenty-five years her senior, which had never interfered with her amours in either England or America. Shedding the husband, she soon become engaged to the Marquess of Donegall, who had been courting her for several years. It was an impressive rise from London's East End to prospective marchioness, but she was only half-hearted about Donegall and did not intend to sit alone in Hollywood while back in England he worked to overcome his mother's objections to a non-U woman, a divorced one at that. (Another ambitious divorcée had just seduced Edward VIII from the British throne.)

Sheilah Graham was a self-created woman, her personal history a work of fiction. For years she had pretended to a fashionable background and genteel education. Her name itself was an invention: she was actually Lily Sheil. "My mother was a woman who lied all her life," her daughter later observed.[33] Graham would eventually write three books about her affair with Fitzgerald. In the first and best-known, *Beloved Infidel,* she recounts that, as they danced together for the first time, he asked her age. "'Twenty-seven,' I said, lying by a year." But even her admission of lying was a lie; she was thirty-two.[34]

Beloved Infidel describes an earlier "terrible moment" at St. Moritz, the Swiss mountain resort: ". . . I had gone skating with Lord Long of Wraxall and his mother. They introduced me to a lovely dark-eyed woman. . . . 'Let's skate together, shall we?' she suggested with a smile. Arm in arm we moved rhythmically across the ice. We were quite alone. Without slackening her pace she said, 'You're an adventuress, aren't you?'"[35] But mostly Graham's imposture succeeded. The Marquess of Donegall had no idea that his future marchioness was a cockney from a poor Jewish family.

They were engaged only briefly, however. Remaining on the lookout, she quickly found a more interesting prospect. She was on Donegall's arm at a Hollywood party held to celebrate their engagement when she first saw Fitzgerald.

Their first conversation came a little later, at a Hollywood nightspot and casino. In all three of Graham's accounts of this fateful evening, she describes their immediate rapturous connection. In *The Real F. Scott Fitzgerald* she recalled, "Our attunement to one another . . . was something instantaneous and without calculation. We danced and danced, waiting on the floor for the music to begin again. The rest of the people at the Clover Club seemed to be murals. . . . When the orchestra stopped, we returned reluctantly to our table, but with eyes only for each other."

"Without calculation" seems unlikely. ". . . Despite Scott's commitments to the past [that is, Zelda] and mine to the future, there must have remained in each of us a receptiveness to new romantic risk and experience," Graham remarked with discreet understatement.[36]

She made no secret of her own receptiveness. "I was a girl on the town and enjoyed it," she recalled of her first two years in Hollywood. Intrigued by his reputation and pallid good looks, she quickly marked Fitzgerald as an eligible conquest. Just arrived in California, he was lonely and craved womanly company. Laura Guthrie would not have been surprised, and Graham too would discover that "there had to be a girl in his life" and he "needed more than the companionship of friends. The center of his life always had to be a woman."[37]

Beyond mutual attraction, they had little in common. Though Graham was eight years younger and careful of propriety, her sexual résumé was more extensive and she aggressively initiated their affair. At their first meeting it was she who asked him to dance, she who soon after pushed herself into a dinner with him and the visiting Scottie, and she who at the end of that evening pulled him into her house, in a seduction glowingly described in both *The Real F. Scott Fitzgerald* and, as follows (condensed), in *Beloved Infidel:*

> He stood at the door, saying good-by. I felt utterly lonely and on the point of tears. . . . He said good night. I did not want him to go. . . . In the half light, as he stood there, his face was beautiful. . . . I wanted desperately to recapture the enchantment that had been and I heard myself whisper, "Please don't go, come in," and I drew him in and he came in and as he came in he kissed me. . . . it was as though this was as it should be, must be, inevitable and foreordained.[38]

And in Hollywood terms, a fade-out.

Fitzgerald knew Graham was no debutante but perhaps flattered himself that, given her just-ended marriage to a much older man, he was the first to awaken her desire. Casually asking about earlier lovers, he was startled when she tossed out a rough estimate: eight. Actually she had lost count, and "this struck me as a good approximation." She had slept around before and during her fifteen-year marriage, for both recreation and advancement. "I had been married and had been on the stage and had worked in New York," and in Hollywood, too, she might have added, for she had recently had an affair with the director King Vidor.[39] (Later, both children of her second marriage would suspect their fathers to be men other than her husband.)

Graham was shocked in turn when after Fitzgerald's death she "took the photograph I had given him of myself from its frame. Scrawled across the back was the inscription, 'Portrait of a Prostitute.'"[40] Probably memorializing a drunken rage, the slur nonetheless suggests Fitzgerald's uneasiness with her amorous past. In a calmer hour he would write a fifty-six-line stanzaic poem on the subject. For example:

> Some kisses nature doesn't plan—
> She works in such a sketchy way—
> The child, though father to the man,
> Must be instructed how to play.
> What traffic your lips had with mine
> Don't lie in any virgin's ken—
> I found the oldest, richest wine
> On lips once soft for other men.[41]

The tag concluding each stanza, "other men," stresses Fitzgerald's role as latecomer to her bed. Though ostensibly a poem celebrating Graham's graduate education in lovemaking, its emphasis on her many liaisons betrays divided feelings.

Despite the fairy-tale prospect of becoming Lady Donegall, Graham for her part was doing well in Hollywood and knew that its promiscuous mix of high *chic* and vulgar glitz, of fantasy, ambition, breezy manners, and crude money-making, was more in her line than the clannish circles of titled English aristocracy. She had visited England only once since arriving in America, to see a divorce lawyer, and had no wish to return.

As frequently evident in her several memoirs, she had a generous opinion of her own desirability. "Both Zelda and I were glamorous women. . . . men were often falling in love with me," she remarks. Asking rhetorically, what did Fitzgerald see when first encountering her at the engagement party?—she answers, "a woman . . . who was at the center of the party, radiating the sense of her own beauty and importance that is part of every Fitzgerald heroine's nature." Fitzgerald plainly found her, if not ravishing, tolerably attractive.[42]

Neither was in a position to be over-particular. Despite her many lovers, Graham had attracted few serious suitors in Hollywood, and Fitzgerald at forty was no film Romeo nor even a prominent director like King Vidor. "He was married, with no hope of a divorce, an author whose books were not in demand," she recalled. "He often drank to excess. There were not too many women who could be happy with these circumstances." He himself lamented, a year after arriving in Hollywood, that "what I am doing here is the last tired effort of a man who once did something finer and better."[43]

He nonetheless struck Graham as a promising combination of attractive, unattached, and willing. By the time she understood that he was unlikely to divorce Zelda, she had fallen into a "hypnotic devotion." She would dearly have liked to bear his children, and put up with drunkenness and abuse that would have sent most legal wives out the door.[44]

When *Collier's* Littauer turned down *The Last Tycoon,* Fitzgerald's drunken abuse did send her out the door, temporarily. In both *The Real Scott Fitzgerald* and in richer detail *Beloved Infidel,* Graham narrates a confused incident involving hoboes, tomato soup, broken china, taunting, screaming, slapping, kicking, police, a hidden gun, threats, harassing phone calls and letters and telegrams, and theft of a fox-fur jacket, all fueled by frustration, disappointment, and gin. It might have filmed well—part melodrama, part Marx Brothers.

Graham walked out and stayed away for a month, then relented. Fitzgerald promised to stop drinking: "Don't just take my words, Sheilah. Test me."[45] Their reconciliation and his pledge provide the turning point in the first, "romanticized version" of her affair with Fitzgerald, *Beloved Infidel.* "This was our happiest time," she reports of their last, calmer, year together. "Scott did not drink."[46]

At least not often. One evening, treating Frances Kroll and her brother to dinner at a Sunset Boulevard restaurant, he ordered a bottle of wine. Neither of his guests drank. Proceeding to drain the bottle himself, "Scott did most of the talking" and eventually "started to ramble" about Princeton. "By the end of the dinner . . . he was glowing." Inviting the Krolls back to his apartment and bringing out a bottle of gin, "he was convivial with glass in hand, even as his eyes grew glazed."[47] Graham was out of town.

Mostly, however, he was a private drinker. Kroll learned his habits well, spending her days with him, taking dictation, doing his typing and bookkeeping, running errands, fixing bacon and eggs for his breakfast, and heating canned turtle soup for his lunch. "The drinking was under control," she testified of his last year. ". . . From the number of bottles that were trashed since the move [from Encino to a Hollywood apartment in May 1940], his consumption appeared to be minimal."[48]

With Fitzgerald largely sober after their January 1940 reconciliation, he and Graham settled into a quiet domestic routine. They maintained separate apartments but spent evenings and weekends together, comfortable and sedate, a slightly irregular version of an old married couple: she a loyal, protective, encouraging ersatz wife, he an eccentric valetudinarian. They had begun Sheilah's educational self-improvement program, described in her memoir *College of One,* with an ambitious reading list he spent hours compiling; it was actually a college of two, for his own college education had been fitful. The project brought out his pedagogic strain, mostly wasted until then on lecturing letters to Scottie at Vassar, and in his last year he devoted as much time to Sheilah's curriculum and tutorials as to his novel.

She played tennis three times a week, but "he was too tired and ill for tennis or swimming." He lacked energy and money for Sunset Strip nightlife. There were occasional dinners out or quiet evenings at the homes of friends. Living a discreet block apart after he moved into Hollywood, he and Graham shared a maid who cooked their joint evening meal, alternating between apartments. Afterwards they might walk down the street to

Schwab's "to buy the morning papers, flip over the magazines, and drink a chocolate malted milk sitting on the high stools at the counter."[49] In June, like two small-town tourists, they visited the Golden Gate Exposition on San Francisco's Treasure Island, where they bumped into Humphrey Bogart.

"For the first time for both of us," Graham recalled, "we were leading average lives, working by day, reading or walking in the evening after the same dinner prepared for us every night by our housekeeper, a thin T-bone steak (at 35 cents a pound!), a baked potato, peas, and a grapefruit jelly."[50]

For Graham it was almost too average. She had enjoyed her sabbatical from Fitzgerald in the weeks following his violent breakdown: "It was pleasant, those first days of 1940, to be free to enjoy all that Hollywood had to offer—to go out again with young men, to be once more a part of the movie colony. . . . And it was fun to flirt again, to dine each evening at another restaurant, table-hopping and gratifyingly conspicuous, to dance each evening at [a] different nightclub." After they reconciled she had trouble adjusting to "our new quietude." "Sometimes in that last year of tranquillity," she admitted, ". . . I was restless, wishing for a little more excitement in our lives."[51]

"My restlessness was fitful and short-lived," she quickly added, though recalling vividly when it had struck one early spring day as she drove to Fitzgerald's house in Encino, "where everything was blooming in the premature heat." Looming ahead, perhaps, lay an evening with a Keats ode or early Henry James novel. "Before my time with Scott," she reflected wistfully, "there had always been several men delighted to take me out to dinner or to the theater or to special events, or to flirt with me."[52] "But I knew that this quiet existence was good for Scott and his work," she sighed.[53] It was wholly unlike his and Zelda's noisy lives in the 1920s.

In that final calm year, 1940, he worked on several short-term screenwriting contracts, but his ambitions were focused on two larger projects. Writing a screenplay loosely based on his 1931 story "Babylon Revisited" occupied him off and on through the summer, and he had resumed his Hollywood novel, dormant since *Collier's* rejected it. Picking it up again early in 1940, after "The Great Binge" as Graham called his final bender, he worked on it before turning to the "Babylon Revisited" screenplay, returning to the novel in the autumn.

"Scott's invalidism disappeared when he was doing something he liked to do," Kroll observed, and Graham noted, "In his last thirteen months of sobriety the TB rather mysteriously disappeared." After a year's planning, plotting, outlining, diagraming and note-jotting, he began writing in earnest.[54]

". . . It was now urgent that he get it all down on paper," Kroll recalled, knowing in retrospect just how urgent.[55] Though living modestly and temperately, he was just scraping by, largely on stories for *Esquire*. Even more pressing than money, though, was his desire to restore his reputation with a masterful novel of the movie industry.

I t was a clear step forward," Perkins wrote of the unfinished novel after Fitzgerald's death. ". . . It has a kind of wisdom in it, and nobody ever penetrated beneath the surface of the movie world to any such degree. It was to have been a very remarkable book."[56]

The year after Fitzgerald's death, his drafts and notes, organized by Edmund Wilson, were published as *The Last Tycoon*. Praising its "power" and the "intensity and reality" of the protagonist, Wilson asserted that "*The Last Tycoon* is thus, even in its imperfect state, Fitzgerald's most mature piece of work" and "far and away the best novel we have had about Hollywood."[57] Scribner's catalog blurb—getting the narrator's name wrong, mistaking her for the heroine, and inventing a marriage that never happens—announced that it "might well have been his greatest novel." *The New York Times*'s J. Donald Adams asserted that "one would be blind indeed not to see that it would have been Fitzgerald's best novel and a very fine one." In the *Saturday Review,* Stephen Vincent Benét concurred: "Had Fitzgerald been permitted to finish the book, I think there is no doubt that it would have added a major character and a major novel to American fiction. As it is, *The Last Tycoon* . . . shows the full powers of its author, at their height and at their best."[58]

The critical merit of such panegyrics remains moot: Fitzgerald left behind less an unfinished novel than notes and sketches for a novel. Only seventeen of a projected thirty episodes had been written, and even they would have been revised, rewritten, and reorganized; some dropped and replaced. A week before his death he predicted a complete first draft "some time after the 15th of January [1941]," but his forecasts were invariably over-optimistic. With almost half the novel yet to be written, a full draft lay at least months ahead.[59]

Amidst choral praise for *The Last Tycoon* fragment, one dissenting voice was, no surprise, Hemingway's. Jealous, disdainful, blunt, sometimes petty, he was seldom guilty of overpraising fellow writers. Yet if nothing else, his overbearing self-confidence insulated him from crowd opinion.

"I am happy the book had such a fine review by J. Donald Adams in the Sunday Times," he wrote to Perkins, but—

> . . . To someone who knew Scott truly well and is in the same trade, the book has that deadness, the one quality about which nothing can be done in writing, as though it were a slab of bacon on which mold had grown. . . .
>
> When you wrote Martha [Gellhorn, Hemingway's third wife], you said that Hollywood had not hurt Scott. I guess perhaps it had not be-cause he was long past being hurt before he went there. His heart died in him in France, and soon after he came back, and the rest of him just went on dying progressively after that. Reading the book was like see-ing an old baseball pitcher with nothing left in his arm coming out and working with his intelligence for a few innings before he is knocked out of the box.[60]

The analogies to moldy bacon and baseball pitcher were more poetic than rigorously analytical; but Hemingway was, as he modestly put it, "in the same trade," and his criticisms—extending well beyond the lines quoted—forcefully challenged the "unfinished masterpiece" argument.

Shortly before his death, Fitzgerald had criticized Hemingway's own latest novel, comparing it unfavorably to *A Farewell to Arms. For Whom the Bell Tolls,* he told Zelda, "doesn't seem to have the tensity or the freshness nor has it the inspired poetic moments."[61] Each had detected the other's fading powers.

*T*he Last Tycoon's love interest is commonly said to be based on Sheilah Graham. Graham herself said it repeatedly. "Almost as overwhelming to me [as Fitzgerald's 1940 sobriety] was my discovery that I was in Scott's novel," she disclosed in *Beloved Infidel*. In fact she was (she claimed) the heroine, Kathleen: "He had never told me he was writing about me—that Stahr, the central character of the book, would fall in love with an English girl who was based on me. . . . When Scott read to me, night after night, what he had written during the day, I began to realize that the love affair between Kathleen and Stahr—the very heart of the novel—was *our* love affair."[62]

A forgivable vanity, but overstated. Though borrowing details from Graham's background and their early encounters, Fitzgerald on first meeting her had felt nothing of Stahr's immediate, almost mystical connection to Kathleen. With Stahr's first glimpse of Kathleen he sees "the face of his dead wife, identical even to the expression." His lost Minna rises from her grave: "Across the four feet of moonlight the eyes he knew looked back at him, a curl blew a little on a familiar forehead, the smile lingered changed a little according to pattern, the lips parted—the same. An awful fear went over him and he wanted to cry aloud. Back from the still sour room, the muffled glide of the limousine hearse, the falling concealing flowers, from out there in the dark—here now warm and glowing." Graham was struck by her own "eerie resemblance" to the young Zelda.[63] Photographs fail to reveal much likeness.

What Fitzgerald actually seems to have seen in Graham at first glimpse, as he sat lonely and ill at ease at a smoky chattering party of Hollywood wits, was an unattached blonde on the make. Zelda, the belle of Montgomery, had been fresh, dashing, sparkling—a prize. Graham was available and eager.

In *Beloved Infidel*, she quotes a long passage from *The Last Tycoon* describing Stahr's meeting with Kathleen at the screenwriters' ball, a charged moment of erotic attraction: "But she was deep in it with him, no matter what the words were. Her eyes invited him to a romantic communion of unbelievable intensity." Graham was touched: "Was this not our encounter at the Writers Guild dance, as magically recreated by Scott?"[64]

But rather than magically recreated, it was recycled. As often, Fitzgerald was "stripping" a passage from an earlier story. In "Magnetism," a dozen years earlier, he had described an encounter: ". . . if they rushed toward each other there would be a romantic communion of almost unbelievable intensity."

In *The Real F. Scott Fitzgerald,* Graham points to another passage in *The Last Tycoon,* describing their immediate mutual attraction: "Stahr's eyes and

Kathleen's met and tangled. For an instant they made love as no one ever dares to do after. The glance was slower than an embrace, more urgent than a call."[65] But in "The Love Boat," a man and woman also "locked eyes," and "For a moment they made love as no one ever dares to do after. Their glance was closer than an embrace, more urgent than a call." The story had appeared in the *Post* in 1927, ten years before he met Graham.

Z elda and Sheilah brought different gifts to Fitzgerald. Graham was later reassured by Edmund Wilson that she had not been Fitzgerald's "mistress. You were his second wife."[66] There is some truth in this: she provided Fitzgerald with routine, stability, encouragement—all of which he now needed, and all of which Zelda flagrantly lacked. Sheilah found his California houses and apartments for him, shared her housemaid and cook with him, deferred to him, praised him, sent him cut flowers, played eager pupil to his earnest schoolmastering. She kept his name current by frequent mentions in her widely read columns, plugging his screenwriting assignments on six different films. Eventually she even managed to bring his drinking under control.

What she could not do was reanimate a tired imagination or arouse the "unbelievable intensity" of 1919. It was not, of course, wholly her fault. Fitzgerald was not twenty-one, ardent and effervescent, but forty, chastened, and subdued. In the first of her columns mentioning him, she chaffed: "Personal nomination for the unhappiest looking male in Hollywood—Author Scott Fitzgerald." He could no longer respond with the ardor and excitement of twenty years earlier. ". . . He loved me with all that was left of his capacity for love," she later admitted sadly.[67]

The young Zelda had been a whirlwind of excitement, a white-hot source of romance, desire, pursuit, longing, ambition, hope, misery, despair, triumph. Her personality "was always a vast surprise." Her very defects—her recklessness, instability, unpredictability, and irresponsibility—were stirring. She fascinated. "She is without doubt the most brilliant & most beautiful young woman I've ever known," a New York friend wrote in 1921. "Winston Churchill was her slave (in conversation) for several hours at a party," Fitzgerald later claimed. In a much-quoted witticism, Ring Lardner

remarked, "Mr. Fitzgerald is a novelist and Mrs. Fitzgerald is a novelty."
"She was alive with sultry excitement," a friend remarked of her during her
Montgomery days. "She knew no conventional bounds. She was a veritable
witch of the Southland."[68]

None of this could be said of Sheilah Graham. Like many women in
Hollywood she was aggressive, industrious, opportunistic. Stronger and
steadier than Fitzgerald, she was in practical terms a vastly better helpmeet
than Zelda and provided the companionship, managerial skills, and domesticity he needed, channeling his disorderly life into regular and sober habits. But she was too conventional, *vin ordinaire,* to generate much emotion
beyond comfort and gratitude.

Two bath anecdotes suggest their different influence. In 1920 or 1921,
a Princeton friend, Lawton Campbell, visited the Fitzgeralds at New York's
Plaza Hotel:

> When I entered, the room was bedlam. Breakfast dishes were all about;
> the bed was unmade; books and papers were scattered here and there;
> trays were filled with cigarette butts and liquor glasses from the night
> before. Everything was untidy and helter-skelter. Scott was dressing and
> Zelda was luxuriating in the bathtub. With the door partly open, she
> carried on a steady flow of conversation: "Scott," she called out, "tell
> Lawton 'bout . . . tell Lawton what I said when. . . . Now . . . tell Lawton
> what I did. . . . This badinage went on until Zelda appeared at the bath-
> room door, buttoning up her dress.[69]

Characteristic Zelda: the room a chaotic mess, she lounging in the bath with
the door open, casually regaling a visitor with chat about once and future
mischief.

Fitzgerald "had great difficulty in finding the time and place to write
with Zelda around," Campbell observed. "Yet, Zelda was absolutely essential to him in those days. She was both his inspiration and his anathema."

Another bath anecdote, this time Graham. Early in their affair, she recalled, "I was in his bungalow at the Garden of Allah [a Hollywood hotel]
taking a bath. Scott came into the bathroom carrying a little pillow, which
he placed carefully under my head without looking at my submerged body.

He then slipped out to leave me to my comfort and to my deep appreciation of this small gesture of tenderness and consideration. It bound me to
him—forever."[70] What thrilled her as much as the pillow was that he tactfully averted his eyes from her nude body, though at this point they had
been sleeping together for several months. Despite her history of liaisons,
Graham clung to a curious modesty, almost prudery. "I don't believe we ever
saw one another completely naked," she disclosed. "Because I have suffered
life-long embarrassment concerning the largeness of my breasts, I always
kept on my bra. As for Scott, I retain the image of him walking about the
bedroom in his boxer shorts and sleeveless undershirt"—an image suggesting not two eager lovers, but elderly grandparents turning in.[71]

   Zelda had no such inhibitions. "Do you remember," Fitzgerald recalled
in a 1935 poem addressed to her,

   That I hated to swim naked from the rocks
   While you liked absolutely nothing better?[72]

Zelda had been the risk-taker and daredevil, the stimulus, the "great and
moving" experience never repeated. Perhaps at forty he was too drained for
a great experience; or perhaps Sheilah Graham was simply not the woman
to ignite one. With *The Last Tycoon*'s romance between Monroe Stahr and
Kathleen Moore, Fitzgerald was laboring to conjure up an amorous intensity he had never felt for Graham, and had felt for no one at all for years.

   Rather than excitement, Graham contributed a cockney earthiness.
In *Beloved Infidel* she scoffed at Fitzgerald's "straitlaced, almost puritanical
streak," with examples. "He *had* been shocked when I spoke so casually to
him of other men I had known," she complained, evidently using "known"
in the biblical sense. "At parties he was acutely uncomfortable if anyone
told a suggestive story. . . . He winced each time I forgot myself and used
any of the colorful language I had picked up from my friends in the British
aristocracy, or from the chorus girls backstage at the Pavilion." John O'Hara
would later deprecate Fitzgerald's "fastidiousness."[73]

   In a 1945 essay the critic Lionel Trilling noted the same chaste quality:
"No one, I think, has remarked how innocent of mere 'sex,' how charged
with sentiment is Fitzgerald's description of love in the jazz age." His earlier

fiction never enters the bedroom, seems in fact to shrink from physical intimacy. In *This Side of Paradise,* Amory Blaine's first youthful kiss plunges him
into "sudden revulsion . . . disgust, loathing"; several years later, when a casual pick-up, a chorus girl named Axia, leads him to a friend's flat, lays "her
yellow head on his shoulder," and allures him with a "sidelong suggestive
smile," all with obvious intent, Amory bolts in horror. In *The Great Gatsby,*
when Tom Buchanan and Myrtle Wilson disappear, with no further details,
into the bedroom of their love nest, Fitzgerald worried that it was "raw." After *Tender Is the Night,* he regretted Dick Diver's taunting remark "I never did
go in for making love to dry loins," as "definitely offensive" and "out of Dick's
character," and wished to eliminate it from any future edition.[74]

The coarseness was out of Fitzgerald's character, too. Among more than
2,000 entries in his *Notebooks,* the category "Rough Stuff" contains seven
items, mostly mild: in one, the roughness is a reference to someone picking his nose; in another, to squirrels mating. "Descriptions of Girls," by contrast, includes 133 entries.

But by 1940, his romanticism was ebbing—with time and disappointment, with immersion in Hollywood, with Sheilah Graham. She had risen,
as one critic put it, through "a rather stunning career of imposture and social climbing," and, one might add, sleeping around.[75] With her greater experience she provided consultation on lovemaking technique for *The Last
Tycoon.* "I knew too well from my first marriage how to deal with sudden
impotence," she explained: "'The only way to make the man perform is for
the girl to be obviously inferior to him,' I told Scott. 'She [Kathleen] would
become coarse so that Stahr would at once feel superior and lose the tenseness. The blood would come down from his head to the proper area.'"[76]
The Last Tycoon's seduction scene incorporates this veteran advice. Finding
Stahr trembling as they begin making love, Kathleen "spoke to him coarsely
and provocatively and pulled his face down to hers. . . . He was not trembling
now." It is the only scene in Fitzgerald's fiction to describe a sexual encounter.

While critics and biographers have praised *The Last Tycoon* as a would-
have-been great novel, they often recoil from Fitzgerald's Pat Hobby
stories, written concurrently, as embarrassing potboilers.

In the 338 pages of Arthur Mizener's pioneering biography of Fitzgerald, the Hobby stories rate a single perfunctory sentence. Andrew Turnbull's 323-page biography allots them an even shorter sentence. At almost 500 pages, Matthew Bruccoli's *Some Sort of Epic Grandeur* dispatches them in a single indifferent paragraph. In Scott Donaldson's *Fool For Love,* Pat Hobby gets a half-sentence nod. A twenty-first-century biography, David Brown's *Paradise Lost,* redresses the neglect with several pages of discussion but concludes with a conventional dismissal of the Hobby stories as, finally, only "a kind of minor-key apprentice piece for the greater work"— *The Last Tycoon.*[77]

Written specifically for *Esquire,* the seventeen Hobby stories follow the misadventures of an aging has-been screenwriter. By accident they match in number *The Last Tycoon* fragment's seventeen episodes, a coincidence inviting comparison. Taken one by one, the stories are amusing baubles; strung together they form a picaresque saga, spoofing and enjoying the misadventures of a seedy Hollywood hack, Fitzgerald's most purely comic hero.[78]

Unlike the over-planned, over-plotted, over-outlined *Last Tycoon,* the Hobby stories were dashed off quickly. Since *Esquire* editor Arnold Gingrich accepted them without demur and promptly wired payment regardless of length or quality, there was little reason to spend time revising and polishing. Nonetheless Fitzgerald was attentive to their quality, and though dispatching them quickly to raise funds, he sometimes followed up with revisions and urged Gingrich to publish the stronger stories first, with the idea of improving or replacing the weaker before they saw print.

Neglect of the Hobby stories is a critical mistake. Short as each is, collectively they fill a 158-page book, and along with a handful of other *Esquire* stories, they were the only fiction Fitzgerald published during his last three years. And while he complained (and others echo) that his earlier stories were cramped by the family readership of the *Saturday Evening Post,* the Hobby stories suffer no such handicap. *Esquire* was a worldly men's magazine, and Pat Hobby is a drunk, a gambler, a womanizer, a con artist, a liar, and a cheat.[79]

He is, in fact, the antithesis of *The Last Tycoon*'s admirable Monroe Stahr, and the incongruity has disturbed those who wish that Fitzgerald had died while clasped in the arms of a serious novel, not two-timing her with a com-ical strumpet. Professor Bruccoli protests indignantly against any likeness between Hobby and his author: ". . . Fitzgerald has often been incorrectly identified with this character. Pat Hobby is not a self-portrait of Fitzgerald in Hollywood. An illiterate ex–gag writer, Hobby survives through petty dishonesty," and so on.[80]

The anxiety is misplaced. Though a rogue, Hobby is likeable, unlike *The Last Tycoon*'s cocky narrator Cecelia Brady. Hobby is a hack, a boozer, a skirt chaser, a fake—the list goes on. What he is *not* is complacent or smug. Once successful, now superannuated and down-at-the-heels, lacking ability and energy, Hobby—like the boll weevil "jus' lookin' for a home"—is just looking for a paycheck.

Bruccoli's dislike—"only two" of seventeen Hobby stories "generate sympathy for Pat"—suggests a somewhat anemic comic sensibility. Though ironic, the narrative voice of the Hobby stories is neither unsympathetic nor censorious. While Hobby is an unrepentant scoundrel, he and his author—both failed, hard-up screenwriters driving old cars and struggling to stay afloat with short-term writing gigs—have unmistakable parallels.

In a story called "No Harm Trying," Hobby is "at 'the end of his resources'— though this term is too ominous to describe a fairly usual condition in his life." For the past five years it had been a regular condition in Fitzgerald's too. Yet also like Fitzgerald, Hobby had known luxury and leisure— swimming pools and limousines and blondes, when "he had arrived at the studio in his car driven by a Filipino in uniform," when his office at the studio "had a room for the secretary and was really a director's office," and when he had once been invited to lunch with the president of the United States in the studio executives' private dining room.

Like some well-known actors and actresses, Hobby had failed to make the transition from silent films to talkies, rather as Fitzgerald had failed to make the transition from fiction-writing to screenwriting, or from the Jazz Age 1920s to the gloomier 1930s. Hobby's nostalgic glances backward echo Fitzgerald's wistful memories of Riviera days with the Murphys—whom he had recently hit up for a loan to pay Scottie's Vassar tuition. Like Fitzgerald, Hobby favors gin and whiskey.

Despite all this, he is less autobiographical caricature than comic antihero expressing an irreverent, cynical view of Hollywood, which—living with a Hollywood gossip columnist, enmeshed in moviemaking culture, and conveniently distant from wife and daughter—Fitzgerald had no intention of leaving. He called the Hobby stories satiric, but rather than moralistic they are facetious and anarchic, often betraying affection for their scapegrace hero.

Pat Hobby is the court jester who mocks Fitzgerald himself—the romantic, aspiring Fitzgerald of *This Side of Paradise* and *The Great Gatsby,* even the Fitzgerald of *The Last Tycoon.* At forty-nine, with hair thinning and bloodshot eyes, Hobby has no ideals, no principles, no scruples, no talent, no illusions, no pretensions, no steady job, and no money. His interests are liquor, young blondes (who now all look alike to him), and the ponies running at Santa Anita. Though a writer, he has "scarcely opened a book in a decade"; his library comprises two books, a ten-year-old edition of the *Motion Picture Almanac* and *Barton's Track Guide, 1939.* He has either two or three ex-wives. In one story he is said to live over a delicatessen; in another he seems to be homeless. His only tender sentiment is a maudlin nostalgia for his heyday of "wives and Filipinos and swimming pools."

The broad farce of the Hobby stories, their low-life humor, their zany, sometimes slapstick action, their anecdotal, joke-like plots, their raffish hero—all have chilled biographers and critics. How to justify scholarly books about a career ending with throwaway comic piffles? The critical emphasis on *The Last Tycoon* as Fitzgerald's crowning work has as much to do with its aspirations and pretensions as with actual merit. The biographical narrative of Fitzgerald suffering a knockdown crack-up, rising from the canvas to resume the fight, and leaving behind a tragically unfinished masterpiece does not jibe well with a clown-hero with unsettling resemblances to Fitzgerald himself.[81]

Yet satirizing Hollywood through Hobby's bleary eyes is no less valid than seeing it as a solemn arena of heroic endeavor and tragedy. *The Last Tycoon* presents Hollywood at the exalted level of a legendary producer at the greatest of studios—Hollywood at the top. The Hobby stories observe it from below, with the worm's-eye view of a dogface in the trenches. Like thousands of Hollywood hopefuls, hangers-on, and has-beens, Hobby belongs to the movie industry's proletariat.

While the Hobby stories were improvisational and anecdotal, Hobby himself remains consistent. He hangs around a nameless MGM-like studio, sometimes on short-term contracts, sometimes scrounging for employ-ment. He has no visible acquaintance or life outside the studio. Other char-acters are mentioned often and now and then appear: Lou the studio bookie, for example, whom Hobby during his flush years freely patronized; now less so. Money is a constant interest: almost all the stories note Hobby's modest weekly pay when working on studio contracts—usually $250, just what *Esquire* paid Fitzgerald for a Hobby story. The stories lack all romance, though Hobby has a hungry eye for women. Actresses are far above him, but at various times secretaries, a nurse, and a lost tourist from Boise spark his interest.

A typical story begins with Hobby finding or happening onto a dodge to make money, often by illicit or sketchy means, and often involving the theft of someone else's work or idea. He is open to any promising hustle. In "The Homes of the Stars" he poses as a tour guide to bilk Kansas City tourists; in "Pat Hobby's Christmas Wish," the first of the stories, he attempts to black-mail a producer. Fitzgerald regretted that this story "characterizes him in a rather less sympathetic way than most," for though "a complete rat," Hobby here seems "a little sinister which he is not."[82]

In several stories he is innocent of chicanery, and merely embarrassed—once, in a false beard, mistaken for Orson Welles; another time compelled to pose in the nude for a female portrait painter—whom, it is true, he had hoped to seduce. The stories usually end with Hobby detected, exposed, disappointed, humiliated, or defeated. In "Pat Hobby Does His Bit," when drafted as a stunt man he is run over by a car and left abandoned and strait-jacketed overnight in "a hinged iron doublet." In "Pat Hobby, Putative Father," he is promised a generous monthly allowance for life, only to lose it the next morning.

Several stories include private jokes. In "Teamed with Genius," Hobby takes credit for a script he did not write, "Ballet Shoes"; three years earlier, Fitzgerald had written a film treatment, never sold, titled "Ballet Shoes." In "Pat Hobby's Secret," Hobby worms himself into the secret of how, in a plot known only to another screenwriter, "a live artillery shell got into Claudette Colbert's trunk." Fitzgerald had recently sketched out a film sce-nario in which a girl discovers "a forty-five pound, 156 mm. artillery shell" in her steamer trunk.[83] After inveigling the drunken scriptwriter to disclose his secret, Hobby promptly forgets it and loses a $1,000 payoff. (With a frenetic, involved plot, Fitzgerald's film scenario never makes the matter quite clear, either.)

Beset by problems, feeling forgotten, and anxious about failing powers, to the end Fitzgerald retained high ambitions. Overshadowed by Hemingway, competing with a younger generation of 1930s writers, he was eager, even desperate, to reclaim his status as a major novelist, to be "extravagantly admired" again. His college program for Sheilah Graham suggests his earnestness. Though idiosyncratic, the reading list was massive, amounting to tens of thousands of pages, with the ultimate goal of plodding through the two volumes of Spengler's *Decline of the West* as translated into dense English from the twelve-hundred-page German original. No program of self-improvement could have been more somber.

The Last Tycoon exhibits a similar ambition. It was to be "the work of integrity," in Graham's words, as opposed to the "inferior stories."[84] Though not so ponderously self-improving as Graham's reading list, it was despite the narrator's breezy glibness intended to be the tragedy of a hero crushed by greed and fate. It would speak for the idealist and romantic Fitzgerald, but also for Fitzgerald the moralist, favored by critics.

But if Monroe Stahr expresses Fitzgerald's idealism and earnestness, Pat Hobby also speaks for his author, mocking the high-flown pretensions of the novel Fitzgerald was simultaneously writing. In both Stahr and Hobby—hero and cynic, artist and washed-out hack—there is much of Fitzgerald. "I talk with the authority of failure—Ernest with the authority of success," he observed during these years. "We could never sit across the table again."[85] The same is true of Hobby and Stahr—except that at Fitzgerald's writing table they *did* meet and converse, in a dialogue between two sides of Fitzgerald himself.

David Brown, the biographer most attentive to Pat Hobby, wonders how much of himself Fitzgerald "put into Pat," and predictably concludes, "not much." A better answer would be: plenty. If Hobby is cynical about Hollywood yet immersed in it, retains a weakness for alcohol and women, is just scraping by now and tearfully nostalgic for golden days of yore—in such qualities he closely echoes Fitzgerald. Hobby is one of many characters— with Stahr, the last—infused with Fitzgerald's own impulses and feelings. "My characters are all Scott Fitzgerald," he had told Laura Guthrie, a dictum as true of the shabby has-been Hobby as of the self-absorbed Princetonian

Amory Blaine, the ambitious midwesterner Gatsby, the disintegrating Dick Diver, the striving, tired, dying Monroe Stahr.

In a 1937 letter to Harold Ober lamenting his bleak finances, Fitzgerald concluded hopefully, "Ah me—well, perhaps I've learned wisdom at forty at last." Readers who wish away Hobby's affinity with Fitzgerald should, instead, appreciate the humor and wisdom of a self-mocking character who suggests perhaps something like humility—not previously conspicuous among Fitzgerald virtues. "The humility that came with failure," Graham remarked, "made him nicer."[86]

Neither Pat Hobby nor Monroe Stahr best represents Fitzgerald in his last year, though. His most fitting valedictory is "Last Kiss," a story written and rewritten during his final year and half. In it he returned for a final time to the larger scale of his *Saturday Evening Post* stories; at six thousand words "Last Kiss" is similar in length to "The Last of the Belles" and "The Rough Crossing" of a decade earlier, and three times longer than the usual Hobby story. More notably, it returns to Fitzgerald's perennial and most potent themes, love and loss.

Kisses had a long history in his fiction. In *This Side of Paradise* they had marked stages in Amory Blaine's romantic life. In the stage directions of the novel's little playlet, "The Debutante," for example, "kiss" occurs seven times, as his passion for Rosalind Connage begins lightheartedly but ends mournfully when she jilts him for a wealthy suitor and sends Amory out the door with a sorrowful final kiss.

Five years later, in one of *The Great Gatsby*'s soaring lyrical passages, Jay Gatsby anticipates his first kiss with Daisy: "He knew that when he kissed this girl, and forever wed his unutterable visions to her perishable breath, his mind would never romp again like the mind of God. So he waited, listening for a moment longer to the tuning fork that had been struck upon a star. Then he kissed her. At his lips' touch she blossomed for him like a flower and the incarnation was complete." A transcendent kiss, leading through devious windings to his death. It was fitting, then, that at the end Fitzgerald returned to the kiss.

"Last Kiss" is a story of three kisses punctuating the failed romance of

Jim Leonard, a Hollywood film producer, and young actress Pamela Knighton. Predictably, Knighton is often identified with Sheilah Graham. Both are English, both have made their way to Hollywood as ambitious gold-diggers. At one point Knighton taunts that "English people don't commit suicide when they don't get what they want," to which Jim replies, "I know. They come to America"—an inside joke for Graham.[87]

More pertinent, though, are their differences. At twenty—a dozen years younger than the Graham that Fitzgerald knew—Pam Knighton radiates head-turning loveliness. Walking into New York's high-chic 21 Club, her agent claims, she stole attention from the stunning Hedy Lamarr. Newly arrived in America, Knighton is "sad and a little lost," but hopeful and eager; inexperienced but cynically exploitive; willful and indiscreetly critical of Americans. The willfulness makes her difficult to work with and soon ends her Hollywood career—in which failure the out-of-work actress more closely resembles the out-of-work screenwriter than the thriving journalist Graham.[88]

Pam Knighton's story is told from the perspective of thirty-five-year-old Jim, whom we meet at a moment of professional success, just promoted to producer at a nameless film studio. "It was a fine pure feeling to be on top," the story begins, in words which will prove ironic.

Despite his new eminence, Jim remains unmarried and lonely, "still trying to match every woman with a lost childhood love" (in an earlier draft, "a childhood love who died"). Mourning this lost love, he joins a line of grieving Fitzgerald lovers beginning with Amory Blaine, continuing with Gatsby, and concluding with *The Last Tycoon*'s Monroe Stahr mourning his dead wife Minna. Bereft lovers were more than simply a routine plot staple: Fitzgerald had lost Zelda twice and took it "hard" both times. In Asheville, Laura Guthrie and Beatrice Dance had been victims of his loneliness; in Hollywood it made him an easy conquest for Sheilah Graham.

Jim is instantly struck by Pam Knighton, "a girl almost as tall as he was, with opaque brown eyes and cheeks as delicate as a Chinese tea-cup." (Graham was half a head shorter than the five-foot-eight Fitzgerald.) Dancing with Knighton, Jim "felt a rising exultation." When she signs a contract with another producer, "He flew East next day, looking for a young actress just like Pamela Knighton. . . . It seemed rather a desperate matter that he should find some one exactly like this girl." Like Monroe Stahr seeking a look-alike for his lost Minna, Jim replaces the haunting image of his childhood love with the fresh and breathing Knighton. When she walks into the room, "her glowing beauty, borne in from outside like something snatched from wind and weather, made Jim breathless for a moment."

Yet though she leaves him exultant, desperate, and breathless, Jim fails to court Knighton, even shrinks from her. When she writes, twice, to remind him of a promise to find a role for her, he brushes her off. Encountering her in "his neighborhood drugstore," no doubt Schwab's, he "wished he could pretend not to see her," and turns aside to avoid recognition. When they leave the drugstore together and she asks which way he's walking, he silently thinks, "The other way from you," and only reluctantly escorts her home.

True, she has informed him earlier that "I'm not free now. . . . I'm engaged," but the fiancé is in England, and no determined suitor with the advantage of I'm-here-he's-not would be deterred by a transatlantic rival. Graham was engaged when Fitzgerald met her, and even the weary Monroe Stahr, "lonesome as hell," pursues a woman with a distant fiancé somewhere.

Though a rising producer, only hesitantly does Jim give Pamela Knighton a "little part" in a movie, though it was common practice for movie-industry powers to advance their wives and lovers. Fitzgerald's Hollywood hero, MGM production head Irving Thalberg, had shamelessly promoted his wife Norma Shearer. "How can I compete with Norma when she sleeps with the boss?" her MGM rival Joan Crawford is said to have complained. But inexplicably, Jim lets Knighton slip away. Strangely passive, inert, reluctant—does he reflect Fitzgerald's own flagging energies?

Their first kiss is nominally a soporific. After the drugstore encounter Jim and Pamela are about to part outside her bungalow, when she unexpectedly asks:

"Are you married?"
"No."

"Then kiss me goodnight."

As he hesitated she said, "I like to be kissed good night. I sleep better."

Innocence and eroticism mingle: a child's need for bedtime ritual and reassurance, a woman's invitation to closer communion, perhaps seduction. Jim is tentative:

> He put his arms around her shyly and bent down to her lips, just touching them—and thinking hard of the letter on his desk [rejecting her for a movie role] which he couldn't send now—and liking holding her.
> "You see it's nothing," she said, "just friendly. Just good night."

Repeating to himself, "Well, I'll be damned," he apparently feels something more than "nothing."

Two weeks later, after watching her act in a play in Pasadena, he gives her a lift back to Hollywood in his chauffeur-driven limousine. Though Jim suggests this second kiss, she again engineers it. As they drive along, she "looked at him appraisingly. Oh, she could do something with him all right"—the narrative switching briefly to her point of view. "She let her hand rest upon his."

With this tacit invitation, he suggests, "Kiss tonight?"

> Pamela glanced at the chauffeur, insulated in his compartment.
> "Kiss tonight," she said.

This kiss does not seem soporific.

W e might expect the next and final kiss to dissolve into a fairy-tale conclusion—"third time lucky"—but "Last Kiss" is a story of two lonely people who should but don't connect. Pamela's embryonic acting career founders. Immature, headstrong, stubborn, falling under the sway of a bitter and jealous adviser, she disrupts the filming of the movie in which Jim has secured her a role. He attempts to counsel and warn her, but finally resigns her to failure and turns away. She "did not realize that this very minute was opportunity and she was losing it forever." Turning away himself, though, Jim lets his own opportunity slip away.

Attempting to dissuade her from her willfulness, Jim had reflected, "Had they been in love, had it ever seemed the time to encourage the spark between them, he might have reached her now." Instead, he walks out. "But it was too late," he concludes, leaving her to the malignant adviser. When she dies soon after, he recognizes his mistake. If not in love earlier, he is now—when it *is* too late.

Eager to reach the culminating kiss, Fitzgerald arranged a quick and arbitrary off-stage death for Knighton. Learning she has died, Jim drives out to mourn at her fresh grave, then returns to the studio to watch film clips of her. After their last unhappy parting, "she had called him twice on the phone, he knew, and he had wanted to see her. But he could do nothing for her and could not bear to tell her so"—a weak excuse for pushing away a girl who fascinated him then and haunts him now. "I am not very brave," he reflects. She was too young and brash; he, too timid: "Even now there was fear in his heart that this"—losing Pamela—"would haunt him like a memory of his youth, and he did not want to be unhappy."

In the final scene, a girl in the drugstore where Jim had earlier encountered Knighton is looking at the *Illustrated London News,* which Knighton too had been flipping through. In Jim's fancy the girl *becomes* Knighton. Leaving the drugstore "he turned the wrong way, her way, and he heard her following—so plain that he slowed his pace with the sense that she had trouble keeping up with him":

> In front of the apartment court he took her in his arms and drew her radiant beauty close.
> "Kiss me goodnight," she said. "I like to be kissed goodnight. I sleep better."

"When you brought your beauty here I didn't want to throw it away," Jim tells the phantom Pam Knighton, "but I did somehow."

In failing to seize his opportunity, Jim anticipates *The Last Tycoon*'s Monroe Stahr, who also lets the appointed woman slip away. The last of Fitzgerald's heroes along with Pat Hobby, Stahr was two different characters: masterful and enterprising Hollywood tycoon, and tired lonely man seeking a lost love. Fitzgerald knew one of them well. The mind and temperament of a studio baron were outside his range, but he understood desire and regret; knew weariness and loneliness. "If Stahr the producer was meant to be Thalberg," Sheilah Graham wrote, "Stahr the lover was always Scott."[89]

EPILOGUE

Nothing left . . . but sleep.
—"LAST KISS"

While living in Hollywood, Fitzgerald saw Scottie during a handful of cross-country visits, he to the East and she to California. Otherwise they corresponded, and while mostly ignoring his letters, she retained them.

He had become a concerned, stern parent, happier with the long-distance fathering that allowed him to write or lecture Scottie without the stress of daily interaction. Despite his poignant story of a rueful father longing to reclaim his daughter, "Babylon Revisited," he did not much enjoy Scottie's company. One letter mentions "the irritations, exasperations and blow ups of the past winter"; another complains, "Living with you in Baltimore . . . represented a rather too domestic duty forced on me by your mother's illness." He discouraged her from joining or often visiting him in California. When he left for Hollywood in July 1937, she was fifteen; the following year, at sixteen, she entered Vassar.[1]

Though peppered with affection and occasional praise, his letters brim with scolding, criticism, lecture, sententious wisdom, and above all, paternal advice—on manifold topics, including driving, at which he was bad (". . . if you have the occasion to drive, I forgot to tell you that in the rain *don't depress the clutch*—use the brake *only*"); and spelling, at which he was worse. Mostly the advice was social and academic, however, as through Scottie he revisited his Princeton years. He advised, for example, that "What *is* important" during her first week at Vassar, "is to go to the library and crack your first book—to be among the 5% who will do this and get that much start and freshness," and "you must be in the library every day. Your college work comes first. . . ." (In *This Side of Paradise,* Amory Blaine visits the Princeton library only once, parenthetically, "browsing" rather than studying.)

Fitzgerald warned Scottie against snobbery, overindulgence in theatricals, New York debutante parties, overspending, drinking ("every boy I know who drank at eighteen or nineteen is now safe in his grave"), and smoking ("I didn't begin to be a heavy smoker until I was a sophomore but it took just one year to send me into tuberculosis . . ."). He gave her worldly counsel on campus politics and social climbing, on boys, on marriage.

Despite the years between them, and though Scottie was a young woman at a women's college, he had difficulty thinking of her experience as differing much from his. Just weeks before his death, he wrote: "Listening to the Harvard-Princeton game on the radio with the old songs reminds me of the past that I lived a quarter of a century ago, and that you are living now." Quoting a reviewer of his published letters—"Fitzgerald wasn't writing those letters to his daughter at Vassar; he was writing them to himself at Princeton"—Scottie agreed. "I was an imaginary daughter," she recalled, "as fictional as one of his early heroines."[2]

In May 1939, three months before the Soviet-German nonaggression pact triggered World War II in Europe, he considered sending her to Russia "with a group of girls on an economically organized tour." Naively imagining that a gaggle of American girls would be allowed freely to wander about Stalinist Russia "for three or four weeks," he encouraged her to go and "form your own opinion about how the [Soviet] experiment might work out." Nothing came of the idea.

Characteristically, he was better informed about a parochial Princeton issue, the eating clubs. Though he had eagerly joined Cottage in 1915, he now railed against "the God-awful system," "a lousy cruel system"; but when Margaret Turnbull's son Andrew, a Princeton sophomore, was deliberating among clubs, he advised her at length, in detail, and with gusto on their relative prestige and advantages. "Nothing would please me better than that the whole snobbish system be abolished," he asserted piously, but went on to advise, snobbishly, that "it would be a little better for Andrew's future if he joined one of the so-called 'big clubs'"—like Cottage.

His more candid sympathies emerge not in pious sentiments and calculating advice, but in more meditative and generous reflections. He rec-
ommends to Scottie "the old virtues of work and courage and the old graces
of courtesy and politeness." He often looks back to a past that held much to
recall fondly, much to lament, the latter frequently revisited in complaints
about Zelda—she had been spoiled and irresponsible, she had wrecked his
youthful "dream," and so on. But recognizing her present loneliness in an
Asheville sanitarium, he commands Scottie to spend time with her mother
during school and college breaks. Recommending that Scottie study botany,
he veers off into the sadness of Zelda's life: "Think of the enormous pleasure
amounting, almost, to the consolation for the tragedy of life that flowers
have been to your mother and your grandmother."

That thought prompted other regrets: "I felt all my life the absence of
hobbies except such, for me as abstract and academic ones, as military tac-
tics and football. . . . And after reading Thoreau I felt how much I have
lost by leaving nature out of my life." Another letter recalls an occasion at
Princeton when a classical scholar "got up and rolled out the great lines of
Horace: '*Integer vitae* . . .'" and he reproached himself. "I knew in my heart
that I had missed something by being a poor Latin scholar, like a blessed
evening with a lovely girl" (the simile incidentally revealing his lingering
attachment to "young love").

With both regret and hope, he reflected on himself as a writer. Of *The
Last Tycoon,* he wrote in 1939, "Look! I have begun to write something that
is maybe great. . . ." But he admitted that he had been "crippled by . . . my
inability to handle money" and "my self-indulgences of the past," and acknowledged the fatal mistake of slacking off after *Gatsby:* ". . . I wish now, I'd
never relaxed or looked back—but said at the end of *The Great Gatsby:* 'I've
found my line—from now on this comes first. This is my immediate duty—
without this I am nothing.'"

He recognized, too, that his gift was not discursive or intellectual, but
lyrical, wistful, elegiac. "The talent that matures early," he advised Scottie,
"is usually of the poetic, which mine was in large part. The prose talent de-
pends on other factors—assimilation of material and careful selection of it,
or more bluntly: having something to say and an interesting, highly developed way of saying it." In defining the prose talent he was probably thinking

of *The Last Tycoon,* less lyrical than *Gatsby* but presumably with "something to say." He would revert to the idea a few months later, observing of Thomas Wolfe's recently published *You Can't Go Home Again:* "His awful secret transpires at every crevice—he did not have anything particular to say!"

He had used the same phrasing in an earlier letter. "If you have anything to say," he told Scottie, ". . . anything you feel nobody has ever said before, you have got to feel it so desperately that you will find some way to say it that nobody has ever found before, so that the thing you have to say and the way of saying it blend as one matter—as indissolubly as if they were conceived together." It was a definition of that marriage of strong feeling and storytelling mastery he had achieved in *The Great Gatsby.* In the autumn of 1940, he struggled to do it again.

L iving with her mother in Montgomery, two thousand miles away, Zelda may have suspected another woman in Fitzgerald's life, but in their correspondence Sheilah Graham remained tacitly nonexistent.[3] There is a poignancy in the letters they exchanged during his final months—in the unsuspecting ordinariness of domestic and family talk, in his apologies for a meager Christmas, in his hopes for completing his novel.[4]

He wrote dutifully, usually weekly—an obligation, but something more too. "His devotion to me is a noble and moving manifestation of faithful faith in an idea," Zelda paid tribute after his death. "I was his wife and he wanted not to lose the precious associations of what the same could have meant."[5]

Though they were now drifted apart, a lingering intimacy persisted in their recollections of happier early days, in their common concern for Scottie. He might chat with Graham about Hollywood gossip and "college-of-one" readings, but his happiest and most intensely lived years had been spent with Zelda, and they shared memories beyond Graham's reach. "Once we were one person and always it will be a little that way," he had written to Zelda two years earlier.[6]

His letters to Zelda that last autumn invariably report on his novel. It was "hard as pulling teeth. . . . I feel people so less intently than I did once. . . ." It was "growing under my hand—not as deft a hand as I'd like but growing." It will "be nothing like anything else as I'm digging it out of myself like uranium—one ounce to the cubic ton of rejected ideas."

"Everything is my novel now—it has become of absorbing interest," he wrote two weeks before his death. He had little to say about his days otherwise, quiet as they were, and entangled with Graham's. Zelda's life too was quiet. ". . . I seldom go anywhere save to church," and ". . . I don't do anything." Mrs. Sayre's eightieth birthday was the notable event of the autumn: "We have been *en fête* and with gala all week."

They talked of Scottie. In his final letter to Zelda, accompanying a Christmas gift, he expressed his anxiety that, despite the expense, Scottie "finish this year at college at least," adding with uncharacteristic *pietas* that "The thing for which I am most grateful to my mother and father are my four years at Princeton. . . ."

As with memories of the good gone days with Zelda, he carried his love of Princeton to the grave; but while she was now relegated to the sidelines, Princeton still played football. In early November, "Listening to the Harvard and Princeton game on the radio reminds me of the past that I lived a quarter of a century ago . . ." (as he had also told Scottie), and two weeks later, "I'm sitting listening to Yale-Princeton. . . ."

The past was much on his mind. In October he reported on a tea hosted by Dorothy Parker, where he encountered "a lot of the past": the actress Fay Wray, whom he had probably met in Hollywood in 1927, "Deems Taylor who I hadn't seen twice since the days at Swopes" (in the early 1920s), and "Frank Tuttle of the old Film Guild."

That same month, "A letter from Gerald [Murphy] yesterday. He has no news except a general flavor of the past. To him, now, of course, the Riviera was the best time of all." (The Murphys' 1930s had been worse than the Fitzgeralds'.) A week later, "I saw the two Duncan Sisters [a vaudeville act] both grown enormously fat in the Brown Derby. Do you remember them on the boat with Viscount Bryce and their dogs?"—an encounter on the Fitzgeralds' second Atlantic crossing, almost twenty years earlier.

Zelda too regretted old times. "Mamma's little house is so sunshine-y and so full of grace," she wrote; "the moated mornings remind me of twenty-five years ago when life was as full of promise as it is now of memory."

Hemingway's *For Whom the Bell Tolls* was published that autumn, and "he is making a fortune out of it," Fitzgerald wrote. Though politely thanking Hemingway for an inscribed copy, he remarked to Zelda on its inferiority to *A Farewell to Arms.* "I suppose," he concluded, thinking of himself too, that "life takes a good deal out of you and you can never quite repeat." Hemingway's financial bonanza evoked memories of the obscure young writer of 1925: "Rather a long cry from his poor rooms over the saw mill in Paris."

In his next-to-last letter to Zelda he told her of "a letter from Katherine Tye [that is, Tighe, of Saint Paul days] the other day, a voice out of the past. Also one from Harry Mitchell who was my buddy at the Barron G. Collier Agency" (in 1919).

He was conscious of aging and fading. At Dorothy Parker's tea, "I felt very passé and decided to get a new suit." Besides guests he knew from earlier times, there was "a younger generation there too," perhaps prompting his reflection a week later that "the nine years that intervened between the *Great Gatsby* and *Tender* hurt my reputation almost beyond repair because a whole generation grew up in the meanwhile to whom I was only a writer of Post stories."

His health was poor, but despite his extensive history of medical complaints, real and imagined, his letters reveal little anxiety about what would actually kill him, heart disease.[7] In the last few days of November 1940 he suffered a mild attack or spasm, and his doctor recommended bed rest. ". . . I am angry that this little illness has slowed me up," he told Zelda. "I've had trouble with my heart before but never anything organic. This is not a major attack but seems to have come on gradually and luckily a cardiogram showed it up in time."

He continued to work on the novel, sitting up and writing on a custom-made bed desk. "The cardiogram shows that my heart is repairing itself but it will be a gradual process that will take some months," he reported in mid-December. He added a medical note that his physician must have offered by way of encouragement: "It is odd that the heart is one of the organs that does repair itself."

A week later, he was dead. Sheilah Graham was the only witness of his sudden death in her Hollywood apartment a few days before Christmas, ending all his earthly loves, ills, weaknesses, struggles, and disappointments.

He would not finish the novel that he hoped would revive his fortunes and reputation. He missed by less than a year Pearl Harbor, the dark months following, and the vast two-front war in which he would eagerly have participated as armchair strategist.[8] He would not live to see Scottie graduate from Vassar and marry a Princeton alumnus, nor hear of Zelda's death by fire in an Asheville sanitarium in 1948. And he would not live to see his reputation revive and flourish after the Second World War, and the *Great Gatsby's* elevation to an American classic.

While his body lay in the William Wordsworth Room of a Los Angeles mortuary, the immediate problem was where to bury him. You can't go home again if you have none.[9] "He left the estate of a pauper and the will of a millionaire," his friend John Biggs "growled when Fitzgerald died after naming him Executor," but the will expressed no instructions about interment.[10] Sheilah Graham recalled that "he really hated California" and would have liked "to be buried where his father is buried because he admired him." Edward Fitzgerald lay with Mollie in the churchyard of old St. Mary's in Rockville, Maryland, but as Fitzgerald had long divorced himself from the Church, permission to bury him there was denied.[11]

He had not been back in Saint Paul for almost twenty years and no longer had close family ties there. Rockville's public Union Cemetery was chosen for the burial. At least it was in Maryland, where he had spent several years in the 1930s and to which he felt a family connection. North Dakota's Jay Gatsby is buried on Long Island, but for Fitzgerald—another ambitious, homeless midwesterner—Maryland was better.

His funeral service, conducted in Pumphrey's Funeral Home in Bethesda by an Episcopalian divine, was dispiriting, "one of those most dreadful funeral home funerals," Perkins told Elizabeth Lemmon.[12] Andrew Turnbull, Scottie Fitzgerald's old La Paix playmate, also attended: "It was a meaningless occasion, having no apparent connection with the man. . . . In the airless hall and communicating rooms of the funeral parlor were a few spindly poinsettias, while here and there a cheap print of a winter scene or autumnal forest decorated the walls. . . . The coffin was closed. . . . and then the voice of the clergyman droning the Protestant burial."[13]

The clergyman himself blandly observed that "the funeral was nothing big to me. I was bombarded with questions from those who thought I should have been excited; but I was merely performing my duty."[14] As at Gatsby's burial, it was raining.

A little over seven years later, Zelda was buried with Fitzgerald, but Rockville's Union Cemetery would not be their final resting place. In the 1970s their remains were transferred across the road, to a plot beside his parents' at St. Mary's. By this time the small 1817 church Fitzgerald knew was dwarfed by a 1960s clamshell replacement nearby, squatting amidst a suburban labyrinth of highways, roads, and parking lots.

Soon after Fitzgerald's death Zelda had written to Peggy Finney, mother of Scottie's friend Peaches, to thank her for hosting Scottie in Baltimore during the Christmas holidays. Commenting on his burial, Zelda wrote: "His people came from Maryland and he always felt that getting back to those flowering and peaceful slopes was to be going home. He loved the hospitable white roads and the immaculacy of the bright green fields, and always hoped that someday he would be able to live there forever."[15]

Long gone are the quiet friendly roads and green fields, but happily spared demolition, the old St. Mary's remains. With back turned to the modern church, one may stand in the small churchyard and meditate on the shared grave of Francis Scott Key Fitzgerald and his wife Zelda Sayre.

Earlier, Hemingway had composed an epitaph: "Poor old Scott," he wrote to Perkins: "He is the great tragedy of talent in our bloody generation."[16] The actual epitaph, inscribed at Scottie's direction, is the last sentence of *The Great Gatsby:* "So we beat on, boats against the current, borne back ceaselessly into the past."

Also fitting would be the final line of "Last Kiss": "There is nothing left for you now but sleep."

NOTES

Fitzgerald's novels and stories are available in multiple editions. Unless otherwise noted, quotations from his writings refer to the comprehensive Cambridge Fitzgerald edition, edited by James L. W. West III.

Fitzgerald's published letters are scattered among several overlapping volumes, included below as *Letters, Correspondence, DSDM, DSDZ, LL,* and *LHD.* As the most recent general collection and perhaps most readily available, *LL* has been cited when it contains the letter being quoted.

ABBREVIATED TITLES FOR FREQUENTLY CITED SOURCES

AEY	*As Ever Yours: The Letters of Max Perkins and Elizabeth Lemmon,* ed. Roger L. Tarr. University Park: Penn State UP, 2003.
Against	Frances Kroll Ring, *Against the Current: As I Remember F. Scott Fitzgerald.* San Francisco: Donald S. Ellis, 1985.
As Ever	*As Ever, Scott Fitz—: Letters Between F. Scott Fitzgerald and His Literary Agent Harold Ober 1919–1940,* ed. Matthew J. Bruccoli. Philadelphia: Lippincott, 1972.
Beloved	Sheilah Graham and Gerold Frank, *Beloved Infidel: The Education of a Woman.* NY: Henry Holt, 1958.
Buller	Richard P. Buller, *A Beautiful Fairy Tale: The Life of Actress Lois Moran.* New Jersey: Limelight Editions, 2005.
College	Sheilah Graham, *College of One.* NY: Viking, 1967.
Conversations	*Conversations with F. Scott Fitzgerald,* ed. Matthew J. Bruccoli and Judith S. Baughman. Jackson: UP of Mississippi, 2004.
Correspondence	*Correspondence of F. Scott Fitzgerald,* ed. Matthew J. Bruccoli and Margaret M. Duggan. NY: Random House, 1980.

DSDM	*Dear Scott / Dear Max,* ed. John Kuehl and Jackson R. Bryer. NY: Scribner's, 1971.
DSDZ	*Dear Scott, Dearest Zelda,* ed. Jackson R Bryer and Cathy W. Barks. NY: St. Martin's, 2002.
FHA	*Fitzgerald/Hemingway Annual.* Washington, DC: Microcard Editions, 1969–79.
FSF	*F. Scott Fitzgerald.*
FSFR	*The F. Scott Fitzgerald Review.* University Park: Penn State UP, 2002–.
GK	Ginevra King letters: F. Scott Fitzgerald Papers, C0187, Manuscripts Division, Department of Special Collections, Princeton University Library.
Hemingway Letters	Ernest Hemingway, *Selected Letters 1917–1961,* ed. Carlos Baker. NY: Scribner's, 1981.
Kalman	Charles Oscar Kalman Correspondence with F. Scott Fitzgerald and family and Fitzgerald memorabilia, Minnesota Historical Society.
Lanahan	Eleanor Lanahan, *Scottie, The Daughter of . . . : The Life of Frances Scott Fitzgerald Lanahan Smith.* NY: HarperCollins, 1995.
Last Kiss	*Last Kiss,* ed. James L. W. West III. Cambridge, UK: Cambridge UP, 2017, in *The Cambridge Edition of the Works of F. Scott Fitzgerald.*
LG	Laura Guthrie Journal: Laura Guthrie Hearne Additions; F. Scott Fitzgerald Additional Papers, C0188, Manuscripts Division, Department of Special Collections, Princeton University Library.
LHD	*Scott Fitzgerald: Letters to His Daughter,* ed. Andrew Turnbull. NY: Scribner's, 1965.
LL	*F. Scott Fitzgerald: A Life in Letters,* ed. Matthew J. Bruccoli. NY: Scribner's, 1994.
LLG	*Letters from the Lost Generation,* ed. Linda Patterson Miller. New Brunswick, NJ: Rutgers UP, 1991.
Letters	*The Letters of F. Scott Fitzgerald,* ed. Andrew Turnbull. NY: Scribner's, 1963.
Mizener	Arthur Mizener, *The Far Side of Paradise: A Biography of F. Scott Fitzgerald.* 1951; rev. ed., Boston: Houghton Mifflin, 1965.
MLC	*My Lost City: Personal Essays, 1920–1940,* ed. James L. W. West III. Cambridge, UK: Cambridge UP, 2005, in *The Cambridge Edition of the Works of F. Scott Fitzgerald.*

Notebooks	*The Notebooks of F. Scott Fitzgerald,* ed. Matthew J. Bruccoli. NY: Harcourt Brace, 1978.
OTTC	*The Only Thing That Counts: The Ernest Hemingway / Maxwell Perkins Correspondence 1925–1947,* ed. Matthew J. Bruccoli. NY: Scribner, 1996.
Piper	Henry Dan Piper Papers, Special Collections Research Center, Morris Library, Southern Illinois University.
PUL	Manuscripts Division, Department of Special Collections, Princeton University Library.
Real FSF	Sheilah Graham, *The Real F. Scott Fitzgerald Thirty-Five Years Later.* NY: Grosset & Dunlap, 1976.
SEP	*The Saturday Evening Post.*
SSEG	Matthew J. Bruccoli, *Some Sort of Epic Grandeur: The Life of F. Scott Fitzgerald.* 1981; 2nd rev. ed., Columbia: U of South Carolina P, 2002.
Turnbull	Andrew Turnbull, *Scott Fitzgerald.* NY: Scribner, 1962.
Zelda	Nancy Milford, *Zelda: A Biography.* 1970; paperback ed., NY: Avon Books, 1971.

PROLOGUE

1. Quoted in Michael LaPointe, "The Racy Jazz Age Best Seller You've Never Heard Of," *Paris Review,* www.theparisreview.org/blog/2019/02/12/the-racy-jazz-age-best-seller-youve-never-hea rd-of/.

2. "In the Darkest Hour: A Poignant Romance of Chaos and Leadership," *Redbook* 63 (October 1934): 15–19, 94–98; reprinted in *The Price Was High: The Last Uncollected Stories of F. Scott Fitzgerald,* ed. Matthew J. Bruccoli (NY: MJF Books, 1979), 512–29.

3. *As Ever,* 206.

4. LG, 106. The other names on *Redbook*'s September 1935 cover were actually those of Arthur Somers Roche and P. G. Wodehouse.

5. F. Scott Fitzgerald, "Introduction," *Last Kiss,* xviii; Scottie Fitzgerald Smith, "The Colonial Ancestors of Francis Scott Key Fitzgerald," "Afterword" in *SSEG,* 495.

6. Adams, *The Epic of America* (Boston: Little, Brown, 1931), 404.

7. In an entry in his *Notebooks* Fitzgerald mentions "the American dream" in a passage about "the most beautiful history in the world"—America's. "It is the history of all aspiration—not just the American dream but the human dream and if I came at the end of it that too is a place in the line of the pioneers" (#2037). With its mention of a new arrival named "Sheilah," the entry dates from no earlier than July 1937, when he met the Englishwoman Sheilah Graham in Hollywood, six years after Adams's *Epic of America.*

8. *LL,* 472.

9. *F. Scott Fitzgerald:* The Great Gatsby, ed. Nicolas Tredell (NY: Columbia UP, 1999), 4; Maureen Corrigan, *So We Read On: How The Great Gatsby Came to Be and Why It Endures* (Boston: Little, Brown, 2014).

10. John L. Micek, "Re-reading *The Great Gatsby* and the enduring appeal of a love story of the one percent," *Patriot-News* (Harrisburg, PA), August 3, 2014, C1.

11. *Correspondence,* 139, 145.

12. "Preface," *The Great Gatsby,* "The Authorized Text," ed. Matthew J. Bruccoli (NY: Scribner, 2003), vii–xvi.

13. Corrigan, *So We Read On,* 15–16.

14. David S. Brown, interviewed for "Book Q&As with Deborah Kalb," March 17, 2017, deborahkalbbooks.blogspot.com/2017/03/q-with-david-s-brown.html, discussing Brown's *Paradise Lost: A Life of F. Scott Fitzgerald* (Cambridge, MA: Harvard UP, 2017).

15. Interview with Maxwell Perkins, June 22, 1945, Piper. *OTTC,* 210. Interview with Michael Fisher, May 24, 1947; with Margaret Culkin Banning, April 7, 1947, both in Piper.

16. *OTTC,* 84; interview with Maxwell Perkins, June 22, 1945, Piper; *LL,* 269; C. Lawton Campbell, "The Fitzgeralds Were My Friends," F. Scott Fitzgerald Additional Papers, C0188, PUL; printed in *FHA,* 1978, 37–54.

17. *Beloved,* 184; "Football & Fitzgerald," *Princeton Alumni Weekly* 56, no. 20 (March 9, 1956): 11.

18. "One Hundred False Starts," *SEP* 205 (March 4, 1933), reprinted in *MLC,* 82–90.

19. Matthew J. Bruccoli, "Foreword" in Mary Jo Tate, *F. Scott Fitzgerald A to Z: The Essential Reference to His Life and Work* (NY: Facts on File, 1998), viii.

20. *LL,* 123.

21. *DSDM,* 203–4.

22. *As Ever,* 221.

23. LG, 118. A contracted spelling ["thots"] expanded, a typo ["morn" for "mourn"] corrected.

24. *Notebooks,* #1072.

25. *Hemingway Letters,* 408.

26. *LL,* 187.

27. *LL,* 368.

28. *LL,* 368.

29. *LHD,* 137.

30. *Chicago Tribune,* August 27, 1918, 11.

31. Fitzgerald's handwritten ledger records details of his writing, publications, and income, as well as an abbreviated monthly log of people, places, and incidents. He acquired the blank ledger in the early 1920s, filled in his first twenty-five years or so from memory or other records, and thereafter kept it more or less current until 1935. Now held at the University of South Carolina, the ledger is an invaluable source for biography and bibliography, though its entries are often cryptic, its dating unreliable. For more on the ledger, see James L. W. West III, "Interpreting Fitzgerald's Ledger," in *F. Scott Fitzgerald in Context,* ed. Bryant Mangum (Cambridge, UK: Cambridge UP, 2013), 16–23.

32. "A Scrap Book Record, Compiled From Many Sources of Interest to and Concerning One F. Scott Fitzgerald," 96, PUL.

33. Twenty years later Fitzgerald would admit that he had *never* kissed Ginevra.

34. PUL. "R" was Fitzgerald's Saint Paul friendly rival Reuben Warner; "Bug," Ginevra's Westover friend Marie Hersey.

Highly literate in a flighty, exclamatory, hopscotching way, Ginevra's letters are of interest even apart from their recipient, as the extemporaneous effusions of a bright, spirited young woman and a revealing, if narrow, social history of the First World War era. Her diary and the typescript of her letters are held at Princeton. Selective diary entries are printed in James L. W. West III's *The Perfect Hour: The Romance of F. Scott Fitzgerald and Ginevra King, His First Love* (NY: Random House, 2005).

35. *Arthur Mizener* Papers, PUL.

36. Printed in Roger Lewis, "Ruth Sturtevant and F. Scott Fitzgerald (1916–1921)," *FHA,* 1979, 16.

37. As the remark about poor boys and rich girls is directly preceded by "Peg Cary stands straight," Ginevra's friend Margaret Carry might be its source. A decade later a *Saturday Evening Post* story, "Presumption," echoes the observation, its hero Juan remarking, "Perhaps all poor boys who are in love with wealthy girls are presumptuous." But, "Rich girls can't live on air," another character reminds Juan, and Fitzgerald agreed.

38. West, *Perfect Hour,* 42.

39. "My Lost City," *Cosmopolitan* 131 (July 1951), reprinted in *MLC,* 106–15; *LL,* 338, 340.

40. *LL,* 131.

41. *LL,* 465.

42. Quoted in Vernon McKenzie, *These Stories Went to Market* (NY: Robert M. McBride, 1935), xviii.

43. One of Amory's flames, Clara, is hardly a "girl" in a narrow sense; rather, a "remarkable woman" and widow with two young children. Yet "girl" was the word Fitzgerald and his characters almost invariably use when speaking of young women, including Clara. In the sense of young woman, "girl" occurs some eighty times in *This Side of Paradise,* over fifty times in *The Great Gatsby.*

44. *LL,* 209.

45. Sara Mayfield, *Exiles from Paradise: Zelda and Scott Fitzgerald* (NY: Delacorte P, 1971), 2.

46. "How to Waste Material," *Bookman* 63 (May 1926), reprinted in *MLC,* 77–81.

1. A DREAM OF THE SOUTH (1918–1920)

1. *LL,* 314.

2. *Zelda,* 372; *LL,* 453.

3. Minnesota Department of Natural Resources, Climate Data, www.dnr.state.mn.us/climate /historical/daily-data.html?sid=217370&sname=ST.%20PAUL%20DOWNTOWN%20AIRPORT&s date=1896-09-01&edate=1917-12-31.

4. Buffalo snow data from Northeast Regional Climate Center, www.nrcc.cornell.edu/wx station/nowdata.html. Data for Syracuse do not begin until 1902.

5. *Correspondence,* 127; FSF to Oscar Kalman, February 2, 1933, typed letter, Kalman; *LL,* 271.

6. "A Scrap Book Record," 138. Army horsemanship standards were lax or nonexistent during the 1917 mobilization. An acquaintance with whom Fitzgerald went riding earlier that year reported that "Scott was a terrible horseman, but determined to ride at all costs. Once he was given an old nag who habitually bolted for home whenever he passed a certain familiar corner. Scott took a bad spill, but got up dusty and determined, and insisted on climbing back

on. We all cheered and admired his courage, but it was clear he would never make a good horse-man." Elizabeth Beckwith MacKie, "My Friend Scott Fitzgerald," *FHA,* 1970, 21; High Plains Regional Climate Center, climod.unl.edu/; *Letters,* 455.

7. "The Cruise of the Rolling Junk," in *Last Kiss,* 338. Fitzgerald was at Camp Gordon in full southern spring, and it seems odd that a Minnesotan would find it "chilly."

8. *LL,* 64.

9. *LL,* 461–62.

10. *"The Romantic Egotist,"* typescript, PUL, 4, findingaids.princeton.edu/catalog/C0187_c00046; "The Cruise of the Rolling Junk," *Motor* 41 (February, March, April 1924), reprinted in *Last Kiss,* 295–342; "My Generation," *Esquire* 70 (October 1968): 119, 121, reprinted in *MLC,* 192–98; "The Death of My Father," *Princeton University Library Chronicle* 12 (Summer 1951): 187–89, reprinted in *Last Kiss,* 418–20.

11. "Wait Till You Have Children of Your Own!" *Woman's Home Companion* 51 (July 1924): 13, 105; reprinted in *MLC,* 66–76.

12. *The Apprentice Fiction of F. Scott Fitzgerald 1909–1917,* ed. John Kuehl (New Brunswick: Rutgers UP, 1965), 36–38; *F. Scott Fitzgerald's St. Paul Plays, 1911–1914,* ed. Alan Margolies (Princeton, NJ: Princeton University Library, 1978).

13. *Correspondence,* 601.

14. *LL,* 461–62. Mary Surratt, related to Fitzgerald's father by marriage, was accused of conspiring in Lincoln's assassination and hanged.

15. *Letters,* 453.

16. *LL,* 41.

17. *LL,* 450.

18. The Sayres' house at 6 Pleasant Avenue was demolished in the 1970s; only a flight of steps leading up from the street remains.

19. John B. Scott Jr., "The Bell Building," *Montgomery County Historical Society Herald* 17, no. 2 (Spring 2009), lostinmontgomery.files.wordpress.com/2009/07/herald-bell-building.pdf.

20. Telegrams pasted into Zelda's scrapbook, Zelda Fitzgerald Papers, C0183, PUL.

21. *Zelda,* 33–34.

22. Fitzgerald later told an interviewer, perhaps half-truthfully: "I met her at the Country Club at a dance. . . . we quarreled. I sorter enjoyed quarreling with her. . . . A few nights later we met and had another pitched battle—words the weapons used. . . . Then I went back home—we quarreled the night I left" ("Bart" Fulton, "Fitzgerald, Flapperdom's Fiction Ace . . . ," *Montgomery Advertiser,* March 19, 1923, 6; reprinted in *Conversations,* 33).

23. *DSDZ,* 214–15.

24. Besides Zelda, May Steiner, and Helen Dent, Fitzgerald's ledger mentions a fourth Montgomery girl, Roberta Jones. Jones, Dent, and Steiner were evidently good friends, their names often appearing together in the society paragraphs of the local newspapers. Reporting a country-club dance, one article mentions "a merry party" consisting of "Miss Helen Dent, Miss Roberta Jones and Miss Mae Steiner and three French officers, Lieutenants Lapravotte, DeCuverville and Sergeant Foraz" (one of whom was probably "Helen Dent's Frenchman"). The society paragraphs often mention Zelda Sayre, too, separately.

25. "Cruise of the Rolling Junk," 340.

26. "Brilliant 'Folly Ball' Given by Members of Les Mysterieuses," *Montgomery Advertiser,*

April 25, 1919, 6; "Pretty Montgomery Girl Creates Stir in Atlanta," *Montgomery Advertiser,* June 24, 1919, 6.

27. John Chapin Mosher, "That Sad Young Man," *New Yorker,* April 17, 1926, 20; *Letters,* 455–56.

28. *Correspondence,* 45; "Who's Who—and Why," *SEP* 193 (September 18, 1920): reprinted in *MLC,* 5.

29. *DSDZ,* 37–38; "Cruise of the Rolling Junk," 339.

30. *Correspondence,* 48

31. *Correspondence,* 49.

32. *Editor* 52 no. 2 (July 1920): 121–22.

33. Rather than returning directly to Saint Paul, he went on to New York.

34. *Correspondence,* 44–45.

35. "Early Success," *American Cavalcade* 1 (October 1937), reprinted in *MLC,* 187.

36. *Correspondence,* 125.

37. FSF to Oscar Kalman, undated [May 1936], typed letter, unsigned (copy), Kalman.

38. *LL,* 448.

39. *Letters,* 461.

40. *SSEG,* 619, 21.

41. *DSDZ,* 24–25.

42. In Zelda's *Save Me the Waltz,* the heroine's name is Alabama; her older sister's, Dixie.

43. Tom Ensey, "Buried History: Oakwood Cemetery," *Prime Montgomery* 5 (October 2014): 18–21, issuu.com/primemontgomery/docs/primeoct2014digital.

44. *Correspondence,* 44–45.

45. For images of the Wreford vault in Oakwood Cemetery: www.findagrave.com/memorial /8285596/samuel-phippen-wreford.

46. *DSDZ,* 12; *LL,* 363.

47. Not just the early chapters: *Save Me the Waltz* concludes with Alabama keeping vigil at her beloved father's deathbed in her Alabama hometown.

48. *OTTC,* 166; *DSDZ,* 116, 129.

49. *DSDZ,* 212–13.

50. LG, 118.

2. HONEYMOON YEARS (1920–1924)

1. *The Nassau Herald: Class of Nineteen Hundred and Seventeen* (Princeton, NJ: Princeton UP, 1917); "Early Success," 185.

2. *DSDZ,* 12; "Who's Who—and Why," *SEP* 193 (September 18, 1920), reprinted in *MLC,* 5. The frieze of rejection slips became a favorite anecdote; for example, interviews in *Conversations,* 70 and 79.

3. "My Lost City," 109.

4. *LL,* 93.

5. "Early Success," 186; "Table of Contents," *Tales of the Jazz Age,* vii, reprinted in *Cambridge Edition of the Works of F. Scott Fitzgerald.*

6. "My Lost City," 112.

7. *LL,* 315.

8. *As Ever,* 19.

9. In 1950 there were almost four hundred bookstores in Manhattan: gothamist.com/arts -entertainment/map-manhattans-disappearing-bookstores.

10. "Table of Contents," *Tales of the Jazz Age,* ix.

11. *Correspondence,* 71.

12. *Correspondence,* 77.

13. "Early Success," 188.

14. *DSDZ,* 35.

15. "What I Think and Feel at 25," *American Magazine* 94 (September 1922), reprinted in *MLC,* 24.

16. *The Vegetable* (NY: Scribner's, 1923), reprinted in *Last Kiss,* 39.

17. *LL,* 93, 131. Thirty as the pivot between youth and decay may have represented Fitzgerald's retreat from an even younger pivot. John Peale Bishop relates that once "I complained to him that I thought he took seventeen as his norm, making everything later a falling off. For a moment he demurred, then said, "If you make it fifteen, I will agree with you" ("The Missing All," in *Collected Essays* [NY: Scribner's, 1948], 67). Hemingway was contemptuous of Fitzgerald's cult of youth, calling it "this little children's, immature, misunderstood, whining for lost youth death-dance . . ." and remarking that "It was a terrible thing for him to love youth so much that he jumped straight from youth to senility without going through manhood" (*OTTC* 209, 237).

18. Fulton, "Fitzgerald, Flapperdom's Fiction Ace . . . ," 33.

19. "My Lost City," 110.

20. "Books," *New York Tribune,* May 7, 1920, reprinted in *Conversations,* 5.

21. *Letters,* 476.

22. John William Tebbel, *George Horace Lorimer and the Saturday Evening Post* (Garden City, NY: Doubleday, 1948), 45.

23. "Early Success," 189.

24. *Letters,* 460.

25. Turnbull, 108. Turnbull does not cite his source.

26. Quoted in Turnbull, 112–14.

27. *LL,* 189–90.

28. *LL,* 41.

29. *LL,* 41; "Table of Contents," *Tales of the Jazz Age,* vii, reprinted in *Cambridge Edition of the Works of F. Scott Fitzgerald; DSDM,* 32.

30. Turnbull, 114.

31. Turnbull, 114.

32. *LL,* 47. H. L. Mencken's 1917 essay "The Sahara of the Bozart" ridiculed the rural culture of the South. Flattered by his attentions in the early 1920s, Fitzgerald often truckled to Mencken.

33. *DSDM,* 44.

34. *LL,* 49; *DSDM,* 51.

35. *Correspondence,* 246.

36. *LL,* 63.

37. *DSDM,* 67–68.

38. *LL,* 363.

39. *LL,* 59.

40. *LL,* 65; "'Great Neck is Like a Cemetery': Ring Lardner to Thomas Boyd," *FHA,* 1979, 231.

41. "What a 'Flapper Novelist' Thinks of His Wife," *Conversations,* 48, reprinted from the Louisville *Courier-Journal,* September 30, 1923. In 1935 Fitzgerald told his secretary Laura Guthrie that after an abortion Zelda "wanted a child very badly to span over the futility of life, but tho she tried six times it always ended in miscarriages as she could not carry a child again." In a paragraph retailing several doubtful stories, this statement is likely exaggerated. Another time he told Guthrie "of having a [fertility] test made in 1929, and he was practically sterile!" (*LG,* 50, 146).

42. *Correspondence,* 472.

43. *Letters,* 465; Katherine B. Trower, "Letters to the Hoveys," *FHA,* 1978, 58; *Correspondence,* 90; *LL,* 62; *As Ever,* 32, 33.

44. *DSDM,* 51; *LL,* 53, 62

45. *LL,* 121; *DSDZ,* 122. "'The Sensible Thing'" was originally longer, before an editor at *Liberty* "cut [it] to pieces" (*LL,* 80). As printed in both *Liberty* and the 1926 collection *All the Sad Young Men,* it is about fifty-three hundred words, less than half as long as "'O Russet Witch!'"

46. "My Lost City," 108.

47. "'Rosalind' is really flesh and blood—I married her eventually," Fitzgerald wrote in 1920 (*Correspondence,* 71).

48. *DSDZ,* 39 (misdated "Fall 1919," the letter dates from spring 1919, before Zelda broke their engagement).

49. *LL,* 285. "Kinney" may have been Montgomery resident Kate McKinney, "an author and poet who used the pen name of Katydid" and who took inspiration from "the trees and the flowers and the brooks." Fitzgerald's ledger mentions her in 1931.

50. *LL,* 467–68.

51. *DSDZ,* 40.

52. *Real FSF,* 57.

53. Quoted in Jackson R. Bryer, "'Better That All of the Story Never Be told': Zelda Fitzgerald's Sister's Letter to Arthur Mizener," *FSFR* 15 (2017): 6; Campbell, "The Fitzgeralds Were My Friends," 44.

54. "My Lost City," 108; *Notebooks,* #552.

55. In response, he sent her abortifacient pills. "I simply *can't* and *won't* take those awful pills—so I've thrown them away," she wrote back (*DSDZ,* 44).

56. *Notebooks,* #1377. "Paul Lagrand" was probably Zelda's Montgomery contemporary Paul Legrand. His name appears with hers in several society-page paragraphs, including one in August 1919 about "a camping party" for select "members of the younger set" at Whetstone's Lake "for the remainder of the week" (*Montgomery Advertiser,* August 20, 1919, 6). Zelda's story "The Magnolia Tree" does not survive, at least under this title.

57. *Correspondence,* 559.

58. *Correspondence,* 53.

59. Quoted in *SSEG,* 183; "How to Live on $36,000 a Year," *SEP* 205 (March 4, 1933), reprinted in *MLC,* 33.

60. Quoted in "Introduction," *The Vegetable,* ix; *As Ever,* 38.

61. *Letters,* 471; Ray Lewis White, "Ben Hecht on *The Vegetable:* A Lost Chicago Review," *FHA,* 1978, 97–98.

62. "How to Live on $36,000 a Year," 33; "My Ten Favorite Plays," *New York Sun,* September 10, 1934; reprinted in *FHA,* 1978, 61–62.

63. *As Ever,* 75.

64. "How to Live on $36,000 a Year," 31; quoted in *SSEG,* 183.

65. *LL,* 67; *As Ever,* 69.

3. *THE GREAT GATSBY* (1925)

1. H. L. Mencken, "As H.L.M. Sees It," *Baltimore Evening Sun,* May 2, 1925, reprinted in *F. Scott Fitzgerald: The Critical Reception,* ed. Jackson R. Bryer (NY: Burt Franklin & Co., 1978), 211–14.

2. *SSEG,* 217, 133.

3. This exchange is printed in *DSDM,* 99ff.

4. *LL,* 141.

5. "My Lost City," 108. One of *Gatsby*'s earliest admirers was the critic Gilbert Seldes, who recognized the novel's confluence of deep feeling and (in Fitzgerald's words) "artistic achievement." "The technical virtuosity is extraordinary," Seldes wrote, but even more, the novel revealed "a consuming passion. *The Great Gatsby* is passionate as *Some Do Not* [Ford Madox Ford's 1924 novel] is passionate, with such an abundance of feeling for the characters . . . that the most trivial of the actors in the drama are endowed with vitality" ("Spring Flight," *Dial,* August 1925, 162).

6. *LL,* 67; *Correspondence,* 517.

7. *LL,* 65–67.

8. *LL,* 100.

9. The two manuscript pages sent to Cather are held at PUL. Facsimiles are printed in Matthew J. Bruccoli, "'An Instance of Apparent Plagiarism': F. Scott Fitzgerald, Willa Cather, and the First *Gatsby* Manuscript," *Princeton University Library Chronicle* 39 (Spring 1978): 171–78.

10. *LL,* 28.

11. *LL,* 113, 118–19.

12. LG; *Correspondence,* 78.

13. *Willa Cather in Person: Interviews, Speeches, and Letters,* ed. L. Brent Bohlke (Lincoln: U of Nebraska P, 1986), 44.

14. *LL,* 65.

15. *The Selected Letters of Willa Cather,* ed. Andrew Jewell and Janis Stout (NY: Knopf, 2013), 370.

16. *LL,* 76; draft manuscript pages sent to Cather.

17. *Letters,* 509.

18. "A Scrap Book Record."

19. *LL,* 98–100.

20. *LL,* 113, 68.

21. *Motor* 41 (February, March, April 1924).

22. *SSEG,* 143.

23. *As Ever,* 48.

24. *Letters*, 478.

25. *LL*, 67.

26. *LLG*, 208.

27. *LL*, 91.

28. *Letters*, 478. The Cambridge edition of *The Great Gatsby* gives a fuller discussion of the history of the novel's title in appendix 2, 206–8.

29. *LL*, 95.

30. *DSDM*, 84, 94,118.

31. Fitzgerald assigned Gatsby a distinctive feature, too, a "radiant and understanding" smile, mentioned at least seven times, but less successfully than Daisy's voice.

32. *LL*, 87.

33. *LL*, 91. The Fuller case is summarized in Henry Dan Piper, "Gatsby and E. M. Fuller," in *F. Scott Fitzgerald's* The Great Gatsby: *A Literary Reference* (NY: Carroll & Graf, 2000), 26–30.

34. *LL*, 126; *A Literary Reference*, 27.

35. *MLC*, 108–9.

36. The deleted passage appears in *Trimalchio: An Early Version of* The Great Gatsby, ed. James L. W. West III (Cambridge, UK: Cambridge UP, 2000), 90.

37. *Letters*, 480.

38. *Correspondence*, 159.

39. *Correspondence*, 159–60. Perkins too found an "indefinable" quality in *Gatsby*, writing to Ring Lardner that "there is in it a sort of strange mystical element . . . an element that comes partly, perhaps, from once having been a Catholic." Quoted in *Letters from Ring*, ed. Clifford M. Caruthers (Flint, MI: Waldon P, 1979), 189.

40. "My Generation," *Esquire* 70 (October 1968), reprinted in *MLC*, 198. In the *Gatsby* typescript, Fitzgerald used Cather's word "incommunicable": ". . . what I had almost remembered was incommunicable forever" (*Trimalchio*, 91). In the published *Gatsby*, the phrase appears in the final sentence of chapter 6, with "incommunicable" now "uncommunicable." Burlingame's phrase, "a nostalgic quality, indefinable, not specific," suggests a similar ineffable feeling.

41. *Letters*, 477; *Correspondence*, 142.

42. A decade later Laura Guthrie reported Fitzgerald thinking that Zelda had been "unfaithful in her mind."

43. *LL*, 80.

44. *LL*, 187, 209.

45. *Notebooks*, #839.

46. *As Ever*, 64.

4. THE RIVIERA, THE ACTRESS, AND FOOTBALL (1926–1927)

1. *LL*, 125.

2. Ernest Hemingway, *A Moveable Feast: The Restored Edition* (NY: Scribner's, 2009), 125–51.

3. *Letters*, 484.

4. *LL*, 114.

5. *LL*, 139.

6. Sara Murphy may have advised Hemingway differently. In 1939 he would write to her, "You gave me some good advice once about 14 years ago that I didn't take." Pauline Pfeiffer began a stealthy seduction of Hemingway in 1925; his marriage fell apart the following year (*LLG*, 19, 22–23, 244).

7. *A Moveable Feast: The Restored Edition*, 215; *Letters*, 495; PUL, facsimile in *Reader's Companion to F. Scott Fitzgerald's* Tender Is the Night, 6.

8. *LL*, 68; *Correspondence*, 142.

9. *Letters*, 485; *LL*, 126; *Correspondence*, 200 (Picasso and Mistinguett were not American, however); *LL*, 137, 139.

10. *LL*, 131, 192.

11. For these and other details on the film industry in the 1920s, see www.filmsite.org/20s intro.html.

12. "Lipstick," *FHA*, 1978, 3–35.

13. "Lipstick," 35.

14. *LL*, 330; *As Ever*, 96.

15. This sketch of Lois Moran's early life is drawn mostly from Buller.

16. *Letters*, 415–16; *LL*, 330; Buller, 3–4.

17. Carol Johnston, *Motion Picture Classic*, January 1928, 51, 86. The title of this puff piece is ironic, but plays on the popular idea of Moran as lacking sex appeal.

18. Mizener Papers.

19. Buller, 107. Only after meeting Fitzgerald did Moran read *This Side of Paradise* and *The Great Gatsby*.

20. Mizener Papers.

21. Buller, 138–41.

22. Ten years later, compiling a joke résumé, he listed "AFFAIR (unconsumated) with ACTRESS (1927)" (*Correspondence*, 480).

23. LG, 103. They had actually been married only four years when Zelda met Jozan.

24. *Montgomery Advertiser*, March 9, 1927, 16; "Show Mr. and Mrs. F. to Number —" *Esquire* 1–2 (May–June 1934), reprinted in *MLC*, 122.

25. These snapshots are reproduced in *The Romantic Egoists*, ed. Matthew J. Bruccoli, Scottie Fitzgerald Smith, and Joan P. Kerr (Columbia; U of South Carolina P, 1974), 154. Fitzgerald's parents had retired to Washington, DC.

26. Seymour I. Toll, *A Judge Uncommon: A Life of John Biggs, Jr.* (Philadelphia: Legal Communications, 1993), 98–100. Biggs was a noted raconteur whose anecdotes are sometimes dubious. Maxwell Perkins and his wife visited Ellerlie several months later. He had dreaded the visit ". . . on account of cocktails, & made up girls, & smoke, & talk. Things I hate & am told I ought to like." He enjoyed himself, though: "I never saw a finer house, or one so restful. . . . It was like remembering something pleasant of a long time ago." He liked Zelda, too, "a girl of character, meant for a far better life than she has led" (*AEY*, 84–86).

27. Buller, 119.

28. Quoted in Buller, 114.

29. *LL*, 193. Apparently unaware of Zelda's jealousy, Moran saw the Fitzgeralds as an "enchanting" unity. "There was a very definite 'togetherness,' they traveled on the same golden cloud—It wasn't possible to love just one of them. You loved them both. Or, at least, I did" (Mizener Papers).

30. *LL,* 187. Later he told Laura Guthrie that "he loved Lois Moran more than she did him."

31. *LL,* 211.

32. LG, 56. The break perhaps occurred in New York in January 1933, when Moran was playing in the Broadway musical *Of Thee I Sing* and Fitzgerald, visiting the city, went "on a terrible bat." A ledger mention of her in February may misdate a January meeting.

33. Mizener Papers; *Correspondence,* 403–4.

34. LG, 56.

35. Mark Bernstein, *Football: The Ivy League Origins of an American Obsession* (Philadelphia: U of Pennsylvania P, 2001), 25.

36. Quoted in Bernstein, *Football,* 8.

37. "YALE OUTPLAYS TIGER IN 3-3 TIE," *New York Times,* November 16, 1913, S1.

38. Hobey Baker, also an outstanding hockey player (the Princeton hockey arena is named after him), served with distinction as a US Army aviator in France during the First World War but died in a crash a month after the Armistice.

39. "Princeton," *College Humor* 13 (December 1927), reprinted in *MLC,* 8.

40. "Sleeping and Waking," *Esquire* 2 (December 1934), reprinted in *MLC,* 166.

41. *"The Romantic Egotist,"* with author's corrections, *PUL.* Another instance of Fitzgerald's brawny aggressive Yalie is Harry Bellamy of "The Ice Palace."

42. Bruccoli, Smith & Kerr, eds., *Romantic Egoists,* 20.

43. "Handle with Care," *Esquire* 5 (April 1936), reprinted in *MLC,* 153; "The Crack-Up," *Esquire* 5 (February 1936), in *MLC,* 139.

44. *LL,* 85.

45. "Lipstick," *FHA.* 1978, 3–35.

46. "Early Success," 189.

47. "Princeton," in *MLC,* 6, 15.

48. The son of a Maryland family with Confederate sympathies, Poe was a legendary Princeton football player of the 1890s, killed in France (not Flanders) in 1915. Sharing Poe's Maryland roots, Fitzgerald probably sympathized also with his modest frame—five-foot-five, 143 pounds— and academic woes: Poe was first suspended and then expelled for poor grades.

49. The stream of telegrams to Ober about "The Bowl" is printed in *As Ever,* 100–104.

50. *OTTC,* 66–67.

51. After his October 1927 Ellerslie visit, Perkins wrote to Ring Lardner, expressing concern about Fitzgerald's "nerves" and wondering if he might benefit from a cure at Muldoon's sanitarium, run with boot-camp discipline and rigor, in White Plains, New York. "There are two things which Professor Muldoon hates," a journalist reported. "Whisky is one and cigarettes the other" (*New Ulm Review,* September 4, 1907). Lardner dissuaded Perkins.

52. The "scholarly undergraduate" glances at Fitzgerald's two most literary Princeton friends, Edmund Wilson and John Peale Bishop. A Princeton professor who knew Wilson as an undergraduate recalled, "Later Wilson confessed that his college education had been all wrong. He did nothing but sit in his room & study while everyone else was off at a party or a game" (interview with Francis McDonald, December 7, 1947, Piper).

53. "As kingfishers catch fire . . . ," *The Poems of Gerard Manley Hopkins,* ed. W. H. Gardner and N. H. MacKenzie (4th ed., Oxford, UK: Oxford UP, 1970), 90.

54. LG, 99.

55. *Notebooks,* #1071.

56. Quoted in Toll, *A Judge Uncommon*, 95–96.

57. This incident is retold in the early pages of *Tender Is the Night*, assigned to the young actress Rosemary.

58. *LL*, 54. "The Diamond as Big as the Ritz" was initially twenty thousand words, cut to fifteen thousand when Ober had difficulty selling it to magazines (*LL*, 50).

59. To Ina Claire, undated holograph note, www.invaluable.com/auction-lot/F.-Scott-Fitzgerald-2-Autograph-Letters-Signed-8030-c-ED54001B47?utm_source=alerts&utm_medium=email&utm_campaign=inv_kwalert&utm_term=2; *Letters*, 492; "Autobiographical Sketch," quoted in *Zelda*. Fitzgerald had seen Ina Claire when she played the title role in *Quaker Girl* in New York in 1911. He was fifteen. Of her and another actress he would recall, "Confused by my hopeless and melancholy love for them both, I was unable to choose between them—so they blurred into one lovely entity, the girl" ("My Lost City," 106).

60. *Correspondence*, 403.

61. Quoted in *Zelda*, 300.

62. "Offside Play" was rejected by the *Post* and never sold. *Tender Is the Night* mentions an enthusiast similar to Percy Wrackham—"Elkins, who would name you all the quarterbacks in New Haven for thirty years."

63. Turnbull, 249; *Beloved*, 330.

5. RESTLESSNESS AND HIGH SEAS (1928–1929)

1. *LL*, 169.

2. *Tender Is the Night* features a similar age disparity: Dick Diver is thirty-four at the opening; Rosemary, the young actress who seduces him, just turned eighteen.

3. *Correspondence*, 403.

4. *LL*, 188, 193.

5. *LL*, 188; *DSDZ*, 86–87.

6. Lanahan, 26; *Correspondence*, 238, 283; "A Letter from Zelda Fitzgerald," ed. Taylor Littleton, *FHA*, 1975, 5.

7. *LL*, 188; *Letters*, 496; "A Weekend at Ellerslie," in Edmund Wilson, *The Shores of Light: A Literary Chronicle of the Twenties and Thirties* (NY: Farrar, Straus, 1952), 375; *OTTC*, 81.

8. Toll, *A Judge Uncommon*, 98.

9. *LL*, 188.

10. *LL*, 193.

11. "The Rough Crossing" recalls a transatlantic voyage Fitzgerald later described, with flourishes, to Laura Guthrie. "Zelda and he got very drunk the first thing. . . . Zelda had the bright idea of calming a terrible storm by propitiating the gods of the tempest. . . . And all of a sudden she decided to throw some valuable overboard and did throw her diamond engagement ring!" (LG).

12. The fourth, "The Swimmers," is a story of a French wife's flagrant and multiple adulteries, the only story of the six which ends with the man and younger woman presumably destined for marriage.

13. *Montgomery Advertiser*, January 5, 1927, 7; April 22, 1923, 19.

14. While stationed earlier at Fort Leavenworth, Fitzgerald had noted in his ledger a "Knowles," and later the same month, "Admiration for Knowles." The ledger mentions no Knowles in Montgomery.

15. F. Scott Fitzgerald, *Poems 1911–1940,* ed. Matthew J. Bruccoli (Bloomfield, MI: Bruccoli and Clark, 1981), 137.

16. "A Scrap Book Record." 141.

17. *DSDZ,* 226–27.

18. In both typescript and the *SEP,* Andy reports that "This ["that" in *SEP*] was ten years ago"—not fifteen. Ten would make better sense: "fifteen years ago" places Andy in 1933, four years after "Belles" was published.

19. The "incompatibility" keeping Ailie and Andy apart was unclear even to Fitzgerald. The typescript explains, "In spite of every incompatibility, of our complete inability to condone each other's mental processes . . ."—but this murky passage, canceled, hardly clarifies (*F. Scott Fitzgerald Manuscripts,* ed. Matthew J. Bruccoli [NY: Garland, 1991], vol. 6, pt. 1: 478).

6. A NOVEL STALLS, ZELDA CRASHES (1930)

1. *LL,* 90.

2. *LL,* 111, 125; *DSDM,* 120.

3. *LL,* 126, 127, 129.

4. *LL,* 131–32, 136, 140, 146, 148, 149, 152, 156; *DSDM,* 141, 144.

5. *DSDM,* 147.

6. *DSDM,* 149, 150.

7. *DSDM,* 151; *LL,* 158.

8. *LL,* 193.

9. Mayfield, *Exiles from Paradise,* 15.

10. *LL,* 159; *DSDM,* 154.

11. *LL,* 161.

12. Matthew J. Bruccoli, *The Composition of* Tender Is the Night: *A Study of the Manuscripts* (U of Pittsburgh P, 1963), xvii.

13. *DSDM,* 120; *LL* 140–41.

14. *LL,* 376.

15. Fitzgerald's admiration for Sara Murphy might also have provided better material for his novel. On a scrap of paper dating from 1940, he compiled a list of "Fixations," beginning at age fourteen. More than a dozen names or initials appear, most easily identifiable—"G.K." for Ginevra King; "D.P." for Dolly Powers, a brief Saint Paul flame in 1916; "Z" for Zelda; "M" in 1927, for Lois Moran. But for two periods, 1925–27 and 1928–31, when the Fitzgeralds were mostly in Europe, the "fixation" is abbreviated "H.Q.S.," which is enigmatic. It might somehow refer to Hemingway, whom he first met in 1925; it might refer to "quiet" Sara Murphy ("Her reticence . . . her power / Of feeling what she had not put in words"—Archibald MacLeish, "Sketch for a Portrait of Mme. G— M—"); "half-baked" was a joke between her and Fitzgerald. "Half-baked quiet Sara"? Long after their Riviera days, Fitzgerald wrote Sara what could be described only as a love letter. "I used you again and again in *Tender,*" he noted, citing as example (slightly misquoted)

a line describing the novel's Abe North: "He had been heavy, belly-frightened with love of her for years" (*LL*, 287–89).

16. *OTTC*, 73.

17. Fitzgerald himself testified later that 1928, 1929, and 1930 were "all devoted to short stories" (*As Ever*, 221).

18. *OTTC*, 70–71.

19. Honoria Murphy Donnelly, *Sara & Gerald : Villa America and After* (NY: Times Books, 1982), 37.

20. *LL*, 164–67.

21. *Hemingway Letters*, 424–25. Fitzgerald's suggestions were "well meant," Hemingway conceded several years later (*OTTC*, 219).

22. *Letters*, 305.

23. *Letters*, 304; *Hemingway Letters*, 304–5.

24. Seldes's review appeared in *the Dial* in August 1925. Its praise of *Gatsby* may have rankled with Hemingway because of its assertion that with *Gatsby* Fitzgerald had left behind "all the men of his own generation and most of his elders." In *The Sun Also Rises*, which Hemingway was writing that August, Seldes's phrase "irony and pity" is ridiculed at length. "They're mad about it in New York" (home of *the Dial*'s offices), the character Bill Gorton scoffs, and extemporizes a foul-mouthed jingle based on it.

25. *LL*, 169.

26. *LL*, 169.

27. *Hemingway Letters*, 262, 273.

28. *OTTC*, 69.

29. Scott Donaldson, *By Force of Will: The Life and Art of Ernest Hemingway* (NY: Viking, 1977), 145.

30. *Hemingway Letters*, 285.

31. *DSDM*, 156.

32. "Personals," *Montgomery Advertiser*, December 3, 1929, 6. After Christmas in Montgomery they planned to spend two months in New York.

33. "Show Mr. and Mrs. F. to Number —," *Esquire*, May–June 1934, reprinted in *MLC*, 116–29. The photos are reproduced in Bruccoli, Smith, and Kerr, eds., *Romantic Egoists*, 169. *LL*, 189.

34. Quoted in *Zelda*, 207.

35. Quoted in *Zelda*, 205.

36. Quoted in *Zelda*, 215.

37. LG, 64.

38. LG, 103.

39. *Correspondence*, 293.

40. *LLG*, 6.

41. "Pasting It Together," *Esquire* 5 (March 1936), reprinted in *MLC*, 149.

42. Linda Patterson Miller, "Fanny and Honoria Remember: September 1994," *FSFR* 8 (2010): 16.

43. The smokestack sentence was a handwritten afterthought in the typescript. In 1923 Gerald Murphy had notoriously painted and exhibited an eighteen-by-twelve-foot canvas of a liner's smokestacks, titled *Boatdeck*, now lost.

44. Both Fitzgeralds apparently *did* stay to watch the dancers in Bou Saâda, Zelda recalling the occasion in "Show Mr. and Mrs. F. to Number —": "The Ouled Nails were very brown and clean-cut girls, impersonal as they turned themselves into fitting instruments for sex by the ritual of their dance, jangling their gold . . ." (in *MLC*, 126).

45. *OTTC*, 133.

46. Quoted in *Zelda*, 148; *OTTC*, 97. H. L. Mencken, who sometimes saw Fitzgerald during the latter's Baltimore days in the early 1930s, echoed Hadley Hemingway: "He has a playful habit of calling those [doctors] he knows at 3 a.m. and demanding treatment, i.e., something to drink. How he manages to get any work done I can't imagine" (*The Diary of H. L. Mencken*, ed. Charles A. Fecher [NY: Knopf, 1989], 63).

47. Boswell's *Life of Johnson*, April 17, 1778.

48. *Letters*, 471; Turnbull, 223.

49. Lanahan, 36, 46 (ellipses in original). The Newman Smiths were living in Belgium.

7. THE VINE-CURTAINED VERANDA MEETS THE JAZZ AGE (1931–1934)

1. *Correspondence*, 429. Sara Murphy had earlier chastised Fitzgerald for arrogance: "Consideration for other people's feelings, opinions or even time is *Completely* left out of your makeup. . . . why,—for instance *should* you trample on other people's feelings continually with things you permit yourself to say & do—owing partly to the self-indulgence of drinking too much . . . unless from the greatest egotism, & sureness that you are *righter* than anyone else?" (*LLG*, 87).

2. *Correspondence*, 308.

3. *Correspondence*, 283.

4. "Cruise of the Rolling Junk," 307; *Diary of H. L. Mencken*, 45. Though paying homage to his Maryland forebears, Fitzgerald only dabbled in genealogy. Scottie, however, in later life compiled "about six hundred pages of genealogical research . . . in a three-inch-thick looseleaf notebook," her daughter reported. "She had gathered all her findings not only on our Fitzgerald and Sayre colonial antecedents, but on the Lanahans and Bonsals [Scottie's first husband's family] as well" (Lanahan, 458). One product of Scottie's researches, "The Colonial Ancestors of Francis Scott Key Fitzgerald," greatly condensed from the six hundred pages, is printed as an appendix to *SSEG*.

5. *LL*, 291.

6. *OTTC*, 170, 174.

7. A volume of Eliot's poem of conversion, *Ash Wednesday*, "Inscribed to Scott Fitzgerald with the author's homage," is now held at the University of South Carolina. In 1926 Fitzgerald professed his "profound admiration" for Eliot as "the greatest living poet in any language," but apart from the much-discussed *Waste Land* (1922), there's little evidence that he was very familiar with Eliot's poetry, including *Ash Wednesday* (*LL*, 139).

8. Quoted in Barbara Lehman Smith, *Elizabeth Sparhawk Jones: The Artist Who Lived Twice* (Denver: Outskirts P, 2010), 96. Fitzgerald's *Notebooks* include a reference to the "fearlessness" of an unnamed woman, apparently Margaret Turnbull: ". . . consider M . . . T . . . who was a

clergyman's daughter—and equally with the others [three other women, including Zelda] had everything to lose and nothing to gain economically. She had the same recklessness" (552). The reference to "recklessness" and masking of her identity suggest sexual transgression. Other evidence suggests that Margaret Turnbull led a chaste life as wife, mother, hostess, and chatelaine of Trimbush. Writing to her, Fitzgerald did not switch from "Dear Mrs. Turnbull" to "Dear Margaret" until he had left La Paix. His surviving letters reveal that their conversations ranged from the domestic to the political and philosophical. Yet a short 1935 letter Fitzgerald wrote to her, mostly about a Thomas Wolfe novel, closes, with abrupt urgency, "I want to see you soon" (*Correspondence* 404). Mrs. Turnbull attended Fitzgerald's funeral with her son Andrew. "Afterwards, we drove to the cemetery in the rain," he would recall, "and when the casket had been covered, my mother laid some pine branches from La Paix over the red earth" (Turnbull, 322). She later requested of Scottie a personal memento of her father—"something like a penknife or a paper weight . . . maybe even just a pencil" (quoted in *Against*, 128).

9. *Letters,* 439.

10. *Diary of H. L. Mencken,* 45.

11. "Malcolm Cowley, The Art of Fiction No. 70," ed. John McCall, *Paris Review* 85 (Fall 1982).

12. Quoted in William Katterjohn, "An Interview with Theodora Gager, Fitzgerald's Private Nurse," *FHA,* 1974, 75–85.

13. Mrs. Owens's account of her years as Fitzgerald's secretary, in John F. Kelly, "Fitzgerald: recollections of a novelist in decline," *Baltimore Sun,* December 21, 1982, B1, B4.

14. Turnbull, 222.

15. *Letters,* 437.

16. Turnbull, "Further Notes on Fitzgerald at La Paix," *New Yorker,* November 17, 1956, 154.

17. For a first-person memory of the fire: www.baltimoresun.com/news/bs-xpm-1996-09-24 -1996268139-story.html

18. *LL,* 268.

19. *Correspondence,* 494.

20. *The Saturday Evening Post* altered this mention of "S.A." to "I never had the sort of thing that Amanda and Jean had."

21. "Show Mr. and Mrs. F to Number —" reprinted in *MLC,* 127.

22. "The Sanitariums," *Fortune* 11 (April 1935): 197.

23. *Diary of H. L. Mencken,* 45.

24. *Correspondence,* 315. At the end of *Tender Is the Night* Fitzgerald joked about the novel's endless gestation: Dick Diver "always had a big stack of papers on his desk that were known to be an important treatise on some medical subject, almost in process of completion."

25. *DSDM,* 194, 189.

26. All in *DSDM.*

27. *Correspondence,* 327.

28. *OTTC,* 181, 205; *LL,* 278.

29. *Correspondence,* 323; *OTTC,* 207; *LL,* 259.

30. *Hemingway Letters,* 407; *OTTC,* 209; interview with Arnold Gingrich, March 29, 1944, Piper; typed letter, signed, to Gerald Murphy, July 30, 1962, Sara and Gerald Murphy Papers, Beinecke Rare Book and Manuscript Library, Yale University.

31. *OTTC,* 211; *Letters,* 510.

32. *Correspondence,* 361.

33. *LL* 181; *Letters,* 526; LG, 120.

34. *Letters,* 419; *DSDM,* 221; *Notebooks* #1031, 1034; *Correspondence,* 590; *Conversations,* 36.

35. *Letters,* 256; *As Ever,* 205–6.

36. *Diary of H. L. Mencken,* 62.

37. *Letters,* 524.

38. *Letters,* 530; *LL,* 290–91.

39. Quoted in Matthew J. Bruccoli, *The O'Hara Concern* (NY: Random House, 1975), 99. Fitzgerald's ledger notes "Parker & O'Hara" in March 1934.

40. *AEY,* 127, 118.

41. *AEY,* 122.

42. *DSDM,* 203–4. Insomniac the night before, he read "an old account of Stuart's battles for an hour or so."

43. *Aeneid* 1.405 ("et vera incessu patuit dea"); *DSDM,* 203.

44. *Correspondence,* 259. Bert Barr later donated her Fitzgerald mementos to Princeton; see Matthew Bruccoli, "Epilogue: A Woman, a Gift, and a Still Unanswered Question," *Esquire* 30 (January 1979): 67.

45. *Correspondence,* 262–63, 408.

46. *Correspondence,* 408; LG; *DSDM,* 224.

47. LG. Harriman's *Times* obituary mentions only two marriages. The current husband had just moved out. After abandoning her at the Algonquin, Fitzgerald wrote in palliation, ". . . I thought you'd think I'd run out on *you,* instead of on my own wretched state of mind and health." As Harriman moved in fast, emancipated circles, Fitzgerald, fearing syphilis, considered her the probable source.

48. LG. Either Fitzgerald or Laura Guthrie got the name wrong; Guthrie's journal calls her "Anne Cunningham."

49. Quoted in Scott O'Brien, *Elissa Landi: Cinema's Empress of Emotion* (Orlando, FL: Bear-Manor Media, 2020), 135. Though she was later registered as born in Venice, Elissa Landi's birthplace is disputed. Her parents were Austrian. Family legend promoted by Landi's mother, Caroline, held that she, Caroline, was the illegitimate daughter of Habsburg Empress Elizabeth of Austria, making Landi Empress Elizabeth's granddaughter. Landi married an English barrister in 1928, but when she left for America he remained in England and after 1930 they saw little of each other. Culturally she was an overmatch for Fitzgerald, who was probably dazzled not only by her looks and air but also by her intelligence and cosmopolitan background. There is no mention of Landi in his ledger and no evidence they had met before 1935. When he arrived in Hollywood two years later, she was leaving for the East to resume her stage career.

50. *LHD,* 10, 11.

51. Landi avoided Hollywood social life, living modestly with her parents, brother, and sister-in-law, riding for recreation, and writing between acting assignments.

52. Quoted in James Fox, *Five Sisters: The Langhornes of Virginia* (NY: Simon and Schuster, 2000), 463.

53. Fox, *Five Sisters,* 25, 215. Fitzgerald quotes "a heart like a hotel" in *Notebooks,* #1740.

54. *New York Times,* January 13, 1913, 1.

55. "YALE'S MUSICAL CLUBS HAD FINE WESTERN TRIP," *New York Times,* January 5, 1913, X8; Fox, *Five Sisters,* 215–16.

56. "Milestones," *Time Magazine,* July 27, 1931.

57. *Notebooks,* #552, 541.

58. *Letters,* 546. The Flynns hosted Scottie on another occasion as well, Fitzgerald writing his Baltimore secretary in 1936, "Scotty is with the M. B. Flinns in Tryon & well taken care of for four or five days anyhow" (autograph letter to Isabel Owens, signed, n.d. [around November 1936], sold at auction May 26, 2022, Written Word Autographs, Tamworth, NH).

59. *LG,* 120.

60. *DSSM,* 217.

61. "The Crack-Up," *Esquire* 5 (February 1936), reprinted in *MLC,* 143.

62. *LG,* 14.

63. *LG,* 14.

64. "Gossip of All the Studios," *Photoplay,* February 28, 1928, 96.

65. *Correspondence,* 495.

8. CRACK-UP DRAMA (1935–1936)

1. All references to Guthrie's journal: Subseries 6D: Laura Guthrie Hearne Additions; F. Scott Fitzgerald Additional Papers, C0188, at Princeton's Firestone Library. The journal is supplemented by other material Guthrie donated—letters, notes, memoranda, snapshots, and poems. A published record of this same summer of 1935, written forty years later, Tony Buttita's *After the Good Gay Times,* is wholly unreliable.

2. *DSDM,* 223, 224.

3. *Correspondence,* 413.

4. *Letters,* 526.

5. *LL,* 189; ALS to Laura Guthrie, postmarked July 29, 1935, PUL.

6. *Hemingway Letters,* 407.

7. The auto-accident story in *This Side of Paradise,* revised for Guthrie, was inspired by reports of two auto accidents fatal to Princeton contemporaries. Fitzgerald later repeated it for Sheilah Graham (*Real FSF,* 84). In April 1917, during Fitzgerald's final spring at Princeton, Robert Sniffen was killed in an accident in Lawrenceville, New Jersey, while returning from Trenton with two other undergraduates. A day later, Charles Wiegand, who had just dropped out of Princeton to join the Navy, was killed in an accident in Newport, Rhode Island. Though noting both deaths in his ledger, Fitzgerald was present at neither.

8. Bimini and Tahiti are eight thousand nautical miles apart, but possibly Fitzgerald or Guthrie confused them.

9. Facsimile of a manuscript note charting Fitzgerald's various times together with Hemingway, reproduced in *College,* 61.

10. *Correspondence,* 421–22.

11. FSF to Oscar Kalman, September 19, 1936, typed letter, Kalman. When Fitzgerald returned to Hollywood in 1937, the now-widowed Shearer brushed him off. "When he telephoned Norma Shearer," Sheilah Graham recalled, ". . . she did not return his call. . . . 'She doesn't want anything to do with me,' Scott said resignedly, after writing her a letter that she did not answer."

12. Even earlier, not every woman found Fitzgerald a "stud." One, a West Virginian who met him when he was twenty, recalled summer-evening canoe rides on the Shenandoah with Fitzgerald, during which "he talked and talked." But, she continued, "The southern boys I knew,

despite their verbal lethargy, at least understood what it was all about, and were more aggressive and emotionally satisfying. In 1917, I'm afraid, Scott just wasn't a very lively male animal." A private nurse at La Paix in 1932-33, Theodora Gager, remarked that Fitzgerald "wasn't too virile a man. You know some men just live for sex, but Scott Fitzgerald didn't. I could see that distinction." MacKie, "My Friend Scott Fitzgerald," 20; Katterjohn, "An Interview with Theodora Gager," 83.

13. *AEY*, 133, 253.

14. *DSDM*, 208.

15. Margaret Culkin Banning, "Scott Fitzgerald in Tryon, North Carolina," *FHA*, 1973, 151-54. Earlier, Banning had remarked, "The Flynns heard he was a celebrity & took him up—then learned he was a 'has been' and let him down" (interview with Margaret Culkin Banning, April 7, 1947, Piper).

16. Interview with Zelda Fitzgerald, March 13-14, 1947, Piper.

17. Quoted in Rodger L. Tarr, "Marjorie Kinnan Rawlings Meets F. Scott Fitzgerald: The Unpublished Accounts," *Journal of Modern Literature* 22 (Autumn 1998): 173-74.

18. Tarr, "Rawlings Meets Fitzgerald," 173.

19. Tarr, "Rawlings Meets Fitzgerald," 173.

20. *Selected Letters of Marjorie Kinnan Rawlings,* ed. Gordon E. Bigelow and Laura V. Monti (Gainesville: University Presses of Florida, 1983), 311.

21. André Le Vot, *F. Scott Fitzgerald: A Biography* (Garden City, NY: Doubleday, 1983), 285.

22. *Correspondence,* 419.

23. Just before marrying, Beatrice wrote in her diary: "Were I to write my meditations upon the eve of my wedding, I should be forced to admit not an all absorbing love or respect for DuPre." She had at least twice postponed the wedding (private collection).

24. ALS to Dupré Dance, postmarked June 7, 1935, private collection; Edmund Spenser, *Faerie Queene,* book 3, canto 12, stanza 21.

25. Beatrice and Hop remained married and active in San Antonio country-club circles until his death in 1962; Eleanor married a clergyman in 1937. Fitzgerald and Beatrice never met again.

26. *OTTC,* 224; *Correspondence,* 420.

27. *Correspondence,* 310. *Aisment* should probably be *aisance.*

28. Returning to Asheville the following year, Fitzgerald asked Guthrie to resume working with him. She declined (ALS, April 14, 1936, PUL). During summer 1936, Fitzgerald's chief companions were nurses hired to help control his drinking, and after he broke a shoulder in a diving accident and was encased in a body cast, to minister to his incapacity. See Helen DeVinney, "Evidence of a Previously Unknown Fitzgerald Nurse: Correspondence from F. Scott Fitzgerald to Pauline Brownell," *FSFR* 2005, 190-96.

29. ALS to Laura Guthrie, October 25, 1935, PUL.

30. *LL,* 292-93.

31. Interview with Nora Flynn, February 24, 1947, Piper.

32. The three "Crack-Up" essays were written in late 1935 and published in successive issues of *Esquire* in 1936: "The Crack-Up" (February), "Pasting It Together" (March), and "Handle with Care" (April); reprinted in *MLC.*

33. *Letters,* 533. After they appeared, he advised one reader, "don't take that little trilogy in *Esquire* too seriously (*Correspondence,* 427); another, "Don't put too much credence in them" (*Correspondence,* 452); another, "I am not at all the sort of person I pictured in those articles.

They were written in the utmost sincerity but definitely in a 'mood' which endured about four months—parallel to a man being one person when drunk & another when sober." Quoted in James L. W. West III, "F. Scott Fitzgerald and American Psychiatry: A New Letter," *American Imago* 68 (Spring 2011): 59–65.

34. Mizener, 290, 277.

35. Turnbull, 269–70.

36. Henry Dan Piper, *F. Scott Fitzgerald: A Critical Portrait* (NY: Holt, Rinehart & Winston, 1965), 234–26.

37. Introductory note, "A Summer with F. Scott Fitzgerald," a mangled extract from Laura Guthrie's journal, *Esquire,* December 1964, 160.

38. Brown, *Paradise Lost,* 279.

39. Kirk Curnutt, communication on the manuscript for this book.

40. He acknowledged his debt to Nora Flynn (by name) in a letter to Sara Murphy the following year: "She helped me over one black week when I thought this was probably as good a time to quit as any" (*LLG,* 159).

41. The alcoholic's memoir was William Seabrook's *Asylum.*

42. Fitzgerald's ledger breaks off monthly entries in March 1935, with a final isolated entry two months later, "Reached Ashville May 16th."

43. *OTTC,* 237.

44. *Hemingway Letters,* 407–9.

45. James L. W. West III, "The Lost Months: New Fitzgerald Letters from the Crack-Up Period," *Princeton University Library Chronicle,* Spring 2004, 489.

46. West, "Lost Months," 488.

47. *The Letters of Thomas Wolfe,* ed. Elizabeth Nowell (NY: Scribner's, 1956), 542.

48. "The Other Side of Paradise," *New York Post,* September 25, 1936, 1; *LL,* 308–9.

9. FITZGERALD'S LAST CHAPTER: HOLLYWOOD (1937–1940)

1. *LL,* 330.

2. *LL,* 330.

3. *LL,* 334.

4. *Letters,* 556; *LL,* 340–41.

5. *LL,* 341.

6. *LL,* 49.

7. *Letters,* 559.

8. *LL,* 339.

9. *LL,* 342.

10. *LL,* 343.

11. *LL,* 352.

12. Quoted in Aaron Latham, *Crazy Sundays: F. Scott Fitzgerald in Hollywood* (NY: Viking P, 1971), 123–24.

13. Quoted in Kenneth L. Geist, *Pictures Will Talk: The Life and Films of Joseph L. Mankiewicz* (NY: Scribner's, 1978), 89–90. Mankiewicz later claimed that his rewriting of *Three Comrades*

was spurred by Margaret Sullavan, the female lead, who complained that, in Fitzgerald's script, "many of her speeches were unspeakable."

14. *Correspondence,* 565, 516.

15. At a 1931 Hollywood party hosted by Thalberg's wife, Norma Shearer, Fitzgerald's tipsy performance of "Dog! Dog! Dog!"—a favorite recitation piece—was snubbed by other guests. The fiasco inspired his 1932 story "Crazy Sunday." Unabashed, he declaimed the same doggerel verse for Laura Guthrie in 1935. "Dog! Dog! Dog!" is printed in *Poems 1911–1940,* 141–42.

16. *Correspondence,* 556.

17. *Correspondence,* 565–66.

18. *LL,* 429.

19. *Correspondence,* 582.

20. Budd Schulberg, *The Disenchanted* (NY: Random House, 1950).

21. Manley Halliday's vocative "baby" occurs almost fifty times in *The Disenchanted.* Laura Guthrie and Sheilah Graham also note Fitzgerald's use of it.

22. *College,* 67; *As Ever,* 387; *DSDZ* 279.

23. *Letters,* 583.

24. *LL,* 393.

25. *LL,* 395; *Correspondence,* 536. The Winter Carnival binge had not involved Zelda.

26. With her husband on sea duty as a Navy officer, Scottie also spent most of World War II with the Obers.

27. *LL,* 395, 396; *LLG,* 238, 254.

28. *LL,* 403. To "Mrs. Horton," October 20, 1939, typed letter, signed, www.invaluable.com/auction-lot/fitzgerald-f-scott-1896-1940-703-c-2f449f7bc1.

29. *Against,* 32.

30. *LL,* 404.

31. *Against,* 34–35.

32. For the Littauer-Fitzgerald exchange, see *Correspondence,* 550, 561, 562.

33. Wendy W. Fairey, *One of the Family* (NY: Norton, 1992), 54.

34. *Beloved,* 178.

35. *Beloved,* 132.

36. *Real FSF,* 27, 24.

37. *Beloved,* 169; *Real FSF,* 177, 26.

38. *Beloved,* 182.

39. *Real FSF,* 19.

40. *Real FSF,* 18.

41. "To the Beloved Infidel," in *Poems 1911–1940,* 150–51.

42. *Real FSF,* 67, 27.

43. *College,* 56; *LL,* 363.

44. *Real FSF,* 16.

45. *Beloved,* 309.

46. *Beloved,* 309, 314. Graham's third memoir of Fitzgerald, *The Real F. Scott Fitzgerald,* sketches a more ambiguous portrait, with remarks like "there would always be a soft, deteriorated side to his nature that could not be repaired because it had been destroyed" (24–25), and the scoffing question, "But was Scott ever a strong character?" (177).

47. *Against,* 96–97.

48. *Against,* 91.

49. *College,* 145; *Real FSF,* 201.

50. *Real FSF,* 201.

51. *Beloved,* 306–7; *Real FSF,* 201.

52. *Real FSF,* 202.

53. *Real FSF,* 201.

54. *Against,* 93; *Real FSF,* 44; *LLG,* 84.

55. *Against,* 95.

56. *The Sons of Maxwell Perkins,* ed. Matthew J. Bruccoli (Columbia: U of South Carolina P, 2004), 312.

57. "Foreword," *The Last Tycoon,* [ed. Edmund Wilson] (NY: Scribner's, 1941), ix–x.

58. "Scott Fitzgerald's Last Novel," *New York Times Book Review,* November 9, 1941, 1; "The Last Tycoon," *Saturday Review of Literature,* December 6, 1941, 10.

59. *DSDM,* 268.

60. *OTTC,* 314.

61. *DSDZ,* 374.

62. *Beloved,* 318.

63. *Real FSF,* 27.

64. *Beloved,* 318.

65. *Real FSF,* 27–28, quoting from *The Last Tycoon.* Graham misquotes slightly: "The glance" should be "Their glance."

66. Quoted in *Real FSF,* 16.

67. *Spokesman-Review* (Spokane, WA), July 27, 1937, 5; *Real FSF,* 144. Graham's comment about the unhappiest male undercuts her later raptures about instantaneous and electrical mutual attraction. Printed three days after first meeting Fitzgerald, the column appeared on the same day she first led him to her bedroom, as narrated in both *Beloved Infidel* and *The Real F. Scott Fitzgerald.* Also challenging Graham's claims of instant rapturous connection was Fitzgerald's interest three months later in Ginevra King, now Mrs. John Pirie. After their luncheon reunion, "For the next few days I was besieged with calls," she recalled, "but . . . he soon gave up the pursuit" (Mizener Papers).

68. *Notebooks,* #569; quoted in *Zelda,* 109; LG; Ring Lardner, "The Other Side," *Liberty,* February 14–March 14, 1925; Campbell, "The Fitzgeralds Were My Friends," *FHA,* 1978, 43. Lardner composed two doggerel odes to Zelda, mostly jokes and nonsense, but lines like

Of all the girls for whom I care,
And there are quite a number,
None can compare with Zelda Sayre, . . .

may betray genuine admiration. When the Fitzgeralds left Great Neck for France in April 1924, he sent another, beginning

Zelda, fair queel of Alabam',
Across the waves I kiss you!
You think I am a stone, a clam:

You think that I don't care a damn,
But God! how I will miss you!

(*Letters From Ring*, 170, 177). "Queel" was a joke deriving from the story of a drunken toast to Queen Victoria: "Gen'lemen—the queal!" (Richard Winslow, "Fitzgerald's 'Favorite Story,'" *FHA*, 1978, 67).

69. Campbell, "The Fitzgeralds Were My Friends," *FHA*, 1978, 47.

70. *Real FSF*, 32. "Knowing my shyness about my body he took care to look only at my head!" (120).

71. *Real FSF*, 120. "Our love, I have thought, was like being in a warm bath," she added.

72. "Lamp in a Window," *New Yorker* 11 (March 23, 1935): 18. A slightly different version is printed in *Last Kiss*. Even walking on the beach, Fitzgerald wore shoes and socks (*Beloved*, 33).

73. *Beloved*, 248; typed letter, signed, O'Hara to Gerald Murphy, July 30, 1962, Sara and Gerald Murphy Papers, Beinecke Rare Book and Manuscript Library, Yale University. In *Real FSF*, Graham wrote, "I have often had the thought that Scott's nature was more spiritual than my own, which I always considered earthy" (119).

74. Lionel Trilling, *The Liberal Imagination* (NY: Viking, 1950), 246; *Letters*, 540.

75. Midge Decter, "Fitzgerald at the End," *Partisan Review* 26 (Spring 1959): 304.

76. *Real FSF*, 180.

77. Brown, *Paradise Lost*, 317.

78. A self-mocking precursor of Pat Hobby, Finnegan of "Financing Finnegan" (1938) is an erratic, excuse-making, chronically indebted writer who unmistakably satirizes Fitzgerald himself.

79. Sheilah Graham recalled Fitzgerald enjoying the Hobby stories: "Between studio jobs Scott would write another Pat Hobby story for *Esquire;* some of these gave him great amusement" (*College*, 130). Frances Kroll recalled that, the more Hobby stories Fitzgerald wrote, "the more attached to him he became" (*Against*, 53).

80. *SSEG*, 469. Bruccoli loathed Pat Hobby and thought enjoyment of the stories symptomatic of diseased psychology: "The morbid interest in Fitzgerald's work for the [Hollywood] studios has resulted in the overrating of the Pat Hobby stories" (Bruccoli, "Foreword" to Mary Jo Tate, *Critical Companion to F. Scott Fitzgerald: A Literary Reference to His Life and Work [NY: Facts on File, 1998]*).

81. As early at 1937, Perkins had recognized the appeal of the comeback angle: "If he will only begin to dramatize himself as the man who came back now, everything may turn out rightly" (*OTTC*, 252).

82. *LL*, 426–27.

83. "Love Is a Pain," in *I'd Die for You and Other Lost Stories*, ed. Anne Margaret Daniel (NY: Scribner, 2017).

84. *Real FSF*, 21.

85. *Notebooks*, #1915.

86. *LL*, 319; *Real FSF*, 43.

87. "He tended to downgrade the British, insisting that Americans were better, but I was then too fresh from England to take his criticism without contradiction" (*Real FSF*, 124).

88. In *College*, Graham wrote: "*Collier's* magazine in 1949 had published Scott's short story

'The Last Kiss,' originally titled 'Pink and Silver Frost,' which I recognized as a hostile version of Kathleen in *The Last Tycoon*" (7). But though flawed, Pamela Knighton hardly suggests hostility.

89. *Real FSF,* 177.

EPILOGUE

1. Fitzgerald's letters to Scottie are printed in *Letters* and *LHD,* both edited by Andrew Turnbull.

2. "Introduction," *LHD,* xv. Scottie is quoting Malcolm Cowley.

3. "Zelda's sisters suspected there might be another woman, but they were as careful as Scott to keep this fact from Zelda" (*Real FSF,* 68).

4. For the Fitzgeralds' exchange of letters, see *DSDZ.*

5. "A Letter from Zelda Fitzgerald," ed. Taylor Littleton, *FHA,* 1975, 3–6.

6. *Correspondence,* 500.

7. An entry headed "*List of Troubles*" in Fitzgerald's notebooks includes nineteen medical issues ranging from "Tingling Feet" to "Depression and Melancholia." It is probably a list of his own complaints (*Notebooks* #929).

8. He would have had a family interest in the war, too. Scottie married a Navy officer in 1943, and two of Fitzgerald's brothers-in-law, Rosalind Sayre's husband Colonel Newman Smith and Annabel Fitzgerald's husband Rear Admiral Clifton Sprague, distinguished themselves.

9. One witness left a description of Fitzgerald's body as it lay in an open casket at Pierce Brothers Mortuary: "Not a soul was in the room. Except for one bouquet of flowers and a few empty chairs, there was nothing to keep him company except his casket. . . . Not a line showed on his face. His hair was parted slightly to one side. None of it was gray. . . . His hands were horribly wrinkled and thin. . . . Others must have come in during the day, but the fact remains that nobody was there when we were" (Frank Scully, *Rogues' Gallery: Profiles of My Eminent Contemporaries* [Hollywood: Murray & Gee, 1943], 267–70).

10. "Dedication," Bruccoli, Smith, and Kerr, eds., *Romantic Egoists.*

11. *As Ever,* 423. In a late codicil (evidently ignored) to her will, Mollie Fitzgerald had requested burial in the McQuillan lot in Saint Paul.

12. *AEY,* 184.

13. Turnbull, 321–22.

14. Quoted in Perry Deane Young, "This Side of Rockville," *Washington Post Sunday Magazine,* January 14, 1979, 8–15.

15. Quoted in Lanahan, 133.

16. *OTTC,* 175.

INDEX

"Absolution" (Fitzgerald), 84–85

Adams, James Truslow, 5–6

Adams, J. Donald, 277–78

agrarian sentimentality, 81–82

alcoholism, 5, 86, 179, 187, 203–6, 232–38, 254–55, 257–59, 265–69, 274–75, 280

Algeria, 185

American Dream, 5–6, 19, 92, 305n7

Antibes, France, 86, 110, 112

Asheville, North Carolina, 226–36, 243, 248–56, 258–59, 267, 323n28

Atlantic City, New Jersey, 75–76

"At Your Age" (Fitzgerald), 156–57

"Babylon Revisited" (Fitzgerald), 16, 167, 196, 200, 214, 276, 295

Baker, Hobey, 121–24, 315n38

Balmer, Edwin, 1, 3–4

Baltimore, Maryland, 21, 45, 159, 200–204, 211–14, 216–17, 222, 227, 235, 255, 319n46

Banning, Margaret Culkin, 245–46, 323n15

Barr, Bert, 218–19, 321n44

"Basil and Cleopatra" (Fitzgerald), 29

Basil stories, 125, 156, 178–79

Beautiful and Damned, The (Fitzgerald), 5, 7, 56, 61, 65, 66, 78, 89, 263

Bell Building, Montgomery, 26

Beloved Infidel (Graham), 271–72, 274–75, 279, 282, 326n67

Benét, Stephen Vincent, 277

Biggs, Anna, 160

Biggs, John, 118–19, 135, 160, 301, 314n26

Bishop, John Peale, 86, 100, 176, 185, 213, 310n17, 315n52

"Bowl, The" (Fitzgerald), 127–38, 155–56, 315n49

Broun, Heywood, 58

Brown, David, 7, 256, 284, 288

Bruccoli, Matthew, 7, 10, 38, 159, 179–81, 256, 284–85, 327n80

Bryn Mawr, Baltimore, 205

Buffalo, New York, 22, 307n4

Burlingame, Roger, 103–5, 313n40

California. See Hollywood

Cambridge Edition of the Works of F. Scott Fitzgerald, 4

"Camel's Back, The" (Fitzgerald), 61

Campbell, Lawton, 281

Camp Gordon, Georgia, 22, 308n7

Camp Sheridan, Alabama, 22, 26–28, 30, 36, 39, 167, 171

Camp Taylor, Kentucky, 22

Capri, 77, 113

Carry, Margaret, 307n37

Cather, Willa, 78–84, 105, 312n9, 313n40

characters, 9–10, 17, 37–38, 91, 100, 288–89

Civil War, 23–24

Claire, Ina, 136, 316n59

class, 7, 14, 97–98

College of One (Graham), 275

Collier's, 269–70, 276, 327n88

Colman, Ronald, *144*

Conrad, Joseph, 81, 104

Considine, John W., Jr., 114

Conte Biancamano, 160–63

Cottage Club at Princeton, 47, 58–59, 129, 132, 296

"Count of Darkness" stories, 1–4, 75, 215

"Coward" (Fitzgerald), 24

Cowley, Malcolm, 203–4

"Crack-Up" articles, 199, 222–23, 225–27, 233n32, 253, 256–59

Craig House, Beacon, NY, 210–11, 214

"Crazy Sunday" (Fitzgerald), 325n15

Crisler, Fritz, 8

"Cruise of the Rolling Junk, The" (Fitzgerald), 87–88, 201, 308n7

Cuba, 267

Dance, Beatrice, *152,* 247–53, 257–58, 323n23, 323n25

Dance, Dupré ("Hop"), 248–49, 251–53, 323n25

Dance, Eleanor, 247–53, 258, 323n25

"Dance, The" (Fitzgerald), 28

Dartmouth Winter Carnival, 266–67, 325n25

"A Debt of Honor" (Fitzgerald), 24

Dent, Helen, 308n24

"Diamond as Big as the Ritz, The" (Fitzgerald), 51, 136

Disenchanted, The (Schulberg), 266–67, 325n21

Doctors Hospital, New York, 267

Donaldson, Scott, 284

double perspective, 91

Editor, The, 31, 33, 42

Egorova, Lubov, 160

Eliot, T. S., 202, 319n7

Ellerslie, 117–18, 126, 127, 136–37, 158–60, 162, 177–79

emotion in writing, 9–11, 32, 78, 100. *See also* love and loss

emotions, 126

Encino, California, 268–76

"End of Hate, The" (Fitzgerald), 24

Esquire, 187, 225, 256–57, 277, 284, 287

Europe, 50, 62, 65, 89, 105, 113, 125, 158–60, 166, 179

expenses. *See* money

A Farewell to Arms (Hemingway), 155–56, 182, 184, 219, 278, 300

"Fate in Her Hands" (Fitzgerald), 229

Finney, Peggy, 302

Firestone Library, Princeton, 50, 179, 225

first-person narration, 48, 80–89

Fitzgerald, Edward (father), 23, 54, 201, 301

Fitzgerald, Elise (aunt), 24

Fitzgerald, F. Scott, photographs, *144, 147, 151, 153, 154*

Fitzgerald, Scottie (daughter), 295–98, 301–2, 328n8; Baltimore years, 203–5, 255; Christmas season photo description, 112–13; on "Count of Darkness" stories, 4; early 1930s, 199–200; early years, 62–63; with the Flynns, 221, 322n58; genealogy, 319n4; girlhood, 195–96; with the Obers, 268, 325n26; photograph, *147;* in Tryon, North Carolina, 219–21; and Zelda, 23, 64–65

Flynn, Maurice "Lefty," 220–24, 245–46

Flynn, Nora, 220–24, 232, 240, 245–46, 255, 257, 324n40

Fool For Love (Donaldson), 284

football, 8, 120–34, 137–38

Fort Leavenworth, Kansas, 22, 317n14

Fortune magazine, 210

For Whom the Bell Tolls (Hemingway), 278, 299–300

France, 62, 89, 109, 124–25, 158–61, 177–78

Fuller, William M., 100

Fuller-McGee case, 100

Gager, Theodora, 204, 323n12

genealogy, 319n4

Gingrich, Arnold, 213, 256, 268, 284

Graham, Sheilah, 8, 73, *153,* 267, 270–71, 274–75, 278–83, 288–91, 294, 298–301, 305n7, 322n7, 322n11, 325n21, 327n79

Great Gatsby, The (Fitzgerald), 5–7, 76, 77–107, 297–98; and Cather, 77–84; class in, 97–99; dramatic and film rights, 78, 110, 181; and emotion, 99–104; football in, 120; and Great Neck, 63–65; influences on, 81–84; Jay Gatsby's army posting, 22–23; lyric impulse, 92–95, 213, 289; narration in, 78–80; new angle for, 79–80, 84–85, 107, 184–85; Nick Carraway as narrator, 84–87, 89–91; and nostalgia, 104–5; novel's title, 95–97; post-*Gatsby* years, 108–9, 175–77; and Seldes, 183, 312n5, 318n24; self-effacing narrative voice, 86–88; sex in, 283; shirts, 101–4; southern sympathies, 46; and theater, 65–66; themes, 7; and "Winter Dreams," 18; and youth, 57, 125

Great Neck, New York, 63–65, 76, 100

Grove Park Inn, Asheville, *150*, 226–30, 232–34, 246–53, 259

Guthrie, Laura, 218, 225–59, 272, 313n42

"Handle with Care" (Fitzgerald), 257, 323n32

Harriman, Margaret Case, 218–19, 321n47

Harvard, 120–21, 133

Hayward, Leland, 265–66

"Head and Shoulders" (Fitzgerald), 25, 48–50

Heart of Darkness (Conrad), 81, 104

Hecht, Ben, 75

Hemingway, Ernest, 5, 10, 109–11, 136, *149*, 155–56, 181–84, 191, 193, 202, 212–13, 215, 238, 240–41, 246, 258, 278, 299–300, 302, 310n17, 314n6, 318n21, 318n24

Hemingway, Hadley, 110–11, 184, 193, 319n46

Hendersonville, North Carolina, 255–58

"Her Last Case" (Fitzgerald), 24, 245

Hobby stories, 283–89, 327nn78–80

Hollywood, 113–20, 187, 259, 260–94, 295

Holmes, Oliver Wendell, Jr., 121

Honeycutt, Anne, 219

horsemanship, 307n6

"Hotel Child, The" (Fitzgerald), 200

"How to Live" articles, 89

Hyères, 111

Hyman, Bernie, 265

"Ice Palace, The" (Fitzgerald), 26, 31–46, 49, 167, 170, 173, 174, 315n41

"Image on the Heart" (Fitzgerald), 106, 254

income. *See* money

"In the Darkest Hour" (Fitzgerald), 1–3

"Intimate Strangers, The" (Fitzgerald), 222–24

"Jacob's Ladder" (Fitzgerald), 16, 156–58

"Jelly-Bean, The" (Fitzgerald), 28, 40

Johns Hopkins's Phipps Psychiatric Clinic, 159, 200, 210

Jones, Roberta, 308n24

journals of Guthrie, 225–26, 230–34, 242–43, 246, 247–54

journals of Moran, 116–17

Jozan, Edouard, 105–7, 111, 180, 192, 314n23

Kalman, Oscar, 65

King, Charles Garfield, 11

King, Ginevra, 11–17, 19, 25, 125, *140*, 167, 306n33, 307n34, 326n67

Kingdom Come Farm, 11, 16

Kroll, Frances, 269–70, 275, 277, 327n79

Lake Forest, 11, 13–15

Landi, Elissa, 219, 321n49, 321n51

La Paix, *148*, 202–4, 206–7, 210–11, 320n8

Lardner, Ring, 65, 280–81, 313n39, 315n51, 326n68

"Last Kiss" (Fitzgerald), 16, 289–94, 302, 328n88

Last of the Belles, The" (Fitzgerald), 16, 25, 27, 125, 166–74, 289, 317nn18–19

Last Tycoon, The (Fitzgerald), 46, 274, 277–80, 282–86, 288, 290, 293–94, 297–98, 328n88

Law, Buzz, 122–23

ledger (Fitzgerald), 12–14, 22, 26, 28–29, 31, 50, 62–63, 66, 85, 105–6, 108–9, 111, 114–15, 124–26, 128, 155, 163, 166–69, 177–78, 182, 185–86, 193, 200, 203, 205–6, 210, 221–22, 240, 257, 306n31, 308n24, 311n49, 315n32, 317n14, 321n49, 324n42

Legrand, Paul, 311n56

Lemmon, Elizabeth, 216–17, 244–45, 301

Le Vot, André, 247

"Lipstick" (Fitzgerald), 125, 127, 260

Littauer, Kenneth, 270, 274
loans, 66, 214, 268, 285
Lorimer, George Horace, 49, 58
"Lost Decade, The" (Fitzgerald), 256
Lost Lady, A (Cather), 79–80, 84
love and loss, 16, 289–94
Love Boat, The" (Fitzgerald), 156–57, 280
Lyon, France, 109–10

"Magnetism" (Fitzgerald), 155–57, 279
Mankiewicz, Joseph, 263–65, 324n13
Mayer, Louis B., 262
Mayfield, Sara, 178
McCall's, 222–23
McKaig, Alexander, 59–62
McKinney, Kate, 311n49
McQuillans, 85–86
Mencken, H. L., 77, 175, 201, 203, 211, 215,
    242, 310n32, 319n46
Men Without Women (Hemingway), 183
Metropolitan, 55
MGM, 261–66
Milford, Nancy, 27
Mission Hospital, Asheville, 254–55
Mizener, Arthur, 256, 284
money, 4–5, 49–50, 77–78, 89, 110, 113, 155–56,
    159–60, 186–87, 203, 240, 261, 269, 277, 287.
    See also class
Montgomery, Alabama, 19–20, 22–23, 25–33,
    36, 39, 45, 62–63, 70–71, 74, 87, 99–100, 113,
    141, 166–71, 174, 200, 298
Moran, Lois, 114–20, 134–37, *144,* 156–58,
    161–65, 244, 260, 314n15, 314n17, 314n19,
    314n29, 315n30, 315n32
"More Than Just a House" (Fitzgerald),
    206–10
Motor magazine, 88
A Moveable Feast (Hemingway), 109–10, 241
Murphy, Gerald, 110–12, *146,* 181, 187–88, 211,
    213, 268, 299
Murphy, Sara, 110–12, *146,* 181, 187–88, 199,
    211, 213, 246, 314n6, 317n15, 319n1
My Ántonia (Cather), 81–83, 105
"My Lost City" (Fitzgerald), 101

Nassau Literary Magazine, 126
new angle for *Gatsby,* 79–80, 84–85, 107,
    184–85
New Jersey, 22, 322n7
New York, 14, 21, 30–31, 45, 47–56, 59–60,
    62–65, 69, 73–74, 76, 85, 90, 101, 117–19, 166,
    210–11, 218–19, 266–68, 281, 315n32
New Yorker, 49, 204
New York Post, 259
New York Times, 121–22, 220
New York Tribune, 58
"No Harm Trying" (Fitzgerald), 285
North American Newspaper Alliance, 270–71
North and South, 32–43
nostalgia, 104–5, 120, 125–26, 170–74, 241,
    285–86
Notebooks (Fitzgerald), 221, 283, 305n7, 319n8,
    328n7

Oak Hall, Tryon, NC, 219
Oakwood Cemetery, Montgomery, 39–40
Ober, Anne, 261–62, 268
Ober, Harold, 31, 51, 64, 127–28, 131, 215,
    258–59, 261, 267–68, 316n58
"Offside Play" (Fitzgerald), 137, 316n62
O'Hara, John, *154,* 213, 216, 282
"One Hundred False Starts" (Fitzgerald), 9–10
"One Interne" (Fitzgerald), 202
"One Trip Abroad" (Fitzgerald), 187–98,
    215–16
"On Schedule" (Fitzgerald), 202
"'O Russet Witch!'" (Fitzgerald), 51–56
Our Type (Fitzgerald), 175–79
Owens, Isobel, 204, 320n13, 322n58

Paradise Lost (Brown), 284
Paramore, Edward E., 262–65
Paris, France, 105, 109, 111–13, 158–60, 167,
    175–78, 181–88, 193, 218
Parker, Dorothy, 216, 299–300
Parrott, Ursula, 1
passion, 78, 101, 103, 104, 312n5
Perkins, Maxwell: and Elizabeth Lemmon,
    216–17, 244–45; Ellerslie visit, 127, 159–60,

314n26; on Fitzgerald, 8, 315n51, 327n81; and *The Great Gatsby,* 77–78, 95–96, 100, 313n39; La Paix visit, 202; and *The Last Tycoon,* 277; photograph, *149;* praise for *Save Me the Waltz,* 45; and *Tender is the Night,* 176–79, 181, 183–84, 211–14; and *The Vegetable,* 66, 75

Photoplay, 224

Piper, Henry Dan, 256

plays. *See* theater

Poe, Johnny, 126, 315n48

Prangins clinic, Switzerland, 187, 218

"Presumption" (Fitzgerald), 307n37

Princeton, 8, 11–14, 22, 47–48, 58–59, 65, 120–34, 138, 299

"Princeton" (Fitzgerald), 127

Princeton Tiger, 129

Pumphrey's Funeral Home, Bethesda, MD, 301

Rawlings, Marjorie Kinnan, 246–47

Real F. Scott Fitzgerald, The (Graham), 271–72, 274, 279–80, 325n46, 326n67

Redbook (magazine), 1–4, *139,* 215, 305n4

"Rich Boy, The" (Fitzgerald), 108, 136

Ringer, Paul, 227, 254–55

Riviera, 105–7, 110–13, 180–82, 187–88, 195

"*Romantic Egotist, The*" (Fitzgerald), 81, 124

Ross, Harold, 49

"Rough Crossing, The" (Fitzgerald), 156, 161–65, 184, 289, 316n11

Ryan, James E., 171

"Sahara of the Bozart, The" (Mencken), 308n24

Saint Paul, Minnesota, 13–14, 21–22, 30–33, 35, 47–48, 50, 62–66, 70, 85, *143,* 301, 328n11

Saint Paul City Directory, 85

Saturday Evening Post, 186–87, 214–15, 217, 258, 284, 320n20; "The Bowl," 127, 136, 155; "Head and Shoulders," 48–49; "How to Live" articles, 89; "The Ice Palace," 31; "The Love Boat," 280; "More Than Just a House," 206; "Presumption," 307n37

Saturday Review, 277

Save Me the Waltz (Sayre), 25, 27–28, 45, 61, 106, 168, 178, 309n42, 309n47

Sayre, Rosalind, 73–74, 195, 200

Sayre, Zelda, 4–5, 10–11, 15–16, 20; absence of, 215–16, 224; in Africa, 185; in Asheville sanitarium, 258–59; and ballet, 136, 158, 160, 178, 185–86, 193; in Baltimore, 201–6; and Camp Sheridan, 171; in Craig House, 210–14; and "The Cruise of the Rolling Junk," 87–89; in Cuba, 267; death of, 302; and Ellerslie, 117, 127, 136–37, 158–60; in France, 109, 111–13, 178; in Great Neck, 63–65; health collapse, 185–87, 195–96, 199–200; in Hollywood, 113–14; and "The Ice Palace," 32–34, 37; income, 155; and Jozan, 105–7, 111, 180, 192, 314n23; Lardner's odes to, 326n68; long-distance engagement, 47–48; marriage in New York, 50–51, 59–63; and Montgomery, 25–31, 38–39, 166, 200, 298–300; motherhood, 62–63, 311n41; and Nora Flynn, 246; Oakwood Cemetery, 39–40; "'O Russet Witch,'" 55; photograph, *142, 144, 147;* reluctance to marry, 73–74; *Save Me the Waltz,* 25, 27–28, 45, 61, 106, 168, 178, 309n42, 309n47; and Scottie, 297; and "The Sensible Thing," 66–73; and Sheilah Graham, 280–82; at Sheppard Pratt, 214, 216, 255, 258; and the South, 21, 45–46; and "The Vegetable," 75–76; and Youth, 56–57

Schulberg, Budd, 266–67

Scott and Zelda Fitzgerald Museum, Montgomery, 200

scrapbooks (Fitzgerald), 49–50, 86, 117, 167, 169, 185, 249

screenwriting, 187, 259, 261–68, 276

Scribner's, 30, 47–48, 50, 66, 75, 81, 108, 155, 261, 277

Scribner's Magazine, 182, 212

Seldes, Gilbert, 136–37, 183, 312n5, 318n24

"'The Sensible Thing'" (Fitzgerald), 16, 66–73, 79, 100, 311n45

sexual equality, Fitzgerald's views on, 242

Shearer, Norma, 244, 291, 322n11, 325n15

Sheppard Pratt, Baltimore, MD, 214, 216, 255, 258

Skylands Hotel, Hendersonville, NC, 255

Smith, Newman, 195, 328n8

"Snows of Kilimanjaro, The" (Hemingway), 184, 241

Some Sort of Epic Grandeur (Bruccoli), 38, 159, 284

Song of the Lark, The (Cather), 78

southern sympathies, 21–46

So We Read On (Corrigan), 6

Sparhawk-Jones, Elizabeth, 202

Steiner, May, 29, 167–70, 308n24

Stella Dallas (film), 114–15

St. Mary's Church, Rockville, MD, 301–2

St. Moritz, Switzerland, 271

St. Raphael, France, 105, 111

"Swimmers, The" (Fitzgerald), 156, 316n12

Syracuse, New York, 22, 307n4

Tales of the Jazz Age (Fitzgerald), 64–65

Talmadge, Constance, 114

Taps at Reveille (Fitzgerald), 136, 158, 214, 217

Tarleton graveyard scene in "The Ice Palace," 39–44

Taylor, Cecilia (cousin), 24, 63

Tender Is the Night (Fitzgerald), 4–5, 15, 111, 120, 165–66, 179–85, 212–14, 283, 316n2, 316n62, 320n24

Thalberg, Irving, 244, 265, 291, 294

theater, 65–66, 78, 110. See also *The Vegetable* (Fitzgerald)

thirty as pivot between youth and decay, 4, 56–57, 125, 310n17

This Side of Paradise (Fitzgerald), 5, 240; auto-accident story in, 322n7; boyhood interests and enthusiasms, 19; broken engagement in, 69–70, 73; and emotion, 11, 16; "girl" occurring in, 307n43; and "The Ice Palace," 32, 44; narrative voice, 81; and Princeton, 123–24, 126, 134; romance in,

283, 289; sales of, 77; Scribner's acceptance of, 30; and the South, 23–24

Three Comrades (film), 262–65, 324n13

Time Magazine, 259

Triangle Club, 65, 124, 129

Trilling, Lionel, 282

Trimbush, 202–3

Tryon, North Carolina, 219–22, 232, 245–46

Turnbull, Andrew, 59, 137–38, 195, 204–6, 256, 284, 296, 301

Turnbull, Margaret, 202, 319n8

Turnbull family, 202–6

Union Cemetery, Rockville, 301–2

United Artists, 113

Vanderhoef, Harman, 223

Vanderhoef, Isabel, 246

Vegetable, The (Fitzgerald), 56–57, 66, 75–76, 78–79, 88–89, 110, 166

Welbourne, 216–17, 244–45

West, James L. W., III, 4, 15

Westport, Connecticut, 51

Wheeler, John, 271

White Bear Lake, Minnesota, 63

Wilson, Edmund, 62, 75, 159, 213, 262–63, 277, 280, 315n52

Winter Carnival (film), 267

"Winter Dreams" (Fitzgerald), 16–19, 73

Wolfe, Thomas, 6, 10, 217, 259, 298, 320n8

women in Guthrie's journal, 242–44

Wordsworth, William, 4, 56

World War II, 5, 301, 325n26

Wray, Fay, 299

Yale, 13–14, 120–37, *145,* 220

Yeats, William Butler, 8–9

You Can't Go Home Again (Wolfe), 6, 298

Youth, 4, 56–58, 125, 157, 310n17